The
American
Novel of War

THE AMERICAN NOVEL OF WAR

A Critical Analysis and Classification System

Wallis R. Sanborn, III

McFarland & Company, Inc., Publishers
Jefferson, North Carolina, and London

Excerpt from "Song of Napalm" from *Song of Napalm* © 1988 by Bruce Weigl. Used by permission of Grove/Atlantic, Inc.

Excerpts from "Tu Do Street" and "The Edge" from *Pleasure Dome: New and Collected Poems* © 2001 by Yusef Komunyakaa. Reprinted by permission of Wesleyan University Press.

Excerpt from "Hwy 1" from *Here, Bullet*. Copyright © 2001 by Brian Turner. Reprinted with the permission of The Permissions Company, Inc. on behalf of Alice James Books, www.alicejamesbooks.org, and Bloodaxe Books, 2007.

LIBRARY OF CONGRESS CATALOGUING-IN-PUBLICATION DATA

Sanborn, Wallis R., 1964–
The American novel of war : a critical analysis
and classification system / Wallis R. Sanborn, III.
p.   cm.
Includes bibliographical references and index.

ISBN 978-0-7864-3863-1
softcover : acid free paper ∞

1. War stories, American — History and criticism.
2. War and literature — United States — History.
3. War in literature.   I. Title.
PS374.W35S26 2012   813.009'3581— dc23   2012034270

BRITISH LIBRARY CATALOGUING DATA ARE AVAILABLE

Front cover image © 2012 Shutterstock

Manufactured in the United States of America

*McFarland & Company, Inc., Publishers
Box 611, Jefferson, North Carolina 28640
www.mcfarlandpub.com*

my intellectual and scholarly evolution. And Debbie Nash at Outreach Extended Studies aided in developing my particular vision of American postmodernism. At UT Permian Basin, Shawn Watson gave me my first job, fresh out of graduate school, and she allowed me to teach a lovely variety of vita-building courses. Also, Billy Rodriguez was a fine friend and professional peer during my time in Odessa. At Oregon State, Tracy Daugherty was a wonderful boss and remains a fine gentleman. At Angelo State, Nancy Allen, John Wegner, and Laurence Musgrove each served as English chair, and as such kept me employed as I obsessed and toiled over this project. Also, Jeff Schonburg, Diane Spraggins, Julie Gates, Mark Hama, Linda Kornasky, Chris Ellery, Terry Dalrymple, Mary Ellen Hartje, Gabby Serrano, and Nicole McDaniel, among others, were wonderful peers during my time at Angelo State, and Julie, Mark, Linda, and Diane have earned my enduring gratitude through their assistance with my professional development.

I would be remiss if I did not mention Rick Wallach, the Cormac McCarthy Society, and the *Cormac McCarthy Journal*. Rick has been a tremendous friend to my work, and "the Society," as it is known by Cormackians, has been a tree of knowledge for me upon which I have feasted on intellect and criticism of all things McCarthy and sundry things life-manifested, while the journal was the literary locus of my first post-graduate publication. Special thanks to Dianne C. Luce, Chip Arnold, David Cremean, John Wegner, again, Jay Ellis, Stacey Peebles, Robert Jarrett, Marty Priola, and Peter Josyph, each of whom has helped me develop as a critic and thinker.

Relative to poetry permissions for the poems discussed in chapter 1, special thanks go out to Dara Hyde at Grove/Atlantic; Suzanna Tamminen at Wesleyan University Press; Frederick T. Courtright and Frank Giampietro at The Permissions Company and Alice James Books, respectively; and Suzanne Fairless-Aitken at Bloodaxe Books.

And now the personal. My mother, Judy Sanborn, has unfailingly supported my efforts to be a writer since the decision was made on 16 July 1986. Since that day, she has never wavered, never lost faith in me, even though it took me a while to get my sea legs. She has been an outstanding mother, and for that I say thank you, very much. My late father, Wallis Sanborn, loved AA and the Marines, and I too have spent my time with each organization. So, thank you, Wal, wherever you are.

Even a misanthrope has a friend or two, and I have two specifically to thank here. My brother in soul and psyche, if not in blood, Ruben Treviño taught me what true emotional and physical toughness is, and I doubt that I would have made it through MCRD San Diego and School of Infantry without his pragmatic lessons. Thank you, Ruben. My friend Will Brannon likewise deserves kudos for, at the very least, listening to me whine when the depth and breadth of this project wore upon me. And, as he is quite well read, he was my discussion partner and sounding board as I moved through these war texts. So, thank you, too, Will.

"ANY work of literature which has war as its subject should be much more than a bald and bare recounting, detailed or otherwise, of the battle, the tactics and strategy, the advance or retreats, the weapons and machines employed, the names of the commanding general and his staff, or the name of the private who is awarded a medal for heroism. All this is mere reporting."

— E.R. Hagemann 356

To all those who have served —
past, present, and future

Table of Contents

Acknowledgments

Of course, no project of this scope is created in a vacuum, and no scholar learns how to create such a project alone, so I have many people and organizations to credit, acknowledge, and thank.

First among all is Professor Patrick W. Shaw, who has been my teacher, mentor, and friend for many years. I owe a debt to Dr. Shaw that cannot be repaid. Dr. Shaw has been instrumental, even crucial, in my evolution as a writer, researcher, and scholar, and without his guidance, this project, as well as my first book, *Animals in the Fiction of Cormac McCarthy* (McFarland, 2006), would not exist. For Dr. Shaw introduced me to Cormac McCarthy, and he taught me, too, how to create a set of finite and focused defining characteristics by which and through which one can critically evaluate a text within a given literary genre. He also introduced to me the literary and chronological parameters that evince American literary modernism and postmodernism, and for that I am indeed indebted, as I use those parameters in this work and on a daily basis. Further, Dr. Shaw taught me how to organize and write a book — no small feat, of course. The skills of organizing a project, and researching and gathering and actively reading and culling primary and secondary sources, with a finished effort in mind, are skills that were brought to me by Dr. Shaw. So, simply, sir, you have changed my life. Thank you.

No project initially composed of 400 non-novel primary and secondary sources and 100 novels can be created without the help of university libraries and professional academic library staffs, so I have to offer honest thanks to the interlibrary loan staff, the reference librarians, and the good people who work the circulation desks at three academic libraries specifically — the University Library at Texas Tech University, the Valley Library at Oregon State University, and the Porter Henderson Library at Angelo State University. Gathering sources was a nearly painless endeavor; an overwhelmed scholar and author suffers enough as a project is organized, so the systematic efficiency practiced at these libraries assisted me greatly as I sought, located, and gathered sundry sources and source types while this project was in its nebulous phases.

I have many peers, mentors, and faculty members to thank at the universities where I have studied and worked — Texas Tech University, the University of Texas of the Permian Basin, Oregon State University, and Angelo State University — some of whom have moved on, and some of whom still work where our paths once crossed. At Texas Tech, Dean Madone Miner was English chair when I was a doctoral candidate, and she, amazingly, let me teach undergraduate literature courses of my own design, one of which was a sophomore-level American Novel of War course, which, with Professor Shaw's assistance, evolved into this work. Also, Bruce Clarke, David Troyansky, Don Rude, and Leon Higdon were crucial in

"ANY work of literature which has war as its subject should be much more than a bald and bare recounting, detailed or otherwise, of the battle, the tactics and strategy, the advance or retreats, the weapons and machines employed, the names of the commanding general and his staff, or the name of the private who is awarded a medal for heroism. All this is mere reporting."

— E.R. Hagemann 356

my intellectual and scholarly evolution. And Debbie Nash at Outreach Extended Studies aided in developing my particular vision of American postmodernism. At UT Permian Basin, Shawn Watson gave me my first job, fresh out of graduate school, and she allowed me to teach a lovely variety of vita-building courses. Also, Billy Rodriguez was a fine friend and professional peer during my time in Odessa. At Oregon State, Tracy Daugherty was a wonderful boss and remains a fine gentleman. At Angelo State, Nancy Allen, John Wegner, and Laurence Musgrove each served as English chair, and as such kept me employed as I obsessed and toiled over this project. Also, Jeff Schonburg, Diane Spraggins, Julie Gates, Mark Hama, Linda Kornasky, Chris Ellery, Terry Dalrymple, Mary Ellen Hartje, Gabby Serrano, and Nicole McDaniel, among others, were wonderful peers during my time at Angelo State, and Julie, Mark, Linda, and Diane have earned my enduring gratitude through their assistance with my professional development.

I would be remiss if I did not mention Rick Wallach, the Cormac McCarthy Society, and the *Cormac McCarthy Journal*. Rick has been a tremendous friend to my work, and "the Society," as it is known by Cormackians, has been a tree of knowledge for me upon which I have feasted on intellect and criticism of all things McCarthy and sundry things life-manifested, while the journal was the literary locus of my first post-graduate publication. Special thanks to Dianne C. Luce, Chip Arnold, David Cremean, John Wegner, again, Jay Ellis, Stacey Peebles, Robert Jarrett, Marty Priola, and Peter Josyph, each of whom has helped me develop as a critic and thinker.

Relative to poetry permissions for the poems discussed in chapter 1, special thanks go out to Dara Hyde at Grove/Atlantic; Suzanna Tamminen at Wesleyan University Press; Frederick T. Courtright and Frank Giampietro at The Permissions Company and Alice James Books, respectively; and Suzanne Fairless-Aitken at Bloodaxe Books.

And now the personal. My mother, Judy Sanborn, has unfailingly supported my efforts to be a writer since the decision was made on 16 July 1986. Since that day, she has never wavered, never lost faith in me, even though it took me a while to get my sea legs. She has been an outstanding mother, and for that I say thank you, very much. My late father, Wallis Sanborn, loved AA and the Marines, and I too have spent my time with each organization. So, thank you, Wal, wherever you are.

Even a misanthrope has a friend or two, and I have two specifically to thank here. My brother in soul and psyche, if not in blood, Ruben Treviño taught me what true emotional and physical toughness is, and I doubt that I would have made it through MCRD San Diego and School of Infantry without his pragmatic lessons. Thank you, Ruben. My friend Will Brannon likewise deserves kudos for, at the very least, listening to me whine when the depth and breadth of this project wore upon me. And, as he is quite well read, he was my discussion partner and sounding board as I moved through these war texts. So, thank you, too, Will.

Introduction

War literature — in song, in verse, in narrative account, in dramatic form — has a long history (nearly all of recorded history, in fact), and accounts of war, in the novel and other narrative forms, occupy the American best-seller lists and the stacks of public and academic American libraries. In times of war and in times directly after war, war literature is written, published, sold, consumed, and critically analyzed. As such, in the American history and popular culture, there exist numerous — too many to count — published war stories, war poems, war novels, war dramas, war memoirs, and so forth. As well, there exists the scholarship that naturally follows the creation of such primary texts. A thorough survey of the extant and contemporary criticism of modern and postmodern American war literature reveals that there is a need for a genre-wide study of the literary modern and postmodern American novel of war and that the creation of such a critical text will fill this scholarly niche and need. Presently, there are critical studies — in essays, anthologies, and book-length efforts — that focus on the literature of the Civil War, the literature of World War I, the literature of World War II, the literature of the Korean War, the literature of the Vietnam War, the literature of the Gulf War, and even the literature being born of the wars in Iraq and Afghanistan. What this scholarship tends to do, though, in focus and in study, is look at the literature of a specific war or conflict. Thus, a study of the recorded literature of World War I will not touch upon the literature of the Vietnam War, or the Korean War, or World War II. Further, many of these studies focus on the literature of the given war, rather than on a specific genre within the literature — the novel, for example. Finally, many of these studies, even when looking at the war novels of record, fail to examine the texts specifically as American novels of war — novels in the American vein that can be grouped, regardless of war, by a specific set of war literature-centric defining characteristics.

The purpose of *The American Novel of War* is to create and articulate a set of standards by which the American novel of war, both modern and postmodern, can be qualified and classified, and thus critically analyzed. Using a pragmatic set of chronological, philosophical, structural, and stylistic defining characteristics, the study will first categorize the modern and the postmodern American novel. Then, the text will classify the American novel of war using the author's thematic and content-based defining characteristics of the American novel of war. In addition to a chapter in which said defining characteristics will be applied to other American works of the literature of war, each rhetorical chapter of the study will address a specific defining characteristic of the American novel of war, the extant criticism related to that defining characteristic in the literature of war, and the defining characteristic as it exists in a number of American novels of war. The result will be an *oeuvre*-and war-wide study, one that encompasses American modernism and postmodernism via the genre of the American novel, via the sub-genre of the American novel of war. Currently, no such scholarly text exists.

What follows are the author's defining characteristics of the modern and postmodern American novel(s) and the author's defining characteristics of the American novel of war (Sanborn xiv–xxii).

American literary modernism and the modern American novel can be dated to 1850 and the publication of Nathaniel Hawthorne's *The Scarlet Letter*. This novel of a woman shunned and ostracized by her own community is, at its very essence, modernist because the work places the alienated individual against family, community, and, more importantly, society. And this alienation of the individual, of one who is rejected by his or her society, or of one who consciously chooses to reject society, is at the heart of the modern American novel. In the study at hand, Stephen Crane's seminal Civil War war novel, *The Red Badge of Courage* (1895), and the World War I novels of Edith Wharton, John Dos Passos, Thomas Boyd, and Dalton Trumbo—*The Marne* (1918), *One Man's Initiation* (1920), *Through the Wheat* (1923), and *Johnny Got His Gun* (1939), respectively—clearly present this alienated and modern individual. In each of these five works, the text's protagonist is an alien among peers, an outsider ostracized secondary to the decisions he makes before and during a time of war.

While *The Scarlet Letter* was written in the nineteenth century, set in the seventeenth century, and published at the dawn of the American Industrial Revolution, and is, as such, a transitional text, both modern and premodern, it is the post–*Scarlet Letter* Industrial Revolution that affects the modernist novels that follow Hawthorne's work. Mark Twain's *The Adventures of Huckleberry Finn* (1885) takes the alienated individual and places him in a setting where the modern and the premodern collide. As Robert Fulton's steamboats are moving up and down the Mississippi River, the transcontinental railroads are pushing westerly and easterly, and Eli Whitney's cotton ginning process is revolutionizing agricultural production, rural nineteenth-century America is forced to modernize, willingly or not. One of the results of this forced industrial, economic, and agricultural modernization is the American Civil War (1861–1865), the first war fought with mass-produced weaponry. Stephen Crane's classic and handy tome illustrates the carnage of the modern battlefield; thousands of men, armed with thousands of weapons, slaughter their opposites in bloody modern mayhem, and Amy Kaplan argues that "Crane wrenches the war from its earlier contexts, not to banish history from his 'Episode' but to reinterpret the war through the cultural lenses and political concerns of the late nineteenth century.... Crane's is a book about social change, about the transition not only from internecine to international conflict or from preindustrial to mechanized forms of warfare, but also from traditional to modern rules of representation" (118–19). Through the U.S. Civil War and *The Red Badge of Courage*, modern warfare is born and fought, is written of and published, and is notably well read and well received; further, the seminal modern American novel of war has been created.

What Crane, Wharton, and Dos Passos have in common, other than being novel-writing American early moderns, is the common theme of the rural and urban individual alienated against his own family and/or society in an era of war. This theme of alienation is one that is made manifest on a number of different levels. As Harmon and Holman note, "*Modern* implies a historical discontinuity, a sense of alienation, loss and despair. It rejects not only history but also the society of whose fabrication history is a record. It rejects traditional values and assumptions, and it rejects equally the rhetoric by which they were sanctioned and communicated. It elevates the individual and the inward over the social and the outward." The individual in the modern American novel is one who is not only alienated from society, but also is alienated from family, tradition, history, and home. To be an individual in a modern society is to be utterly and absolutely alone, even, or especially, among family and peers; the modernist individual is an isolated alien who is geographically, culturally, and socially decentered, and in the modern American novel of war, this alienated individual is one who is removed from rural or urban home and is placed on a battlefield on foreign soil and tossed into the madness, chaos, and brutality of modern war. Then and there is one who is abjectly, physically, psychically, and terrifyingly alone.

In addition to focusing on a central isolated individual, modern American novels are usually narrated by a single narrator, and from a single narrative perspective. This narrator might be a character in the text, and as such will use first-person narration, or, more commonly, the narrator will be a formal third-person narrator. But what is important here is the fact that in a modern American novel, a single narrator is used through the entirety of the book, and a single tale is narrated. Overwhelmingly, war novels, and the texts in this study, use third-person limited omniscient narration, with a third-person objective over-narrator and a focus on a particular character's—the isolated individual's—thoughts and optic. As Joseph Chuman argues, "The modernist values objectivity [of narrator]" (13), and Crane's text uses the third-person point of view, while Wharton, Dos Passos, Boyd, and Trumbo also use the modernist third person. Yet, remember, "[t]he modern temperament is individualistic" (Chuman 13); hence, the use of the optic of one specific textual character. The use of the objective narrator and the individual character's optic allows the author the opportunity to present mass conflicts from the perspective of the individual, and thus, allows the author to humanize that which is not human, and to stabilize that which is not stable—modern warfare.

Next, a modern American novel is most often told in a linear narrative. The story is told as the events happen, or have happened, from beginning to middle to end. Also, the action in a modern novel usually occurs within a single temporal span; that is, the action occurs primarily or exclusively within the linear narrative and the temporal confines of the linear narrative. As such, both temporality and narrative run parallel and in sequence of events occurring. While back-story and flashbacks may be found in the text, as in Trumbo's savage *Johnny Got His Gun*, there is neither slippery temporality nor chronological leaps back and forth through time as there are in many postmodern novels. Some works take excruciating pains to chronicle linear narrative and contiguous temporality, but novels such as the Crane, Wharton, and Dos Passos texts conjoin narrative linearity with temporal contiguity to create a unified and coherent text. Of course, the nexus of narrative and time allows for the early modern reader, often a passive reader, to be easily centered in the text; it also allows the author to present his or her rhetoric sans explicit intellectual challenges to the reader, and as such the text is, per Ihab Hassan, a "*Lisible* (Readerly) ... Narrative/ *Grande Historie*" ("Postface" 87) and is clearly modern in design, construct, and execution.

Further, the protagonist of the modern American novel is very often a Kierkegaardian proto-existential individual, one who encourages the individual over society and belief in self over belief in others, and one who believes that it is a positive trait to be a social nonconformist. Henry Fleming, Troy Belknap, and Martin Howe join the war effort before being forced to, and thus exhibit self-belief beyond any belief in peers or society; this self-belief is the drive that allows these proto-existential "individuals to discover their own unique identities" (McDonald). By voluntarily entering the war effort, Fleming, Belknap, and Howe evolve from "pseudo-individuals" (McDonald) to individuals. Additionally, in joining the ambulance service, Troy Belknap goes against his societal caste and is among a number of moderns who evolve "beyond their socially imposed identities" (McDonald), and, in so doing, gain individual self-identity. Collectively, Fleming, Belknap, and Howe contribute to the dawn of individual subjectivity in the modern American novel of war by presenting Kierkegaard's rhetoric in literary form. Each character makes an existential choice that is a bold — and modern — statement in and of self-identity.

More often than not, the modern novel is one that is told in a reality-based setting, not a fantasy, psychedelic, psychotic, or drug-induced hallucinatory setting; the events happen in this world, in real time, in a real-life setting. And, of course, any modern American war novel is going to deal with naturalism — as a literary philosophy and in practice — as the modern battlefield is a Darwinian environment where survival demands both fitness and luck. Malcolm Bradbury correctly argues that World War I "undoubtedly changed style, and it helped ratify modernism. It enforced the naturalist insights; it also intensified the sense of historical disorder and irony that many experimental writers had begun to probe.... And of the great transition into the modern place, modern time, modern indifference, modern hardness, the war [World War I] was the ultimate symbol" (193–94). War (in this case, World War I), and its literary representation, is the modern. Modern war is indifferent, and modern war is brutal and hard, and modern war leads to the proto-existential, Stirnerian nihilism of William Hicks at the close of Boyd's *Through the Wheat*—"No longer did anything matter, neither the bayonets, the bullets, the barbed wire, the dead, nor the living" (266)—and to the physical destruction of Joe Bonham in Trumbo's *Johnny Got His Gun*: he has lost his arms, his legs, his eyes, his ears, his face, as well as the abilities to see, to speak, to smell, to taste, to hear. So, nature is indifferent; war is indifferent; warriors become indifferent; and reality-based Naturalism is the delivery device of the carnage of modern war in the modern American novel of war.

The modern American novel is primarily textual prose; that is, the story is told from beginning to end without the explicit and overt intrusion of other types of documents— Internal Paratext. For example, with postmodern American novels, many texts contain, in addition to the narrated prose, non-embedded newspaper blurbs, letters, song lyrics, poems, and other non-narrated or character-spoken items; this Internal Paratext serves to assist in the storytelling while it calls attention to the concept of the postmodern world as a fragmented world (Chuman 14). Additionally, the Internal Paratext in the postmodern American novel is necessary for the structural integrity of the work. That is, the work is not complete without the Internal Paratext. The modern American novel, however, is likely a complete text in prose, and the occasional use of a shard of Internal Paratext is a rhetorical addition used to complement the prose, rather than an absolute conditional necessity to the telling of the greater story. For example, *The Red Badge of Courage*, *The Marne*, and *Through the Wheat* are composed nearly entirely of narrated prose and dialogue but for a quatrain of doggerel, Shakespeare, and cadence call, respectively. As such, the story narrated in each novel exists utterly and absolutely as narrated prose and dialogue. The use of Internal Paratext is a bit more liberal in the Dos Passos text, as *One Man's Initiation* contains a number of examples from contemporary song lyrics. Nonetheless, and authorial effect aside, *One Man's Initiation* exists overwhelmingly as modernist prose rhetoric.

The isolated individual in a modern American novel is often a hero or heroic figure to himself and/or to others— readers especially — who overcomes some tragedy, or, of course, exile or societal alienation or near death experience, that results in an epiphany of sorts.

This epiphany may or may not be consciously experienced by the character but may be presented in the text for the reader. The protagonists of Wharton's *The Marne*, Troy Belknap, and Dos Passos' Martin Howe begin their initiation into war as members of the volunteer ambulance corps, serving the wounded French, British, Belgian — and even German — soldiers of the day. Service of this sort came under fire, of course, and artillery or gas cared nothing for who was affected, maimed, or poisoned. It bears mention that Wharton's text is explicitly propagandistic, while Dos Passos' is less so. Regardless, Belknap and Howe are heroic characters in volunteering to risk all upon foreign soil, as the contemporary American government and the social peers of each practice neutrality and objection to American entrance into the war. And while the heroic figure of the modern American novel of war is not the perfect hero of the medieval romance or quest, he is nonetheless not the absolute existentialist of the postmodern novel, and even warrior-come-lately Henry Fleming and Stirnerian nihilist William Hicks possess heroic qualities (in varying degrees, of course), in the context of the fighting and necessary killing of the battlefield. Trumbo's Joe Bonham might be the most ideally heroic of the five modern protagonists in this discussion, as he is maimed beyond comprehension and external communication, yet he creates an internal world to maintain his sanity, and then realizes the ability to communicate with the caregivers of his body through tapping Morse code out with his head.

Finally, the modern American novel often places the isolated individual against the machinery of the modern era. Mass transit, mass communication, mass media, mass industry, and the modern cityscape — all machines of a sort — affect the modernist individual, often in ways beyond said individual's human power and ability to reason. In the modern American novel of war, the isolated individual is at war with, and at the mercy of, the mass-produced weapons of war. While Spencer carbines and Henry repeating rifles were used primarily by Union cavalry, Union infantry used breech-loading rifles, as Crane accurately presents: "The steel ramrods clanked and clanged with incessant din as the men pounded them furiously into the hot rifle barrels" (37). What is noteworthy in this passage is the use of the word "rifle"; up to this point in the history of war, hand-held long-weapons did not have rifled barrels, and as such were highly inaccurate. With the advent of mass-produced weapons with rifled barrels, accuracy of shot and distance of accuracy of shot were greatly increased, and as such, until tactics caught up with weaponry, slaughter, secondary to frontal assaults, was the order of the day. Artillery or cannon, smoothbore and rifled, were also mass produced by the North secondary to the American Industrial Revolution, and Crane notes the presence of artillery batteries on the battlefield as shells "hurtled" (43) over Henry's head. The evolution of science and technology before and during World War I led to the creation of ghastly weapons and exponential battlefield carnage. High-rate-of-fire machine-guns, massive artillery, lethal and non-lethal gases of all sorts, flamethrowers, hand grenades, and tanks, planes, and submarines contributed to the wholesale lethality of World War I, while ambulances, motorcycles, field hospitals, trucks, and trains moved and served weapons, warriors, and civilian men, women, and children alike. The presence of this mechanized mass movement, and pre- and post-movement mass slaughter, is readily apparent in nearly all novels of World War I, and the Wharton, Dos Passos, Boyd, and Trumbo texts are not exceptions to this literary commonality. The Boyd text in particular is a catalog of modern weaponry and the violence and destruction thus produced. Collectively and individually, and as novels of war, the five example novels of the modern American novel properly present the mechanized weapons and machinery of modern war.

Crane's seminal American novel of war, and of modern war, *The Red Badge of Courage*, slots nicely into all of the defining characteristics of the modern American novel (circa 1850–1944), while Wharton's *The Marne*, Dos Passos' *One Man's Initiation*, Boyd's *Through the Wheat*, and Trumbo's *Johnny Got His Gun* are quintessential examples of the modern American novel. A number of other novels in this study are quintessential examples of the postmodern American novel (circa 1945–present): Peter Bowman's *Beach Red* (1945), Norman Mailer's *The Naked and the Dead* (1948), Joseph Heller's *Catch-22* (1961), Leslie Marmon Silko's *Ceremony* (1977), Gustav Hasford's *The Short-Timers* (1979), Cormac McCarthy's *Blood Meridian, Or the Evening Redness in the West* (1985), Tim O'Brien's *The Things They Carried* (1990), and Chaim Potok's *I Am the Clay* (1992) are postmodern in era, tone, and defining characteristics. Another novel, a text that uses an astounding 113 first-person narrators to tell 113 vignettes, William March's *Company K* (1933), falls a decade before the postmodern era but is so uniquely postmodern in tone and in structure that it must be grouped with the postmodern war novels rather than with the modern.

The postmodern American novel is a fragmented, anarchic construct, born of a fragmented, anarchic society, world, and era, an era with no boundaries and no center, an era in which man can destroy mankind and Earth — and all life upon it — an era in which the laws of physics and nature no longer matter. Idealized and revisionist views and interpretations of post–World War II America have created a mythos of happy suburbia — a suburbia filled with early TV and drive-ins and carhops and the fulfillment of the post-war American Dream. However, due to the post–World War II division of ideologies and nations between the Democratic West and the Communist East, the bipolar Cold War created an omnipresent case of mass fear. Mutually Assured Destruction (MAD) assured that, if the United States started a nuclear war with the Soviet Union (USSR), or the USSR with the West, the retaliatory strikes would be so devastating that known life on Earth would cease to exist. The Cold War meant that life on this planet was at stake. Thus, after the Trinity blast of 16 July 1945 and the atomic bombings of Hiroshima and Nagasaki, Japan, on 6 August and 9 August 1945, man — American man — had demonstrated the unique ability to destroy all life on Earth, as the atomic bomb was the great postmodern machine, one whose force no civil individual or federal collective had the power to control. And after the Soviet Union's First Lightning detonation of 29 August 1949, the Americans were no longer alone in destructive capability. The result of MAD and of the Cold War, and of all this powerlessness over one's individual and collective fate, was an American public that lived in an ongoing state of ever-present stress.

The world could end at any moment, and as such, the already alienated individual now had to worry about atomic immolation — instant death — or radiation poisoning — gruesome and long-acting death. The result, as Harmon and Holman dryly note, was that the "fundamental philosophical assumptions of modernism, its tendency toward historical discontinuity, alienation, asocial individualism, solipsism, and EXISTENTIALISM [Harmon and Holman's caps] continue[d] to permeate contemporary writing, perhaps in a heightened sense." One can consider postmodernism as an exponentialized modernism; one takes all of the fears and anxieties of the isolated, alienated modernist individual, and adds the constant threat of the end of the world, and the result is, well, the postmodernist individual. Add to this individual's psyche Hassan's "horrendous facts of postmodernity ... diasporas, migrations, refugees, the killing fields, [and] a crisis of personal and cultural values seemingly without parallel in history" ("Beyond Postmodernism" 5). And of course, with the impending end of the world always right around the corner, and with the postmodern individual at the mercy of the great postmodern machine — the atomic, then hydrogen, then nuclear bomb(s)—the postmodern individual lives in a universe that has no order; this lack of universal order leads to life and art and literature that is highly fragmented, sans the aesthetic and structural boundaries of its predecessors. The constructed, long-form result of this social, cultural, scientific, and artistic fragmentation is the postmodern American novel, a novel that is aesthetically, structurally, and philosophically different from the modern American novel.

The modern American novel is usually narrated by a single narrator, in most cases exclusively in the first-person or the third-person limited omniscient voice, with the narrator serving as a fictive device whose purpose is to be a conjunction between story and reader. The postmodern American novel is often consciously metafictive, and as such, the narrator is aware that he or she is writing or telling a story; the story is often about the telling of the story, or the power of the telling of the story, or the process of the telling of the story, and of course, in the case or cases that the metafictive narrator, protagonist, or author is a war veteran, the act of telling the story is a cathartic act for the traumatized narrator, protagonist, or author. As Nigel Hunt notes, "In the case of writers with battle experience, they [war novels] may tell us something about what it is to be traumatized ... [and] our understanding of war trauma is enhanced by the study of works of literature, novels and poems written by war veterans" (211–12). William March's *Company K* is one such veteran-authored novel. As the postmodern novel will often have multiple narrative points of view or multiple narrators, this means that the story is told or seen through the eyes and minds of more than one narrator or character. This multiple-point-of-view narration allows the reader to see the pre-battle, battle, and post-battle action as it affects different characters in the novel. Additionally, multiple narrators allow such postmodern American novels to have more than one narrative structure; when one narrator is narrating the action, one type of literary text is used, such as very long, formal sentences, but when another narrator is narrating, short, choppy sentences are used, and so on. March's seminal text uses 113 first-person narrators—the members of World War I Marine infantry Company K—to tell 113 vignettes of war abroad and at home. The different styles of narration and capsulated storytelling allow the reader to glean the various narrators' educational backgrounds, fears, tertiary emotions, beliefs, opinions, thoughts, and so forth. The narrative fragmentation and antiform in this early or proto-postmodern American novel reflect the disjunctive post-war existence for March, a highly decorated combat veteran of World War I. Further, the 113 narrators and sketches are prescient in their heralding of the social and cultural rupture of the postmodern American existence.

In a postmodern world, the form of the modern narrator, and his or her unified, comprehensive narrative, is no longer valid. The linear narrative of the modern novel has lost its efficacy. Consequently, the postmodern narrative is often a non-linear narrative. Novels no longer are told, written, or narrated in a linear manner. The postmodern American novel will often have a narrative that leaps around in what seems to be a lack of cohesive order, and Tim O'Brien's *The Things They Carried* certainly does just this. The novel opens *in medias res* as the first paragraph of the first chapter of the work plops the reader directly into the Vietnam War and the daily activities and toils and burdens of an American infantry company. The second chapter leaps forward to a post-war meeting between the primary narrator and the commanding officer of the company, while the third chapter is a series of metafictive vignettes that occur during the war. The fourth chapter occurs prior to the narrator's wartime experiences, and the fifth chapter returns the reader to the war. And on the text continues, chapter by chapter, in-war, out-of-war, pre-war, post-war—even the narrator's childhood experiences with death and post-war visit to Vietnam become links in the seemingly unchained narration of the work. There is a lack of order in the postmodern universe, and there seems to be a lack of order in the postmodern narrative. Lucas Carpenter argues that "the postmodern [interpretive] approach to Vietnam, however, also lays claim to Vietnam as a quintessentially postmodern event to be imitated in a postmodern manner" (31). Hence, postmodern social and cultural disjunction leads to artistic and narrative disjunction, and a decentered, decentering world and war lead to a decentered, decentering art and novel.

Further, time is neither constant nor linear in the postmodern American novel. Time may shift within a chapter, a scene, a paragraph, or even a sentence to a future or past event or era. This slipperiness of temporality is analogous to the denial of universal order in a postmodern universe. Thanks to atomic science, the laws of nature no longer exist, and there is no logical natural order in the postmodern universe. As such, there need not be any order, even temporal order, in the postmodern American novel. On the battlefield, of course, universal order has been supplanted by universal chaos—or so it seems—and the logical measurements of time passing and chronological order are askew before, during, and after battle, as Silko shows so expertly in her masterwork, *Ceremony*. The first prose paragraph of the text is set after World War II, but it occurs during World War II, AND before World War II, AND after World War II (5–6), and Silko is so adept at temporal slipperiness that such time travel often occurs even within a single sentence. Tayo, Silko's protagonist, is a slave to time and trauma-induced time travel, and the reader travels the perilous journey, powerless to help Tayo or him- or herself. As such, both Tayo and the reader realize, in war and in the postmodern era, "that one is a meaningless pawn in the larger (though equally meaningless) game of history" (Carpenter 31). Man is powerless over history, and as such, man is powerless over time. Bowman's *Beach Red* explicitly argues for this time slavery, but does so quite differently than does *Ceremony*. While Silko's text is temporal slavery secondary to temporal anti-linearism, Bowman's text is sixty minutes long and is told minute-by-minute as a countdown to death—the final sixty minutes of the protagonist's life. Each two-page chapter is one minute in time—tick, tick, tick—so while Bowman's time is linear, his protagonist is just as powerless over time as is Silko's, a pawn to time, to war, to history, to postmodernism.

As the modern American novel has the protagonist as proto-existentialist or Stirnerian nihilist, the postmodern American novel has the true, Sartrean, post–World War II, existentialist—one who believes in experience over essence—or the post-war, post–Nietzschean, existential nihilist—one who believes in nothing ... utterly and absolutely, without corruption and without bias. As Alan Pratt notes, "Existential nihilism begins with the notion that the world is without meaning or purpose. Given this circumstance, existence itself—all action, suffering, and feeling—is ultimately senseless and empty" ("Existential Nihilism"); thus, "life has no intrinsic meaning or value" ("Origins"). For example, in Mailer's *The Naked and the Dead*, a novel that "recalls the naturalist novel in its narrative sprawl and sheer bulk" (Dawes, "American" 56), Intelligence and Reconnaissance platoon leader Staff Sergeant Sam Croft is a near-perfect existential nihilist—"I HATE EVERYTHING WHICH IS NOT IN MYSELF [Mailer's caps]" (164), and Red Valsen is an excellent example of a practicing existentialist—"You know, I'll tell ya something, I don't believe in God" (224). Valsen's existentialist believes in a daily human existence, but Croft's nihilist will not even admit to a life of experience over essence. An ultimate showdown between the two shows the power of nothing over the power of existence (694–96), as Valsen submits to Croft's will rather than his rank; Croft will willingly kill his peers, and does so when necessary, while Valsen only wants to live, and so, rather than die at Croft's hand, Valsen chooses submission and life over disobedience and death. As the modern world no longer exists and the postmodern world's end is pending, thinks the nihilist, why believe in anything but oneself? Thinks the existentialist, if this is existence, so be it.

Rather than present life in a manner of realism, the postmodern novel often presents life in a manner of anti-realism. Anti-realism is a narrative removal from reality that includes the reader; many Vietnam-era novels of war include anti-realistic passages in which characters escape reality by ingesting psychedelic, narcotic, or hallucinogenic drugs, or suffer post-traumatic psychosis. While not a focus of this study, Larry Heinemann's *Paco's Story* (1986) and Tim O'Brien's *Going After Cacciato* (1978), both National Book Award winners, are excellent examples of postmodern novels of war that use anti-realism. Literary representations of combat veterans can also experience post-war or peri-war hallucinatory dream sequences. The "Private Manuel Burt" (245–53) episode of *Company K* is an splendid early example of a combat veteran's post-traumatic or traumatic psychotic mental illness presented as a journey into an anti-realistic setting; the narrator — Burt — sees and experiences and communicates with a German soldier he had killed during World War I, up to the point that he has a psychotic break from reality. One wonders to whom Burt is narrating, and the immediate and obvious answer is a psychoanalyst of some sort. In times of war, with death at hand each day, reality can be too much of a burden, and thus anti-realistic escapes such as drugs and fantastical dreams are needed in order to cope. Further, in times after war, because death was at hand each day, reality can still be too much of a burden, and thus anti-realistic escapes are psychically manifested, so as to attempt to cope, consciously or unconsciously.

While the modern American novel is created primarily of narrated text, the postmodern American novel is created of narrated text and Internal Paratext. As "para" means beyond or beside, Paratext means text beyond or beside the text proper, and Internal Paratext is paratext that is contained within the first and last pages of the story but is not embedded in the prose. As well, to be considered true Internal Paratext, the non-prose text must contribute materially to the rhetorical purpose of the work. Thus, in order to fragment and further the story, the postmodern American novel often will contain advertisements, footnotes, song lyrics, newspaper articles or editorials, poems, letters, lists, and many other types of Internal Paratext. For example, Mailer's *The Naked and the Dead* uses lyrics from myriad popular songs of the World War II era to enhance the moods of homesickness and feelings of isolation felt among the men who are fighting in the jungles of the Pacific isles, and Hasford's *The Short-Timers* uses excerpts from the "Marine Hymn," examples of boot camp drill cadence, and sundry USO letters from American schoolchildren to enhance and contrast the rhetorical effect of the brutal and ultra-violent prose. Further, the use of Internal Paratext is also a postmodern denial of the validity of the modern novel form; the prose narrative story, as once was written, is not sufficient in a postmodern world, and Silko's *Ceremony*, with its bifurcated text of alternating poetry and prose, uses the ancient to create the postmodern, not unlike McCarthy's *Blood Meridian*, which cloaks its postmodern premise of historical American over-violence within the model of a middle-nineteenth century novel, with each numbered chapter containing a pre-chapter, hyphenated, sentence-subject synopsis. Such is the advent and sometimes overuse of Internal Paratext in the postmodern American novel.

As the modern has the hero or semi-heroic figure, the postmodern has the anti-hero, the very flawed but occasionally heroic figure. In a postmodern world, no one is a hero; the order of heroes and villains is out of time and place and date. As well, one era's hero may be another's villain. However, in the postmodern universe, the flawed or the very flawed individual can act heroically or nobly, if only temporarily and within a given context, and postmodern American war novels are rife with anti-heroes, those who act heroically in isolated instances but behave antisocially on a serial basis, but very few Sergeant Alvin Yorks are to be found. So, Heller's *Catch-22* contains, among others, Captain John Yossarian, a bombardier who has flown seventy-one (411) combat missions, yet deserts to Sweden (461–63)—not without good reason, of course—and a character who mirrors Hassan's postmodern anti-hero as "rebel-victim" ("Character" 3), one whose ethic is "defined existentially by his actions and even more by his passions" (4). Yossarian's existential actions are, of course, motivated by a passion for staying alive; hence, the desertion. McCarthy's *Blood Meridian* contains a number of differently anti-heroic figures. Judge Holden, pederast, intellect, and murderer, a marble among malignancies, stands out as perhaps one of the greatest characters in all of postmodern American fiction, or all of American fiction for that matter, while the kid and Tobin and Toadvine, and other members of John Joel Glanton's gang, possess heroic qualities in the context of the novel—if heroism is defined as the willingness to kill or die beside one's fighting peers. Potok's *I Am the Clay* shows that refugees, powerless but selfish in their drive to survive, can possess heroic qualities, such as helping a wounded child, while also possessing anti-heroic qualities, such as letting others starve. Clearly, then, the postmodern anti-hero is not a single, specific type but a chameleon of anti-heroic qualities, subjectified by authorial need, which, of course, is suitably postmodern.

Obviously, then, the postmodern American novel is a very different construct than is the modern American novel—in characterization, in narrative structure, in theology and philosophy, in prosody, in chronology, in reality, and in psychological setting—and, of course, both the modern American novel canon and the postmodern American novel canon contain novels that can be conjoined in the novel sub-genre of American novel of war. In the study at hand, 23 novels will be examined as American novels of war. Five of the novels are explicitly modern, nine are explicitly postmodern, and nine are "tweeners"—novels written during postmodern era, but that are, nonetheless, structurally, aesthetically, and philosophically modern. As Ihab Hassan notes, "Modernism and Postmodernism are not separated by an Iron Curtain or Chinese Wall; for history is a palimpsest, and culture is permeable to time past, time present, and time future" ("Postface" 84). The dated Cold War analogy notwithstanding, it is, of course, perfectly plausible that a work might possess literary and/or structural aspects out of the typical modern/postmodern oppositional dyad, and such is the case with a number of works in this study: Pat Frank's *Hold Back the Night* (1952), Ernest Frankel's *Band of Brothers* (1958), Edward Franklin's *It's Cold in Pongo-Ni* (1965), Richard Hooker's *MASH* (1968), Terrence D. Haynes' *Desert Norm: A Journal/Novel About the Gulf War* (2002), Charles Sheehan-Miles' *Prayer at Rumayla: A Novel of the Gulf War* (2001), E.L. Doctorow's *The March* (2005), Cole Bolchoz's *A Medic in Iraq: A Novel of the Iraq War* (2007), and Karl Marlantes' *Matterhorn: A Novel of the Vietnam War* (2010). While written during the postmodern era, all of the works except for Doctorow's are set during the postmodern era. Further, each of these works follows a linear narrative line as well as temporal contiguousness, and each text has a neatly fixated beginning, middle, and end. Historically, and in order of publication, these postmodern-cum-modern texts complete a recursive post–World War II cycle that begins with Mailer's text and ends with Marlantes,' a cycle that runs from one post-atomic epic to another.

Now, relative to the texts that are included in this study, some modern, some post-modern, some structured in modernity but written and published in the postmodern era, and all American, a brief mention must be made of texts and types of texts not included in this study. Of course, as this work is a study of the American novel of war, novels written by non–American authors or expatriate authors relocated to the United States are not included. As such, many fine World War I novels written by British, French, and German authors are not presented here, novels such as Richard Aldington's *Death of a Hero* (1929), Henri Barbusse's *Under Fire* (1916), and Erich Maria Remarque's seminal modern master-piece *All Quiet on the Western Front* (1929). As a rule, novels that are from and of the Cold War, and novels focused on the spy game, are not included here, such as Tom Clancy's mega-selling *Hunt for Red October* (1984), *Patriot Games* (1987), and *Clear and Present Danger* (1989), and Milt Bearden's *The Black Tulip: A Novel of War in Afghanistan* (1998). As a rule, novels commonly known as war novels but that take place primarily out of the war zone or have primary non-war thematic elements like "love in a time of war" or "issues at home during a time of war" or farcical non-war premises are not included, novels that include such out-standing works as Willa Cather's *One of Ours* (1922), Ernest Hemingway's *A Farewell to Arms* (1929), James Jones' *From Here to Eternity* (1951), William Styron's *The Long March* (1953), Leon Uris' *Battle Cry* (1953), John Oliver Killens' *And Then We Heard the Thunder* (1963), George Sidney's *For the Love of Dying* (1969), Kurt Vonnegut's *Slaughterhouse-Five* (1969), James Webb's *Fields of Fire* (1978), Robert Stone's *Dog Soldiers* (1974), Bobbie Ann Mason's *In Country: A Novel* (1985), and, more recently, Christian Bauman's *The Ice Beneath You* (2002), Luke S. Larson's *Senator's Son: An Iraq War Novel* (2008), Toni Morrison's *Home* (2012), and Ben Fountain's *Billy Lynn's Long Halftime Walk* (2012). Also not included are war series texts such as Herman Wouk's *The Winds of War* (1971) and *War and Remembrance* (1978), and the works of John Jakes, W.E.B Griffin, and Jack Terral. Simply put, the works mentioned above, while all war novels or novels that include war or are written by writers of war fiction, do not meet the defining characteristics of this study, and as such are not included.

So, what is war, and what is a novel? According to James Der Derian, "War is a form of organized violence conducted by states, with commonly accepted (if not always observed) rules against bombing, assassination, armed assaults, kidnapping, hostage-taking, and hijacking of civilians" (98). This definition, concise and succinct and on target (so to speak), serves the purpose of this study, and all of the texts in this study contain war, as is defined by Der Derian. While terrorism, as defined by Der Derian, is "a strategy of intimidation and violence [that] relies on unpredictable, randomized violence to achieve it various objec-tives" (98), what sets terrorism apart from war is war's conduction by states—that is, nations. Esoterically, and historically, and geopolitically, one can argue whether or not states sponsor terrorism, but such an argument is not the goal or focus here, and as such, war (more spe-cifically, war in which Americans have participated and of which Americans have written) is the focus here: war as "a form of organized violence conducted by states," in which and of which Americans have participated and written. Relative to the second query in the topic sentence (what is a novel?), one could write a book rather than a paragraph, of course, but suffice to say, all of the works in this study are book-length prose or prose-poetry constructs of a narrative nature that contain the central thematic element of physical war and, in some cases, the results thereof. Many of these texts follow a central character or characters who undergo a passage from "innocence to experience involving some combination of fear, courage, brotherhood, sacrifice" (Carpenter 31), violence, and loss of life. Quite often, the warrior/character's earned results of this passage from innocence to experience are peri-

and post-war bitterness, hostility, and hopelessness. It bears mention, too, that one can assume that each novel's author is attempting to document that which he or she sees to be the truth of war — that is, the true war story, or the truth of the war story. This is what war is, the war novelist argues. And these are what the American novels of war are, this author argues.

The first defining characteristic of the American novel of war is that the war at hand is the central theme or defining action of the text. All of the novels in this study centralize the theme and topic and actions and results of war. One asks, would the novel exist sans the war at hand? If the answer is no, then the novel is not in this study. But, if the central thematic action of the text is war, if the locus of the guts of the work is the war zone, if the optic of the philosophy of the novel is the view of war, then, obviously, the work is a novel of war. Thus, were it not for the real wars covered in the fiction, these novels would not exist, and while not every author here is a combat veteran, every novel here is by and of combat — in theme, in topic, in element. For example, in *Blood Meridian*, Cormac McCarthy presents the child, then the kid, then the filibuster, then the scalphunter, and finally the post-war man, who, in the end, cannot or does not live without war. What is more, the American novel of war is a presentation of war, and in the McCarthy text — as well as in each text in this study — war is the protagonist, not the judge, nor the kid, nor Captain White, nor even John Joel Glanton. "War is god" (249), says the judge, and the judge is right, as war is the creator of each novel of war. Further, each novel used for analysis in this study has been chosen for its literary presentation of war, and while a number of texts here will not be historically noted for literariness — however that may be critically or popularly defined — all of the texts here present war in a literary fashion. A novel of war must have war and the physical, psychological, spiritual, social, and cultural effects of war; otherwise, it is not a novel of war. A novel of war must be born of war; otherwise, it is not a novel of war.

Next, the violence in the American novel of war is real, not symbolic, not metaphorical, not verbal, not imagined, not cold — hence the absence of Cold War tomes in this study. The violence is real and present and is written out on the page and experienced by the characters in the text. The novel's violence exists on the battlefield first, if not primarily; then, after the battlefield violence occurs, the war violence resonates in the minds of the participants. All of the novels of war in this study have extended scenes of battlefield violence, and all of the texts deal with the physical, psychological, emotional, and intellectual traumas that the combatants undergo before, during, and after battle. In order of combat era or war, *Blood Meridian*, *The Red Badge of Courage*, *Through the Wheat*, *Ceremony*, *Band of Brothers*, *The Short-Timers*, *Matterhorn*, and *Prayer at Rumayla* each present the violence of war realistically and without compromise. *Blood Meridian* and *The Short-Timers* are texts composed of historically verifiable and nearly omnipresent violence, and the former text is a masterwork of artifice and verisimilitude, while the latter is an explosion of boot camp and war zone rage and conflict. *The Red Badge of Courage* and *Through the Wheat* are seminal texts in that each work, early in the American canon, showed the violence — and bloody cost — of war realistically for a readership that, up to that particular time in history, had not been exposed to war violence in such a realistic mode. Late nineteenth-century readers of the Crane text assumed that Crane was a veteran of the U.S. Civil War, while readers of the Boyd text knew that Boyd certainly was. Further, *Ceremony*, *Band of Brothers*, and *Matterhorn* each present interpolated but extended battle scenes of exquisite violence, on a grand and petite scale, in which the American combatants face elemental dangers as well as hostile enemies. *Prayer at Rumayla*, alone in this study, expressly presents tank warfare and the human carnage resultant thereof. Inherently and intrinsically, man is violence—man is war, and a novel of war must have the violence of war, and the effects of the violence of war; otherwise, it is not a novel of war.

An American novel of war must also contain the rhetoric of war. The narrator and characters must continually use such rhetoric—war lingo, war slang, war clichés, war abbreviations and acronyms, and, of course, war propaganda and obfuscation—to refer to war equipage, war nomenclature, war stuff, and war incitation and justification; this language of war is a constant part of the dialogue and narration and is spoken both by the warriors who fight the wars and the politicians who declare and order the wars. The rhetoric of war is fascinating, funny, and infuriating, and is also very much era specific and war specific. As such, the rhetoric of war from the Civil War—the early 1860s—is quite different from the rhetoric of war from the Vietnam War—the late 1960s—and a collation, examination, and analysis of the rhetoric of war from *The Red Badge of Courage* (infantry men's argot), to *Blood Meridian* (the language of the Monroe Doctrine and Manifest Destiny) to *Johnny Got His Gun* (official government rhetoric and obfuscation) to *The Short-Timers* (omnipresent, page-by-page, text-wide Marine jargon), to *The Things They Carried* (a "hard vocabulary" [20] section), to *Matterhorn*'s 31-page, post-text "Glossary of Weapons, Technical Terms, Slang, and Jargon" (569–600) shows that, while the rhetoric of war may change with the era and the particular war, the presence of the rhetoric of war during war is constant; as such, the presence of the rhetoric of war in the American Novel of war is constant, and is constantly evolving. Warriors talk about war while fighting war, and politicians talk about war while declaring, promoting, and justifying war; hence, the presence of the rhetoric of war in all of the novels of war in this study.

In conjunction with the omnipresent rhetoric of war, the tools and equipment and weapons of war are consistently at hand in the American novel of war. The Civil War was the first war to use mass-produced weapons, which led to mass death, of course, and from Crane's text onward, novels of war catalog the equipage of war; interestingly, and obviously, each war introduces new weapons with which and by which men can destroy one another, so each war introduces war-relative weapons and equipment. All soldiers need beans, brass, bullets, bandages, and like manner of weapons to fight a war, and as technology is created and evolves, warriors need planes, and tanks, and ships, and artillery, and mortars, and automated weapons, and so on, to support the ground fighting. For what is a war without the weapons of war? And what is a novel of war without the weapons of war? By chronological order of war, *The Red Badge of Courage, One Man's Initiation, Company K, Through the Wheat, Beach Red, Band of Brothers, Hold Back the Night, The Things They Carried,* and *Desert Norm* each present extended catalogs of the weapons and equipment of war, relative, of course, to each war's historical era. By presenting this system of era- and war-specific nomenclature, the authors are juxtaposing the Civil War warrior's tools with the World War I warrior's tools with the World War II warrior's tools, and so on, through the Korean War to the Vietnam War to the Gulf War to the Iraq War; each war is of a different era, and each war is fought with different tools of destruction. So, the gross artillery and the musketry and muzzle-loading riflery of the U.S. Civil War are contrasted with the massive artillery and machine-guns and grenades and gas of World War I, which thereby are contrasted with the automatic hand-held weaponry and wired radio communication of World War II, which are then contrasted with the helicopters and wireless radio communication of the Korean War, which are contrasted with the wholesale helicopter use and jungle-war equipment of the Vietnam War, which are explicitly contrasted with the desert-relative and early digital-era equipment of the Gulf War, and so it goes. Business is booming, yes? With each successive war, there is technological innovation, and there are new ways to fight and to kill. Further, by presenting this systemized nomenclature of war, the authors of the American novel of war are juxtaposing the warrior's task with the farmer's or the carpenter's or the merchant's. The warrior's task, of course, is death and dying, and these are his tools.

In war — in any war — fighting peers die. Without fail, in the American novel of war, a significant number of fighting peers — primary as well as secondary characters — will die, individually or *en masse*, before the close of the text. *Blood Meridian*, *Band of Brothers*, *Hold Back the Night*, *Matterhorn*, and *The Short-Timers* each has a diminishing cast of characters — as does every text in this study. In *Blood Meridian*, a remarkable number of scalp-hunters, never mind filibusters, do not live until the end of the text; in fact, all are gone but for the judge and perhaps Tobin, and the filibusters and scalphunters are killed in battle; are shot, stabbed, hanged, and mortally wounded in a variety of ways; are captured and tortured and killed; are ambushed and sniped; and occasionally are killed by each other. The two Korean War texts here contain a remarkable number of dying combatants, named and unnamed, and in each text, American combatants die by the hundreds — or thousands — as 1st Division Marines of X Corps attempt a strategic but unbelievably brutal withdrawal through overwhelming numbers of Chinese and North Korean forces from the Chosin Reservoir to the Port of Hungnam. Conversely, the two Vietnam War texts here contain a limited number of peer deaths, and the deaths concern named characters, characters with which the reader is engaged. Not that the deaths of primary characters in *Band of Brothers* and *Hold Back the Night* are sans pathos, but a number of character deaths in *Matterhorn* and *The Short-Timers* are especially shocking and emotionally evocative. Fighting peers die in all wars, and the American novel of war must and does present this facet of war.

In war, and in the American novel of war, warriors are not the only people who die: noncombatants die, too. On purpose and through accident, men and women civilians, children, entire families, and whole populations of villages and towns are killed, secondary to the war and regardless of the lines of battle. The death of noncombatants is a facet of all wars, and therefore must be a facet of all accurate novels of war. In *Blood Meridian*, *I Am the Clay*, *The Short-Timers*, *The Things They Carried*, and *A Medic in Iraq*, the life of a noncombatant in a war zone is most terrifyingly presented, and the texts show that, regardless of era or war or location of war, noncombatants in war zones die. In all of these texts, both allies and enemies of those who try to exist in areas overrun by battle kill local peoples who are not armed and active participants in the war. That is, the strong and armed kill the weak and unarmed. For example, in *Blood Meridian*, Apaches, Comanche, Yumas, and contracted scalphunters kill unarmed and noncombatant Anglos, Apaches, Mexicans, and Gileños. In *I Am the Clay*, both the invading Chinese forces as well as the occupying American forces use mechanized warfare to kill numerous rural peasant Korean civilians. And in *The Short-Timers* and *The Things They Carried*, American weaponry in the form of tanks, air support, and infantry kill children, women, and old men. Meanwhile, the narrator of *A Medic in Iraq* laments the fact that Iraqi civilians "do not have the luxury of choosing whether or not to be blown up in their markets" (Location 1595 of 1666). In a war zone, routine daily activities are deadly, life expectancy is short, and families in a war zone do not survive the war intact. The parents, grandparents, siblings, and children of the local young men who are partaking in war are casualties of the war, killed through combat, but not counted as combat casualties. Rhetorically, human lives become "collateral damage," and the war goes on for all but the dead, while the living are not even allowed to properly mourn their lost family members.

In addition to the combat deaths of fighting peers and the deaths of noncombatants, there is omnipresent death and destruction in war and in the American novel of war, not merely the deaths of noncombatants and combatants, but also the destruction of animals houses, farms, schools, hospitals, villages, towns, cities, roads, highways, bridges, railroads, cars, trucks, planes, helicopters, boats, ships, and entire nations. War is death, and war is destruction; this is a fact of every war, and omnipresent death and destruction is a defining characteristic situated in every true and accurate modern and postmodern novel of war. And of course, in the works studied here, many animals are slaughtered, and a number of nameless and named towns and villages cease to exist, while wells are poisoned and hamlets are burned into nothingness. Each of the 23 novels in this study uses this omnipresent death and destruction thematic element, but a survey of *The March, One Man's Initiation, The Marne, Catch-22, I Am the Clay, The Things They Carry,* and *Prayer at Rumayla* shows the timelessness, breadth, and scope of omnipresent death and destruction during war — any war, every war. In *The March,* General William Tecumseh Sherman and his Union troops ride and run through Georgia, South Carolina, and North Carolina, and sack and burn, and collect and conquer; no town, nor city, nor countryside that faces Sherman's troops escapes the destruction and death borne of an army 60,000 strong. *The Marne* and *One Man's Initiation* describe repeated scenes of devastation and carnage secondary to relentless artillery barrages that go on for years at a time, and Wharton is especially adept at presenting imagery of destroyed villages, while Dos Passos is equally skilled at offering mimeography of savaged forests and gutted mules. *I Am the Clay* offers the tools of mechanized war — jets, tanks, helicopters—versus ancient villages and livestock, both of which become litter under rocket or tread or machine-gun. *The Things They Carry* and *Prayer at Rumayla* carry the theme of omnipresent death and destruction into the late postmodern era. The former text does so in an old-fashioned way, though, as American troops (not without cause?) drop dead animals into village wells and burn thatched-hut villages to ashes. The latter text renders the results of the American incursion into Iraq during the Gulf War "a trail of burning vehicles and broken bodies hundreds of miles long" (98). In any era, in any country, in every war, the result of war is the same — omnipresent death and destruction. As such, in every American novel of war this thematic element is readily apparent.

Of course, local noncombatants who are not killed secondary to battle are quite often displaced from their regions or homes and are thus forced to become refugees in their own nation or land. The omnipresent death and destruction secondary to modern and postmodern warfare inevitably leads to large-scale relocation of those in the way of the war machine, and in the American novel of war, if noncombatants are present — and living — then the displacement of locals to refugees automatically takes place in the text. One must move or die. This thematic element of war and the novel of war is timeless, trans-war, transnational, and trans-religious. *The March, The Marne, Hold Back the Night, I Am the Clay, The Short-Timers,* and *Prayer at Rumayla* present a comprehensive survey of this enduring war theme. *The March* and *I Am the Clay* show — in the middle nineteenth and twentieth centuries, respectively, and in the United States and Korea — the steamrolling effect of the war machine upon the local populations, both Christian and Buddhist — the former, from an optic that is broad and deep and sweeping; the latter, from the finite and localized point of view of the refugee. Further, the theme of the refugee occurs in wars great and limited; *The Marne* and *Prayer at Rumayla* present the theme of the Christian and Muslim war refugee in the early and late twentieth century, in Europe and in the Middle East. Finally, *Hold Back the Night* and *The Short-Timers* illustrate the effects of internecine war among the local population as Chinese and American invader/occupiers ally with political comrades in arms to oppose political combatants in arms. What all of these texts have in common is the argument that war begets refugees, as does the American novel of war.

Naturally, in war, and in the American novel of war, there is an oppositional dyad between the occupying/invading forces and the indigenous/local peoples. Even without the war-born deaths of noncombatants, and the omnipresent death and destruction, and the displacement of refugees, the presence of non-native, non-national armed forces is a cause of great social, cultural, political, racial, and religious enmity between the occupier/invaders and the local/indigenous peoples. Historically, and in the literature of war, this oppositional dyad is a fact of all wars. An inherent lack of trust between those who have come and those who have been invaded or occupied also enters the socio-cultural fray and leads to a supposition that no one — on either side — can be trusted by the other. *The Red Badge of Courage*, *Company K*, *Band of Brothers*, *The Short-Timers*, *Desert Norm*, and *A Medic in Iraq* show that this oppositional dyad between invader/occupiers and the locals is one that runs from the nineteenth century to the twenty-first century and occurs wherever war occurs. A brief passage in *The Red Badge of Courage* posits a corpulent Union soldier against a civilian young lady as the soldier arrogantly attempts to steal the woman's horse, and multiple sketches in *Company K* posit war-exhausted French civilians against new-to-war American Marines. And so, even when allied, occupiers and the indigenous do not seem to want one another. *Band of Brothers*, *The Short-Timers*, and *Desert Norm* show that the locals and the occupiers, even when invited by the government of the occupied, in the Far East or in the Middle East, in the twentieth or in the twenty-first century, tend not to get along — to the point of killing each other. And finally, *A Medic in Iraq* offers the explicit hatred of the local populace toward the uninvited American invaders whose quid pro quo toppled a dictator but invited the terrorist. Clearly, then, invited or invading armed occupiers are resented to the point of hatred by the indigenous occupied. This facet of war is common to all wars and of course is common to the American novel of war.

Another oppositional dyad that exists in the American novel of war is an oppositional dyad between the officers and the enlisted men. This dyad between officers and enlisted goes back hundreds if not thousands of years and is time-honored in the literature of war, American and otherwise. The conflict between the officers and the enlisted men is complex and historical and involves tensions related to education level, command level, military experience and service in relation to rank, combat experience in relation to battlefield command, pay scale, and food and housing discrepancies, and can be seen explicitly in *The Red Badge of Courage*, *Company K*, *One Man's Initiation*, *Through the Wheat*, *The Naked and the Dead*, and *The Short-Timers*. In the American novel of war, the result of this tension between the officers and the enlisted entities within a fighting unit can be catastrophic as well as comedic, contingent upon the novel. *Company K*, *The Naked and the Dead*, and *The Short-Timers* show the catastrophic, the act of fragging an officer (that is, killing the officer — the term comes from using a fragmentation grenade to do so), with the chosen actions of enlisted men leading to the deaths of officers, directly or indirectly, while *One Man's Initiation* and *Through the Wheat* offer the oppositional dyad in a lighter tone, as the former presents a decorated officer as less than honorable, and the latter shows a major general as a bumbling buffoon. *The Red Badge of Courage*, the seminal American text containing this thematic element, uses a number of scenes of a low-ranking officer — a company lieutenant, in particular — beating the enlisted ranks, and also of hapless, confused generals, to pillory the officer class. And as officers are often drawn as incompetent and clownish in novels of war, enlisted men are just as often drawn as murderous and vengeful. Time and battle — and text — tested, the oppositional dyad between officers and enlisted men is a ready literary device in the American novel of war.

As war, and the American novel of war, most often includes the deployment of American forces on foreign soils, the foreign terrain or weather becomes an enemy or a battlefield opponent. Extreme heat, extreme cold, jungles, mountains, deserts, rain, ice, sleet, snow, wind, dust, rivers, oceans, and lakes all adversely affect the warrior's mission and life and combat conditions, as do indigenous flora, fauna, and disease. Each and all add misery to the daily existence of the warrior, no matter the rank, age, gender, land in question, service branch, or war. That said, novels written about specific wars and eras share the intertextuality of the locus of the war. *Blood Meridian* explores the hostilities of the Chihuahua desert, "a terra damnata of smoking slag" (61) and dead men and animals, while early in *The Red Badge of Courage*, Henry Fleming's regiment fights only the cold as it waits out the months of the harsh winter in Washington, D.C. Novels set in Europe during World War I, such as *One Man's Initiation, Company K,* and *Through the Wheat,* share the related natural elements of that war — rain, mud, lice — while novels set in the Pacific theater during World War II, such as *Beach Red, Ceremony,* and *The Naked and the Dead,* share the hostile elements of Pacific jungle warfare — rain, heat, humidity, disease-ridden insects, and "Jungle law" (Bowman 57). Novels set during the brutal winter campaigns of the Korean War, such as *Band of Brothers, Hold Back the Night, I Am the Clay,* and *It's Cold in Pongo-Ni,* share the thematic element of the cruel Korean winter, and in each text, the hostile winter weather — death-inducing weather — becomes a character in the text as the works clearly illustrate how the severe cold can kill warriors as effectively and efficiently and heartlessly as an enemy combatant. Jungle law returns in the Vietnam War novels, as evidenced in *Matterhorn* and *The Things They Carried,* novels in which animals and insects and leaches and triple-canopy jungle and monsoon rains are unarmed, uncombatable enemies in war. This motif of the terrain or weather becoming an enemy is one that is found in American novels of war because it is one that is found in American wars; truth finds its way into art, verisimilitude into artifice.

Another truth found in war and in the American novel of war is the burning or fire motif. In war, all sorts of things and animals and people and places burn and are burned. Modern and postmodern war machines run on fuel, and fuel burns and explodes; modern and postmodern war machines likewise run on explosives, and, of course, explosives explode and lead to the collateral burning of humans, vehicles, buildings, towns, cities, regions, states, and nations. War and burning are conjoined, shackled, and bonded to one another, and war and fire exist in a destructive and symbiotic relationship. Especially shocking are scenes of humans burning and burned, and *Prayer at Rumayla* shows what postmodern incendiary weapons can do when such weapons are unleashed upon human flesh, while *I Am the Clay,* with a recurrent and explicit burning motif, seems to be a panegyric to the Holocaust and to all those who lost their lives in the fires of World War II and the Korean War. Conversely, *The March,* contextually, seems to be aware that fire is indeed a physical and psychological component of the new modern warfare; in this way, Doctorow's text seems a harbinger of the war-manifested holocausts to come. Yet, obviously, fire as a tactic to terrorize and destroy is not a new war tactic, and many cities and places and people have burned in ancient, pre-modern, and early modern times, so historically fire is not a new weapon, and the fire or burning motif is liberally present in the other nineteenth-century settings of *Blood Meridian* and *The Red Badge of Courage*. What makes the fire or burning motif elemental in modern and postmodern warfare and the modern and postmodern American novel of war are the tools used to conduct fire- and burning-specific warfare. *Through the Wheat* shows how World War I mustard gas led to severe, debilitating, excruciating — and often fatal — burns after it came into contact with one's skin. *Beach Red* offers the results of what happens when a man meets a flamethrower, and *It's Cold in Pongo-Ni* introduces the chemical effectiveness of white phosphorus hand grenades and napalm. In war, and in the American novel of war, fire, chemically enhanced or not, beats, and burns, and immolates man, and places, and things.

And along with fire, can there be war and warriors— and texts of war — without prostitution? Prostitution is nearly always present in the American novel of war, and only *The Red Badge of Courage* does not explicitly mention prostitution in any way — although one scene does warrant attention, analysis, and speculation. Of course, the woman's body as commodity is a motif or thematic element in literature that can be easily traced to pre-Classical eras and texts, as is the motif of the woman prostitute in time of war. For when a woman is a refugee, when a woman has no money, or home, or food, or possessions, or anything else materially or socially, a woman still has one commodity — her sexualized body — and male warriors (on all sides of every war) seek sexual release from the life-and-death pressures of war. As such, prostitution thrives in times of war, and nearly every novel of war researched and read for this study, American and otherwise, contains the presence of prostitutes and prostitution. Of importance here, *MASH* and *Catch-22* show thriving and organized prostitution operations that are text-wide and fully thematic in nature. *MASH* shows that organized prostitution activities befit organizational names— The Famous Curb Service Whorehouse and Dr. Yamamoto's Finest Kind Pediatric Hospital and Whorehouse — and operate "regardless of the [brutal] Korean weather" (14) and often with philanthropy in mind. Prostitution is so omnipresent in *Catch-22*, and the American airmen spend so much time with Italian prostitutes, that the trope of the man in love with the whore occurs repeatedly AND is reversed, as the character of Nately's whore falls in love with Nately, who is subsequently killed on a bombing run; Nately's unnamed whore then spends the rest of the novel trying to murder Yossarian, who had broken to her the news of Nately's death. Regardless of the text's comic absurdity, *Catch-22*'s prostitution theme is sad and enlightening; *Company K* presents prostitution in a similar way, as a young sexually indoctrinated member of Company K is introduced to carnality by a diseased prostitute — as a joke played upon him by his company peers— and is later court-martialed for failing to "report for a [medicinal, post-coital] prophylactic" (107) at the hospital dressing station. *I Am the Clay* also presents the sadder, yet necessary, role of wartime prostitute, as women who have nothing in a time of war are rarely far from the compounds of American soldiers. And so, while prostitution might not be necessary for the combat of war, prostitution is a necessary by-product of the situation of war. As these and numerous American novels of war show, thriving and organized wartime prostitution operations are situated where men of war are situated.

Finally, in the American novel of war, the absurdity of war is presented, often generously or with savage irony, often with comic absurdity or with abject tragedy. While the absurdity of war is found in many American novels of war, frequently the absurd situations are so seriously presented that one may not notice the absurdity of the given scene and situation because of the life-and-death nature of the goings-on in the text. In some war texts, the absurdity is laughable, but, however, as the locus is war, in many instances the comic absurdity leads to the death or deaths of the allied combatants, so the reader does not readily notice the absurd. While *Catch-22* and *MASH* immediately come to mind when one thinks absurdity of war and war text, *Company K, Johnny Got His Gun, It's Cold in Pongo-Ni*, and *Desert Norm* all deal overtly with the absurdity of war, comic and tragic. Of course, *Catch-22*'s title is born of the ever-increasing number of bombing missions that Yossarian and his peers must undertake before being transferred to a safe, non-combat billet, while the comedic absurdity in *MASH* is nearly overwhelming and rhetorically counterproductive in its exponentially explicit and less-than-subtle nature. Less humorous, though, is the fact that the in-theatre surgical hospitals in *MASH* exist to mend battered warriors so that the battered can return to battle, and in *Catch-22*, each increase in flight count leads to more deaths of pilots, co-pilots, and flight-crew members, so beneath each comic text lies a rage, an incipient anger at war and its deathly absurdity. *Company K* and *Johnny Got His Gun* are also texts that howl with fury. The former, a very serious text, is littered with vignettes of comic and seriocomic absurdity; for example, officers get morphine sulfate for pain, while enlisted men do not; some prostitutes service officers only, and a man with sniping skills taunts an enemy sniper, and endangers his own life, by altering his gait and attitude as he moves about the allied trenches. *Johnny Got His Gun*, a text absolutely seething with rage, presents a narrative protagonist who is so maimed from war that he cannot even commit suicide; this situation is absurd, but not untrue, nor unrealistic. Like *MASH*, *It's Cold in Pongo-Ni* uses the motif of inter-unit American football to present the comically absurd; in the latter text, a starting fullback is sent on a combat reconnaissance mission — the combat purpose of the book — so it is imperative that he survive the mission. At the conclusion of this deadly mission, the man is called upon to play football; no doubt in each text there is present the absurdity in the rhetorical and over-used analogy between the game of football and the "game" of war. Finally, in *Desert Norm*, the narrator refers to the Gulf War as a TV war, one offered to the public AND to the warriors by satellite and cable TV; this television-ization of war makes celebrities of those on TV, especially the commanding generals. These examples show that one should not necessarily conjoin the absurdity of war with the humor of war; the absurdity of war can be tragic, of course, and it often is, while it can also be comic (and often is). While humor is often present in war novels — both literary and pulp — many serious American novels of war do not contain humor; that said, most, if not all, do contain the serious absurdity of war.

In closing, one can see, then, that the American novel of war is a self-standing subgenre of the greater genre of American literature of war, which includes memoirs, short stories, songs, poems, drama, and the like. Further, one can see that the American novel of war can be identified in both modern and postmodern American novel form. The stated goal of this author, with the publication of this critical study, is to create a set of standards by which and with which the American novel of war, both modern and postmodern, can be qualified, classified, and critically analyzed. In so doing, the author hopes to add to the corpus in some small way.

I

The Defining Characteristics of the American Novel of War as Found in American Poems, Short Stories, Dramas, and Memoirs of War

The defining characteristics of the American novel of war can be found not only in novels, of course, but also in other — genre-specific — literature of war. The difference between the use of the defining characteristics in the novels and in the non-novel works is the breadth and depth of the presence of the defining characteristics in the literary works. Partly because of length — with poetry, short story, drama, and some short memoir — and partly because of rhetorical focus, the novel-centric defining characteristics used in this study are not always elevated to the point of thematic concern in non-novel literature of war. However, many, if not most, of the shorter non-novel works of literature of war here, regardless of genre, do include many of the study's defining characteristics of the novel of war, but at the motif rather than thematic level. As well, because of brevity of length, it is common for the shorter works of war not to use all of the defining characteristics, but rather to fully develop one or two of the defining characteristics within the work. As such, some shorter works of war analyzed here use sundry defining characteristics within the work at an undeveloped level, while others use one or two of the defining characteristics at a wholly developed level. The poetry of war, the short story of war, the drama of war, and the memoir of war are the task at hand, and, almost exclusively, the works in this chapter were written by those who participated in war as combatants or in a medical capacity or viewed the war first-hand as war correspondents. Thus, the common mitigating factor among most of the authors of these literary works of war is direct war participation of some sort, and in shape, form, or genre, the works in this chapter are born of and are specific to the U.S. Civil War, World War I, World War II, the Korean War, the Vietnam War, the Persian Gulf War, the Iraq War, and the War in Afghanistan. There is even a brief foray back to the War of 1812 (18 June 1812–18 February 1815). As such, the documents here present a broad survey of the non-novel American-authored war literature of note from the early nineteenth century to the early twenty-first century. Further, each of the non-novel texts here utilizes the defining characteristics of the American novel of war, albeit at a level less prominent than in the novels of war analyzed in this study. The poetry, short story, drama, and memoir discussed in this chapter are relative to the novels discussed in the forthcoming chapters in the sense that each genre of American war literature contains similar thematic elements and motifs — the thematic elements and motifs of war.

Historically, direct experience of war is a common signifier in the poetry of war, regardless of era or war, and Philippa Lyon argues that for readers and critics, the "desire for a connection between war poetry and the 'real' experience of war is still very strong" (1), even in the twenty-first century. In fact, if one looks back and then forward, one can see clearly that the American soldier-poet's rhetorical influence is a force of war and the pen conjoined with poetic form to transcribe the effects of the battlefield upon warrior, civilian, and nation. One need look no further than the poem "In Defence of Fort McHenry," written in September 1814, to see that elements of war can be used as stirring symbols in a timeless manner: "And the rockets' red glare, the bombs bursting in air, / Gave proof through the night that our flag was still there" (5–6); of course, these lines are from Francis Scott Key's poem now commonly known and set to music as "The Star Spangled Banner." After the British forces burned Washington, D.C., on 24 August 1814, Key, a British captive, was witness to the bombardment of Fort McHenry, Maryland, on 13–14 September ("Star Spangled Banner and the War of 1812"). And while most Americans know only the verse of the first stanza, the poem, with the War of 1812 as the central action of the text, also mentions other timeless effects of war in addition to nineteenth-century mortar and rocket fusillades: "the havoc of war and the battle's confusion" (18) and the need for the free warrior to place himself between "loved home and the war's desolation!" (26). Rockets' red glare, bombs bursting in air, havoc of war, battle's confusion, war's desolation — each and all refer to elements of war seen through time and literary genre. The "rockets" and "bombs" are, of course, tools and equipment of war utilized in the violent outpouring of war and are used to inflict death and destruction upon civilian and military populations, and the "havoc" and "confusion" and "desolation" of war are secondary to the violence, and omnipresent death and destruction, of war waged upon a nation by externally based invading forces that are now internally based. So, even in this early American poem — pre–American literary modernism — a number of the defining characteristics of the American novel of war are explicitly presented.

Segueing from the historical and literary pre-modern to the literary modern as well as the modernity of war, Walt Whitman's "The Wound-Dresser" — originally titled "The Dresser" — from *Drum-Taps* (1865), presents modern war and the destructive results thereof centrally in the text. Whitman's war work in poetry was the result of his work in war; Whitman worked as a medical aide and "visited Washington area hospitals from late 1861 until June 1862, when his physical collapse brought doctor's warnings that he must not return" (Linderman 28). No doubt, Whitman's collapse was not merely physical. Post-traumatic wound infection and vermin infestation were more common than not, and apparently "Whitman was so unnerved by the sight of so many wormy, mortifying Wilderness wounds that he became ill and had to be evacuated to the North" (Linderman 128). Apropos to his role as the nation's poet, Whitman chronicled his horror at the effects of the nation's war in verse:

> On, on I go, (open doors of time! Open hospital doors!)
> The crush'd head I dress (poor crazed hand tear not the bandage away),
> The neck of the cavalry-man with bullet through and through I examine,
> Hard the breathing rattles, quite glazed already the eye, yet life struggles hard
> (Come sweet death! Be persuaded O beautiful death!
> In mercy come quickly).
>
> From the stump of the arm, the amputated hand,
> I undo the clotted lint, remove the slough, wash off the matter and blood,

> Back on his pillow the soldier bends with curv'd neck and side-falling head,
> His eyes are closed, his face is pale, he dares not look on the bloody stump,
> And has not yet looked on it.
>
> I dress a wound in the side, deep, deep,
> But a day or two more, for see the frame all wasted and sinking,
> And the yellow-blue countenance see.
> I dress the perforated shoulder, the foot with the bullet-wound,
> Cleanse the one with a gnawing and putrid gangrene, so sickening, so offensive,
> While the attendant stands behind aside me holding the tray and pail [39–55].

Viewed through the optic of the wound-dresser, the scene evokes an image of bed-after-bed-after-bed-after-bed of carnage, of mangled and dying soldiers and cavalry-men, a scene in which death is sweet, beautiful, and merciful because life is sour, rotting, and malodorous. The work seems to be one of metonymy, whereby this wound-dresser and these wounded are but some of the many, and the locus here, the Civil War field hospital, is the result of the violence of war — the place where maimed fighting peers go to die. And do not forget that it is not only trauma secondary to violent war that causes death; wound infection also causes death. As such, post-wound disease is an elemental enemy of the warriors. Walt Whitman, America's first modern poet, joins the U.S. Civil War, America's first modern war, and, through free verse and open stanzaic form, pens America's first modern war poetry.

Alan Seeger, whose "I Have a Rendezvous with Death" was written in 1915 and published posthumously in *Poems* starting in 1917, fatalistically writes of a fighting peer's death — his own. In so doing, ironically, Seeger, "America's only noteworthy poet of the Great War" (Matthews 228), juxtaposes spring with death rather than with life and foreshadows his own death on the battlefields of World War I: "I have a rendezvous with Death" (1, 5, 11, 20), the speaker claims in line 1 and thrice more repeats. In the poem, death plays the role of fated lover — "It may be he shall take my hand" (7) — and the speaker the role of willing accomplice — "And I to my pledged word am true, / I shall not fail that rendezvous" (23–24). Relative to this study, though, in addition to the (correctly) foreshadowed death of the speaker, are references to omnipresent death and destruction and the presence of the fire or burning motif: "I have a rendezvous with Death / On some scarred slope of battered hill" (11–12), and "I have a rendezvous with Death / At midnight in some flaming town" (20–21). Lines 11 and 12 conjoin death and locus and refer to the land-based devastation brought on by month-after-month-after-month of artillery barrages. Seeger's use of two adjectives shows a need to present the destruction as great and small, grand and petite. Every inch of the land is destroyed and thrashed. Lines 20 and 21 conjoin death and locus again and present the war-born fire motif. War is fire, and fire is war, and, as previously noted, fire and burning occur in all wars, and with the technological advances brought forth in World War I, the immolation of towns and cities was commonplace: artillery explodes; heated metal and fingers of flame light combustible material; oxygen fuels the flames. As well, Seeger shows that one can die in the country — on a hill — or in the borough — in a town — and as such, the omnipresence of death, the inescapability of death, both the speaker's and others,' is duly and appropriately noted, and fated.

While Seeger may have been the only American poet of artistic repute to come out of World War I, several poets of note from World War II and the Korean War deserve mention before moving on to the examination of a number of poets from the Vietnam War and the Iraq War. World War II brought full-scale aerial warfare, and two poets need to be recognized. Of course, Randall Jarrell claimed poetic immortality with "The Death of the Ball-Turret Gunner." To die in a ball-turret of a B-17 or B-24 bomber and to be so destroyed physically that one must be washed out with a steam hose is to be utterly disengaged from life and corporeal being; what is implied but not stated in the five-line poem is that after the steam cleaning, another ball-turret gunner would man the turret, and then the cycle would begin anew — fly, fight, die, wash, replace, repeat. Another lesser-known poet whose work centers on the air war of World War II is Richard Eberhart with "The Fury of Aerial Bombardment." In the work, Eberhart uses a Cain and Abel analogy to question the existence of God as well as the behaviors of man in war; the poem closes with a quatrain listing dead fighting peers by name whose faces the speaker cannot remember but whose knowledge of fighting equipment he can. As well, World War II produced John Ciardi, whose "The Pilot in the Jungle" is one of the seminal poetic works of war that uses the thematic element of the jungle terrain as an enemy. Finally, the work of W.D. Ehrhart and Philip K. Jason must be recognized. Their anthology of poetry and short fiction, *Retrieving Bones: Stories and Poems of the Korean War* (1999), is a treasure of the creative writing born of the Forgotten War. Warrior-poets whose work in the anthology is notable and worth mention are William Childress ("Letter Home," "Combat Iambic," "The Long March"); Rolando Hinojosa ("The Eighth Army at the Chongchon," "Night Burial Details"); Reg Saner ("Flag Memoir"); William Wantling ("Korea 1953," "The Korean," "I Remember," "Pusan Liberty," "The Day the Dam Burst"); and Keith Wilson ("The Captain," "The Girl"). These poems all use defining characteristics found in this study, and as such, are worthy of mention, if not analysis. What is more, Ehrhart and Jason deserve kudos for assembling and publishing these poets and poems and granting literary immortality and substantiality to poets and works that, sadly, might otherwise have been ignored and forgotten.

The works of two poets of the Vietnam War deserve recognition in the context of this study — Yusef Komunyakaa and Bruce Weigl. Both men served in Vietnam, and both men have written copiously about the war since that service. Milton J. Bates argues, "It would ... be a mistake to think that black America can make sense of its Vietnam experience in isolation from white America" (69), and in "Tu Do Street," a poem that Bates calls possibly "the best single dramatization of black-white [and Vietnamese] relations during the war" (69), Komunyakaa uses the in-war prostitute as a conjunctive device to present the nexus of the black and white American soldier. Komunyakaa begins the poem using racial segregation as a point of demarcation: "I close my eyes & can see / men drawing lines in the dust" (2–3); "America pushes through the membrane / of mist & smoke, & I'm a small boy / again in Bogalusa. *White Only*" (4–6). The America of the speaker's boyhood and young adulthood is one of racial lines drawn, but in war there are no such lines: "We have played Judas where / only machine-gun fire brings us / together" (15–17). The violence of war makes American men, black and white, betray their race and race roles, as does the lure of sexual release in wartime:

> There's more than a nation
> inside us, as black & white
> soldiers touch the same lovers
> minutes apart, tasting
> each other's breath,
> without knowing these rooms
> run into each other like tunnels
> leading to the underworld [27–34].

The prostitute, in conjunction with the violence of war, becomes the nexus, the literal point of convergence, between white American soldier and black American soldier. As such, the Vietnamese prostitute, in time of war, has done what no great society has been able to do — conjoin the African American and the Anglo American. War makes for strange bedfellows, indeed.

Komunyakaa's poem "The Edge" also explores the role of prostitute in time and locus of war: "When guns fall silent for an hour / or two, you can hear the cries / of women making love to soldiers" (1–3). Of course, that "love" is carnality only; there is no genuine love involved, only commerce for one and release for the other: "'You want a girl, GI?' / 'You buy me Saigon Tea?' / Soldiers bring the scent of burning flesh / with them — on their clothes & in their hair" (21–24). The men reek of death — the burned flesh of Vietnamese soldiers and civilians — yet the women, through the abject circumstance of war, prostitute themselves and participate in intercourse with those who are killing — accidentally and with malice aforethought — their countrymen, and countrywomen, and native children. So, the prostitutes must smell the immolated bodies of their peers when engaging in intercourse with the American soldiers. Though not explicitly stated, the poem posits the desperation and desperate circumstances of the unnamed prostitutes in the text. Additionally, with the mention of the "scent of burning flesh," Komunyakaa smoothly places the burning motif into this poem of war. Komunyakaa's poems of war are aesthetic and sensory explorations of war that clothe brutality in beauty.

Bruce Weigl's works do the opposite and clothe beauty in brutality. The poem "Song of Napalm" is an exploration in brutal imagery that, nonetheless, contains beauty among the horrors brought on by war and the tools of war, and the very title is paradoxical, as the song produced by napalm — jellied gasoline used to burn things and places and people — is one of horror and agony and death. Yet the song is also the poem, as it exists, so the poem is the song of napalm, but the song is additionally the burning and death of a girl in Vietnam, a noncombatant whose village has been bombed by U.S. forces: "Still I close my eyes and see the girl / Running from her village, napalm / Stuck to her dress like jelly, / Her hands reaching for the no one / Who waits in waves of heat before her" (23–27). The speaker, writing from the perspective of post-war life in the United States, cannot escape the image of the girl on fire, the girl napalmed, the song of napalm, and he imagines a scene in which the girl rises like a bird and flies away, but that scene is false:

> The lie works only as long as it takes to speak
> And the girl runs only as far
> As the napalm allows
> Until her burning tendons and crackling
> Muscles draw her up
> into that final position
>
> Burning bodies so perfectly assume. Nothing
> Can change that; she is burned behind my eyes [35–42].

The excerpts from this powerful and brutal poem display, among other things, a number of the defining characteristics of the literature and novel of war: The equipment of war — napalm via aerial disposal; omnipresent death and destruction — the decimation of a peasant village; death of noncombatants — the immolated girl; the burning or fire motif — the burning of the village and the girl, and the use of napalm to do so; unstated refugee status of locals, as those who survive the bombing will no longer have a home; and, of course, the oppositional dyad between indigenous peoples and their occupiers—their allies. Weigl's "Song of Napalm" is a sublime effort that narrates the stunning violence of war.

Finally, to show that the defining characteristics of the literature of war in war poetry are neither time, nor locus, nor war specific, Brian Turner's poetry of the Iraq War warrants examination. Turner's poems are set in the Middle East in the twenty-first century, and are, situationally, representative of the War in Iraq, yet the works are also representative, metonymously, of the greater body of war poetry and the even greater body of war literature. As such, poems such as "Hwy 1" marry the ancient and historical with the postmodern: "It begins with the highway of death, / with an untold number of ghosts / wandering the road at night, searching / for the way home ... / This is the spice road of old, the caravan trail / of camel dust and heat" (1–4, 7–8). An ancient trade route is now a home to ghosts near and recently dead, ghosts born of war and the violence thereof. The ancient trade route is now a numbered and nicknamed highway upon which military convoys run "past the ruins of Babylon and Sumer, / through the land of Gilgamesh where the minarets / sound the muezzin's prayer, resonant and deep" (16–18). Again, the speaker offers the juxtaposition, comparison, and contrast of the ancient and the postmodern. In time of war, though, omnipresent death and destruction trumps the beauty and serenity of the (idealized) historical:

> Cranes roost atop power lines in enormous
> bowl-shaped nests of sticks and twigs,
> and when a sergeant shoots one from the highway
> it pauses, as if amazed that death has found it
> here, at 7 A.M. on such a beautiful morning,
> before pitching over the side and falling
> in a slow unraveling of feathers and wings [19–25].

The thematic element of omnipresent death and destruction in war and in war literature is as timeless as the Euphrates River, and Turner's poem, like many American works of war literature before it, shows American military killing indigenous fauna. In so doing, Turner presents the facet of war as a conduit for the killing not merely of human beings but also of that which is before the sights—animals included, of course.

The poetry of war, like all literature of war, contains elements relative to war, which are related as thematic elements or motifs in the literature of war. Short stories of war, prose asides of the "truths" of battle, most often told in the manner of realism that incorporates naturalistic tendencies, as befits dramas of life and death, are more readily accessible to a readership that values prose over the poetic. As Holger Klein correctly notes when discussing the literature of World War I, though his point can be applied to all modern and postmodern literature of war, "as prose is the most frequently read genre in the modern [and postmodern] era, this is the medium in which ... war had its widest impact on the reading audience" (4). Prose sells; prose is accessible; prose allows itself to the nineteenth-, twentieth-, and twenty-first-century reader, and all of the wars from the U.S. Civil War to the Iraq and Afghanistan Wars have produced prose literature of critical and popular importance. Further, fictional non-novel war prose—the short story of war—is itself a timeless and important sub-genre of the prose literature of war. As such, an examination of the fictive non-novel war prose is in order, and the focus immediately is on the short story of war. As will be shown, the short story of war uses the same defining characteristics of the American novel of war—in a limited capacity due to length, of course—and, as such, is further evidence, as with the poetry of war, of the validity of the author's defining characteristics as a model through which and by which the critic and the reader can clearly identify a work of war literature.

As Sharon L. Gravett notes, "Literally thousands of works of fiction have been written about the Civil War and its aftermath" (603), but when discussing the lasting prose literature of the U.S. Civil War, and the nineteenth-century authors thereof, three names continue to merit popular and critical reception, even into the twenty-first century. Those names, of course, are Stephen Crane, Ambrose Bierce, and Harold Frederic. While Crane's short stories set during the Spanish-American War (25 April–12 August 1898) are worthy of admission, Crane's most important short war works are the seven short stories of the Civil War: "A Mystery of Heroism" (August 1895), "A Gray Sleeve" (October 1895), "Three Miraculous Soldiers" (March 1896), "The Little Regiment" (June 1896), "The Veteran" (August 1896), "An Indiana Campaign" (September 1896), and "An Episode of War" (December 1896). Of these seven short stories, "A Mystery of Heroism" is suitably relative to this study, as the work utilizes a number of the defining characteristics of the American novel of war — as do all of the short stories addressed in this chapter, of course. Ironically, it was not until after he had penned his great Civil War works that Crane, as a war correspondent, was first witness to war through viewing the Greco-Turkish War of 1897 and the Spanish-American War.

"A Mystery of Heroism," written after *The Red Badge of Courage* and the first of the seven Civil War short stories, is the story of one man's thirst and his acts of heroism born of such. Infantryman Fred Collins desires a drink of water — water is a component of the necessary equipment of war, of course — and thus is given permission to risk his life to acquire the thirst-quenching elixir of life, under heavy enemy fire. Kevin J. Hayes argues that Crane's work "reduces the conflict between two warring nations [*sic*] to an individual episode in one man's life" (12); however, of note here is the fact that Crane immediately presents many of the defining characteristics of the American novel of war, and, of course, does so quickly and concisely: the two armies are "wrestling" (1) in battle, their artillery "arguing in tremendous roars" (1); guns, caisson, and horses outline the sky; a horse and bugler fall to the bombardment (1). So, in the opening paragraphs of the text, Crane offers the violence of war, the equipment of war, war as central thematic element of the work, and the death of fighting peers. Still on the first page of the story come omnipresent death and destruction and displacement of locals to refugees: "Beyond it [a green meadow below the company] was the grey form of a house half torn to pieces by shells and by the busy axes of soldiers who had pursued firewood.... A shell had blown the well-house to fragments. Little lines of grey smoke ribboning upward from some embers indicated the place where had stood the barn" (1). Additionally, Crane uses the fire motif and the oppositional dyad between indigenous peoples and occupying/invading forces, and he does so all on the first page of the story. Crane even sees fit to include the oppositional dyad between officers and enlisted men: after Collins risks his life to gather a bucket of water for himself, a mortally wounded man, and his peers — under heavy fire, no less — two immature lieutenants jostle over the bucket, drop it, and spill the contents. And while the story ends on the oppositional dyad between the officers and Collins— an enlisted man — Michael Schaefer argues that the "import of Collin's compassion for the wounded officer" (111) is the central and heroic element of the story. As such, Schaefer argues for a conjunctive dyad between officer and enlisted man. However, although Crane identifies the fallen man as an officer, would not Collins stop to give water to any Union soldier? So, his act of compassion is Union to Union rather than enlisted to officer. That said, what is not debatable is Crane's readily apparent use of the defining characteristics of the American novel of war in the Civil War short story "A Mystery of Heroism."

While Crane wrote only seven Civil War short stories, Ambrose Bierce's output was a bit more prolific, and as Thomas Bonner, Jr., notes, "Stylistically, both writers provide ample evidence of irony and satire in their fiction, Bierce's being the darker of the two" (52). Between 1880 and 1910, Bierce, a veteran of nearly four years of Civil War combat (Duncan and Klooster 21), wrote upward of seventy-five extant and verifiable documents on the Civil War (Duncan and Klooster vii–ix), twenty-five of which are acknowledged as short stories (Hopkins 261). Two of which bear acknowledgment here — "Two Military Executions," for its use of the oppositional dyad between officer and enlisted man, and "Chickamauga," for its use of a number of this study's defining characteristics, among which are omnipresent death and destruction, the death of noncombatants, and the fire or burning motif — are explicitly provided. "Two Military Executions" presents Private Bennett Story Greene, a young volunteer who has "committed the indiscretion of striking his officer" (380), and who, as a result, "was promptly arrested on complaint of the officer, tried by court-martial and sentenced to be shot" (380–81). The officer and the private, it seems, were once familiar as civilians: "You might have thrashed me and let it go at that ... that is what you used to do at school, when you were plain Will Dudley and I was as good as you. Nobody saw me strike you; discipline would not have suffered much" (381). The lieutenant concurs and asks Greene for his forgiveness, which he does not grant. Greene is executed by firing squad the next morning. Thus, an enlisted man is executed for an act committed against an officer, an act that, while insubordinate, was not witnessed, and thus was not catalogued, except for the lieutenant's complaint. Of course, Bierce has some fun with the pair's names, as Lieutenant Will's will is done, and Ben Greene is never allowed the chance to mature past his salad days of youth. Further, Greene exacts his revenge, as Bierce allows in ghostly manner, for the ghost of Greene snipes Lieutenant Dudley during the sergeant major's morning roll call, and after answering the call of the name "Greene" (381–82). Hence, the oppositional dyad between officers and enlisted men exists even after death.

"Chickamauga," on the other hand, is as serious a short story as Bierce produced. The Battle of Chickamauga (18–20 September 1863) was the last major Confederate victory of the war and resulted in more than 34,000 uniformed casualties ("Chickamauga"), but Bierce's optic is focused on one child and that child's experiences during a day of war. Edmund Wilson argues, correctly, that in "Chickamauga," "Bierce manages to make us feel the indignity and absurdity of war and at the same to suggest the nullity from the point of view of a being who should not have any stake in it" ("Ambrose Bierce" 619–20). The story begins as the child, a Southern boy of "about six years, the son of a poor [but slave-owning] planter" (313), plays and then gets lost in the woods about his home. Meanwhile, slaves and freemen and his mother search for the boy, while "thunder" (314) beckons in the background. After crying himself to sleep, the boy wakens at dusk to note large beings wandering through the forest, moving slowly and strangely, if not unnaturally. These beings are wounded and maimed Union soldiers, "by dozens and by hundreds" (315), moving north in post-battle retreat. The child is at first amused, and then is horrified by what he sees, and as night falls, "[i]nstead of darkening, the haunted landscape began to brighten" (316), as beyond the immediate scene a fire rages: "The fire beyond the belt of the woods on the farther side of the creek, reflected to earth from the canopy of its own smoke, was now suffusing the whole landscape" (317). The child walks toward the fire, the ground littered with the equipment of the fighting and fallen — a blanket, a knapsack, a rifle. The dead, too, lie where they have fallen. The child moves to the light: "the red illumination ... the blazing ruin of a dwelling. Desolation everywhere!" (318). Again, the child is in awe of the spectacle, and again, awe and interest turn to horror as the child realizes that it is his very own home that is on fire. On the ground lies a dead woman: "The greater part of the forehead torn was away, and from the jagged hole the brain protruded, overflowing the temple, a frothy mass of gray, crowned with clusters of crimson bubbles— the work of a shell" (318). This is Bonner's darkness, the darkness that Crane does not use, perhaps because Crane did not see combat prior to writing his Civil War works. The story closes as the child realizes the death of his mother: "Then he stood motionless, with quivering lips, looking down upon the wreck" (318). In six pages of prose fiction, Bierce clearly evidences the omnipresent death and destruction of war, the fire or burning motif, the death of noncombatants, the violence of war, the displacement of locals to refugees, the oppositional dyad between occupying/invading forces and indigenous peoples, and the absurdity of war. Bierce's skill as a portrayer of the realistic truths of war is unmatched by any Civil War writer, perhaps because of his experience during war. Nonetheless, Harold Frederic does deserve some recognition for his writing central to the internecine conflict.

The late-nineteenth-century novelist Harold Frederic, best known for his non-war novel, *The Damnation of Theron Ware* (1896), wrote seven Civil War stories in 1892 and 1893 (O'Donnell and Franchere 106), the last of which, "A Day in the Wilderness," is the only one of the seven to take place entirely in a war zone with all of the characters in uniform (Wilson, "Introduction," *The Civil War Stories* xiv). As the entire text takes place on the battlefield, before, during, and after a battle, "A Day in the Wilderness" obviously uses the thematic element of war as the central action of the text. In addition, at various levels, Frederic uses the violence of war, the equipage of war, death of fighting peers, oppositional dyads between officers and enlisted men, the terrain or weather as the enemy, onmipresent death and destruction, and the burning or fire motif to clearly identify the short story as an explicit text of war. As the tale opens, a "moving human flood" (229) flows down a road toward battle; artillery can be heard, and smoke fills the air with the stench of burnt gunpowder as men move *en masse* toward violence and death. Like Bierce's story of the Battle of Chickamauga, Frederic's work is set during a real battle — the Battle of the Wilderness (5–7 May 1864), a Virginia battle in which there were more than 29,000 casualties ("Battle of the Wilderness"). However, writing retrospectively, sans participation, Frederic could only imagine the events, but he does so effectively. The hostility of the battleground is set:

> It was a vast, sprawling forest district, densely covered with low timber, scrub-oak, dwarf junipers, and tangled cedar and pines, all knit together breast-high and upward with interlacing wild vines, and foul underfoot with swamp or thicket.
> In this gloomy and sinister wilderness men did not know where they were, nor whom they were fighting. Whole commands were lost in the impenetrable woods. Mounted orderlies could not get through the underbrush, and orders sent out were never delivered [234].

The terrain is the enemy. It is hostile to the outsiders, and it impedes both forward progress and means of communication. Once the battle starts, the destruction of the treescape begins— "Some were hanging to the trunks by their bark; everywhere the splinters were white and fresh ... a big branch not far away shook violently, then toppled downward" (235)—and so does the death of peers, as after the battle Lafe Hornbeck, the drummer-boy from the brigade band, notices twenty-six blue uniformed men "lay sprawled in unnatural positions, flat on the green earth" (243). The dead have been robbed of their "muskets, knapsacks, [and] canteens" (243), as well as their boots. After a lengthy and melodramatic aside in which the body-looting villain, also a "bounty-jumper" (246)—one who enlists for an enlistment bounty and then deserts—is caught and waylaid by Foldeen Schell, the brigade band flautist, the drummer-boy Lafe unites with and saves his cousin, Lieutenant Lyman Hornbeck, who has himself been waylaid by Red Pete, the bounty jumper. Finally, and back to war-relative historical truth and fictive verisimilitude, "Lafe saw above the tree-tops nearest him, piling skyward on the wind, a great writhing wall of black smoke.... The woods were on fire!" (263). Lafe and the lieutenant escape the flames, thanks to Lafe's efforts—and to Romanticism's—and the story concludes on a happy note. While Frederic's story may be a bit melodramatic and tinged in Romanticism, the document nonetheless exists as a working example of the short story of war and, as such, certainly and effectively utilizes a number of the defining characteristics of the American novel of war.

While Dorothy Canfield Fisher's *Home Fires in France* (1918) is perhaps the best recognized American-authored short story collection endemic of World War I, it is Ellen Newbold La Motte's 13-story collection *The Backwash of War* (1916) that deserves contemporary recognition for its unbridled Naturalism and accurate representation of truth in war. La Motte's text, subtitled *The Human Wreckage of the Battlefield as Witnessed by an American Hospital Nurse*, and born of her time as a nurse in a French military field hospital in Belgium, "stresses absurdity [through] the ironic triumphs of surgery [and] the empty postwar hopes of shattered survivors" (Solomon 855). Additionally, among the defining characteristics of the American novel of war, the oppositional dyad between officers and enlisted men, the death of noncombatants, and the death of fighting peers feature prominently in the text. The result of La Motte's use of vicious irony to project the absurdity of war is especially "antiheroic, antireligious, antihumanistic acceptance of man's fate" (Solomon 855), via the modern fiction of the modern world war. Conversely, Canfield Fisher's work, while it does promote "the idea of the strength and courage of women in wartime" (Stout 55) (see, for example, Ellen Boardman in "A Little Kansas Leaven") also emphasizes a sort of idealistic propagandizing (see "Notes from a French Village in France," for example) that was created "for rallying American philanthropic and political responses to the plight of western Europe in the late years of the War" (Ryder 143). While Canfield Fisher's goal of helping her French friends through the Great War was indeed noble, for prior to publishing *Home Fires in France* as a collection, she "sent a steady stream of articles and stories home to America for publication" (Washington 159), La Motte's rhetorical goal was to present the ugliness "churned up in the wake of the mighty, moving forces" of war, the lives made "weak, hideous, repellent" (v) by combat—that is, in La Motte's jargon, "the Backwash of War" (v).

In her short stories of war, La Motte often uses a savage, almost postmodern, irony to present the absurdity of war. For example, in "A Citation"—and this is a motif that recurs in war literature as modern medicine advances through the twentieth and into the twenty-first century—a surgeon's particular surgical skills lead to the prolonged suffering of a wounded soldier:

[A]nd in course of time he [Grammont, the wounded soldier] arrived one day at the hospital with a piece of shell in his spleen.

He was pretty ill when brought in, and if he had died promptly, as he should have done, it would have been better. But it happened at that time that there was a surgeon connected with the hospital who was bent on making a reputation for himself, and this consisted in trying to prolong the lives of wounded men who ought normally and naturally to have died. So this surgeon worked hard to save Grammont, and certainly succeeded in prolonging his life, and in prolonging his suffering, over a very considerable portion of time [59].

"All the while Grammont remained in bed, in very great agony" (59), and "After about three months of torture, during which time he grew weaker and smelled worse every day, it finally dawned on the nurse that perhaps this life-saving business was not wholly desirable" (61). As the story and the "treatment" progress, Grammont, a former social outcast, convicted criminal, and thug, while still dying a bit every day, becomes polite, kindly, worthy of a citation, but alas, 20 minutes before the decorating general is to arrive, Grammont dies — the irony of situation and war. La Motte layers her ironies so that it is not merely bad enough to be kept artificially alive (in agony, no less), through medical malpractice; a criminal, from a convict battalion, is to be awarded a medal for heroism — a rare occurrence, and essentially for being a compliant patient — yet that man, poor Grammont, dies just prior to the award ceremony.

La Motte uses the absurdity of war so often and in so many of her stories that the absurdity of war becomes a thematic element of the text. In "Heroes," the opening story of the text, a wounded deserter who has attempted desertion through suicide — a bullet to the mouth — must be saved so that he may meet his proper end: "He was a deserter, and discipline must be maintained. Since he had failed in his job, his life must be saved, he must be nursed back to health, until he was well enough to be stood up against a wall and shot" (1). In "A Surgical Triumph," a young soldier is maimed and loses his arms, his legs, his face, and his eyes in battle, yet he is saved by the surgeons, who are proud of their work and of their patient. But their patient, their "surgical triumph" (55), upon arriving home, "kept sobbing, kept weeping out of his sightless eyes, kept jerking his four stumps in supplication, kept begging in agony: 'Kill me, Papa!'" (55), but alas, his father cannot. As a nurse in a front-line field hospital of World War I, La Motte witnessed the absurdity of war, the special irony that comes with surgical evolution: surgical advances lead to suffering and the unnecessary prolonging of life. *The Backwash of War* is a tremendously valuable literary artifact of World War I. Explicitly Naturalist, the work is also one of the seminal fictive works that effectively presents the absurdity of war through the irony of surgical advance.

Returning briefly to *Retrieving Bones: Stories and Poems of the Korean War*, three short stories merit particular attention, relative to the defining characteristics of the American novel of war. James Lee Burke's "We Build Churches, Inc.," Eugene Burdick's "Cold Day, Cold Fear," and Mark Power's "Graves" each contain a number of the defining characteristics of the American novel of war used in this study, and as such, remain important reminders of the human effect of the Korean War as well as the literary legacy thereof. It is not hyperbole to say that with *Retrieving Bones*, Ehrhart and Jason have done a service to Korean War veterans, as well as to the readers of war literature in general and of Korean War literature in particular; the anthology of poetry and prose is the essential collection of the Forgotten War. In much of the literature of the Korean War, the weather, specifically the grinding and wretched cold, is characterized and "becomes more than a literal reality; it gains metaphorical power" (Ehrhart and Jason xxvii), and as such, it becomes "a register both of tangible and intangible conditions" (Ehrhart and Jason xxxi). The cold is, and the cold does. In "Cold Day, Cold Fear" and in "Graves," the nearly unendurable cold, while not personified, exists as an omnipresent character against which the warriors must battle, as seen in the opening paragraph of "Graves": "It was cold: a thermometer at the railhead had read fifteen degrees below zero; he thought perhaps it was colder than that, in the country away from sheltering buildings. Maybe twenty below, twenty-five; a little colder and even a man's urine would freeze before it hit the ground" (115). Power's surreal, temporally slippery, stream-of-consciousness story, which deals with the psychological costs of an officer who has killed a peer whom he was rescuing, opens with cold and closes in kind: "It was fifteen degrees below zero yet all about him the snow glittered strangely as if it were about to metamorphose into water" (126). In between the opening and the closing of the text, Captain Graves, a veteran of World War II and the Korean War, is exposed as a weary and traumatized warrior, who, perhaps justifiably, has come to distrust, dislike, and even hate the indigenous Koreans for whom he is fighting. It is also fairly obvious that Graves has killed the gravely wounded man he was sent to rescue ("I had to do it.... He was so heavy, I had to do it. He wouldn't let me go" [126], and in fact, "Graves" is but one of a number of works in this study — nonfiction and fiction — in which Americans in uniform come to kill their peers, primarily out of mercy for the captured, tortured, or mortally wounded. Graves seems to be looking for some sort of justification from the psychiatrist to whom he is speaking, but that verbal appeasement is not forthcoming. In "Graves," in addition to the weather as the enemy and the absurdity of war and the death of fighting peers, Power also uses prostitution and the burning or fire motif throughout the work.

"Cold Day, Cold Fear" also opens with the cold: "They lay head to head in the ditch. There were a few inches of water in the ditch. An edge of rime ice would form on the water and then be pulled away by the slight current ... he could see his hand under the water ... the blue skin was wrinkled, the thumbnail was dead white, the veins stood out purple. He tried to close his hand and nothing happened" (53). The "they" in the first sentence of the story are two soldiers— an American named Eli and a South Korean named Kee — trapped in the ditch, "Two out of thirty" (53), pinned down by a group of "Communist soldiers" (53). As hypothermia is setting in, Eli and Kee are, of course, freezing to death in the water: "Fear is just like the cold, just exactly" (53), thinks Eli — both immobilize; both paralyze; both can kill, but the former is internal, and the latter is external. While Eli and Kee attempt to stay alive in the cold, the war continues around them as a new tool of war, the jet plane, sends rockets into a communist convoy, setting the vehicles afire. And after dark falls, Eli takes a flashlight from a dead peer and uses Morse code to signal their location to a reconnaissance plane, which then calls for a jet that dumps a "napalm bomb" (61) upon the proximal communist soldiers, immolating the lot of them. After the firebombing, a helicopter, an "ugly beetle" (61), swoops in and rescues the pair. So, in "Cold Day, Cold Fear," the weather as an enemy is featured prominently, as is the new-era equipment of war. Cold and fear are both debilitating, and Eli and Kee must face and defeat each in order to survive.

"We Build Churches, Inc." likewise opens with the abject cold: "Across the frozen fields the brown North Korean hills were streaked with ice and pocked with craters from our 105s" (43). Set in November 1950, on the evening of the massive Communist Chinese offensive, the story, within the first paragraph, is a catalog of violence, death and destruction, rhetoric, and the equipment of war: "We had killed Communists by the thousands all the way across North Korea" (43); the Americans use tanks and F-80s and B-25s and napalm, and phosphorous and incendiaries. A peer dies from a blast from a "potato masher" (43), GI war slang for a hand grenade; 16 marines are found dead in the snow. When the Chinese attack, fire and violence and the deaths of peers overwhelm the text, and the narrator is captured and becomes a prisoner of war for "the next thirty-two months" (51). As a POW, the narrator learns "how political lunatics could turn men into self-hating, loathsome creatures who would live with the guilt of Judas the rest of their lives" (52) for actions committed during wartime, specifically in the POW camps: "I spent six weeks in a filthy hole under a sewer grate, with an encrusted G.I. helmet for a honey bucket, until I became the eighth man of eleven from our shack to inform on an escape attempt" (52). And so the age-old, and absurd, adage of war is again repeated: old men send the young to war, to die and to kill and to live with their actions.

Thom Jones' excellent first short story collection, *The Pugilist at Rest* (1993), opens with a trilogy of Vietnam War–era stories, and the first two stories, "The Pugilist at Rest" and "Break on Through," are set in-uniform and in-country and explicitly present the defining characteristics of the American novel of war. "The Pugilist at Rest" opens at MCRD San Diego— Marine Corps Recruit Depot (i.e., "Boot Camp")— moves on to Vietnam, and closes in the United States after the war. Through the story, the narrator manages to fling Marine Corps rhetoric in a manner rivaled only by Gustav Hasford in *The Short-Timers*. That is, Jones' characters practice the "standard appellations" (3–4) of the corps: a recruit is a "shitbird ... a maggot" (3); a girlfriend back home is "*Rosie Rottencrotch* [italics Jones]" (3); a North Vietnamese soldier is "Luke the Gook" (5), and a fellow Marine is your "buddy" (5), never to be deserted on the battlefield; recruits live in a "squad bay" (3); meals are "chow" (6); lousy recruits are "dropped" (6) from the platoon, and on, and on. In fact, one could read "A Pugilist at Rest" and, through the language Jones uses, come slightly to understand "the tyrannical repression of recruit training" (7), circa August 1966. Again, only Hasford's text, because of the depth, breadth, and length of the novel form, better captures Marine Corps recruit training, but Jones' text does so quite accurately, perhaps because both authors are former Marines. And like the Hasford novel, the Jones story is set in boot camp and then moves overseas to the war zone. In the war zone, as the critic might assume, the equipage of war and the violence of war are liberally presented, and the narrator's closest friend, Jorgenson— among others— dies after "something like twelve minutes total in the theater of war" (26), while a "short-timer" (17) named Lance Corporeal Hanes gets "greased" (17) because a short-sighted Lieutenant had Hanes walking "point" (12). In battle, the men use M-16s, .45s, M-60s, K-bars, and M-79s as mortars fall all around them and AK-47s fire green tracer rounds at them, and Phantom F-4s swoop in and drop HE — high explosive — rounds and napalm, which burn everything and everyone in proximity "to a crisp" (17). Thus, the (unnamed at this point) narrator completes and survives his first battle: "I got over that first scare and saw that I was something quite other than that which I had known myself to be" (19).

The collection's second story, "Break on Through," is also littered with the defining characteristics of the American novel of war. The story starts in Vietnam, focuses on a Marine Corps Reconnaissance team —"Force Recon Team *Break on Through* [italics Jones]" (28)— and closes at Camp Pendleton. As with the first Jones story, "Break on Through" is heavy on the rhetoric of war, the violence of war, and the equipment of war: "hung-down, drug-down and crashing hard after five days of in-country R&R.... The word was out that we were going up-country for a quickie, a little 'sneak and peek'" (28)— a mission to reconnoiter for intelligence, not a seek-and-destroy mission. Even at China Beach, a safe sanctuary, the narrator keeps his "CAR-15 cradled" (28) in his lap, and he cannot escape the memories of excursions recently past, excursions in "the purple field" (29) of the Vietnamese jungle, where he had Claymore anti-personnel mines placed in his fire lanes to kill "Charles" (29); he states that he did not need a "Starlight Scope" (30) to see the Viet Cong because he could "sense" (29) Charlie. After picking up a SEAL with a violent history and a Medal of Honor named Baggit, the team sets out — "motate[s]" (36) — to the "bird" (38) and into the "triple-canopy" (40) jungle and is immediately ambushed upon entering the LZ — the landing zone: "The enemy was waiting for us, and in seconds we were getting chewed up by .31-caliber machine-gun fire. Charles began firing rockets at the choppers, and I knew that if they had rockets they had to be there in numbers. I had seen hot LZs before, but never anything like this" (41). Mason, the team medic, is hit and dies of a "sucking chest wound" (41), and the team separates in the battlefield confusion. After four days, the narrator — here named Tommy — reconvenes with the rest of the team at "a small outpost" (54) deep in the jungle. After the outpost is attacked and a fight takes place between Baggit and another recon member, among other things, the team makes it back to its home base, Camp Clarke, and eventually is rotated back to Camp Pendleton. The story closes as Baggit, on 9 July 1971, kills his "estranged old Lady" (64) and himself while barricaded in a beauty parlor in Salinas, California, listening to the Doors and their late singer, Jim Morrison — whose death had just been publicly announced (64) — perform "The End." The war follows the warrior home, indeed, and perhaps war is the end of the warrior's existence, the door through which the uninitiated pass, forever changed, altered — the door through which one can never return.

Briefly, two dramas of war, set for the stage rather than the reader, are worth examination in the context of this study. Maxwell Anderson and Laurence Stallings' *What Price Glory*, first performed in 1924 (2), and David Rabe's *The Basic Training of Pavlo Hummel*, first performed in 1971 (90), both use a number of the defining characteristics of the American novel of war, albeit in a limited manner, of course. The former text, written after Stallings' return from World War I, and the latter text, written after Rabe's return from Vietnam, both evoke an urgency born of the experience of serving in a war zone in uniform. In fact, the prefacing "note" to *What Price Glory* argues that the drama "is a play of war as it is, not as it has been presented theatrically for thousands of years. The soldiers talk and act much as soldiers the world over" (3), and the drama is realistically presented, even if a love interest is used to provide melodramatic tension between the two primary uniformed characters — Captain Flagg and First Sergeant Quirt. Flagg, the "skipper" (6, 7) — Marine rhetoric for a captain or company commanding officer — of Marine Corps Company L, which is stationed in France during World War I, and Quirt, the new top non-commissioned officer (NCO) of the company, are old peers and old rivals. Flagg is a Mustang (20), a former enlisted man who has received a commission, which, naturally, is a source of contention between the two. Thus, the chief defining characteristic of the American novel of war present in this drama is the oppositional dyad between Flagg and Quirt, and this characteristic is developed thematically through the three acts of the play. As well, the drama also uses omnipresent death and destruction — the French countryside and only proximal road are devastated from artillery, and a company runner notes, "Here's the map. That's the only road there is, and we can't use it. The damn thing is one long shell-hole from last May" (10). The artillery shelling (from which side is irrelevant) has shattered civilian thoroughfares, a not uncommon occurrence during war or World War I, or in the texts of war in general. The equipment of World War I is readily presented — Flagg rides in a motorcycle with a side-car (12) — and "It rains grenades most of the time" (18), which, of course, notes the violence of war, and the men carry "V.B. grenades" (47) and gas masks and wear "*tin hats*" (50) and "*spiral legging*[s] [italics Anderson and Stallings]" (51). Further, the absurdity of war is presented as a general expects Flagg to send a detail of men behind enemy lines to place propaganda posters for the German soldiers to read (42). As well, fighting peers die as the text fore-shadows and progresses: "God knows most of 'em haven't got long to live" (19), Flagg says to Quirt in Act I, while the company is billeted in the rear. Act II is set during battle, in a wine cellar cum sleeping quarter cum field hospital, and wounded men come and go, with a Private Lewisohn dying as the act closes (71). Act III is set in a tavern, two days post-battle, and the melodrama between Flagg and Quirt is reintroduced as the men vie for the tavern owner's daughter's attention. The drama closes as the company is called back to the war. All in all, *What Price Glory* is a fine example of an early modern American drama of war and of a work of the American literature of war, and the drama offers an excellent catalog of the uses of a number of the defining characteristics of the American novel of war.

Like Hasford's *The Short-Timers* and Jones' "The Pugilist at Rest," *The Basic Training of Pavlo Hummel* spends much of the text in basic training and then moves on to deployment in Vietnam, but the title character, while he does make it through boot camp successfully, does not change, does not evolve, so the basic training is for naught. Pavlo Hummel seems to be psychologically and emotionally stunted and static, and this lack of personal growth and ability to evolve eventually leads to Hummel's death in-country—not on the battlefield but in the saloon of a whorehouse. In fact, as per his personal goals, Hummel does show a propensity for honor and duty in times of battlefield stress, volunteers for battlefield assignment, and even attempts to save a mortally wounded peer in a very deadly situation (74–75). While the peer, PFC Jay Charles Johnson Parham, an African American soldier brutally attacked by the Viet Cong, dies, and Hummel is wounded (76), Hummel's inability to assess inter-human relationships on a personal and social level, not a combat level, is what leads to his death, not at the hands of the Viet Cong but at the hands of an American peer over a prostitute. Rabe uses a number of the defining characteristics of the American novel of war at the motif level—omnipresent death and destruction, the oppositional dyad between officers and enlisted men, the oppositional dyad between occupiers and indigenous peoples, the violence of war, of course, and the death of fighting peers, among others—but he uses prostitution at a thematic level, and the opening scene of the drama (5–7), as well as the penultimate scene (82–85), incorporate prostitution with Hummel's lack of foresight and social and common sense. After Hummel pummels a "rear-echelon asshole" (84) in the bar—a Sergeant Wall, one who outranks him, of course—he is given a fragging by the sergeant, who tosses an M-26 A2 fragmentation grenade into the bar, killing Hummel and the prostitute (85). Hummel, who starts the text in Act I as a misfit in Army boot camp, ends the text in Act II as a misfit in American-occupied Vietnam, one who, according to Rabe's "Author's Note," is a lost soul who "has, for a long time, no idea that he is lost" (89), but perhaps realizes this situation when the grenade is in his lap. *The Basic Training of Pavlo Hummel* is an excellent dramatic example of the presentation of the socially isolated, psychically stunted postmodern warrior; further, the play is also an excellent example of the thematic use of the prostitution defining characteristic.

The final sub-genre of the American literature of war to be examined is the war memoir. As with the poem, short story, and drama of war, the memoir of war is a time-tested, oft-repeated literature of war. Often, a book-length narrative will be written in first person by a veteran of a given war, or the war memoir might be a third-person or first-person account written by a journalist who has witnessed a given war first-hand. War memoirs are also collected in edited editions that contain first-person accounts narrated by war veterans. As well, war memoirs can be single, unique texts published in magazines or newspapers. Unlike the "creative nonfiction" memoirs in vogue in the late twentieth and early twenty-first centuries, war memoirs are primarily straight, biased, unfiltered presentations of the narrator's war experience(s). Ambrose Bierce's "What I Saw of Shiloh" is just such a narrative, and while this recounting of the Battle of Shiloh (6–7 April 1862) does not contain the artifice of, say, "Chickamauga," it is "a simple story of a battle; such a tale as may be told by a soldier who is no writer to a reader who is no soldier" (93). Bierce's narrative is also written by an author who is journalist and artist and war veteran. Bierce writes from combat experience, as is evidenced in his art and in his memoir, and he is rare among his peers, but for perhaps Arthur Guy Empey and Tim O'Brien, in his ability to create effective fiction and powerful nonfiction.

In *Patriotic Gore*, Edmund Wilson argues that Bierce "seems rarely to have felt any pity for his dead comrades of the Civil War, and it is characteristic of him that he should write as if in derision ... of the soldiers who fell at Shiloh and who were burned, some while still alive, in a forest fire lit by the battle" ("Ambrose Bierce" 623–24). Wilson, of course, is referring to the oft-cited passage in which Bierce writes of viewing those immolated dead — fighting peers from an Illinois regiment — and does so dispassionately and in "gruesome description" (Wilson 618). First, Bierce presents the omnipresence of fire in the war zone: "In many engagements of the war the fallen leaves took fire and roasted the fallen men. At Shiloh, during the first day's fighting, wide tracts of woodland were burned over in this way and scores of wounded who might have recovered perished in slow torture" (106). Then Bierce, to "gratify a reprehensible curiosity" (106), enters the "valley of death" (106), observes the immolated, and, as journalist, retrospectively reports that which he saw:

> Along a line ... lay the bodies half buried in ashes; some in the unlovely looseness of attitude denoting sudden death by the bullet, but by far the greater number in postures of agony that told of the tormenting flame. Their clothing was half burnt away — their hair and beard entirely; the rain had come too late to save their nails. Some were swollen to double girth; others shriveled to manikins. According to degree of exposure, their faces were bloated and black or yellow and shrunken. The contraction of muscles which had given them claws for hands had cursed each countenance with a hideous grin [107].

Bierce closes the paragraph somewhat cold-heartedly and derisively, per Wilson's argument: "Faugh! I cannot catalogue the charms of these gallant gentlemen who had got what they enlisted for" (107). In *Embattled Courage*, Gerald F. Linderman notes that, during the Civil War, "Soldiers were startled that those wounded in Wilderness combat, but not fatally perhaps but seriously enough to immobilize them, should burn to death in brushfires begun by the battle" (125). In Bierce's writing of the Battle of Shiloh, and the resultant pyre thereof, it is obvious that many of the immolated were not dead prior to the forest fire. "What I Saw of Shiloh," ghastly and sad as it is, is clearly a fine example of the burning or fire motif common to much of the fiction and nonfiction literature of war, and to the American novel of war.

Over the Top (1917), Arthur Guy Empey's book-length account of his time spent as a machine-gunner in the British Army trenches of World War I, is, sadly, little known, but nonetheless, it is an excellent example of the veteran-written, book-length war memoir. After the sinking of the *Lusitania* on 7 May 1914, Empey, already a U.S. Cavalry veteran and National Guardsman, and dissatisfied with the American response, ventured across the pond and joined the Royal Fusiliers (1–5). Written immediately after his discharge, Empey's text, like Karl Marlantes' epic novel *Matterhorn*, concludes with a glossary of the rhetoric of war — in this case, "Tommy's Dictionary of the Trenches" (281–315). Empey's sense of humor stands out in the glossary entries as it does throughout the text, which is as fine an introduction to the boredom and terror and equipment and absurdity of trench warfare as any other text, including the timeless and outstanding *All Quiet on the Western Front* (1929). Empey's work, as a memoir written before the era of "creative nonfiction," is lacking somewhat in character development, but Empey's narrator (himself, of course), keeps the text lively — even when gravely wounded to the face — and the witticisms are ever present. The glossary closes with this nugget:

> **Zeppelin.** A bag full of gas invented by a count full of gas. It is a dirigible airship used by the Germans for killing babies and dropping bombs in open fields. You never see them over the trenches, it is safer to bombard civilians in cites. They use Iron Crosses for ballast [315].

The humor of the first and last sentences notwithstanding, the definition does include some serious points of note. The defining characteristics of the equipage of war — the zeppelin and bombs therein, of course — and the violence of war — aerial bombardment, of course — and the deaths of noncombatants — babies and civilians, of course — are directly referred to in juxtaposition to the lightness of the opening and closing sentences of the entry. Empey, as the author of the memoir and as the editor of the "Tommy's Dictionary of the Trenches," is quite adept at this juxtaposition of the humorous and the tragic. For example, "**Wipers.** Tommy's name for Ypres, sometimes he calls it 'Yeeps.' A place up the line which Tommy likes to duck. It is even 'hot' in the winter time at 'Wipers'" (314). This brief entry is brimming with irony and tragicomic juxtaposition. In Ypres, a locus of mass death and casualties — 550,000 in the third battle alone (Duffy) — and site of massive battles in 1914, 1915, and 1917, one can be wiped from the Earth; one can get the Yeeps — as in creeps, as in yips, as in shakes from fear — because one is so scared, and one is never cold because the area is hot (under incredible and massive and violent fire). Empey's text is pregnant with the comic and the tragic, and the work is so important that it should not be forgotten. While nearly a novel, but for the artifice, some scholars have incorrectly labeled *Over the Top* a work of fiction, but, at its heart, the text is a nonfiction work of war, a memoir of "An American Soldier Who Went" (i).

Ernest Hemingway's tremendous anthology *Men at War: The Best War Stories of All Time* (1942) contains fictional, historical, and first-person non-fictional accounts of war. Relative to this study, and out of respect for the war pilots of the American war efforts through history, the final entry in the text, Walter B. Clausen's brief Associated Press excerpt, "Midway," deserves attention. Clausen, author of the instantly authoritative *Blood for the Emperor: A Narrative History of the Human Side of the War in the Pacific* (1943), in which the piece is expanded and included, introduces the reader to Houstonian "Ensign George H. Gay, Jr., [a] 25-year-old torpedo-plane pilot" (1070), who was shot down on the first day of the Battle of Midway Island (4–7 June 1942). His on-board peers were killed in an assault on the Japanese fleet, and Gay "was the only one of the crew of three to survive the crash of his ship" (1070). While in the water for twenty-four hours or so, Ensign Gay watched the battle's "most violent stages" (1070), and he tells of "watching a line of burning Japanese ships pass by" (1070). Again and again in the account — as dictated by Clausen — the rhetoric of the fire or burning motif is used — burning and flaming and blazing — to describe the Japanese vessels under American attack. Early in the battle, "One of the larger carriers already burned fiercely" (1071), and later "tremendous fires burst from these vessels" (1071), while "internal explosions sent new gushes of smoke and fire belching from the carriers at momentary intervals" (1071). Even in this account, possibly censored to be made fit for mass-public news consumption, the presence of fire in war is readily apparent. Fire is war, and, chronologically speaking, each war is more of a lesson in burning than was the previous. As weapons evolve explosively and as the tools of war grow into massive sea-faring vessels, each with proportional shares of oil and airplane fuel and diesel petrol, as the number of humans engaged in gross-level warfare propagates in the air and on the sea, fire becomes not merely a thing that burns forests and towns and bodies therein, but also part of the explosiveness of world war, literally, and in itself it becomes an analog for the burning of war on a nearly inhuman level, a burning that is at its apex with the atomic bombings of Hiroshima and Nagasaki. In June 1942, man could not yet burn the world, but that would come, and in a few short lines, Clausen, via Gay's testimony, clearly evidences the omnipresence of fire in the late modern war that was World War II.

Marine veteran C.S. Crawford's memoir of the Korean War, *The Four Deuces: A Korean War Story* (1989) — published through Novato, California's Presidio Press, but, interestingly, without an ISBN number on this author's first edition of the text — is of value both to this study and to the corpus of American war literature because the text is one of a number of works that deals with an action that is rarely present in the literature of war — the justifiable killing of a fighting peer by an ally. Wallace Terry's *Bloods* (1984) and Gustav Hasford's *The Short-Timers*, among a limited number of other texts, also contain passages in which some-one, in an impossible situation, must kill a peer to end the mortally wounded peer's suf-fering, and while the Hasford text is fiction, the Wallace and Crawford texts are not. Rarely in fiction or non-fiction, and never in the public's view via news dissemination, does this brutal truth come to light: in some situations, it is better to die than to live. Crawford, a forward observer for a 4.2-inch mortar battery, tells of how a single North Korean sniper team, using a Russian-made 61-millimeter anti-personnel rifle — a massive hand-held weapon, firing from three fortified mountain positions (AKA, "Luke the Gook [in] Luke-the-Gook's castle" [175]) — terrorizes entrenched infantry Company Easy in December 1951. To kill a sniper who is dug into a fortified position — or three positions, in this case — one must use a sniper. Hence the appearance of one to whom Crawford refers as "the Candy Bar Kidd" (177) — a sniper brought in to kill Luke the Gook. On the Kidd's second night of stalking Luke the Gook, the Kidd is caught, and Crawford's description of the situation and of the Kidd (181–82) is both exquisite and horrifying, as well as justifying.

It begins, "[N]o one saw the Candy Bar Kidd out in front of our lines while he was working. But on his second night out we heard him.... Wounded men make different sounds ... but nothing compares to the moaning-mewling sound a wounded man makes when he is out beyond your reach and he knows he can't bandage himself, restricted maybe, because he has broken bones" (180–81). Crawford foreshadows the situation: "the grunt who knows there is no way for him to recover from his wounds, he's the guy who begs, piteously, for release from his agony ... mortal agony" (181). Crawford then describes the sight of the Kidd, who has been staked out on the mountainside, in front of Luke the Gook's castle:

> The face of whoever it was ... was definitely that of a Caucasian with blond hair.... I could see that the puffy face had no eyelids, no nose, no ears, and no lips. The camouflage jacket was ripped open; the rips down his chest and stomach opened to puffy, purple-gray, sluggish worms of intestines pushing through the long slashes. The crotch area of his trousers was hacked out; he was butchered, and whatever had distinguished him as a man was no longer there. We could see no toes on his shoeless feet, no fingers or thumbs on his hands.
> And yet his body moved. Like a grotesque marionette, it twitched convulsively [181–82].

Although the Kidd's body is booby-trapped, the Marines of Easy Company, per the Marine Corps code, must retrieve the Kidd — dead or alive (or in this case, dead and alive) — even at the certain loss of life that the mission will entail. Crawford closes the bloody passage with confirmation of the Candy Bar Kidd's killing at the hand of the (also mortally wounded) company first sergeant: "Later, other men would confirm that the first sergeant had gotten to within five feet of the Candy Bar Kidd, close enough to shoot the Candy Bar Kidd five times with his 45-automatic pistol" (185). War begets terrible choices that men must make, and terrible missions that men must undertake. All told, five men were killed — "KIA" (185) — and ten more were wounded — "WIA" (185) — over the course of the five patrols it took to help end the Candy Bar Kidd's suffering (185) and to retrieve his mutilated corpse. Finally, it bears mention that an M-26 tank was brought up to destroy Luke the Gook's castle.

Moving forward chronologically to the Vietnam War, three texts are relevant to this study. Tim O'Brien's combat memoir, *If I Die in a Combat Zone, Box Me Up and Ship Me Home* (1975), Michael Herr's electric reportage, *Dispatches* (1977), and Wallace Terry's anthology of 20 first-person accounts of the Vietnam War experience from the African American perspective, *Bloods: Black Veterans of the Vietnam War: An Oral History* (1984), are all texts worthy of study on their literary merits, but each text is also representative metonymously as a sub-genre of the non-fiction account of war. O'Brien's text is a book-length memoir written by a combat veteran; Herr's text is a book-length memoir written by a professional journalist, and Terry's text is an *omnium-gatherum* of accounts reflective of the variety of roles accorded African American soldiers, sailors, pilots, and Marines who served in the Vietnam War.

O'Brien's text, the first of his in-country trilogy, is, according to the author, mostly "straight autobiography" ("Two Interviews" 136), even if the text is "an imperfect recollection" ("Two Interviews" 136), with made-up dialogue and a re-ordered chronology of events ("Two Interviews" 136); "the book was written as a novel; that is, the form of the book is fictional" ("Two Interviews" 136). And if one reads the text, the story of a man who is drafted and becomes a soldier in an infantry platoon and completes his service in Vietnam, one could say that the text does, indeed, read like a novel — a realist, modernist, straight-narrative novel with a tendency toward naturalism. And unlike O'Brien's second in-country work, the National Book Award–winning *Going After Cacciato* (1978), a realist-naturalist-fantasy epic that indeed is clearly a novel, and his third in-country work, *The Things They Carried*, a postmodern construct and a masterwork of postmodernism and the Vietnam experience, *If I Die in a Combat Zone* is O'Brien's attempt "to communicate with his reader through straightforward description of sensations and emotions, thematic self-revelation, translation of the argot of the soldier, and simple organization based on sequential military events: induction, basic training, arrival in Vietnam, experience of battle, term in the rear, and return to the States" (Wesley 3). That is, the work is a memoir of war, and as such, the work contains all of the defining characteristics of the American novel of war, liberally presented, in fact, from page one of the text, wherein the reader is thrown into the war and the story *in medias res*: "Snipers yesterday, snipers today"(1).

The war — and the training for such — is the central thematic action of the text, the violence is real, the combatants are well equipped with "Claymore mines, booby traps, the M-60 machine gun, the M-70 grenade launcher, the .45-caliber pistol, the M-16 automatic rifle" (51), and the Grunt rhetoric flows like monsoon rain — for instance, to die is to be "lethalized" (2). Further, death of fighting peers and of noncombatants, omnipresent death and destruction, displacement of locals to refugees, the oppositional dyad between occupiers and indigenous peoples, and between officers and enlisted men, the terrain and weather as enemy, the burning or fire motif, prostitution, and finally the absurdity of war are explicitly located all through the text, so the work is fairly oozing with the defining characteristics of the American novel of war; however, the work is a bit lacking in the constructed artifice of O'Brien's two other in-country efforts. This paragraph, for example, is an excellent illustration of the manner in which O'Brien uses multiple defining characteristics in complicity:

> Mad Mark called in the gunships. For an hour the helicopters strafed and rocketed Tri Binh 4. The sky and the trees and the hillsides were lighted up by spotlights and tracers and fires. From our position we could smell smoke coming from the village. We heard cattle and chickens and dogs dying.... Smoke continued to billow over to our position all night, and when I awakened every hour, it was the first thing to sense.... In the morning another patrol was sent into the village. The dead VC soldier was still there, stretched out on his back with his eyes closed and his arms folded and his head cocked to one side so that you could not see where the ear was gone. Little fires burned in some of the huts. Dead animals lay about. There were no people. We searched Tri Binh 4, then burned it down [84].

O'Brien utilizes characteristics of war fiction for rhetorical effect in his memoir of war. And in so doing, he does, indeed, create a fiction-esque war memoir. The work reads like a novel, is written like a novel, and feels like a novel, yet the events in the work, according to its author, all occurred, if not in said order. Taken in conjunction with *Going After Cacciato*, *If I Die in a Combat Zone* clearly foreshadows the brilliance of *The Things They Carried*, a novel that will be thoroughly analyzed as this study continues.

Herr's *Dispatches* is a work that is nearly alive with the zeitgeist of the Vietnam War and its in-country ethos. Herr spent a year in Vietnam (November 1967–October 1968), and he experienced first-hand the battles of Hue and Khe Sanh and the Tet Offensive, and his text practically vibrates in one's hand, as Herr "writes in an idiom which creatively fuses hippie catchwords, black slang, pop lyrics, military jargon, technical press terms, and the vocabulary and colloquialisms of the American youth and drug cultures" (Walsh, *American War Literature* 206). Herr's narrative is a sort of stream-of-consciousness cum New Journalism mish-mash that is bursting with visual imagery, and thus has a cinematic quality:

> Once I looked at them [dead bodies of the enemy] strung from the perimeter to the treeline, most of them clumped together nearest the wire, then in smaller numbers but tighter groups midway, fanning out into lots of scattered points nearer the treeline, with one all by himself half into the bush and half out. "Close but no cigar," the captain said and then a few of his men went out there and kicked them all in the head, thirty-seven of them. Then I heard an M-16 on full automatic starting to go through clips, a second to fire, three to plug in a fresh clip, and I saw a man out there, doing it. Every round was like a tiny concentration of high-velocity wind, making the bodies wince and shiver. When he finished he walked by us on the way back to his hootch, and I knew I hadn't seen anything until I saw his face. It was flushed and mottled and twisted like he had his face skin on inside out, a patch of green that was too dark, a streak of red running into bruise purple, a lot of sick gray white between, he looked like he'd had a heart attack out there. His eyes were rolled up half into his head, his mouth was sprung open and his tongue was out, but he was smiling. Really a dude who'd shot his wad [18].

Herr describes the scene of the dead North Vietnamese soldiers who were killed trying to breach the base perimeter wire, which is static, but then he adds to the static scene that of the post-description excursion of a "few" men, whittled down to one man's ejaculatory actions, and the scene becomes dynamic and cinematic. Interestingly, and perhaps not coincidentally, Herr later entered the film industry and is one of the credited screenwriters on the film *Full Metal Jacket* (1987), which is based on Gustav Hasford's novel, *The Short-*

Timers. Herr's work is replete with such scenes in which a static becomes a dynamic. Additionally, the text is full of dynamisms of locomotion — of trucks and men and helicopters, and the overriding feeling of the text is one of constant movement and re-movement, all while the mobilization and re-mobilization leads to a lack of progress or even a regression of progress, as the war at hand never seems to come complete. Men transfer back to the world but, as Herr attests and experiences, one never escapes the 'Nam:

> I knew one 4th Division Lurp [Long Range — Reconnaissance — Patrol]....
> This was his third tour. In 1965 he'd been the only survivor in a platoon of the Cav wiped out going into Ia Drang Valley. In '66 he'd come back with the Special Forces and one morning after an ambush he'd hidden under the bodies of his team while the VC walked all around them with knives, making sure. They stripped the bodies of their gear, the berets too, and finally went away, laughing. After that, there was nothing left for him in the war except the Lurps.
> "I just can't hack it back in the World," he said [5].

In this way, and as this passage occurs at the opening of the work, the Vietnam experience is forever, and thus is recursive, as is the text. One begins *Dispatches* in-country, and one ends *Dispatches* in-country, regardless of geographic locale. The experience of war lasts a lifetime, and Herr is not the first to note that, but there is something about the metafictiveness of Herr's work, the self-awareness of the text and its author, that is postmodern and unique to war writing — a seminal thing.

Terry's oral-narrative anthology *Bloods* is also a seminal text. Like Mark Baker's *Nam: The Vietnam War in the Words of the Men and Women Who Fought There* (1981), *Bloods* is an oral history, spoken by a number of those who were in-country, but unlike the Baker text, the Terry text identifies the androcentric speakers by name as well as by photograph, which lends an accountability and authenticity to the text and a responsibility to its speakers. And like Stanley Goff, Robert Sanders, and Clark Smith's *Brothers: Black Soldiers in the Nam* (1982), *Bloods* focuses exclusively on the African American experience during the Vietnam War, but unlike the Goff, Sanders, and Smith text, which tells the story of Goff's and Sanders' experience(s) in the American military and in Vietnam, the Terry text tells the story of 20 disparate African American men who served in uniform during the Vietnam War — in the Army, Navy, Air Force, and Marines, both officers and enlisted men. As such, while *Nam* and *Brothers* are tremendously important texts of the Vietnam War and are noteworthy artifacts, each detailing experiences of note and record, *Bloods* is absolutely unique: in scope of narratives presented, in number of narratives presented, and in accountability of narratives presented. As well, *Bloods* is widely and well received. Jennifer C. James calls the text "the most remarkable record of collective [African American] memory" ("African American Literature") of the Vietnam War, or of any war. Perry D. Luckett notes that there were 20 Congressional Medals of Honor awarded to African Americans during the Vietnam War (1); that African Americans "fought valiantly while recognizing that service in Vietnam would not guarantee full citizenship in the United States" (1), and as such, "most black soldiers [had to] reconcile divided loyalties to function in a white-dominated military" (14), and this social division is explicitly presented in *Bloods*, as nearly all of the narrators express statements relative to the Anglo-centric hegemony and institutional racism of the day. Further, writing in *A Freedom Bought with Blood*, James correctly observes that the history of war in the United States is also the history of African Americans fighting FOR the United States — "5,000 men of African descent followed in [Crispus] Attuck's footsteps, joining the ranks of the Continental army" (3) — and the literature thereof is also the literature of the United States at war, as evidenced by William Cooper Nell's seminal text,

Colored Patriots of the American Revolution (1855), a work "replete with acts of black valor and heroism equal to those of whites" (5). According to James, Nell "recognizes that war was a means for blacks to demonstrate national loyalty, and that narration of war was a means of writing blacks into the national 'historical destiny'" (6). Wallace Terry, a *Time* correspondent in Vietnam from 1967 to 1969 (xiv), of course, concurs with Nell a century later that African American participation in the Vietnam War, and the chronicling thereof, is an act of African American, national, and historical importance. And interestingly, Milton J. Bates offers, while calling *Bloods* "the best example" (65) of narrated oral history of the Vietnam War, the suggestion that African American soldiers "who were lower-ranking enlisted men tell stories of separation, whereas the former officers and senior NCOs tell stories of assimilation" (65). But is this not the case with Anglo and Hispanic and Asian war participants, too? One could argue that to gain rank is to assimilate, regardless of race.

Nonetheless, Terry's effort is a social, military, and historical artifact of unique importance; further, the text, and the narratives therein, contain all of the defining characteristics of the American novel of war. Two oral histories, those of Richard J. Ford III (31–52) and of Arthur E. "Gene" Woodley, Jr. (236–57), merit particular attention because each narrative is a study in the abject truculence of up-close killing — an important facet of all wars. Ford, a LURP, and Woodley, a Special Forces Ranger, each took part in ground-based missions in which hand-to-hand combat and killing were, if not commonplace, not far from routine. As such, each man's narrative bears a particular witness to the Vietnam War. Interestingly, both men refer to the ability of combat to animalize a man — that is, to turn a man into a savage type for whom killing is a *modus operandi* of survival in war. In fact, Ford relates how rear echelon soldiers in a club in Nha Trang saw the LURPs as other than human: "They had girls dancing and groups singin'. They reacted like we was some kind of animals, like we these guys from the boonies" (36). Woodley even sees himself as an animal: "I went to Vietnam as a basic naïve young man of eighteen. Before I reached my nineteenth birthday, I was an animal. When I went home three months later, even my mother was scared of me" (236). This animalization motif is not unique to these men, nor is it unique to the Vietnam War, nor is it unique to the literature of the Vietnam War. In fact, much of war literature refers directly to the need for warriors to become animals to succeed in war; further, it is often necessary to dehumanize one's enemy in order to wage war effectively, and Alfred Bonadeo notes, when referring to Erich Maria Remarque's masterwork, *All Quiet on the Western Front*, and the scholarship born of World War I, that "animal language represents something real ... survival on the Western Front is hard; therefore [Paul Bremer, Remarque's narrative protagonist] fights with superior daring and energy; he fights like an animal.... Peopled by men who have lost their human identity, in Remarque's narrative the front becomes the home of the beast" (410). This beastliness is a facet of war — pre-modern, modern, and postmodern — and it is explicitly expressed and acted out in both of the narratives at hand; in war, one becomes what one must in order to survive, and one does what one must in order to survive. That is war.

Ford's and Woodley's narratives are additionally important to this study because each narrative also presents all of the defining characteristics of the American novel of war, in brief narrative form, of course, and, in so doing, shows the validity and accuracy of the defining characteristics when posited in novel-length war fiction. Novels of war use these defining characteristics to present war truly and accurately. Particularly rhetorically effective in both narratives are descriptions of fighting and killing up close — of enemies, noncombatants, and peers. Woodley writes of his first combat experience, as a "cherry" (236) on patrol, only fourteen days in country: "I heard this individual walking. He came through the elephant grass, and I let loose on my M-16 and hit him directly in his face. Sixteen rounds. The whole clip. And his face disappeared. From the chin up. Nothing left. And his body stood there for 'proximately somewhere around ten, fifteen seconds. And it shivers" (236–37). After the subsequent firefight, Woodley shivers and sweats from fear, but his initiation has begun, and he shows himself to be a superior jungle fighter. Ford tells of a "search and destroy" (42) mission in a free-fire zone, in which the local villagers had been forewarned to evacuate; nonetheless, some — the old and the young — did not do so: "I heard movement in the rear of this hut. I just opened up the machine gun. You ain't wanna open the door, and then you get blown away ... anyway, this little girl screamed. I went inside the door. I'd done already shot her, and she was on top of the old man ... both of them was dead. I killed an old man and a little girl in the hut by accident" (42). Ford is, of course, horrified, and saddened, but the war continues on: "The flamethrowers came in, and we burnt the hamlet. Burnt up everything ... killing animals. Killing all the livestock. Guys would carry chemicals that they would put in the well. Poison the water" (42). Violence, noncombatant death, omnipresent death and destruction, the creation of refugees, oppositional existence between locals and occupiers — these are the defining characteristics of war, and of war literature, in nonfiction and fiction narrative.

Were that not enough, Woodley's narrative contains what Ann Collette identifies as "the single most wretched war story [she has] ever come across" (22): the account of Woodley having to kill a survivor of a helicopter crash who has been captured by the North Vietnamese forces and is discovered alive, but who has been "staked to the ground, flayed, maggots and flies burrowing in his flesh" (22). Like the Marines in Crawford's *The Four Deuces*, Woodley is forced to kill one of his own: "he had been peeled from his upper part of chest down to his waist. Skinned. Like they slit your skin with a knife ... you could see the flesh holes that the animals — wild dogs, rats, field mice, anything — and insects had eaten through his body ... and he started to cryin', beggin' to die" (241). The team has no morphine and is in the middle of a mission, sans support or medevac, and as the LURP team leader, Woodley has to kill the man:

> I put my M-16 next to his head. Next to his temple.
> I said, "You sure you want me to do this?"
> He said, "Man, kill me. Thank you."
> I stopped thinking. I just pulled the trigger. I cancelled his suffering.
> ...
> Then I cried [243].

Faced with, to be trite and cliché, an impossible situation, Woodley does his duty and alleviates the fighting peer's suffering. Woodley, who was awarded an amazing five Bronze Stars for valor, and who "killed around 40 people personally" (250), and even more impersonally — in firefights and the like — remains tortured, not by the overall experience and horrors of his war tenure, but by the act he was forced to commit, taking "someone else's life not in a combat situation" (257).

Anthony Swofford's account of the Persian Gulf War (aerial and ground assault dates: 17 January–28 February 1991), *Jarhead: A Marine's Account of the Gulf War and Other Battles* (2003), while gushingly reviewed — a bit too much so, in fact — is a decent primer into the post–Vietnam era of American war and war literature. While the war in which Swofford fought was short — the ground assault lasted approximately 100 hours (officially 23–27 February 1991) — Swafford's text, nonetheless, offers a unique view of the Marine combat grunt's perspective at the *fin de siècle*, and the text is loaded with the rhetoric of war, the equipage of war, and the omnipresent death and destruction of war, even a short war. Common Marine Corps idiom, known by all current and former Marines— such as doggy, squid, fly-boy (108), thrash (94), pogue (12), skivvies, cover, dickskinner, cum receptacle, go-fasters, moonbeam, ink stick, rack (30), and get some (9)— is liberally and lovingly offered in the text, and Swofford makes it clear that he, like all Marines, has earned the right to use such language. Also liberally presented is the gear common to the grunt of the Gulf War, and while Swofford is an 0311 (an infantryman), he is also a member of a Surveillance and Target Acquisition (STA) platoon, and as such, carries specialized equipment that most Marine grunts do not. A catalog late in the text, during the ground assault, exemplifies the variety and physical burden presented by an STA platoon member's fighting equipment, and in addition to wearing a cumbersome and heavy MOPP suit — a nuclear, biological, and chemical defense outer-suit — Swofford carries the following war-necessary items:

> In or attached to my ruck [backpack], or in my hands, I carry an extra pair of boots and extra fatigues, six MREs [meals ready to eat], six quarts of water, a disassembled M16, a 9mm pistol, the M40A1 sniper rifle, one hundred rounds of boat-tail ammunition for the sniper rifle, thirty rounds of 9mm ammunition, five hundred M16rounds, four M67 fragmentation grenades, two smoke grenades, three green star clusters, two replacement sets of gas mask filters, a map and a patrol-order book inside a map case, a compass, and a GPS system. My gas mask is secured to my hip [221].

Only Tim O'Brien's masterful and comprehensive catalogs in *The Things They Carried* come close to Swofford's efficient listing here. Swafford's prose is tinged with sarcasm, and he seems to question, implicitly and subversively: How the hell can one fight effectively, efficiently, and furiously when one is lugging one hundred pounds of gear?

Juxtaposed with Swofford's comically tinged equipage of war catalog is a less comic and strikingly vivid scene of the omnipresent death and destruction of war:

> [W]e will walk for twenty miles, and the only enemy we see are those who surrendered, gathered now in concertina-wire circles, and their dead friends in trenches and burnt vehicles, men who might've surrendered, or probably would've surrendered, but in order to coax a withdrawal or surrender you must first prove your might, everyone knows, and you prove your might by destroying weapons and equipment and humans. I've never seen such destruction. The scene is too real not to be real. Every fifty to one hundred feet a burnt-out and bombed-out enemy vehicle lies disabled on the unimproved surface road, bodies dead in the vehicles or blown from them. Dozens, hundreds, of vehicles, with bodies inside or out. Perhaps those two burnt men, one missing both arms, perhaps they were thinking they might make it back to Baghdad and their families for a picnic; and that man crushed under the upended T62 turret, he was running from God knows what to God knows what and of all the godfuckin gun lucky space in the desert he stopped and paused right where the turret landed; and he with half a head remaining and maggots tasting through what's left was a staff officer down from Kuwait City to inspect and instruct the troops, to offer support and welfare.
> This is war, I think ... the epic result of American bombing, American might [221–22].

In addition to this destruction, the burning or fire motif is also offered in this passage, as it is in other parts of Swofford's text. As the retreating Iraqi soldiers flee from the onslaught of American might, they, of course, light Kuwaiti oil wells and refineries on fire so that the terms "petroleum rain" (1) and "petrol rain" (211, 213, 214) become rhetorical terms of war unique to the Gulf War and common to this text. Swofford's work, a book-length memoir written by a combat veteran, is a valuable literary asset relative to American war literature in general and to this study in particular, because the text is a transitional one — a bridge, a conjunction — from the texts and war of the Vietnam era, the Cold War, Asia and Europe to the post-postmodern era and locus of American war — one that is digital, one that is situated in the Middle East, one that is fixated on dictatorial and Islamist ideology, rather than situated in communist ideological political dyads. And so Swofford's effort, while hampered and hurt by the distraction born of the torrent of pre- and post-publication critical and popular reception in print, remains, regardless, an important war memoir.

Without doubt, the publication of *Jarhead*, and the proliferation of published memoirs in the first decade of the millennium — AKA, "memoir mania" — allowed for many book- and magazine-length memoirs to be published secondary to the wars in Iraq (2003–2011) and Afghanistan (2001–present), and even the shorter works published in provincial publications like *Texas Monthly* present the defining characteristics of the American novel of war. One such short memoir, Matt Cook's "Soldier" (*Texas Monthly* July 2008), is a first-person narrative of the author's two tours in Iraq with the 187th Infantry Regiment of the 101st Airborne Division — the first in Tal Afar, and the second in Bayji. Especially evident in Cook's work are the oppositional dyad between occupying forces and indigenous/local peoples and the absurdity of war. In Tal Afar, early in the war (2003), "We are feared and loved by most Iraqis" (124), yet Cook writes, "I do not trust them" (124). So, even soon after Saddam Hussein's fall in April 2003, distrust between occupiers and indigenous/local peoples is evident, and the oppositional dyad is being created. When Cook returns to Iraq for his second tour in 2005, the situation has gotten exponentially worse, and the National Guard unit that Cook's unit is replacing is "bone-tired, homesick, and ready to scrub their brains clean.... Their battalion has suffered numerous casualties and hundreds of wounded — the result of IEDs [Improvised Explosive Devices], indirect mortar and rocket fire, and snipers" (125). Cook notes, "Bayji is home to tens of thousands of unfriendly Sunnis" (156), so it is clear that the oppositional dyad at work here is not merely between the occupying forces and the external forces who have come to Iraq to fight, the so-called "Al Qaeda in Iraq." Minority Sunnis, who once made up the majority of Saddam Hussein's ruling Ba'ath Party, have been displaced and, through fear and anger, are hostile to the occupying forces. This hostility toward the occupying forces leads to the continual placement of IEDs and land mines and the hatred of the occupiers toward the local peoples: "We receive our mission brief from their [the National Guard] platoon leader. With a monotonous voice, he speaks frequently about his absolute hatred of Iraqis and the complete hopelessness of our mission" (156). Out on patrol, "Sheepherders graze their flocks near the roads and wave as we drive by. 'They're taunting us, Sergeant Cook,' he says. 'I guaran-fuckin'tee you they're calling *mujah*' — our slang for *mujahid* or 'holy warrior'—'right now to let 'em know we're coming down the road'" (156). So, in shades of Vietnam, those the United States came to save and liberate from tyranny possess an abject hatred for the "liberators." Ironically and absurdly, the forces of the Iraqi Army (IA) are related to the Anti-Iraqi Forces (AIF) — AKA, the enemy — so the AIF will not usually attack the American forces if the IA forces are present (156); after all, why kill a relative when killing an occupier, when patience will lead to the opportunity to kill an occupier who is alone? To make the situation even more absurd, the fluidity of the war allows for insurgents to become informants of allies, and today's enemy can become tomorrow's ally (157). Cook's narrative is loaded with nuggets of the absurdity of the Iraq War — another example: trying to kill an enemy and lethally wounding him, then trying to save him with first aid (161) — and is populated with example after example of the oppositional dyad between occupying forces and indigenous/local peoples. The result of the narrative is explicit: the Iraqis (or at least the Iraqis Cook has come across) hate the

Americans, and the Americans, through Cook's optic, of course, "would rather sweat and bleed in Afghanistan" (125), a locus and war they view as valid.

Colby Buzzell's book-length memoir, *My War: Killing Time in Iraq* (2005), is an outstanding work of postmodern, peri-combat memoir. Unlike Swofford's *Jarhead*, Buzzell's text was written during Buzzell's time in a war zone, and Buzzell did not join the military out of a sense of family tradition and honor and duty but out of a sense of boredom and socio-cultural and professional malaise. Structurally, Buzzell's text stands in opposition to Swofford's, as Swofford's text is very much a modernist text in the tradition of the post-war warrior memoir and constructed in the American modernist structural tradition — see Introduction. Conversely, Buzzell's text is mechanically and philosophically an explicitly postmodern device, one that was begun modernistically as a warrior journal and evolved postmodernistically into an in-war warrior blog Buzzell started writing in opposition to the Army's and popular media's official rhetoric of war — that is, government propaganda fed to media sources and then propagated to the American and world-wide public — while serving in a combat capacity in Mosul, Iraq, from December 2003 to October 2004.

What makes Buzzell's text unique, of course, is that it is written and digitally published, during war, rather than after war. As such, there is a specific urgency to the text, particularly to the blog entries, which are often written immediately after battle or combat service. As Buzzell uses the blog entries to "clarify" the official Army or media-sanitized version of events, the reader will get a propaganda sandwich; for example, in the MEN IN BLACK section (248–65), a section on an AIF attack and subsequent city-wide, battalion-wide battle, CNN's version of the event (248) is three short paragraphs composed of four sentences, while Buzzell's version of the same event (248–60) is nearly 13 pages long, and the Army's version (260–62) less than three pages long. The battle, per CNN, in its entirety, as posted on 4 August 2004:

> MOSUL CLASHES LEAVE 12 DEAD
> Clashes between police and insurgents in the northern city of Mosul left 12 Iraqis dead and 26 wounded, hospital and police sources said Wednesday.
> Rifle and rocket-propelled grenade fire as well as explosions were heard in the streets of the city.
> The provincial governor imposed a curfew that began at 3 P.M. local time (7 A.M. EDT), and two hours later, provincial forces, police and Iraqi National Guard took control, according to Hazem Gelawi, head of the governor's press office in the Nineveh province. Gelawi said the city is stable and expects the curfew to be lifted Thursday [248].

What is interesting about the CNN release is the lack of identification of American forces: an entire battalion was roused from FOB (Forward Operating Base) Marez, yet nary a mention of the presence of American fighting forces is present in the web release. Freedom of the American press aside, censorship — or at least the suggestion of content editing — must be at work here, as the Army's official press release, while lengthier in word count, is nearly as limited rhetorically:

> Task Force Tomahawk Press Release
> Release # 08-13
> FOR IMMEDIATE RELEASE
> Coordinated attacks in Mosul leave 14 civilians dead; Iraqi Security Forces stand their ground against attackers, return stability to the city.
> MOSUL, IRAQ (August 4, 2004) — a series of coordinated attacks in Mosul today targeting Iraqi Police, Iraqi National Guard and multinational forces left more than fourteen Iraqi citizens

dead and 31 wounded. Iraqi Police and Iraqi National Guard soldiers responded quickly and returned stability to the city. No Iraqi security forces were killed in the attacks.

... Multinational forces served in a supporting role, providing additional support where and when the Iraqi leaders involved in the attacks requested it.

... Since the transfer of sovereignty on June 28 [2004], Iraqi Security Forces continue to assume the majority of the responsibility for maintaining the overall security of the region [260–62].

"Multinational forces" are, of course, American forces, and "supporting role," of course, means that they fought the battle, nearly in its entirety.

According to Buzzell, whose account is placed betwixt the two official accounts, "Now here's what really happened" (248). After the battalion was roused and rolled out of FOB Marez and into Mosul, the platoons were ambushed in coordinated attacks brought on by AIF and the Men in Black of the section title — Iranian insurgents: "Bullets were pinging off our armor, all over our vehicle, and you could hear multiple RPGs [rocket-propelled grenades] being fired, soaring through the air every which way and impacting all around us.... My entire platoon was being ambushed. We were stuck in the middle of a kill zone" (251). Buzzell's platoon evacuates the area only to return nearly immediately: "We were taking fire from all over. I fired and fired and fired and fired and fired. At EVERYTHING. I was just 360-ing the .50-cal and shooting at everything. We were taking fire from all over, and every single one of us had our guns blazing. At one time, I saw a dog try to run across the street and somebody shot it" (252). Buzzell also mentions that a watermelon stand is destroyed and a Pepsi bottling plant is burning, so, in passing, the defining characteristics of omnipresent death and destruction and the burning or fire motif are presented within the greater defining characteristic of the violence of war. And Buzzell has this to say about those who "returned stability to the city": "This gunfight had been going on for 4½ hours when the INGs [Iraqi National Guard] showed up to the party (about fucking time) in their ING pick-up trucks, all jam packed with ING soldiers in uniform armed with AK-47s" (256). The fight lasted approximately 12 hours, two of Buzzell's comrades were critically injured and evacuated out, and Buzzell ends the blog entry with this dollop of understated sarcasm: "Note: I don't think CNN's report of only 12 dead is accurate" (260). The blog entry is dated 5 August 2004, the day after the battle. Further, before placing the Army's press release in the text, Buzzell comments, "I've put the events of that day in a shoebox, put the lid on it, and haven't opened it since" (260). Buzzell's work is unlike any preceding warrior-written war memoir, both structurally and philosophically. A seminal artifact of the digital era, and of the soldier's perspective of war during war, and of the Bush-Cheney Doctrine in Iraq, *My War* offers an immediacy so urgent that the nightmares of war come before the post-war sleep.

Turning to the decade long — and ongoing — war in Afghanistan, war correspondent Sebastian Junger's book-length memoir, *War* (2010), and the late Tim Hetherington and Junger's companion film, *Restrepo* (2010), are — like Buzzell's work — texts created and produced while the war examined and presented rages without end. Both texts focus on 2nd Platoon, Battle Company of the 503rd Airborne Infantry Regiment, 173rd Airborne Brigade Combat Team, who were stationed in the Korengal Valley, in the Kunar (AKA, Konar) Province of Eastern Afghanistan, for a fifteen-month tour in 2007–2008. While *War* was very well reviewed (in the *Washington Post* by no less an authority than Philip Caputo, for example), and *Restrepo* was nominated for a 2011 Academy Award for Best Documentary, it is interesting to note, relative to this study, the intertextuality of *War* with Herr's *Dispatches*.

Herr was given the opportunity for a long-term assignment in Vietnam by *Esquire*—a glossy but well-respected publisher of literary and journalistic nonfiction—while Junger was given the opportunity for a long-term assignment in Afghanistan (June 2007–June 2008) by *Vanity Fair*—another glossy but well-respected publisher of literary and journalistic nonfiction. And early in each text, there is a story told to the journalist by a combat soldier that needs no answer (*War* 58; *Dispatches* 6). First, the story from the Junger text: "A combat medic once told me what to do to save a man who's bleeding out" (58). The medic then goes on to tell Junger how to stanch limb-based, life-threatening arterial bleeding—pressure, tourniquet, pack the wound, wrap the wound, start an IV. The medic, per Junger's paraphrased narration, continues: "If you are wounded and there's no one else around, you have to do all this yourself. And you want to make sure you can do it all one-handed" (58). Junger's narrator adds, "When a soldier told me that, I unthinkingly asked him why. He didn't even bother answering" (58). Herr's interpolated story is even more acutely powerful:

> But what a story he [the Lurp from the Herr section cited above] told me, as one-pointed and resonant as any war story I ever heard, it took me a year to understand it:
> "Patrol went up the mountain. One man came back. He died before he could tell us what happened."
> I waited for the rest, but it seemed not to be that kind of story; when I asked him what had happened he just looked like he felt sorry for me, fucked if he'd waste time telling stories to anyone as dumb as I was [6].

Obviously, Junger has read Herr.

One particular event stands out in *War* and *Restrepo*: the Operation Rock Avalanche death of Scout Team leader Staff Sergeant Larry Rougle on 23 October 2007. While fighting peers die in the text(s)—in fact, the film is titled for Juan "Doc" Restrepo, who was killed on patrol on 22 July 2007—it is the death of Rougle that seems to psychologically and emotionally devastate the men of Battle Company, and it is the death of Rougle that seems to be at the heart of the book, if not the film. In the rhetoric of war and in the infantry vernacular, Rougle was a Super Grunt, one who is exceptional at the business of infantry combat and the nomenclature and practice thereof:

> The [Scout] squad leader is a short, strong-looking man with dark eyes and jet-black hair named Larry Rougle. Rougle has done six combat tours in six years [three in Iraq and three in Afghanistan] and is known in Battle Company as a legendary badass and some kind of ultimate soldier. Once [Firebase] Phoenix got hit and Rougle and his men grabbed their weapons at the KOP [Korengal Outpost] and ran down there so fast that [Lieutenant Matt] Piosa was still on the radio calling in the attack when they walked in the wire [80].

What that means is that Rougle and his men ran to the point of attack a kilometer away, counter-attacked, finished the fight, and returned to the outpost before radio support could be called in to offer land and air support to those attacked at the firebase. Rougle is killed when his position is overrun by Taliban forces during Operation Rock Avalanche: "Cortez goes to one knee behind cover with his rifle up and glances to the right and sees a body lying facedown—an American. Walker runs to him and shakes him to see if he's all right, and finally rolls him over. It's Staff Sergeant Rougle, shot through the forehead and his face is purple with trauma" (106). Rougle's men, especially a Scout named Clinard, who shrieks and sobs with grief, are devastated. Men like Rougle are not supposed to die. When Rougle is killed, the randomness of war becomes a very real specter to the men of Battle Company, for if Rougle can die—in an immediate fashion, no less—then anyone can die. No one is safe, neither the pogues nor the super grunts. In Hetherington and Junger's film (Scene 10, 8:00–11:00), the men's fears and grief are properly articulated, but in the book, Rougle's death and its effects are textually articulated, sans the limit of running time, and thus are better explained. Rougle died quickly in an effort to support his men, who were under a high volume of fire, and who, in turn, have survivor's guilt for not taking care of Rougle, who was taking care of them. As a Scout named Raeon says, "Some of them [Scout team members] are takin' it real bad, kind of blamin' it on themselves because we couldn't push over the top. But the thing they got to understand is he was dead instantly — there's just nothin' you could do right there" (113–14). Rougle is dead, as are Juan Restrepo and Timothy Vimoto before him, and all told, 40 to 50 other Americans died in the Korengal Valley — numbers differ according to news and government sources. In April 2010, the American command decided to abandon the Korengal.

To conclude, the defining characteristics of the American novel of war are found not only in novels, of course, but in other — genre-specific — literature of war. As shown, the difference between the use of the defining characteristics in the novels and in the non-novel works is the breadth and depth and scope of the presence of the defining characteristics in the literary works. Because of length — with poetry, short story, drama, and some short memoir — and because of rhetorical focus, the novel-centric defining characteristics used are not always elevated to the point of thematic concern in non-novel literature of war. However, nearly all shorter non-novel works of literature of war, regardless of genre, include a limited number of the defining characteristics of the American novel of war at a motif rather than thematic level. Conversely, some shorter literary works of war do not use a number of the defining characteristics, but rather, fully develop one or two of the defining characteristics within the work. As such, some shorter works of war analyzed use sundry defining characteristics within the work, at an undeveloped level, while others use one or two of the defining characteristics, at a wholly developed level. In either rhetorical situation, relevant is the presence of the defining characteristics of the American novel of war in said non-novel works of the American literature of war, because as all wars contain certain and specific elements of war, all works of war literature contain certain and specific literary elements of war. And of course, in this study, all of the literature is relative to American wars and is written by American authors. Thus, the poetry of war, the short story of war, the drama of war, and the memoir of war present a broad, if necessarily incomplete, survey of the non-novel American-authored war literature of note from the early nineteenth century to the early twenty-first century, and as noted, each of the non-novel texts here utilize the defining characteristics of the American novel of war, albeit at a level less prominent than in the novels of war analyzed in this study. The poetry, short story, drama, and memoir discussed in this chapter is relative to the novels discussed in the forthcoming chapters in that each genre of American war literature contains similar thematic elements and motifs — the thematic elements and motifs of war, American war, as authored by American authors.

II

War as Central Action

The first defining characteristic of the American novel of war is that the war at hand is the central thematic action of the text. All of the novels in this study centralize the theme and topic and actions and results of a specific war or episode of war: the era of Indian Eradication after the Mexican–U.S. War of 1846–1848, the Civil War, World War I, World War II, the Korean War, the Vietnam War, the Persian Gulf War, and the Iraq War. If one asks whether a given novel would exist sans the war at hand, and the answer is yes, then that novel is not in this study. But if the central thematic action of the text is war, if the locus of the guts of the work is the war zone, if the optic of the philosophy of the novel is the view of war, then, obviously, the work is a novel of war fit for this study. Thus, were it not for the real wars covered in the fiction, these novels would not exist, and while not every author here is a combat veteran, every novel here is by and of combat — in theme, in motif, in topic, in element. For example, in *Blood Meridian, Or the Evening Redness in the West,* Cormac McCarthy presents the child, then the kid, then the filibuster, then the scalphunter, and finally the post-war man, who, in the end, cannot or does not live without war. What is more, the American novel of war is a presentation of war, and in the McCarthy text — as well as in each text in this study — war is the protagonist. Further, each novel used for analysis in this study has been chosen for its literary presentation of war, and while a number of texts here will not be historically noted as "high literature" — however that may be critically or popularly defined — all of the texts here present war in a literary fashion and use most, if not all, of the defining characteristics of the American novel of war, and in so doing, earn a place in this study. A novel of war must have war and the physical, psychological, spiritual, social, and cultural effects of war; otherwise, it is not a novel of war. A novel of war must be born by and of and through war; otherwise, it is not a novel of war.

Moving war by war, chronologically, in reference to the texts born of each war, Cormac McCarthy's masterwork, *Blood Meridian,* while a postmodern construct, is set earliest historically, with the majority of the action occurring from the spring of 1849 (5) to the late spring/early summer of 1850 (311–12), a period during which the Chihuahua state government contracted with "Anglo aliens" (Sepich, Rev. ed., 6) to eradicate Comanche, Apache, and other raiding indigenous peoples through the collection of "receipts" (McCarthy 98) — scalps — as proof of death (Sepich, Rev. ed., 5–8), what Timothy Parrish accurately calls "socially sanctioned" (87) killing in gangs whose "goals are to rid the earth of the heathen tribes below the newly formed border and make a little money while doing it" (Wegner 59). Parrish notes that, in the text, "humans wage war against other humans, against things, and against nature [and that] *Blood Meridian* is an expression of existence as an ongoing, total war" (84), while John Wegner correctly posits that "war is the central thesis to

McCarthy's southwestern works" (59). In *Blood Meridian*, the post-war fight against the Apache and the Comanche — and then any who have black hair (Sepich, Rev. ed., 8) — is the central optic through which war is viewed and the locus at which the text is situated. As John Sepich shows in his crucially important study, *Notes on Blood Meridian* (1993, Rev. ed. 2008), McCarthy's text is based on a number of nineteenth-century works; primary among those is Samuel Chamberlain's *My Confession: Recollections of a Rogue* (1956, Rev. ed. 1996), whose history and narrative protagonist serve as the "historical analog" (Sepich, Rev. ed., 105) for the McCarthy text and the kid. Chamberlain (1829–1908), who apparently served with the Glanton gang in a scalphunting capacity from March 1849 until the Yuma Massacre of April 1850 — William H. Goetzmann, editor of the revised edition, argues that Chamberlain's scalphunting episode is "hearsay" (13) — explicitly tells of his year with the scalphunting gang (Rev. ed., 304–32), and in addition to the Yuma Massacre, a number of other episodes found in *My Confession*, including the fight on the Little Colorado and the judge's lecture on geology, are situated in the McCarthy text. And while Chamberlain, who wrote his text from 1867 to 1905 (Rev. ed., 16), might be forgiven for some geographical and dating inaccuracies, that which is historically verifiable is the existence of the Glanton gang — and a number of members therein but not the judge — and its scalphunting role in the war on the Apache and Comanche and other marauding indigenous Indians, and this is the war central to McCarthy's *Blood Meridian*.

According to the *Benét's Reader's Encyclopedia of American Literature*, there have been "more than a hundred thousand volumes" (qtd. in Kaufman 148) published on the U.S. Civil War, and further, Will Kaufman argues, "No single episode in American history has spawned as much literary output as the Civil War" (148). This author, and this study, will address but two of those multitudes — Stephen Crane's seminal text, *The Red Badge of Courage: An Episode of the American Civil War*, and E.L. Doctorow's recent work, *The March: A Novel*. According to Donald Pizer, "The typical Civil War novel of Crane's time concentrated on a Southern belle and a Northern officer whose initial antagonism and final love symbolized the theme of national discord followed by permanent union" (2). As such, the typical "Civil War novel" was a love novel, tinged with Romanticism, rather than a modern American novel of war. Battle scenes were "minimally portrayed" (Pizer 2) and were used for melodramatic heroism, self-sacrifice, and rhetorical effect. Conversely, Crane's text, as it is widely known now, is based on real war, specifically, the battle of Chancellorsville (30 April–6 May 1863) — and thus, is the product of war and the response to war; as well, Crane's use of "various turn-of-the-century 'isms' — impressionism, symbolism, naturalism, expressionism, and so on — as well as his often jaundiced view of human nature" (Pizer 5), identify Crane and the text as prime examples of early American modernism. Further, as Pizer notes, with a nod to contemporary reviewer George Wyndham, the text is "Crane's portrayal of combat through the thoughts and feelings of a young recruit ... the portrayal of the responses to battle by an untried youthful soldier ... [is] both a study of human psychology and a social and moral allegory" (4). As such, *The Red Badge of Courage* is the first modern American novel of war, a novel born of an actual battle that deals with the isolated individual and does so in a way that is both internal and external.

E. L. Doctorow's *The March*, a narrative of William Tecumseh Sherman's November 1864 to April 1865 "March to the Sea" through Georgia, and subsequent run north through South Carolina and into North Carolina, is very much a modernist text in its construct and its execution. The text deals with Sherman's devastating push through the psychological and geographical locus of the Confederate South and the devastation thereof. Historically, as Sherman, with more than 60,000 troops, marched from Atlanta to Milledgeville to Sandersonville to Savannah while living off the loot of the towns and the land, the zeal of his Union troops to wreak havoc upon the South grew, and, as Edmund Wilson reflects, as the march continued, "Sherman who knew the South, who had always got on well with the Southerners and who did not much object to slavery, became more and more ferocious to devour the South" (*Patriotic Gore*, "Introduction" xxxii). The objective of taking Georgia, South Carolina, and North Carolina became such that the local results became not so important as the grand results, and as such, obliteration was the historical rule of the day, culminating in the burning of Columbia, South Carolina, on 17 February 1865. South Carolina was the first state to secede, of course, and the Civil War was born at Fort Sumter on 12 April 1861; thus, Columbia, South Carolina, was a locus of pathological anger for the Northern soldiers, so the troops, with or without Sherman's consent, on accident or on purpose, burned Columbia, the state capital — an event that features prominently in Doctorow's text and in Chapter XIII of this study. Moving north, Sherman's troops crossed into North Carolina and fought their way through Fayetteville to Averasboro to Bentonville to Goldsboro to Smithfield to Raleigh. As with most of Doctorow's works, but for his postmodern masterwork *The Book of Daniel* (1971), which is quite focused on a finite number of characters, *The March* contains a multitude of characters, many of whom run through the entirety of the text, and some of whom appear and are then forgotten; also common to Doctorow's texts is an accurate historicity — dates, locations, and historical figures who appear as major and minor characters are geographically and situationally accurate and verifiable. What is interesting about Doctorow's work, though, is that there is nary a villain in the panoptic presentation of Sherman's March to the Sea and through the Carolinas. A number of secondary characters are villainous and do villainous things, but no one sect or person is in the business of the practice of villainy. Doctorow's claim seems to be that Sherman's March is proceeding, as it should in a time of internecine war.

American novels of World War I can be posited in three distinct categories: those written of pre–American intervention in the war (*The Marne, One Man's Initiation*), those set during the war (*Through the Wheat, Company K*), and those set after the war (*Johnny Got His Gun*). Novels from each category are philosophically, politically, socially, and artistically unique from the novels of the other two categories. Prior to the entrance of the United States into World War I (6 April 1917), Americans who wanted to participate in the war had two options— one, they could join a foreign fighting force, à la Arthur Guy Empey, or two, they could join a volunteer ambulance group and drive an ambulance, à la Ernest Hemingway, e.e. cummings, and, relative to this study, John Dos Passos. From 1914 until 1917, driving an ambulance proximal to the battlefront afforded one — an American specifically — the opportunity to see and experience the war regardless of the fact that the United States had yet to enter the conflict as a combatant nation. Two American authors of note use the trope of the American ambulance driver in war to create novels of war for very different rhetorical purposes. Edith Wharton uses *The Marne* to conjoin "gentility with bloodthirst [and] the mannerisms of the social novelist with the matter of a recruiting poster" (Cooperman, *World War I* 41); that is, Wharton creates a propaganda novel that retrospectively emphasizes the importance and righteousness of American entrance into World War I and the need thereof for American fighting men to heed both the call and the eventual draft, while John Dos Passos, who served as an ambulance driver in Italy before the United States entered the war (Matthews 229), in shades of literary and political rhetoric to come, uses *One Man's Initiation* to "contradict the domestic version of the war" (Matthews 229) and to reflect "growing disillusionment with the patriotic vision of the war effort" (Quinn 180). Wharton's work, in addition to being a propaganda piece, and like Willa Cather's *One of Ours* (1922), is also a screed against American materialism and indifference. While the domestic sections of the Cather text are set in the rural Midwest, the domestic in the Wharton text is set in the bowels of American high society — AKA, New York and the East Coast — and the social elites, but for Troy Belknap, are pilloried as socially and materially selfish, and politically indifferent to the needs of the Europeans in time of war — especially to the needs of the cultured and gentile French, à la Dorothy Canfield Fisher. Dos Passos' work skips the propagandizing and Francophilism — and the hallucinatory or ghost story ending — and focuses on Martin Howe's initiation into the realities of mass conflict, and while the Wharton text is (eventually) set specifically at the second battle of the Marne (15 July–5 August 1918), Dos Passos' work is ambivalent; the war is in France, in 1917, and the war machine is a great beast beyond any man's or any nation's control, so while Wharton's text presents "war casualties as strangely unrelated to human bodies, Dos Passos' pages are strewn with ghastly corpses [and] grotesque wounds" (Matthews 230). Of course, a propaganda novel on war is not going to present the realities of war, while an anti-war novel will explicitly do so.

Relative to the Dos Passos work, peri-war World War I novels, written by combat veterans after the war but set during the war, such as Thomas Boyd's *Through the Wheat* and William March's *Company K*, exponentialize the realities of war as well as the psychological and physical effects thereof. In each text, war is presented as a brutal and carnal act, an act that leads to devastation sans regeneration. Both authors were highly decorated Marine Corps veterans of World War I who volunteered to rescue wounded peers under heavy fire (Beidler, "Introduction" xi; Simmons xii), and each author uses his combat experiences to "debunk the fantasies of heroism which have for so long cast an aura around militarism" (Homberger 177), as each text chronicles the fact that "war [is] dehumanizing, and that heroism and patriotism [are] things which serious people could no longer believe in" (Homberger 176). Additionally, each text "construct[s] the soldier as a sacrificial victim of forces beyond his power" (Cobley 75), as the machine of war deconstructs the machine of individual man. Philip D. Beidler argues that with the novels of Boyd and March — and even Dos Passos — "a realistic fictional depiction of the experience of modern warfare entered American literature as a significant, and even a central topic" (xiii). And the centralization of these realistic literary adaptations of modern war was, of course, the authors' experiences in the First World War. Coincidentally, Boyd and March — whose given name was William Edward Campbell — each served in the United States 2nd Division, 4th Brigade, Boyd in the 6th Marines, and March in the 5th Marines; as such, each Marine cum author fought in the same battles — Toulon/Les Eparges, Belleau Wood, Soissons, Blanc Mont — but they did not know one another, and each was wounded in battle — Boyd was gassed at Blanc Mont (Simmons xii), and March was shot/shrapneled at Belleau Wood and Blanc Mont (Beidler xi, xii). And similarly, each novel "affords a point at which two major World War I literary reactions intersect: rhetorical indictment on one hand, and benumbed negation on the other" (Cooperman, *World War I* 165). So, philosophically, each novel is similar: war is a meat-grinder, and man is meat. This similarity is not hard to fathom, as each author served under very similar circumstances during the war.

Structurally, however, the novels are radically different. *Through the Wheat* begins *in medias res* in March 1918 with William Hicks — no rank yet given — nine months in France and waiting for battle. Boyd's narrative is told in linear form, and chronology follows the narrative while the story unfolds as Hicks and Company C enter and exist in the fields of fire. Nonetheless, the tale is very much the tale of a modernist protagonist, the psychically isolated Hicks, and the novel "focuses on the odyssey of an individual soldier in a particular battle" (Quinn 181). Conversely, *Company K* is, for its day, a radical experiment in structure and form and is told in 113 narrative vignettes, each of which is titled with the name and rank of the narrator and which are articulated by five officers, 15 non-commissioned officers, 92 privates, and one unknown soldier: "The unsentimental sketches are told in the first person and demonstrate repeatedly that war is not glamorous, that it is an economic boon for business back home, and that it is the most horrific phenomenon that man has ever created" (Quinn 182). And while the narrative sketches are told in chronological order, the first sketch is a metafictive, post-war comment by one Private Joseph Delaney, who has just completed a book of his own company that he wants "to be a record of every company in every army" (13). That is, Delaney wants his text to be a metonymous record of war, applicable to all wars and to all warriors, regardless of nation. So, as the Boyd text, written and published immediately after the war (1923), is very much a modernist construct, the March text, published 15 years after World War I (1933), is very much an avant-garde postmodernist construct. Yet, while the earlier text is—structurally—very much in the legacy of American literary modernism, and while the latter text is—structurally—very much in the proto-genesis of American literary postmodernism, both texts are inherently anti-war, as is the final World War I–centric text in this study—Dalton Trumbo's astounding and horrifying *Johnny Got His Gun*.

Trumbo's novel, at once horrifying, savage, brutal, and prescient, is also a text that rails against the rhetoric spewed forth from the lips of politicians who justify war as a noble and comprehensible act. Trumbo's text is "the war novel of rhetorical protest" (Cooperman, *World War I* 241), through which the author, influenced by the carnage of World War I and foreshadowing the potential of greater carnage of World War II, rages against war as a political reaction; in the text, terms such as liberty, democracy, duty, God, country, freedom, and the like are weapons by which the political sect mesmerizes and hypnotizes and influences and guilts the common boy into taking a uniform to support his country in a time of war. As such, the work is "antiwar literature which looks forward as much as back" (Quinn 183), and in so doing, *Johnny Got His Gun* is born of World War I but is very much a warning of World War II. Using interior monologue and an explicit lack of authorial objectivity, Trumbo (who, it should be noted, was a man of great personal, professional, and political courage, and who refused to testify in front of the House Un-American Activities Committee and was subsequently found in contempt and jailed for a year), offers the reader one Joe Bonham, a World War I veteran maimed almost beyond comprehension — Joe's and the reader's, but not the author's—who, following the work's central theme of communicated rhetoric, political and otherwise, seeks a method by which he can communicate with the outside world from his voiceless, sightless, soundless husk of a body. A World War I shell has destroyed Bonham's ability to communicate; nonetheless, Bonham eventually, and after years of isolation entombed within his own body and mind, uses Morse code to communicate—first with a nurse and then with a federal representative. Juxtaposed are the thematic elements of ideological political propaganda and Bonham's inability to communicate, and when Bonham breaks through to the external world, he is told that he will not be able to communicate his thoughts and feelings and experiences of war because he is evidence, and his words would be evidence, of a sort of subversiveness born of being mangled in war; that is, he would not be good for business—the business of recruiting, procuring, and using men in war. Ironically, he would be bad propaganda. The results of war are counterproductive to the promotion of war.

Conversely, World War II, at least from the American perspective, was "an honorable war" (Mailer, "Hubris" 92), a war that pitted democracy against fascism, a war in which "attitudes towards conflict itself were more pragmatic and provided much less ground for the disillusionment of great romantic expectations" (Hölbing 212). And of the 1,500 to 2,200 novels born of the conflict of the Second World War (Hölbing 213), three of the four novels in this study —*Beach Red*, *The Naked and the Dead*, and *Ceremony*— deal with the war in the Pacific, while one —*Catch-22*— deals with the war in Europe. American involvement in the war in the Pacific lasted the entirety of the American involvement in World War II (7 December 1941–14 August 1945), and as such, perhaps allowed American authors an unrestricted ability to present the war as seen and experienced, sans referential Western history; according to Mailer, unlike the European theatre, "the Pacific lent itself to working on a broad canvas. You didn't have to worry about how much you knew" ("Hubris" 92). Thus, sans history, World War II novels of the Pacific allowed one to write expressively rather than in a historical context. And as Mailer notes, "The Japanese had attacked Pearl Harbor in the Pacific. So it was a simple war" ("Hubris" 92). The enemy was the Other, and the enemy had directly attacked the United States. So clearly, in *Beach Red* and in *The Naked and the Dead*, the enemy Other is nameless and faceless and nearly void of dialogue or characterization, but in *Ceremony*, the enemy (genetic predecessors of Laguna Pueblo American Indians), is personified, and thus is personally characterized and villainized.

According to Eric Homberger, "The jungle warfare of the Pacific seemed to American writers [and readers] particularly terrifying because it lacked clear demarcations and sides" (178), and a primary component of the war in the Pacific was the beach landing by Allied forces upon an island occupied by Japanese forces. Peter Bowman's *Beach Red*, written and published before the close of 1945, is an excellent, unique example of the urgency and immediacy brought forth from direct participation in the war in the Pacific. The text is written in a staccato-narrative prose form — often incorrectly referred to as "free-verse narrative" (Hölbing 221)— which is meant to represent the "rigid timing" (Bowman Inside Front Cover) of a military beach landing upon an occupied island. Unique to the work, in addition to the narrative structure (one in which the 60 minutes of elapsed time is presented over 120 pages of text), is the component of the narrative perspective, that of one soldier who thinks about the war and his mission and role, even though he dies at the end of the text. Bowman, who served in the Pacific with the U.S. Army Corps of Engineers during World War II, offers in 120 pages a catalog of the characteristic violence of an island landing, the natural world as the enemy, the equipment used by the infantry and navy of the era, and the adjacency of jungle fighting conditions to the mind of the fighter. Bowman's novel is necessarily short, compact, and condensed, for the hour that passes, the last hour of one man's life, is short, compact, and condensed, and the work, as per the title, is thematically concerned with two issues— the beach landing of an occupied Pacific island and the death thereof.

Conversely, Mailer's work is an opus, explicitly so. As World War II raged on, Norman Mailer was inducted into the Army; while a young man still in basic training, Mailer decided that he "wanted to write the great novel of World War II" ("Hubris" 91), and *The Naked and the Dead* was his effort and primarily successful result. Mailer, who desired to fight in Europe but was sent instead to the Pacific ("Hubris" 91), sets the text on the fictional island of Anopopei, an island at once occupied by the Japanese and invaded by the Americans.

Mailer's work is very much a work of the futility of war on a microcosmic level, as an Intelligence and Reconnaissance platoon is sent to reconnoiter Japanese positions and numbers prior to an island-wide Allied assault. What happens during the mission is astounding but commonplace in war and in American novels of war, as the platoon breaks down psychologically and physically, and the structure of the hierarchy of rank implodes from within. And while the trope of the island invasion is one that becomes commonplace in the World War II novels of the Pacific, as does the melting pot theme — a thematic situation whereby a platoon is composed of a mixture of men of various ethnicities, religions, education levels, socioeconomic situations, and geographic placements — the text is distinctive in that it offers the inner focalizations of many, if not most, of the primary and secondary characters. Further, and uniquely, the work also offers the points of view and personal histories of enlisted men, non-commissioned officers, and officers alike, from private to general. But, of course, what is centralized in *The Naked and the Dead*, as well as in *Beach Red*, is the island-hopping campaign in the Pacific, without which neither of the novels would exist. Interestingly, Mailer would, of course, go on to become, if not a giant, a very important writer of postmodern-era American fiction and New Journalism, while Bowman would go on to serve primarily as a magazine editor and reference library owner. However, while the texts are set during the war of the Pacific and were written by combat veterans of said campaign, *The Naked and the Dead* and *Beach Red* are both explicitly of the post-atomic era, and each text is structurally and philosophically postmodern.

Leslie Marmon Silko's masterwork *Ceremony* is also post-atomic and postmodern, even though its author is neither a military veteran nor a participant of World War II. Nonetheless, Silko's work is a searing work of war fiction, a nexus of a number of historical, cultural, social, and literary influences. *Ceremony*, while seemingly a work of World War II, and set during and immediately after that war, is very much a protest work that rails against the fact that American Indians fought in a world war "on behalf of a nation that still discriminated against them and deprived them of their rights" (Hölbing 217). In this way, the work is derivative of N. Scott Momaday's seminal work, *House Made of Dawn* (1968), a work for which Momaday won the Pulitzer Prize. American Indians are fine to serve in uniform for the United States, but once the war is over, the soldier is again a mere Indian, less than an Anglo in all facets of hierarchical American culture and society. As well, in the Momaday text and in the Silko text, the narrative protagonist (Abel in the former and Tayo in the latter) is severely and psychologically damaged by his participation in the modern cum postmodern form of war. Tayo, a participant in the Bataan Death March, has seen and heard his cousin Rocky's death, while Abel is nearly suicidally reckless in war (102–4) and suffers greatly thereafter. Tayo is also struck by the fact that his captors bear a physical resemblance to him and his cousin Rocky, both of whom are Laguna Pueblo Indian. So Tayo is fighting against those whom he resembles, while he is fighting alongside those who socially repress and disenfranchise him in times before and after war. And despite the fact that Silko's work is set during the Second World War, the text is very much by and of the Vietnam War. Written from 1973 to July 1975 (Silko, "Preface" xii–xvii), *Ceremony* was created in the shadow of a war after which its warriors were ostracized by the very society for which they fought. These combatants, many of whom were poor and/or non–Anglo draftees, came home to a nation in shame rather than pride, and as such, were analogous to Tayo, Harley, Leroy, Emo, and Pinkie in *Ceremony*. And while Silko does not expressly say so, the influence of the Vietnam War experience upon *Ceremony* cannot be denied. Therefore, the work is both a World War II American novel of war (directly) and a Vietnam War American novel of war (indirectly). Further, the novel has enemies external — the Japanese or Vietnamese — and internal — the American Anglo "destroyers" and the American Indian "destroyers."

In Joseph Heller's *Catch-22*, of course, the enemy is external and internal, too. In addition to the external, explicit, uniformed German enemy, there is the internal, initially implicit, uniformed American enemy — the military hierarchy, one that causes the deaths of its own forces. But the German enemy is largely unseen in the novel, and the American enemy is grossly present in the novel. As such, the implicit is the explicit, and the explicit is the implicit. And while Heller flew 60 combat missions as a B-25 bombardier during World War II, the novel is more reflective of the author's sentiments of war and the industry of war as viewed at a distance from his war experiences. As such, the work, while written by an air combat veteran of the European theatre of World War II, is very much a work in which Heller asserts, from a Cold War perspective, that "[w]ar threatens to become a way of life dominated by the business interests of global military-industrial corporations" (Hölbing 218), and that "the old claims of patriotism and loyalty have, for the *Catch-22* generation, lost their power, have indeed become an obscene charade" (Homberger 205). And while Hölbing and Homberger are correct in their claims, the novel is nonetheless set during World War II, in Italy, on the island of Pianosa and in Rome, during the Allied occupation of the former Axis power. And the novel's central thematic element is the theme of mission creep, through which combat missions are ever increased so that a flier can never complete his allotted number of combat missions and then be rotated out of combat. Consequently, to claim the novel is anything other than a novel of war — peri-war — is disingenuous. And as the novel would not exist in its current state sans World War II and Heller's participation as a combat airman in said war, and as the novel contains all of the Defining characteristics of the American novel of war, the novel must be considered an American novel of war.

Five novels of the Korean War that would not exist sans the war are *Hold Back the Night, Band of Brothers, It's Cold in Pongo-Ni, MASH*, and *I Am the Clay*. The first two works deal with the 1st Marine Division's — under X Corps — organized, hasty retreat in November/December 1950 from the Changjin/Chosin Reservoir to Hungnam, North Korea, and the Sea of Japan. Pat Frank's *Hold Back the Night* is a petite view of what remains of a single Marine infantry company, the fictional Dog Company, and the seventeen men left alive after extended fighting from the Reservoir to Hagaru to Koto-Ri through the Asian steppes. By the time the text opens, the company has lost "a hundred and sixty-odd men" (10), is isolated, and those left alive are in danger of starving or freezing to death, or being killed in action, on the way to Hungnam and safety. The text spends much of the time between the opening and closing chapters in backstory mode, as the narration details the lives of a number of primary characters and the events that led to the first chapter of the text — the posting of the company at the Chosin Reservoir, the Chinese attack on 27 November 1950, the destruction of the company, and the hasty movement from Chosin to Koto-Ri to Hungnam. *Hold Back the Night* primarily examines the role of a commanding officer (Captain Sam Mackenzie) under duress and without support, and the manner in which he and his men live and fight and move toward a common goal — that of survival intact as a common fighting unit, albeit one that exists after ninety percent KIA. Frank's text and character development are limited in scope, and thus serve to remind the reader that a war is not merely thousands upon thousands of men fighting and dying on a mass scale; a war is composed of battles, which are of individuals who are living and fighting and dying, one-by-one, even as whole groups die cumulatively and collectively. Frank reminds the reader, through the close examination of a very small number of developed characters, that each man fighting and dying is a man with a history and life and dreams and goals. Frank's text also examines the role and definition of leadership under duress and who is fit to take and practice such leadership as assigned leaders fall in battle.

Conversely, Ernest Frankel's *Band of Brothers* is a grand examination of a Marine company of two hundred and fifty men (Able Company of the 1st Marine Division) and their movement *en masse* from the Chosin Reservoir to Hungnam and the Sea of Japan. While the Frankel text covers the same Marine division and the same battle and hasty retreat as the Frank text, *Band of Brothers* does not start *in medias res* as does *Hold Back the Night*. *Band of Brothers* is told primarily in chronological order from the days prior to the Chinese attack, and Frankel introduces an entire catalog of characters—American officers and enlisted men, Chinese and Korean translators and prisoners and double agents (many of whom do not survive the text, of course). Interestingly, and historically accurate, Frankel includes African American and Hispanic characters in addition to the standard—for the era—literary cum military Anglo hegemony. And unlike *Hold Back the Night*, which opens after what remains of Dog Company has moved beyond Koto-Ri, *Band of Brothers* opens with Able Company still occupying the southwest shore of the Chosin Reservoir (25), on or just before Thanksgiving 1950—23 November. Frankel takes pains and uses hundreds of pages to detail battle scenes and the company's movement from Chosin to Hungnam, and the progress of the company is excruciating, and slow, and violent. What *Hold Back the Night* and *Band of Brothers* have in common, though, other than the common history of 1st Marine Division and the race to the Sea of Japan, is the identification of the Korean winter as murderous in its effects upon the Marines. In fact, all five of the Korean War novels in this study explicitly use the winter as a thematic element in the literature as well as present the Korean weather as hostile to all who are forced to occupy the land in time of war.

Edward Franklin's *It's Cold in Pongo-Ni* uses the weather as a literal threat in addition to using the winter weather as a symbol for the war in Korea. The weather is brutally cold, and the war in Korea is a passionless war for those who are there. The county is stark, barren, rocky, mountainous, and cold, and the only emotion is fear, a cold fear, a fear based not only on the immediacy and presence of death but also on the absurdity of the present state and stalemate of the war and the missions therein and thereof. Also set in November, but of 1951 or 1952, as the opening sentence of the text reads, "It is November again" (9), the novel concerns a combat raid and prisoner snatch to be performed by a team of eight men and a lieutenant—one who is ironically and absurdly assigned the billet of "peace officer." The 38th parallel is established, the peace talks are in mission—as of July 1951—and the trenchlines of the South Koreans and Americans, and the North Koreans and Chinese, are firmly in place. So firmly in place, in fact, that the Korean War resembles the First World War in that it is a trench war of drawn lines rather than mobile lines. Further, the war is a stagnant and stagnating war, a cold-ish war, a war in a vacuum, wherein men snipe one another and kill each other in small numbers. So, in a text-wide theme of absurdity, the peace officer is forced to take a team of eight men, men who are available because they are assigned to mess duty rather than to their rifle platoons, up to The Claw—the Chinese-held position—to kill a few and capture a few. And this combat raid is the central action of the text. On the combat raid to The Claw, the raiders must cross through a deserted and destroyed village, Pongo-Ni. Here, in the text title, conjoined with the village name, there is also symbolism with the use of the word "cold"; the village is a point of no return, a point of demarcation, a point at which allied fire becomes deadly because the village is proximal to The Claw. The village is also cold as in dead, destroyed, deserted, and lifeless. And then there is the weather — November at the 38th parallel. *It's Cold in Pongo-Ni* begins very much as a psychologically taut and sparse work, but evolves into an American novel of war with the defining characteristics and actions of such. Franklin's combat role in Korea in 1951 and 1952 obviously allowed him the knowledge to write the combat scenes, and his post-war education perhaps allowed him to write a text philosophically existential and structurally experimental, yet based on a conventional war.

The final two Korean War texts in this study, Richard Hooker's satirical *MASH* and Chaim Potok's proletariat *I Am the Clay*, are also paradoxical works. Each text gives a voice within war to those often unspoken of or unmentioned in warfare and the annals thereof. The former text, written by former Army surgeon Richard Hornberger and journalist W.C. Heinz under the pseudonym of Richard Hooker, offers the reader the surgeon's-eye view of warfare, and the results and absurdities thereof, away from the battlefield, but secondary to the battlefield. The latter text, written by rabbinical scholar, former Army chaplain, and novelist Potok, offers the peasant cum refugee's view of life among the battlefields. Each text is an American novel of war but is, nonetheless, not of the grunt's-eye view. Regardless, each text is important to this study for that which it does include, the defining characteristics of the American novel of war, with, of course, the Korean War as the central thematic action of the text. *MASH* is important because it catalogs the pre–Vietnam equipment and social and cultural maladroitness that comes from a Western occupier in a Far Eastern nation. As well, *MASH* is relevant because the text offers one of the peculiar absurdities of war and war medicine — that the job of the trauma surgeon in war is to, in addition to saving the gravely wounded, save the less-than-gravely wounded so that they can be returned to the battlefield. To save one in order so that that one can kill or die is one of the ultimate absurdities in war medicine, and while this absurdity is comedically presented in the text, the gravity of the healer's role in the process is a severe one; as "Hooker" notes in the text's foreword, "The surgeons in the MASH hospitals were exposed to extremes of hard work, leisure, tension, boredom, heat, cold, satisfaction, and frustration that most of them had never faced before" (5) — that is, military life in time of war. And it is this presentation of the medical officer in time of war that makes *MASH* an important text, not the film or the television series. Another omnipresent thematic element of the Korean War, and of war and warriors, is the use of prostitutes and the institution of prostitution in wartime, an element readily presented in *MASH*. Of course, *MASH* would not have been possible without Richard Hornberger's time spent as a surgeon with the Army Medical Corps during the Korean War, and the immediacy and urgency of the text, secondary to the omnipresence of the war, humor notwithstanding, is evident and historically accurate.

The Potok work is another Korean War text that accurately presents the war from the perspective of the voiceless, nameless, and faceless. While surgeons may be masked while working, wartime peasant refugees are voiceless, powerless, and silent because of their very situation during war. Refugees are present in every war, but in most novels of war, the refugees, while present, remain silent and secondary characters, often abused, homeless, village-less, and lacking in existence but for their physical presence, which often runs in and out of the scenes of the war novel. In *I Am the Clay*, Potok, who served as an Army chaplain in Korea from 1955 to 1957, gives a dimension to the dimensionless, and he creates dynamic and round characters in a literature that had heretofore created only static and flat characters. Potok also creates primary characters out of those who had only been secondary characters in the literature, and in so doing, Potok humanizes the Other, while he also articulates the suffering experienced by the millions of nameless and faceless refugees who inhabit every pre-modern, modern, and postmodern war. Further, Potok's work, while set during the Korean War and of the Korean War refugee diaspora, is also a text of two wars set during one war. Similar to Silko's *Ceremony*, which is explicitly set during and after World War II but is couched in the Vietnam War and the Vietnam era, *I Am the Clay* is set, of course, during the Korean War but is very much a Holocaust work. Fire, burning, and human immolation are a constant presence in the text, and as the text is set five to seven years after the close of World War II and the *Shoah*, and as Potok is a rabbi and scholar and novelist of the Chosen and their Wandering and suffering and homelessness and Diaspora, it is readily apparent that the Holocaust haunts the novel just as the Holocaust haunts human and Judaic history, and the analogy between the victims of the Holocaust and the war refugees in *I Am the Clay* cannot be cogently denied. As such, *I Am the Clay*, while a very successful literary catalog and presentation of the suffering of the Korean peasant refugees during the Korean War, is also as much a Holocaust text as are Elie Wiesel's *Night*, *Dawn*, and *Day*, or Art Spiegelman's *Maus I* and *Maus II*, or A. Anatoli Kuznetsov's *Babi Yar*, or Tadeusz Borowski's *This Way for the Gas, Ladies and Gentlemen*, or D.M. Thomas' *The White Hotel*, or any other of a number of well-known, well-received Holocaust-themed texts. Nonetheless, critics identify the work as "one of his [Potok's] few novels not centered in the Jewish world" (Fox, "Chaim Potok"). This identification, obviously, is incorrect.

According to Jeffrey Walsh, "Taken collectively, such works [as the five novels in this study] ... constitute a cognitive map of the Korean War and show how Korea anticipated Vietnam in the use of napalm, helicopters, troop rotation, and ideological confusion, especially the mistaken belief that superior firepower would achieve victory" ("American Writing" 227), and as such, none of the five Korean War novels here present any sort of material or military victory, even though all five novels do present a sort of survivalism evidenced by the characters peri-textually. War after World War II is not victory, the thesis seems; war is survival, and survival is victory.

The three Vietnam War novels analyzed here — Gustav Hasford's *The Short-Timers*, Tim O'Brien's *The Things They Carried*, and Karl Marlantes' *Matterhorn* — individually and collectively offer the reader three disparate yet synchronic optics of the same war. Veterans of the Vietnam War author all three texts, but each text offers a perspective unique to its author's Vietnam War experience(s). *The Short-Timers* is an excursion into postmodern savagery, and the brutality of the human animal is found stateside (in Marine Corps boot camp), and overseas (in Vietnam), and in the city (in the Battle for the Citadel of Hue), and in the county (in a battle for death in the jungle). Sadism and violence taken to the most extreme elements during war are the thematic devices of the Hasford text, and there is really very little difference in the sadistic abilities of the allies or enemies in the text, and what is common to all present is the desire, motivation, and joy of killing in a time and locus of war. The text is set in 1967 and 1968, not coincidentally the time in which Hasford was in the Marine Corps and Vietnam, so, autobiographically, the work is born of Hasford's life experiences. In Vietnam, Hasford was a combat correspondent, not unlike the text's protagonist, private/lance corporal/corporal/sergeant Joker. Steffen Hantke argues that one of the elements of the literature of the Vietnam War is that "soldiers [are] transformed grotesquely by the experience of the war" ("Disorienting Encounters" 268), but Hasford seems to be arguing that the warriors are not transformed by war but are rather freed by war to be more violent, which is, ironically, more human. War is the mass animalization of man, but man is, at heart, an animal.

Tim O'Brien, in *The Things They Carried*, the third text of his in-country trilogy — along with *If I Die in a Combat Zone ...* and *Going After Cacciato*— argues that war has no moral; war is war, but he shows that the novel of war does not have to be a lesson in redundancy. Writing "within a discursive field where the dominant conventions are still those of direct combat experiences" (Hantke, "Uses of the Fantastic" 65), O'Brien nonetheless manages to create an absolute postmodern construct, one "whose formal experiments construct war as multifaceted, fragmentary, kaleidoscopic, absurd, and surreal in character" (Walsh, "American Writing" 232). The result is an American novel of war that is metafictively conscious of its self, written by a Vietnam War veteran who is consciously self-aware that he is creating a new form out of an old form. War is what war is, but the war novel is what can be: as created secondary to authorial experience in Vietnam and artistry; the war novel form as it was; and the postmodern palimpsest of form, structure, and philosophy. O'Brien's time as an infantryman in Vietnam from 1969 to 1970 colors all of his works, and *The Things They Carried* is expressly a war novel, yet it is also a protest product born of a war and an era of which and during which dishonesty and ambiguity were the norm, both officially and unofficially. As such, what is moral, and what is truth, and what is real, or what is immoral, and what is untruth, and what is unreal, consistently and constantly are presented and addressed within the text. On a textual level, the reader must ask, what is verisimilitude, and what is artifice? And what is truth, and what is fiction? O'Brien's text is reflective of the Vietnam War, and while the reader is aware that O'Brien served in the Army infantry in the Vietnam War, this much is truth, while the rest is, well, a lesson in postmodern ambiguity.

Conversely, Karl Marlantes' *Matterhorn* is as unambiguous as *The Things They Carried* is ambiguous. Marlantes' work, the result of 30 years of effort, has been gushingly reviewed, and not without reason, yet the text, set in winter/spring 1969, breaks no such artistic ground as does the O'Brien work. Nonetheless, the Marlantes novel is an important American novel of war because it is the epic opus of a former Marine lieutenant, one who was highly decorated for exceptional valor and combat service in Vietnam, and the battle scenes are exquisite — especially an assault of a fortified hill — and autobiographical in nature, and thus are based on the realities of the Vietnam War. That said, the text would not exist without the author's war experiences, and the author's war experiences would not exist without the Vietnam War. Marlantes' novel, while structurally and stylistically decidedly not *avant garde*, which is fine, of course, owes more to World War I and World War II epics than it does to postmodern constructs such as O'Brien's *The Things They Carried* and *Going After Cacciato*. With a linear narrative and chronology, a post-narrative glossary of military terms, jargon, and equipment, and a paratextual, pre-narrative set of maps, *Matterhorn* is derivative of war works such as Arthur Guy Empey's *Over the Top* and Mailer's *The Naked and the Dead*, and while the work is very much a useful presentation of the sociocultural *milieu* of the late 1960s — the racism, classism, drug use, music, rebellion, and so on — the novel is important for its accuracy in dealing with combat and mission futility in Vietnam. For example, the Marines fortify a hilltop only to abandon the hilltop, which is then used by the North Vietnamese Army to assault the Marines. Another important aspect of the work is the respect shown by the narrator, and some characters, for the fighting efforts and skills of the North Vietnamese regulars. Historically, the Viet Cong and the NVA regulars were very different types of fighting forces, and many authors do not convey this fact accordingly.

As the text is told in a linear narrative in chronological order, *Matterhorn* reads very much like a cathartic effort penned, skillfully, by a former warrior, which it is, of course. Therapeutic and cathartic value to its author aside, and regardless of its derivative tendencies, the novel is nonetheless a valuable addition to the thousand or so extant Vietnam novels, and the Vietnam War canon is well served by Marlantes' autobiographical and unambiguous effort.

A war without a fictional corpus is the Persian Gulf War. However, a small body of novels was born of this short war, and two can be posited within this study — Terrence D. Haynes' *Desert Norm* and Charles Sheehan-Miles' *Prayer at Rumayla*. Adi Wimmer argues, "When it comes to artistic representations of the American soldier in the Vietnam war, there has been a remarkable similarity between 'valuable,' 'high literature' texts and texts that we customarily call 'exploitation literature' or 'entertainment'" (41), or "low" texts. This claim can be applied to the literature of any war in which the United States has participated. Consequently, the Persian Gulf War (or First Gulf War, or even Gulf War), as a brief, limited war, conducted in an era of memoir mania, produced very little high literature. Regardless, the Haynes and Sheehan-Miles texts, while not high literature, do have some literary value, both as American novels of war and as testimonials born of participation in the conflict to free Kuwait from Suddam Hussein's clutches. Haynes' goal, as stated in the text's "Introduction," was to present, in literature, "the voice of an educated, black, low-ranking, enlisted soldier, one who was qualified to be an officer but elected not to go that route" (xiii). The author, a graduate of SUNY-Fredonia, served in the Army as a topography specialist during Operation Desert Shield and Operation Desert Storm, and the text is set from December 1990 to March 1991. What makes the work valuable to the body of American war literature, and to this study specifically, is the omnipresence of the Western media in the text — which leads to a video-game war and hero worship of those who are televised — and the intricate explanation of the map-making process prior to the Persian Gulf War ground campaign (23–28 February 1991). As well, the work is also, ironically, a portrait of Christian religiosity during a time of war in a locus dominated by Islam, as the conjunction of piousness and war is always an interesting one.

While *Desert Norm* is set on-base outside of Riyadh, Saudi Arabia, in a combat supporting environment, *Prayer at Rumayla* is a text in which the war is the backstory but remains the dominant influence on the actions of the contemporary present and the post-traumatic stress experienced by the literary protagonist, Chet Brown, a tankloader during the war's ground campaign. Written two years after Sheehan-Miles' service with the 24th Infantry Division during the Persian Gulf War, the work is an angry text, written by an author who "was bitter, angry" (i). As Evelyn Cobley correctly notes, "The war in Kuwait was a carefully orchestrated display of *disciplined* and *impersonal* violence that has been criticized for concealing and sanitizing its destructive force [italics Cobley]" (96), and, of course, the irony is that a telegenic war, one that was broadcast and disseminated by media all over the world, was censored and sanitized for mass consumption. This government-and media-driven censorship and sanitization rightly enrages Sheehan-Miles and his scenes of the material and human carnage secondary to tank warfare are searing and brutal. Also at issue in the novel is the post-combat treatment of those who fought, who are in a combat zone one day, with the mortal dangers therein, and in the rear echelon the next day, with the rules and regulations therein, sans any transitional allowance and assistance. Sheehan-Miles' protagonist Chet Brown is in a rage, the postwar results of which are quite devastating, but more important to this study are the scenes of devastation born of tank warfare.

In her recently published study, *Welcome to the Suck: Narrating the American Soldier's Experience in Iraq*, Stacey Peebles notes, "Though digital technology has dramatically changed the way soldiers' stories about contemporary war are told, [the] war stories themselves are nothing new" (4), and Cole "Doc" Bolchoz's ebook *A Medic in Iraq: A Novel of the Iraq War* is an excellent example of Peebles' claim. Bolchoz's work, published in 2007 via ebooksonthe.net and sold on Amazon Kindle and Amazon Kindle PC, is an instant account of one man's experiences in Ramadi, Iraq, during the Iraq War. But the content therein, while digitally disseminated, is the stuff of war, time-honored, time-tested, true. Bolchoz's work, born of his time as an Army combat medic in a war zone and set primarily in the first seven months of 2007 — while in serious need of professional prose and copy-editing — possesses an amazing urgency and immediacy not readily apparent in most works of war that are created retrospectively in a post-war environment. *A Medic in Iraq* is very much the expressive act of an author who laments the caustic results of war on the human participants and victims of the combat actions, and these victims include both the uniformed combatants and the civilian population in Iraq. Perhaps the strongest aspect of the text is that it offers a view of an Iraqi populace that is victimized by war and enraged by the American presence in the country. The Iraqis view the Americans as invaders and occupiers, and the omnipresent violence of war leads to the deaths and maiming of many civilians and the destruction of their cities, towns, homes, mosques, and marketplaces. Bolchoz does a more than adequate job of presenting the toll that the war is taking on the civilian populace while also showing how the populace loathe the Americans and their presence in Iraq, and the death of noncombatants, omnipresent death and destruction of Ramadi, and the oppositional dyad between occupiers and indigenous peoples are text-wide thematic elements of war in Bolchoz's digital novel.

Clearly then, none of the 23 American novels of war in this study would exist without the war that is the central thematic action of the text. Further, in most cases, the novel's author experienced the war at hand proximally or experientially or in a combat role. As such, without the war, the novel would not exist. All of the novels in this study centralize the theme and topic and actions and results of a specific war or episode of war: The era of Indian Eradication after the Mexican–U.S. War of 1846–1848, World War I, World War II, the Korean War, the Vietnam War, the Persian Gulf War, and the Iraq War. So, the central thematic action of each text here is war, the locus of the guts of each work is the war zone, the optic of the philosophy of each novel is the view of war, and thus, each of the 23 works of war is a novel of war fit for this study. Consequently, were it not for the real wars covered in the fiction, these novels would not exist, and while not every author here is a combat veteran, every novel here is, by and of, combat — in theme, in motif, in topic, in element. What is more, the American novel of war is a presentation of war, and in each text in this study — war is, if not the protagonist, a protagonistic element of the text. Further, each novel used for analysis in this study has been chosen for its literary presentation of war, and while a number of texts here will not be historically noted for presentation as "high art" — however that may be critically or popularly defined — all of the texts here present war in a literary fashion and use most, if not all, of the defining characteristics of the American novel of war, and in so doing, earn a place in this study. A novel of war must have war and the physical, psychological, spiritual, social, and cultural effects of war; otherwise, it is not a novel of war. A novel of war must be born by and of and through war; otherwise, it is not a novel of war, and as well, in this study, a novel of war must be an American novel of war, and all are.

III

The Violence of War

The violence in the American novel of war is real, not symbolic, not metaphorical, not verbal, not imagined. As the central thematic element of each text is war, the violence in each text is real and present and is written out on the page and experienced by the characters in the text. The novel of war's violence exists on the battlefield first, if not primarily; only then, after the battlefield violence occurs, does the war violence resonate in the mind of the reader, and often, too, in the minds of the characters. All of the novels of war in this study have extended scenes of battlefield violence, and all of the texts deal with the physical, psychological, emotional, and intellectual traumas that the combatants undergo before, during, and after battle. In order of combat era or war, *Blood Meridian*, *The Red Badge of Courage*, *Through the Wheat*, *Ceremony*, *Band of Brothers*, *The Short-Timers*, *Matterhorn*, and *Prayer at Rumayla* each present the violence of war realistically and without compromise. *Blood Meridian* and *The Short-Timers* are texts composed of historically verifiable and nearly omnipresent violence, and the former text is a masterwork of artifice and verisimilitude, while the latter is an explosion of boot camp and war zone rage and conflict. *The Red Badge of Courage* and *Through the Wheat* are seminal texts in that each text, early in the American canon, shows the violence — and bloody cost — of war realistically for a readership that, up to that particular time in history, had not been exposed to war violence in such a realistic mode. Late–nineteenth-century readers of the Crane text assumed that Crane was a veteran of the U.S. Civil War, while he was not, of course, and readers of the Boyd text knew that Boyd certainly was a veteran of World War I. Further, *Ceremony*, *Band of Brothers*, and *Matterhorn* each present interpolated but extended battle scenes of exquisite violence, on a petite and grand scale, in which the American combatants face elemental dangers as well as hostile enemies. *Prayer at Rumayla*, alone in this study, expressly presents tank warfare and the human carnage resultant thereof. Inherently and intrinsically, man is violence, man is war, and a novel of war must have the violence of war, and the effects of the violence of war; otherwise, it is not a novel of war.

Relative to the use of textual violence, one must ask a number of questions when analyzing novels of war. What is violence? What is a novel of violence? What is the purpose of violence in novels of war? How does violence differ in novels of war? Do different war text authors use violence for different rhetorical purposes? Patrick W. Shaw's excellent study, *The Modern American Novel of Violence*, is a good place at which to start. Shaw argues, first, that violence is "*any action, premeditated or not, that is performed with the purpose of injuring or killing another living creature, especially another human* [italics Shaw]" (2). So, the goal of violence is to injure, maim, or kill, in most cases, but not always, another human being. This is simple enough, but in the novel of war, animals, too, bear the brunt of man's violent actions. Further, after defining violence, Shaw creates a set of defining characteristics specific to the American novel of violence. First, the violence is androcentric (5–6). Overwhelmingly, and in spite of recent "gains" whereby women warriors are taking more active roles in combat situations, according to Shaw, "Even a fanatic proponent of gender equality would be hard pressed to refute" (6) this claim of androcentricism, and "in the essential violence that instigates eye-to-eye, face-to-face killing, males are still by far the more capable" (6). Thus, historically and in the literature of violence and war, men are the actors of violent acts. Further, according to Shaw, novels of violence have "violence as [the] central narrative focus and as the conflict that energizes the plot" (6). And of course, all of the novels of war in this study, as each is based on and is by and of war, use violence as a central narrative focus. Novels of war are about acts of war, and acts of war are about acts of violence. As well, according to Shaw, novels of violence use "a recognizable vocabulary of violence.... For example: agony, anger, attack, beat, bleed, blood, bones, break, chop, claw, cut, die, flay, gash, gore, groan, guts, hurt, mangle, scream, shredding, slash, stab, tearing, twist, and whip" (6). When applied to the American novel of war, this characteristic evolves into the rhetoric of war — grunt lingo and official obfuscation, relative to the promotion and exercise of war-level violence. There is a language of violence and a language of war in the novel of violence and the novel of war, and this language is readily apparent upon critical textual examination. Shaw — per Sigmund Freud, Frederick J. Hoffman, and others — acknowledges "that violence is an instinct, not learned behavior, and that war is the highest expression" (12) of such. Finally, citing Michael Kowalewski's *Deadly Musings*, Shaw makes it clear to the reader that his definition of violence and the American novel of violence refer only to "depictions of physical violence or pain and its aftermath, not psychological violence or examples of metaphorical, 'discursive' violence" (13). Shaw's parameters are extremely viable and relevant to this study, as the American novels of war in this study are also, and not coincidentally, American novels of violence.

Returning to Freud's cum Hoffman's cum Shaw's argument that "war is the highest expression" of violence, one must consider that war is violence perpetuated "with society's or the state's blessings" (Shaw 12). War is socially sanctioned violence on a grand scale. Looking back at Der Derian's definition ("War is a form of organized violence conducted by states, with commonly accepted [if not always observed] rules" [98]), and Tabea Alexa Linhard's argument that, in war, "a particular governing body — or those who aim to overthrow that same governing body — usually sanctions acts of violence committed in the public arena" (31), one notices that war takes the instinctual act — the act of humanly perpetuated violence — and produces that act on a grand scale that is officially and legally allowed and publicly performed. So, violence is a physical act that aims to injure, maim, or kill, most often, another human being but sometimes an animal, and war is violence on a grand scale that is socially and/or federally sanctioned. Now, as the locus of this study is the American novel of war, and as the locus of Shaw's study is the American novel of violence, is there anything, any characteristic, that makes Americans uniquely violent? Not surprisingly, Shaw argues that there is such an American uniqueness. Shaw believes that there is "a harsh truth about the American character that the general population does not wish to consider" (13), and that truth is "those genes that made us [Americans] intrepid enough to venture into the wilderness [of the New World] were the same genes that intensified the natural tendency to violence. Mixed, mingled, and regenerated, those genes have made America's history a hemophile's delight" (13).

Shaw is not the only critic who feels as such, of course, and Richard Slotkin notes that violence is autochthonous in the American mythos:—"In each stage of its development, the Myth of the Frontier relates the achievement of 'progress' to a particular form or scenario of violent action" (qtd. in Liparulo 88)—and Steven P. Liparulo continues, "This myth applies equally well to the American western frontier of the Indian wars or the global frontier of Third World nations and wars against 'Communist insurgencies'" (88). So, for America and Americans, as is historically verifiable through practice, war is America's "path to achieving its destiny" (Liparulo 88), and violence is "endemic to American life" (Shelton 81). Now, how does one reconcile, or conjoin, the history of the United States, a history of violence and war, with the catalog of American novels of war (novels that are, by the way, American novels of violence)? War is "an atmosphere of violence and death" (Ross 50), and as such, "violence destroys fiction" (Dawes, *Language* 131), but not war fiction, official propaganda and obfuscation, such as the lie that American might makes right. Paradoxically, violence creates fiction, but as truth. As James Dawes posits, "The experience of violence puts tremendous pressure on nations, persons, ideas, and language. Violence thus achieves bare truth negatively" (*Language* 131). The result of violence (and on a greater level, of war) is truth. And for the author of the American novel of war, truth is born in fiction and is the child of war.

Returning to the questions central to this chapter, and after answering the first two—What is violence? What is a novel of violence?—the next three must be addressed: What is the purpose of violence in novels of war? How does violence differ in novels of war? Do different war text authors use violence for different rhetorical purposes? To answer these, one must survey a broad series of American novels of war, and the most efficient way to do so is historically by era or war and then thematically by one particular text. From the first page of the text, Cormac McCarthy identifies *Blood Meridian, Or the Evening Redness in the West* as a novel of violence: "See the child. He is pale and thin.... In him broods already a taste for mindless violence. All history present in that visage, the child the father of the man" (3). Inherently and intrinsically, from birth, from childhood, man IS violence; man is war. Note that McCarthy does not name the child; the child is all of man, all males, all men, all human violence. Timothy Parrish correctly argues that the history of American violence present in *Blood Meridian* is the history of violence present in the history of the United States: "In *Blood Meridian*, the primal given of existence is violence. McCarthy portrays violence not as transcendent but as transhistorical" (83). So, through the novel of war, McCarthy is arguing that man's violence runs through human history, and Parrish argues, further, that American man's violence, specifically, runs through the history of the nation and through the McCarthy work: "*Blood Meridian* depicts American history as a series of violent encounters and ultimately unsuccessful attempts to establish a history other than the murderous one implied when the 'civilized' Europeans enslaved or eradicated the 'savages' they encountered" (85). Thus McCarthy portrays American history, and perhaps all human history, "as the eternal return to violence" (Parrish 85), as European-American man first unleashes "catastrophic violence on Indians (the violent and peaceful alike)" (Harrison 35) and then attacks any others who possess black hair, until, finally, the Glanton gang moves on to kill at will as they travel the Border Southwest. The novel of war's violence exists on the battlefield first and primarily; then, after the battlefield violence occurs, the historiographic war violence resonates in the mind of the reader, rhetorical effect achieved. As John Wegner congruously argues, "History [is] an important, viable character in *Blood Meridian*" (61), and as John E. Sepich articulates in *Notes on Blood Meridian*, much of the text is historically verifiable. Further, Wegner notes that in Mexico, "revolution is continual and ongoing, hence the past is a significant part of the present" (61). Also, past and present is the use of violence to articulate social change — the eradication of the Comanche and Apache, for example. *Blood Meridian* contains a number of gross-level battlefield scenes, of course, starting with the Comanche attack on the filibusters (51–54), moving on to a number of raids by the scalphunters on all manner of peoples, culminating in the Yuma Massacre episode (273–76), and the novel is framed by scenes of the intrinsically violent child (3), who becomes the man, who dies at the hand of the judge (333). According to McCarthy, from childhood to death, all is violence, all is war, and violence and war are the history of man, the history of American man, and the history of the United States of America.

Conversely, in *The Red Badge of Courage: An Episode of the American Civil War*, Stephen Crane takes a limited view — a number of assaults within the Battle of Chancellorsville — and a limited optic — that of neophyte warrior Henry Fleming — to present a grand, and perhaps obvious, statement about modern war and modern violence: War is violent chaos. And per "the striking originality and power of Crane's portrayal of combat through the thoughts and feelings of a young recruit" (Pizer 4), the contemporary reader sees this violent chaos. Crane's impressionistic use of sensory detail, and Henry Fleming's moment-in-time battle experiences and emotions, subjectify the chaos of modern battle violence and introduce the late–nineteenth-century reader to a new history of the modern violence of war, a form of war in which rifled weapons, and artillery batteries, and frontal assaults, create carnage and chaos:

> Presently he began to feel the effects of the war atmosphere — a blistering sweat, a sensation that his eyeballs were about to crack like hot stones. A burning roar filled his ears.
> Following came a red rage....
> Buried in the smoke of many rifles his anger was directed not so much against the men whom he knew were rushing toward him as against the swirling battle phantoms which were choking him, stuffing their smoke robes down his parched throat. He fought frantically for respite for his senses, for air, as a babe being smothered attacks the deadly blankets [36].

The opponent here is not the Southerner but war itself, as Fleming is not truly at war with the Confederates: he is at war with war, with the chaos of war — the smells, the sounds, the sights, the tastes, the emotions, the feel of war. War feels chaotic, and war is chaotic. Crane is adept at showing a mass-level chaos through Henry Fleming's limited optic, and in so doing, Crane is arguing for the chaos of war via Henry's limited battlefield experiences. The passage cited above is Henry's first foray into battle, but ironically, the chaos Henry experiences increases with the next assault, and he deserts (42) at a time when he thinks his line will be overrun. The line holds, but Henry does not. Yet he is drawn back to the chaos; as such, the violence of war is an addictive chaos: "The battle was like the grinding of an immense and terrible machine to him. Its complexities and powers, its grim processes, fascinated him" (52). Interestingly, Henry, as voyeur, is the optic through which the reader can view the chaos and carnage of the violence of the Civil War, through the Battle of Chancellorsville, of course, so while Crane limits the scenes of actual violence in the text, the chaos of such is clearly evident through Henry's impressionistic subjectivity.

In *Through the Wheat: A Novel of the World War I Marines*, Thomas Boyd builds to the first scene of violence (79–83), and from that point forward, the text is as violent as one would expect a realist, modernist World War I tome to be. What is interesting about the violence in the Boyd text is the randomness of death and destruction secondary to the war machine. While this randomness is presented peripherally in the Crane text, in *Through the Wheat*, as in modern and postmodern warfare, life and death and maiming and wounding can be random results of random violence. Men die all around William Hicks, Boyd's Marine protagonist, seemingly without motive or reason. This element of randomness is presented early in the text as Boyd makes the presence of ongoing and constant artillery a fact of life for the Marines, even in the rear: "a long-range gun boomed sullenly in the distance" (4), "an occasional long-distance German shell had given an air of solemn decrepitude [to a smashed building]" (10), "the noses of mammoth artillery unexpectedly rose [from concealed fortresses concealed by greenery]" (19), life in the trenches is dull but for "an occasional shell fired from the artillery" (23), "[o]ccasionally a shell from the German batteries would start lazily off and end up with terrific speed in the platoon's trench" (29), and on it goes, inevitably, until men begin to die: "Once or twice men were killed when the shells struck" (29). There is no alarm on the part of the narrator, or on the part of the men in the text; in a war experienced in static trenches, one in which artillery is a constant act of warfare, and one in which the participant becomes desensitized to the ongoing bombardment, death is a random act, not quite accidental, of course, but random nonetheless. One is alive; then, one is dead. Note the narrator's nonchalance: "Once or twice." Did it happen one time? Two times? While the narrator seems blasé, were they able, the men killed in the attacks might have something to say about the urgency of the narrator's tone. Soon after, on a night raiding party between the trenches, a man is killed, shot by his own machine-gunners (33–35). The randomness of this death, early in the text and prior to wholesale combat, foreshadows deaths to come and illustrates the randomness of death by violence during World War I, something the Marines in the text are aware of, which the narrator refers to as the knowledge of "the eventuality of their being killed" (57). And without surprise, hundreds, if not thousands, of men are randomly killed as Boyd's text and the Marines' mission are completed.

Conversely, in *Ceremony*, Leslie Marmon Silko deals with the violence of war through mutual brutality—the execution of a number of Japanese prisoners (7–8) by American forces, Rocky's execution during the April 1942 Bataan Death March (43–44), and the way of "white warfare—killing across great distances without knowing who or how many had died" (36), culminating, of course, in the atomic bombings of Hiroshima and Nagasaki. Silko also examines post-war violence and seems to argue that violence begets violence, and killing in war leads to killing after war: "Reports note that since the Second World War a pattern of drinking and violence, not previously seen before, is emerging among Indian veterans" (53), and the behavior of the primary characters seems to bear this out, as Tayo stabs Emo (52–53, 63) and Emo kills Harley, Leroy, and then Pinkie (258–59). Silko's argument is that one cannot stop the violence once one has become accustomed to such. Says Emo (retrospectively, of course), "We were the best. U.S. Army. We butchered every Jap we found. No Jap bastard was fit to take prisoner" (61). Tayo notes, "Emo grew from each killing. Emo fed off each man he killed" (61). That said, Silko allows blamelessness for none, for the text opens as Tayo, in the midst of post-traumatic stress and in flashback, re-experiences being ordered to participate as a firing squad member in the execution of a group of Japanese prisoners. Tayo cannot pull the trigger (7), but stands with the firing squad—which includes Rocky—as the prisoners are shot (8). So, Rocky, while perhaps the most honorable character in the text, participates in a mass execution. Later, after being wounded and captured, Rocky's skull is smashed in by a Japanese soldier (44). In the text, no violent actor escapes Silko's swath, and all are labeled "destroyers": "Nothing was all good or all bad either" (11). Perhaps the greatest destructive violence in the text is that resultant of the atom bomb, that bastardization of natural law that creates "heat-flash outlines, where human bodies had evaporated" (37). Anglo, Japanese, and Indian, in *Ceremony*, are all violent destroyers of others and of the natural world, and war is the vehicle of violent actions, but the end of war is not the end of violence, as Tayo, Emo, Harley, Leroy, and Pinkie carry the war home with them, and the U.S. government continues, historically, to find wars to fight.

While Silko posits a small number of very specific acts of violence in *Ceremony*, for specific rhetorical effect, Ernest Frankel uses *Band of Brothers* as a technical coming-of-age manual for Marine Captain Bill Patrick, the green company commander of Able Company, relative to the violence born of the 1st Marine Division's hasty and organized retreat from the Chosin Reservoir to the Sea of Japan. Much of the violence in the text forces Captain Patrick's evolution from incompetent company commanding officer to "Skipper"—a term of respect and acknowledgment but not an official rank designation. Relative to the former, Patrick's Colt .45 1911 A1 semi-automatic pistol is stolen after he—astoundingly—leaves the sidearm on a rock: "As he ducked before the entrance, he remembered his pistol belt. He had left it on the ground by the rock. He found it. But the holster was empty" (23). To a civilian, this might seem to be merely a careless act, but to a Marine, this is a blasphemous and deadly act of incompetence that shows a lack of military professionalism, for all Marines, from the first time they are issued a weapon in boot camp or Officer Candidate School, are taught to never, ever leave their weapon unattended. When Frankel introduces this negligent act in the text, the astute reader is aware that a life will be lost, and in one of the early scenes of deathly violence, an American, Radioman Monk Nelson, is killed by the pistol thief: "Holding his rifle before him, Monk Nelson approached Kao Teh. The prisoner was clutching his throat, groaning" (36). Nelson's final act, an act of kindness, is to offer the prisoner a drink of water, and "in his last conscious moment, he saw the pistol, saw the flash of fire" (36). Nelson is shot, secondary to the CO's gross negligence, and the prisoner is then shot, too, as he tries to escape, in a suicidal act, of course. The company executive officer, First Lieutenant Joe Anderson, a salty combat veteran and the interim CO prior to Patrick's assignment, has this to offer Captain Patrick: "'Here,' he said. 'I found your .45'" (36).

As the text continues, and the company-level violence becomes standard, each battle is an opportunity for Patrick to measure himself against Anderson, and each battle is an opportunity for Patrick to observe Anderson under fire and to evolve as a leader. Ironically, though, through 200 pages of grinding battle, so many men die off during the course of the text—hundreds, thousands, of members of the 1st Marine Division, on the page and off—that the loss of Monk Nelson becomes compartmentalized and almost insignificant in the greater scheme of taking and holding Bad Girl Ridge, an elevation whereby Able Company can slow down the Chinese assaults so that the rest of the battalion can organize and prepare to make the move from Chosin to Hagaru to Hungnam. Frankel spends the first two-thirds of the text in and around Bad Girl Ridge, which gives Captain Patrick time and opportunity to evolve as a battlefield commander, and when Lieutenant Anderson is—inevitably—killed by an artillery round (172), Captain Patrick is sufficiently indoctrinated into combat command, and by the close of the text, when the 1st Marine Division is entering Hungnam, Patrick is competent enough and respected enough to be addressed as "Skipper" (288).

While Frankel uses combat violence to show the evolution of the leadership ability of one company commander, in *The Short-Timers*, Gustav Hasford uses omnipresent and ongoing brutality to evidence the savagery of war, as viewed from the optic of one Marine, combat correspondent cum grunt James "Joker" Davis; as Joker states, "A day without blood is like a day without sunshine" (66). Especially effective and violent are the scenes in which snipers, in the ancient Citadel of Hue and in the bush of the rain forest, deposit rounds into Marines, who are maimed and gruesomely wounded but not killed. In the jungle scene, Hasford, as in *Four Deuces* and *Bloods*, displays mercy killing, whereby Marines have to kill mortally wounded Marines (176–78). This thematic element of sniper violence is foreshadowed in the boot camp section that opens the text, "The Spirit of the Bayonet," in which Gunnery Sergeant Gerheim, the senior drill instructor, orders then–Private Joker into a tree: "I'm a sniper. I'm supposed to shoot the platoon.... If I can see a recruit well enough to name him, he's dead" (12). Later, in-country, Corporal Joker is assigned to Lusthog Squad of 1st Platoon, Delta Company, during the siege of Hue, and "snipers on the wall [of the ancient citadel] fire a round here and there, sighting us in" (97). Then, during the siege, "The snipers zero in on us. Each shot becomes a word spoken by death" (98). Soon, of course, a sniper has the range and shoots a grunt through the knee (106), which begins an extended passage of sniping violence. Says squad leader Cowboy to Joker:

> "T.H.E. Rock was walking point. The sniper shot T.H.E. Rock's foot off. Shot it off. The Hardass Squad went out to get him, one at a time. That sniper shot all their feet off. We were hiding behind graves, those old round graves like baseball mounds, and we had nine grunts down in the street.... Then the sniper started shooting off fingers, toes, ears—everything. He popped T.H.E. Rock's head off and then he put a round through each guy's head" [108, 109].

The terror of the sniper comes from his (or her, in this case), ability to shoot from a concealed position, while doing so accurately with a high-powered weapon. In this case, one sniper kills nine grunts, an excellent kill ratio. Psychologically, a sniper has the ability to destroy the morale of a fire-team or squad or platoon. As well, using the man-made hiding places in a city, a sniper can kill for hours or days sans discovery, and, of course, using grunts to hunt a sniper leads to more deaths. In this case, it takes a tank to destroy the adjacent mansions to locate and expose the sniper, who is then shot repeatedly until dead, and is then decapitated (117, 120). Snipers also operate in the jungle, and in the closing passage of the text (147–80), Lusthog Squad is in the rain forest outside of Khe Sanh, and the scene of precise sniping is repeated as Alice, Doc Jay, New Guy, and Cowboy are sniped. Cowboy, while wounded, kills Doc and New Guy (176) and then Alice (177), and Joker then kills Cowboy (178). This time, though, the sniper — Sorry Charlie — lives to snipe another day, as the squad saddles up and moves back down the trail. Thus, in the city or in the bush, snipers kill grunts, and grunts hate snipers.

While there are a number of short scenes of tank violence in *The Short-Timers*, as well as in a limited number of other works in this study, the presence of tanks in the texts is primarily a peripheral element. However, in *Prayer at Rumayla*, Charles Sheehan-Miles' narrator and protagonist Chet Brown is an M1A1 tankloader during the Persian Gulf War, so the text necessarily contains scenes of the violence of tank warfare. Common to Sheehan-Miles' scenes of tank-driven, vehicle-on-vehicle violence is chaos, and power, and destruction, and fire, and the aftermath of the battle. This early scene, set 26 February 1991, as Brown's tank moves into battle, is a prime example of such:

> [T]he quiet is shattered by a call over the radio.
> "Black six, Red six, we got vehicles to our front! About a dozen armored vehicles, cannot identify, over."
> ...
> A moment later another call comes over the radio. "Black six, red six —"
> The transmission is cut short by a loud explosion. To my right, where first platoon should be, an explosion.

"Black six, Red six, we're taking incoming. Tanks to our front!"

"Weapons free! Weapons free!..."

...

Griggs calls out, "Tank identified!"

Adrenaline jumping, I drop into the turret and raise the arming handle, screaming, "Up!"

"Fire!" calls Sergeant Arno.

I turn away from the main gun as it fires. The concussion knocks me against the back wall, spitting out the spent shell onto the floor.

I hit the knee switch for the ammo door and grab a SABOT round, flipping it over and shoving it into the tube.

"Sabot loaded!"

Arno calls out, "Target, re-engage!"

"Up!"

"Fire!"

The round goes off, and I reload again. Outside I hear machine guns and tank cannons firing. The tank bucks with a loud explosion.

"Shit! We got incoming!"

...

The pounding continues. I stare out into the black through the tiny vision block in my hatch. All I can see is the silhouettes of burning vehicles [92–93].

Chet Brown's introduction into the violence of tank warfare is not yet over. After the tank-on-tank combat, a violent cleaning up is necessitated: "I start firing my machine gun, tracers from it and twelve others saturating the area, cutting down any survivors" (94). Therefore, while the ground assault of the Persian Gulf War may have been short-lived, so too, were the enemy opposites who occupied the Soviet-made T-72 tanks, and even those who escape death during assault are killed via tank-mounted automatic weapons fire — M240 and .50 caliber M2 machine-guns — post-tank-on-tank battle. Through the text, in narrated flashbacks and in dream sequences, Sheehan-Miles presents this type of scene of tank violence. The battle is chaotic, the American firepower, tactics, and teamwork are superior, and the result of the violence is devastation to both opposing vehicles and human beings. When juxtaposed with small-arms violence, M1A1 tank–based violence is a violence of grand decimation.

Conversely, Karl Marlantes' *Matterhorn: A Novel of the Vietnam War* needs no tanks to posit a text-wide theme of Vietnam War violence. Interestingly, and somewhat unique for a Vietnam War novel, the war violence in *Matterhorn* is primarily traditional war violence — that is, violence to take and occupy land. Thus, there is none of the aimless village-to-village patrolling or civilian populace as hostile Other in the text, which, of course, are the most common thematic elements in Vietnam War novels, and the fighting in Marlantes' work comes against highly disciplined and well-equipped North Vietnamese Army regulars rather than the Viet Cong — many of whom were killed off with internecine violence during the Tet Offensive of 1968. Set in the opening months of 1969, Marlantes' text is very much a modernist construct, and Norman Mailer's *The Naked and the Dead* haunts the text, especially during the only extended seek-and-destroy patrol in the work, humorously named "the Trail of Tears Op" (248), during which the grunts of Bravo Company battle the terrain and elements (135–246), and during which, one man is killed and partially eaten by a tiger (158) while another dies of "cerebral malaria" (238). Also derivative of the Mailer text — and many World War II texts, in fact — is the theme of war for land. Relative to the thematic violence in the text, that of traditional war violence directed at taking and occupying land, Marlantes does an excellent job of using rising action to build the violence. Ironically, the true villains of the text, according to the author's note on the copyright page (ii), are the 1st Battalion commanders, Lieutenant

Colonel Simpson and Major Blakely, and the author and the Marines in the text treat the NVA regulars with grudging and explicit respect: "They're fucking pros" (377), Lieutenant Goodwin says. Nevertheless, the men of Bravo Company and the NVA infantry shed the blood, while Simpson and Blakely operate the war by radio (241–42, 335–37). As such, the traditional war violence—combat violence for held terrain—between Bravo Company and the NVA for Matterhorn, a reinforced Fire Support Base, occupies the central elements of the text.

Marlantes slowly and effectively draws the reader into the thematic element of war violence by using traditional rising action, whereby the violence in the text is peripheral—a short retrospective story of a fight (78)—then presented in short bits of violence through small firefights (87–89, 101–3), then presented in longer or more intense violent episodes (171–73, 251–53, 331–32, 334–35), and then presented on a gross level in extended battle scenes (349–58, 370–74, 472–87), during which the goal is to take swaths of occupied acreage. As a result, Marlantes shows that the postmodern Vietnam War was at times a traditional modern war—in violence and in purpose. As such, the traditional view of the Vietnam War as a war of aimless patrols and body count objectives and unseen, non-uniformed enemies is incorrect. According to Marlantes' text, the Vietnam War was like any other war, a war for land, a war in which friends fought for their friends' lives (370–71, 375), not for their country or for their politicians' ideology or for their field officers' goals. Marlantes begins the theme of traditional war violence with a brief terra-centric aside explaining how an M-60 machine-gunner nicknamed Mole—grunts love nicknames, as do grunts turned authors—earned his nickname: "He received the nickname on the DMZ operation. Connolly's squad had been pinned down, and Mole had moved so low to the ground behind rocks and bushes to flank the enemy that the rest of the squad swore he'd gone underground" (78). Mole killed two "NVA" (78) and freed the trapped squad. So, very early in the work, Marlantes is foreshadowing the text-wide theme of traditional, ground-based warfare; the story is of a grunt nicknamed for a terra-centric animal. Further, this aside also identifies the combat enemy as the North Vietnamese Army infantry soldier, rather than the Viet Cong guerrilla. Traditional warfare is the order of the text, against a traditional, uniformed enemy. However, a few pages later, the first small firefight occurs (87–89), a fire fight more in the vein of standard Vietnam War texts—a routine patrol, an unseen enemy, a barrage of M-16 and AK-47 rounds, silence, a made-up body count (91–92). So while this brief aside seems to foreshadow a traditional Vietnam War text, with traditional Vietnam War motifs, the purpose of this small firefight is rising action, rather than a promotion of the standard Vietnam War novel typing. A later firefight continues to build the rising action, while it returns to the traditional war violence theme. What is interesting about this brief scene (101–3) is that it occurs off the page, obscured by the density of the jungle-scape, so the reader does not see the action; also, the objective of the mission is not a routine jungle patrol but is to capture a stationary NVA machine-gun emplacement. Lieutenant Waino Mellas, through whose optic much of the action is viewed, and who commands Bravo Company's 1st Platoon, hears the firefight rather than experiencing it, as it is being fought by a squad from 3rd Platoon. During the narration, Marlantes' narrator suggests that the NVA possess mortars and artillery, so once again traditional warfare is the element of the day, and, of course, of the text—a squad takes out a stationary machine-gun emplacement, and the violence-themed rising action occurs.

Moving forward to the Trail of Tears Op, an extended, company-wide seek-and-destroy mission, which occurs after Bravo Company has, under the orders of Blakely and Simpson, reinforced Fire Support Base Matterhorn and then deserted the bunkered mountain without first blowing the bunkers (129), the company is ambushed (171–73) by the NVA. Uniquely, Marlantes presents the ambush from two perspectives, one of which is the optic of an über-grunt nicknamed Vancouver from 1st Platoon's 1st Squad (171–72), and the other of which is 1st Platoon's CO, Lieutenant Mellas (172–73). First, Vancouver's optic: "Vancouver dropped to his knees and opened up.... Everything was in motion.... Vancouver saw only shadows, but the shadows were screaming back at him with AK-47 automatic rifles.... He heard Connolly shouting for Gambaccini.... He saw the lieutenant, who'd moved forward and was shouting something at Hamilton" (171–72). Now, Mellas' optic: "To Mellas, the whole thing happened so quickly that he didn't even remember thinking. There was a sudden burst of Vancouver's machine gun, and Mellas dived for the ground and immediately started crawling forward to find out what was happening.... Mellas shouted at Hamilton — 'Tell him [Company Commander Fitch] I don't know. I don't know'" (172). By bifurcating the violent and chaotic scene, Marlantes gives the reader a matching vision of the synchronic actions of the participants in a firefight, which is a sort of concurrent postmodern horizontal split-screen vision of the actions of the members of an ambushed platoon, and so, structurally and rhetorically, modernism and postmodernism influence Marlantes' text, to the benefit of the reader. Vancouver, who is walking point, enters the fray, and then so does Mellas. The synchronic perspectives of the single violent action also allow the effect of teamwork under fire and show that Mellas is evolving as a platoon leader. The ambushed members of 1st Platoon — officer and enlisted — work in unison to repel the ambush, and nary a member of the platoon is injured (WIA) or killed (KIA). The violent scene is fast, furious, and chaotic, but the work of the platoon is cohesive, and the bifurcated optics allow the reader to see this cohesion during chaos.

A later violent scene, this one set after the Trail of Tears Op, and while Bravo Company occupies Firebase Sky Cap, formerly Hill 1609, concerns a Security Patrol, as Mellas, Vancouver, forward observer cum radioman Daniels, Doc Fredrickson, and grenadier Gambaccini come upon and wound an NVA soldier, who, while mortally wounded, stubbornly refuses to die (251–53). A Security Patrol's mission is to make sure the terrain surrounding the firebase is secure. The patrol is more of a reconnaissance mission than seek-and-destroy mission; however, to engage the NVA is to kill the NVA. After first contact, during which the NVA soldier is wounded, the men try to "grease" (253) the enemy combatant with a fragmentation grenade, but this, too, is insufficient. The man is obviously mortally wounded — his guts are oozing out from all points — so the patrol leaves the man for the tigers and returns to Sky Cap. This brief scene returns the violence to the theme of land-based warfare, but Bravo Company is pulled back into the bush when a Force Recon team of six Marines is "in contact with a company-size NVA unit" (327) in the valley below Matterhorn, and the company is sent to support and save the Recon team, one of whom is dead and five of whom are wounded (333). The landing zone is hot, and a CH-46 machine-gunner is shot in the face at the drop (331), but the Recon team is rescued. While waiting for medevac, the Recon team leader tells Bravo CO Fitch that Matterhorn, with its reinforced bunkers, is now occupied by the NVA (333), and Bravo is immediately mortared from the mountain (334–35). In this scene, Marlantes completes a number of rhetorical tasks: He reintroduces Matterhorn to the reader, while he also re-posits the thematic element of traditional terra-centric warfare and violence. Further, the rising action is nearly complete, as the title of the text is reintroduced and relativized. The book, the war, the violence, the NVA, the company, the mountain — all are conjoined, shackled, as in traditional war, war over acreage.

Adjacent to Matterhorn, 600 meters to the east, is Helicopter Hill, a hill set at a lower elevation than Matterhorn, a hill also occupied by the NVA, and one that must be retaken before Matterhorn can be retaken. Ironically, Helicopter Hill has been defoliated with Agent Orange, so the assault must be made in the open, and the Marines of Bravo Company walk up the slopes, "waiting for the enemy to open fire" (348), and, of course, the NVA oblige, and the grab for land is on as "Helicopter Hill exploded with the steady, ear-splitting fire of heavy machine guns and the clatter of the solid automatic AK-47 and semiautomatic SKS rifles of the North Vietnamese Army" (350). Note how Marlantes ties in the elements of thematic violence: he names the ground for which the violence is occurring—Helicopter Hill; he identifies the opposing weapons of war—AK-47s and SKSs; he identifies the opposing combatants (the North Vietnamese Army) by name rather than abbreviation (the NVA) so that the reader is aware that Bravo Company is fighting against a regular army not a guerrilla fighting force. As the battle rages, "What, moments before, had been organized movement now disintegrated into confusion, noise, and blood.... A burst of machine-gun bullets cracked over his [Mellas'] head as he ran parallel to the contour of the hill to try and help get the squads back together again" (350, 351). As in the earlier passage (101–3), an entrenched NVA machine-gun bunker is at issue, and through will and blood, and the sacrifice of a number of lives, the men take the machine-gun bunker (350–56), which opens up a hole in the NVA line of defense, through which 2nd Platoon files and subsequently turns the hill into a scene of "methodical and cautious destruction" (357). Helicopter Hill is, once again, in possession of the Marines (358), but the NVA still hold Matterhorn, which must also be retaken, and so it goes. While the reader might think that the retaking of Helicopter Hill is the penultimate act of terra-centric war violence in the text, with the coming retaking of Matterhorn representing the ultimate act of terra-centric war violence, the reader will be both correct and incorrect, as logically, the next mass assault must be the retaking of Matterhorn, and so it is. However, due to a lack of numbers and a lack of air support, secondary to weather, after initially retaking Matterhorn from the NVA (370–74), Bravo Company is forced to give up the mountain (378, 382), so it is the final taking of Matterhorn, actually the re-retaking of Matterhorn (472–87), that is the ultimate act of broad, traditional, terra-centric war violence in the text, and it is this re-retaking of Matterhorn that is the true climax of the text's rising action.

Ironically, after taking Helicopter Hill, Bravo Company begins taking sniper fire from the bunkers on Matterhorn (361)—bunkers that Bravo had built, of course. Matterhorn must be retaken, so Lieutenant Fitch is ordered to do so (366), and he thus orders two platoons—1st and 3rd—to prepare to assault the mountain, while 2nd Platoon remains on Helicopter Hill to guard the wounded (367). Once the assault begins (370), ill timing caused by an incompetent lieutenant who cannot follow a map or a compass, and misinterpreted radio communications, in conjunction with the wiliness of the NVA—who have deserted the bunkers for newly dug fighting holes—lead to an immediate scene of disarray: "from the new holes just above the old bunkers where the NVA unit, reduced in size, had moved during the night, bright fire blazed out of the gloom" (370). The new fighting holes are twenty-five meters behind and above the bunkers, so the Marines must traverse that ground to continue the assault, and in so doing, "one-third of the remaining thirty-four in the platoon went down" (371). But, for those who cross the divide, "attackers and defenders joined together and bellowing, frightened, maddened kids—firing, clubbing, kicking—tried to end the madness by means of more madness" (371). After much sacrifice, and the deaths of a number of named and unnamed characters, Matterhorn is retaken, and the NVA move off the mountain and toward Laos, which is situated due west (374). Nearly immediately, though, the NVA off-site begin to mortar the wounded who are left on Matterhorn, and the rounds leave a "meat-red footprint" (375) wherever a Marine is hit. The penultimate land-based battle is over, but the mountain is not the Marines'. Short of men, too short to hold both Matterhorn and Helicopter Hill, Lieutenant Fitch pulls the Marines off Matterhorn in order to hold Helicopter Hill (378, 382). All the while, the NVA mortar Helicopter Hill and the remaining 97 effectives, and of course, it is the NVA's turn to retake Matterhorn (401), which is painless, as the mountaintop now — and again — lies unoccupied.

While waiting on Helicopter Hill for the weather to clear so that helicopters can fly in with supplies and evacuate the wounded and remove the dead, Bravo Company also faces an assault by the NVA (410–17), which is repulsed at great loss. Eventually, the weather clears, supplies are flown in and the wounded flown out, and the battalion command — that is to say, the villains — choppers on to Helicopter Hill. It is time to re-retake Matterhorn (459), and the field officers want to watch. In a very Vietnam-esque way, the battalion commanders — Lieutenant Colonel Simpson and Major Blakely — want body counts, but in a traditional war violence methodology, land must be taken to produce the bodies. So, in keeping with the text-wide thematic violence of land-based warfare against a traditional uniformed enemy, Marlantes uses the ultimate scene of violence (472–87) — a fifteen-page run of finely written and narrated combat — to restate the theme of terra-centric warfare. And as the text's ultimate assault needs a pre-assault, Marlantes sees fit to describe and detail the pre-assault (461–71), during which a plan is formulated to divide what remains of the three Bravo Company platoons and the limited number of replacements for the assault (461). As the platoons are stationed in the jungle between Helicopter Hill and Matterhorn, just prior to the attack, friendly artillery bombards the bunkers atop the mountain, but to no avail, as "the artillery had been useless against the fortified positions" (467), bunkers built by Bravo, of course. Then, Phantom F-4s are called in to bomb and napalm the mountaintop, but their drops are off (469–71), so the fixed-wing air support is also a failure. The grunts of Bravo Company are alone in their action, sans cover, sans air support, sans supporting numbers.

Marlantes devotes an entire freestanding chapter, "Chapter Eighteen," to the assault and its immediate aftermath, the climax of the text's terra-centric and traditional war violence. Marlantes introduces Battle Time as well, which gives the reader some idea of how many things can go right or catastrophically wrong in mere seconds of a battle. Marlantes also re-introduces the machine-gun emplacement motif, which runs the entire length of the battle and, as such, the entire length of the text's combat violence. It is important to note that fixed machine-guns do terrible physical and psychological damage to men under fire, and the fixed machine-gun motif is present in nearly all war novels situated in World War I, World War II, and the Korean War but not so much in the novels of the Vietnam War. As the battle for the re-retaking of Matterhorn begins, the assault immediately bogs down: "The bunkers winked light, and the ground around the Marines seemed to come alive. The air was split by bullets and by the sound of AK-47's, SKS rifles, and Russian-built RPD 7.62 machine guns" (472). Under fire, and with men dropping, Mellas and a number of his platoon take cover behind a log: "It was suicidal to go farther. The attack, barely started, came to a complete halt" (473). In mere seconds, men attempt to move forward, are shot, and are dragged to cover to die. In mere seconds, Mellas must decide what to do, how to continue the assault, how to take out the machine-gun emplacement killing his Marines. So Mellas decides to rush the bunker(s) directly, using covering fire from one of his own M-60s, and it must be noted here that Marlantes, as a young lieutenant, took a similar action in a similar position, for which he was awarded the Navy Cross, the second highest combat award for valor, surpassed only by the Congressional Medal of Honor: "On March 6 [First Lieutenant Marlantes] initiated an aggressive assault up a hill, the top of which was controlled by a hostile unit occupying well-fortified bunkers.... Delivering a heavy volume of fire, the enemy temporarily pinned down the friendly unit. First Lieutenant Marlantes, completely disregarding his own safety, charged across the fire-swept terrain to storm four bunkers in succession, completely destroying them" ("Navy Cross Citation for Karl A. Marlantes"). Marlantes was wounded but remained in his duty capacity until after the battle was completed. Marlantes' actions resemble Mellas' actions, of course, and even in the postmodern era, it is hard to sever the life of the artist from the art. Mellas rushes the first bunker, and, to his surprise, his men follow him, regardless of the heavy fire: "The whole platoon was swarming up the hill after him" (477). The battle has lasted three minutes. Meanwhile, the enemy, the field officers, watch through binoculars from the safety of Helicopter Hill (478). But still, machine-gun fire continues from a bunker on the edge of the LZ on Matterhorn. A Marine sacrifices his life to take out that bunker (479), and the assault continues. After being grenaded and wounded, Mellas recovers enough to continue to lead (in shades of Marlantes, of course), and "the fight for the LZ moved into its final phase" (485). A final machine-gun emplacement is taken (487), and, at last, "The hill was theirs" (487). However, while the mountaintop is in U.S. hands, the NVA has mined the land, so Marines continue to die and be mangled (488) even after the NVA have removed to Laos—a few kilometers to the west—and even after the text's ultimate terra-centric, and traditional, battle is violently fought.

There is no doubt that Marlantes' novel of war is an exceptional war novel, regardless of some of the derivative aspects therein. Its uniqueness, however, lies in its presentation of the Vietnam War, and the violence born of that war, as traditional, earth-based warfare against a traditional and well-trained professional military opponent. The violence in *Matterhorn* is relative to the taking and giving up of land, rather than the violence born of aimless, endless jungle patrolling against a faceless guerrilla enemy; absent from the text are the Viet Cong and the Vietnamese villages and peasants present in most Vietnam War novels. Thus, Marlantes creates a new optic through which the critic, the veteran, and the reader can view the Vietnam War, and for this, Marlantes deserves kudos.

Returning to the questions central to this chapter of violence in the American novel of war, and the use thereof in such works, it would appear that the questions have been responded to in some way, hopefully successfully. What is violence? "*[A]ny action, premeditated or not, that is performed with the purpose of injuring or killing another living creature, especially another human*" (Shaw 2). All of the novels in this chapter, and in this study, contain actions situated under Shaw's definition of violence, in varying degrees, of course. And more specifically, war is a specialized form of violence—driven to kill human beings, often on a grand scale. What is a novel of violence? According to Shaw, an American novel of violence contains an American ethos of violence, born of the nation's birth in revolution and its people's history of using violence as a means of civilizing. As well, a novel of violence contains violence that is primarily androcentric, violence that is the central narrative theme and plot device of the text, violence that has its own rhetoric and vocabulary, and violence that is physical in nature. So, the American novel of war contains the defining elements of the American novel of violence; thus, all of the works examined in this chapter are American novels of violence in addition to being American novels of war. And what is the purpose of violence in novels of war? Quite often, the purpose of the violence in the American novel of war is to decimate or eradicate an enemy and/or to take land. Very often, the purpose of violence in the novel of war is to show said violence. A war novel without war violence is most likely not a true novel of war.

How does violence differ in novels of war? Violence differs in these novels in both the presentation therein and the severity thereof. Some works, such as *Blood Meridian*, litter the text with violence on nearly every page, but others, such as *Ceremony*, place a limited number of examples of violence in the text, yet nonetheless are also highly effective works of violence and war. Violence can also be presented on a grand scale or on a petite scale, contingent upon war and authorial intent — a sniper might take on a squad, or a company another company. Do different war text authors use violence for different rhetorical purposes? As there is no standard use of violence in the American novel of war, one can easily conclude that different war novel authors use violence for different rhetorical purposes. In *Blood Meridian*, Cormac McCarthy offers the bloody history of the era of geographic American expansion and of the entirety of the history of the United States, while in *The Red Badge of Courage*, Stephen Crane offers a violence born of modern mass-produced weaponry and warfare, through the optic of a single battle and single soldier. In *Through the Wheat*, Thomas Boyd evidences the randomness of death when the individual is placed within a gargantuan war machine, but in *Ceremony*, Leslie Marmon Silko offers mutual peri- and post-war brutality and blame for all destroyers, regardless of nationality, race, or ethnicity. In *Band of Brothers*, Ernest Frankel details the forced evolution of a company commander under severe and violent duress, and Gustav Hasford uses *The Short-Timers* as a study of the savage brutality of war and the power of sniping. Charles Sheehan-Miles offers *Prayer at Rumayla* as a testimony of the chaos and brutality of tank-on-tank warfare and the results thereof, and, of course, with *Matterhorn*, Karl Marlantes reminds reader and critic that the violence of the Vietnam War was often a traditional, terra-centric form of war violence against a well-trained and professional opponent.

In closing and to repeat, inherently and intrinsically, man is violence, man is war, and a novel of war must have the violence of war, and the effects of the violence of war; otherwise, it is not a novel of war. Each of the works examined in this chapter is thus a fine example of the presentation of the violence of war in the American novel of war.

IV

The Rhetoric of War

An American novel of war must also contain the rhetoric of war; more so, the rhetoric of war in the American novel of war is an integral component of the text. The narrator and characters must continually use such rhetoric — war lingo, war slang, war cliché, war abbreviations and acronyms, and, of course, official war promotion and obfuscation and popular war propaganda — to refer to war equipage, war nomenclature, and war incitation and justification; this language of war is a constant part of the characters' dialogue and the author's narration. The rhetoric of war is fascinating, funny, and infuriating, and is also very much era specific and war specific. As such, the rhetoric of war from the era of Manifest Destiny is different from the rhetoric of war from the Civil War era — the early 1860s — which is quite different from the rhetoric of war from the Vietnam War — the late 1960s. Thus a collation, examination, and analysis of the rhetoric of war, from *Blood Meridian* (rhetoric born of the Monroe Doctrine and Manifest Destiny), to *The Red Badge of Courage* (regionalist infantry men's argot), to *Johnny Got His Gun* (official government rhetoric and obfuscation and social propaganda), to *The Short-Timers* (omnipresent, page-by-page, text-wide Marine Corps jargon), to *The Things They Carried* (a "hard vocabulary [of] grunt lingo" [20]), to *Matterhorn*'s 31-page, paratextual "Glossary of Weapons, Technical Terms, Slang, and Jargon" (569–600), shows that while the rhetoric of war may change with the era and the particular war, the presence of the rhetoric of war during war is constant; as such, the presence of the rhetoric of war in the American novel of war is constant, and is constantly evolving. With each new era and war come new slang, jargon, obfuscation, and language — of war and for war — and, of course, war rhetoric is influenced by service branch and locus of war. Warriors talk about war while fighting war, and politicians talk about war while declaring, promoting, and justifying war; hence, the presence of the rhetoric of war in all of the novels of war in this study and the uniqueness in presentation of war rhetoric in each work.

Relative to the rhetoric of war in the American novel of war, one must ask a set of questions. What, exactly, is the rhetoric of war? How is the rhetoric of war both war and era specific? How does literary war rhetoric influence other rhetorics? Do different texts use war rhetoric differently? Do different authors of American novels of war use war rhetoric for different rhetorical purposes? According to Paul Dickson, editor of *War Slang: American Fighting Words and Phrases Since the Civil War*, "From the Revolutionary War to the 2003 Operation Iraqi Freedom, tens of thousands of new words and phrases have been born of conflict, boredom, good humor, bad food, new technology, and the pure horror of war" (ix), and thus "the unavoidable conclusion [is] that wars create great bodies of new language that sound as different as do a musket, an M-1, and a Patriot missile. For every term that becomes part of the larger language there are three that live on only in the literature of a particular period" (x). So, the nexus of conflict, boredom, humor, food, technology, and horror, centralized by military life and war, creates a new language: the rhetoric of war. And this rhetoric of war—conjoined with the experience(s) of war—influences other rhetorics, both during and after conflict. And these post-war rhetorics are literary and social. War is horrifying, and writing in regard to World War I, Paul Fussell, in the classic study *The Great War and Modern Memory*, notes that World War I was so horrifying, so grotesque, so unique, that the language of the nineteenth century, a British language of war written and spoken with a "tendency towards heroic grandiosity" (175), was obsolete, and that "the war was much worse than any [contemporary or historical] description ... could suggest" (174). As such, euphemisms and slang born of the war were created; for example, World War I was "the great venture" (21). These war euphemisms were then appropriated by Western societies, used in popular and scholarly histories, propagated in medicine, commandeered by those on the home front, and even pilfered for other arts, and, Fussell argues, "the diction of war resides everywhere just below the surface of modern experience [and] politics would be a very different thing without military jargon" (189). Take, for example, trenchcoat, rank and file, firing line, over the top, barrage, platoon, breakthrough, no man's land, hold the line, and so forth. People use these terms "without, of course, any sharp awareness that one is recalling war" (189), for these and thousands of other terms and phrases have become part of the non-combat English and American vernacular. The war, as fought in filthy, muddy, vermin-ridden trenches, with assaults over the tops of the trenches, thus influences the rhetoric of the war, which, in turn, influences the rhetoric away from the war.

During World War I, war rhetoric was appropriated and used in a number of different ways, by a number of different types of appropriators. For example, as Mark A. Robison notes, the use of the pejorative label *Hun* was applied to the German combatant in particular, and the German in general (175), and was optimally used in the print media of the day. And while the term was, according to Dickson, first used by Kaiser Wilhelm in 1900—as in "fight like Attila's Huns" (Dickson 70)—Arthur Guy Empey argues that the term was used primarily by journalists and the like as a propaganda piece (Empey 295). Thus, the American popular media used the slang term rhetorically to stoke anti–German feelings back home: "The Germans stood for guttural language, spiked helmets, and jack boots" (Buitenhuis 290). War also influenced art, and proto–World War I–era artists appropriated such language for their artistic means, even before the war was begun. According to Milton A. Cohen, "For beyond merely anticipating or even welcoming a new war, avant-garde artists across Europe drew upon war in its multiple meanings—war as metaphor and as actuality, war as language, as visual images, as models of both organizing and destructive power, and, most of all, war as focused energy" (160), and "At times, modernists borrowed the rhetoric of imperialist generals and politicians" (161). Further, Cohen notes, early twentieth-century modern artists were socially and culturally at war before World War I, and "modernists turned to war and violence for the vocabulary to depict [their aesthetic sociocultural war]" (160). As such, groups and artists such as the German Expressionists—especially Der Blaue Reiter with *Der Blaue Reiter Almanac* (1912)—the Italian Futurists with their *Foundation Manifesto* (1909), and the Vorticists—especially Wynham Lewis with *Blast 1* (1914) and then the peri-war *Blast 2 War Number* (July 1915)—used the rhetoric of war to fight their cultural wars in literary and plastic forms. Cohen emphasizes that the rhetoric was nothing compared to the catastrophic effects of the war upon artists of the era, as "it killed or severely maimed scores of artists, including some of the very best; it drove numerous others to physical or nervous breakdowns and weakened still others to make them vulnerable to the 1918-19 influenza epidemic or pneumonia" (164). Thus, artists might have asked for war rhetorically, and in protest, but the actuality of the war was something else entirely.

Relative to war-centric, medicinal rhetoric, a new physical science came into being through World War I and the proximity of artillery and battle carnage to post-combat surgery: "traumatology" (Pachet 1318) was born, the child of war, and, rhetorically and medicinally, the "invention of new [medicinal] terminology can be viewed ... as part of the creative effort in technology which war encourages" (1318). Thus, new wars produce new languages. And new wars produce new forms of injury and injury-related medical rhetoric—the rhetoric of traumatology—such as "gas gangrene" (Heyman 99), a particularly nasty anaerobic bacterial infection born of closed, unclean wounds. As well, neurological, psychological, and psychiatric medicine benefited rhetorically, and in practice, from the suffering of those in the war: "war-neuroses" (1317), "shell-shock" (1318), and "traumatic neurosis" (1324) were all applied to the psychological trauma men carried secondary to their experiences in the war. So, war-based suffering, physical and psychological, born of modern war, was given a language and a practice. The rhetoric of World War I even affected literary practices through censorship—"the banning, burning, seizing, and censoring in the 1920s, under authority of the obscenity laws" (Willis 468)—long after the war, during a time in which authors of the day, such as Ernest Hemingway, wanted to use the language of war, including anatomical and sexual slang and jargon, in their texts to accurately portray humanity and human behavior in a time of war—that is, "the full lexicon of trench obscenities" (Willis 472). The problem in the 1920s, according to J.H. Willis, Jr., was "how to be faithful to the bitter, life-changing experience of modern warfare in a realistic depiction of both action and dialogue" (470), and the solution was, in many cases, if one wanted to publish in the United States, censorship of language. So, even after World War I, even after (or perhaps because of) the slaughter, the publishers of novels saw a problem with the rhetoric of war—it was too true, too real, not to mention obscene, sexual, carnal. Nonetheless, some honest and true works, such as *Through the Wheat* and *Company K*, were courageously published between the world wars.

So, through the optic of World War I, it is easy to see that specific wars—or in this case, a specific war—create rhetoric relative to the era and the war, and the events relative to the era and war. It is also clear that the rhetoric of war influences other (official and unofficial), social and cultural and medical and artistic and aesthetic rhetorics, before, during, and after a given war. Now, a brief look at the nineteenth century and the twenty-first century is needed, first to see how the rhetoric of war influences history and historical interpretation and then to see how the rhetoric of war influences, well, the rhetoric of war. Webb Garrison notes, "Language evolves from generation to generation. Dozens of word usages that were commonplace during the Civil War have since disappeared from our speech or have changed in meaning" (Garrison and Garrison ix). These claims are obvious enough, and correct, of course, and, when taken with the closing thoughts of Garrison's essay, can be interpreted in the context of this study: "only by rediscovering how words were used during the [Civil War] years can we better grasp what our predecessors recorded of their experiences in the midst of this convulsion in the nation's history" (x). Thus, when analyzing the rhetoric of war, one must analyze it in the context contemporary to the war's era, or else one will not properly and cogently interpret that which is being studied. Further, proper historical context leads to proper post-historical comprehension. For example, a twenty-first-century dictionary will define "straggle" in the context of wander or stray, sans reference to war, but Garrison and Garrison's *Encyclopedia of Civil War Usage* defines a *Straggler* as "a soldier who deliberately wandered away from his REGIMENT, usually to avoid combat" (242). As such, Henry Fleming is not a deserter but a Straggler, and he does not desert, he straggles. Or is Henry actually a *Skedaddler*— one who has "fled the battlefield, discarding his weapons and equipment in the process" (230)? Obviously, when interpreting the use of the rhetoric of war in the literature of war, contemporary context, relative to both the war and the historical era, matters, lest the post-war interpreter misinterpret the rhetoric. So, Stephen Crane, writing three decades after the U.S. Civil War, uses dialogue in *The Red Badge of Courage* for linguistic quasi-historical context, language "that may have struck readers in 1895 as colorful and old-fashioned ... slightly quaint [and] historical" (Habegger 192). As such, "The novel had an overwhelming historical authenticity for [nineteenth-century] readers, not because it revived the history of battles and leaders and official rhetoric, but because it revived, or seemed to revive, the unofficial voices and the unexpressed experiences [of the participants]" (193)— the war novel as historical document, historical record, accurate or not, but truthful, via accurate rhetoric (or that which seems to be accurate). And according to Habegger, Crane's text "contributed to the general representation of how the 1890s thought the 1860s spoke" (192).

Reader response does matter in this regard because historical sentimentality greatly affected the sales of Crane's text as well as his literary legacy as a modernist and an author of the first modern Civil War novel and American novel of war. But what about war rhetoric and war fact? In an amusing *USA Today* piece on the naming of twenty-first-century military operations, in the context of history, Lionel Beehner examines how the (necessary?) naming of war operations— the rhetoric of war — was started by the Huns, er, Germans, during World War I, which led to named American operations during World War II, Korea, Vietnam, the invasion of Panama, the Persian Gulf War, and the wars in Iraq and Afghanistan. The rhetoric of war begets the rhetoric of war. Beehner argues that the naming of military operations is a "puzzling and somewhat pointless exercise [and] is just a clever way of putting a kinder, gentler face on war" ("An Operation by Any Other Name")— Operation Blue Spoon, for example (the invasion of Panama). This said, one can ascertain the differences in the rhetoric of war. There is the contemporary rhetoric created by the combatants and participants, which is born in an attempt to promote the truth of war, or born as the truth of war, via language (and here specifically via written language and novel-length fiction). There is also the rhetoric of war written from a historical, but fictional, context, a presentation of "war as it was." Then, there is the official means of rhetoric, which is used by those in power — in uniform and out — to obscure and obfuscate the realities of war — for example, the recently popular "Kinetic Operations." Finally, there is patriotic propaganda, which is used by all sorts to promote and intoxicate in times of war.

In *Blood Meridian*, the rhetoric of war is the rhetoric of the Monroe Doctrine and of the era of Manifest Destiny (1814–1860). The Monroe Doctrine (2 December 1823) bifurcated the New World and the Old World and attempted to disengage any European powers from assimilating Latin American nations that had freed themselves from Spanish colonial rule. The goal of the doctrine was to entrench American power over the entirety of the western hemisphere — economically, politically, militarily. Manifest Destiny, of course, was the belief that the United States was divinely destined to expand across the geographic entirety of the North American continent and was used to justify the war between the

United States and Mexico, as well as other U.S. appropriations. American expansion, and the moral right to such expansion, was obvious—manifest—and was determined—destiny. The practice of the philosophy of Manifest Destiny also had a devastating effect upon the indigenous peoples of North America, as their lands were initially usurped through the Indian Removal Act, beginning in the South in 1830, and their cultural and social ways were eradicated in the name of God-given destiny and Anglo hegemony. The hammer of Manifest Destiny is war, and in *Blood Meridian*, McCarthy uses his narrator, Judge Holden, and other named and unnamed characters, to present the language and practice of Manifest Destiny. Early in the text, filibuster leader Captain White argues, in regard to the Mexican government and people, "We are dealing with a people manifestly incapable of governing themselves" (34), and "unless we act, Mexico—and I mean the whole of the country [i.e., the United States and Canada, too]—will one day fly a European flag. Monroe Doctrine or no" (35). The use of the word "manifest" and its juxtaposition with the concept of Manifest Destiny, relative to Mexico and its governance, without explicitly saying so, justifies the violent practices of Manifest Destiny. Thus argues Captain White: We, as Americans, are duty- and God-bound to take Mexico, and if we have to eradicate the Mexicans, doing so is for their own good, and the survivors, the United States, and the Western Hemisphere will all be better off for it. And if the word manifest is not explicit enough, McCarthy has White explicitly refer to the Monroe Doctrine.

Part of the practice of Manifest Destiny is the dehumanizing of the opponent, and in the text, the scalphunters collect, not human scalps, but proofs of life taken, for cash payment, as John Joel Glanton orders, in reference to a dead old woman's scalp: "Get that receipt for us" (98). And as the practice of Manifest Destiny and of scalphunting and Indian eradication is a violent one, practiced by violent men, in a time of war and through acts of war, the practitioners are, according to one old man in a Mexican cantina, "socieded de guerra. Contra los barbaros" (102)—that is, the society of war, against the barbarians. In *Blood Meridian*, war is the social practice, and war is the language. And after the battle, the talk is of war—not of the battle held, necessarily, but of war: "It makes no difference what men think of war, said the judge. War endures.... War was always here. Before man was, war waited for him. The ultimate trade awaiting its ultimate practitioner. That is the way it was and will be" (248). While the rhetoric of war may change with the era, the topic of the rhetoric will not. Warriors discuss war. And warriors practice war relative to the era and the era's social, cultural, economic, and political practices. Thus, the rhetoric of war in *Blood Meridian* reflects the era of Manifest Destiny and the practices and philosophies of said era as well as the greater theory and practices of the Monroe Doctrine.

In *The Red Badge of Courage*, Stephen Crane uses the rhetoric of war in a number of different ways; as argued above, the text is an example of how Americans of the 1890s thought that people of the 1860s spoke. As such, for readers in the mid–1890s, the text is a sort of quasi-linguistic primer to the patois and argot of the 1860s, per Crane the author. And while Theodor Ropp argues that the American Civil War was the first war "in which really large numbers of literate men fought as common soldiers" (qtd. in Fussell 157), the reader sees very little of this literacy but for Henry Fleming, who dreams of war as that which he has read of in the classics and in the popular press of the day: "Tales of great movements shook the land. They might not be distinctly Homeric, but there seemed to be much glory in them" (5). Idealized visions of war—Henry's "consuming desire to see the appearance of a real, Greeklike war" (Mulcaire 58)—and rumors of war compel Henry to enlist. The motif of the rumor in war and of war (a type of the rhetoric of war) is introduced in the second and third paragraphs of the work, in which the tall soldier, Jim Conklin, in Conklinese patois, states, "We're goin' t' move t'morrah — sure.... We're goin' 'way up the river, cut across, an' come around behint 'em" (3). Addressing the ongoing motif of rumor in time of war in Crane's text, Marilyn Boyer ponders and asserts the following: "The story begins with a rumor. What is a rumor? Is it a lie or is it a truth? Or, being neither, is it in any way reliable? Existing in the gap between the binary oppositions of truth and falsehood, the rumor of active warfare in the novel functions as a supporting indicator of the unstable nature of war" (6). Of course, anyone who has been a part of a military hierarchy based on a chain of command can attest that, in the military, rumors are the unofficial orders of the day, as the vacuum created by a lack of knowledge must be filled, often with inaccurate information. As such, in the military, before, during, and after times and acts of war, rumors and rumor mongering are persistent, especially among the unenlightened lower ranks; according to Dickson, the term *Scuttlebutt* — originally, the words informally spoken around a ship's water barrel — was coined in the early nineteenth century for military gossip (19), of which Conklin's rumor of war is an obvious example. And while gossip, or rumor, or scuttlebutt may be spoken and spread, the war is coming, the violence is coming, so sooner or later, the rumor of war in amalgamated into the rhetoric of war.

Leaping forward a century, the rhetoric of war born of the Vietnam War is as unique and war and era specific as Crane's post-war rhetoric of the Civil War. According to Dickson, the Vietnam War "did indeed produce a totally new slang — brutal, direct, and geared to high-tech jungle warfare with a rock 'n' roll beat backed up by the throb of chopper engines.... [A rhetoric of war] loaded with raw frustration and bitter cynicism" (260). Social upheaval, political unrest, the draft, the counter-culture, and the ultra-violence of the war all contributed to a deep-seated pessimism relative to American presence in Vietnam. Further, the patois and argot of the Civil War era — viewed through Crane's text — feel ancient stylistically and linguistically, and rhetorically, when compared with the hipster slang, branch-specific jargon, and military rhetoric of the Vietnam-era and the texts endemic to that era and war. *The Short-Timers, Matterhorn,* and *The Things They Carried* each deal specifically with the rhetoric of war born of the Vietnam War, and each text is unique in its presentation of the Vietnam-era rhetoric of war, in part, no doubt, due to the authors' experiences and participation in the war. *The Short-Timers* is trifurcated into three disparate sections — "The Spirit of the Bayonet" (1–33), "Body Count" (35–140), and "Grunts" (141–80). The first section is set in Marine Corps boot camp at Parris Island, South Carolina. The second section is focused primarily around the battle for the Citadel of Hue, and the third section is set primarily in the jungle of Vietnam. Hasford's text, from the first sentence of the first paragraph of the first page of the first section, is a primer in Marine Corps jargon and is obviously written by one who has lived the life of the Corps: "The Marines are looking for a few good men" (3). Sentence two reads, "The recruit says that his name is Leonard Pratt" (3). Sentence three reads, "Gunnery Sergeant Gerheim takes one look at the skinny red-neck and immediately dubs him 'Gomer Pyle'" (3). "Marines ... a few good men," "recruit," "Gomer Pyle"; this rhetoric is branch-specific to the Marine Corps. Also present on the first page of the text: "Three junior drill instructors ... yellow footprints painted in a pattern on the concrete deck ... the United States Marine Corps Recruit Depot" (3). Even to the uninitiated reader, the setting is clear: This is the Marine Corps, and this is boot camp; the rhetoric explicitly says so. Not ironically, John Newman, author of *Vietnam War Literature: An Annotated Bibliography of Imaginative Works about Americans Fighting in Vietnam*, which is an excellent, although thirty years post-publication (1982) and thus incomplete, annotated bibliography on the works born of the war, writes of the Hasford text, "Descriptions of combat are graphic and detailed, although the extensive use of nicknames and Marine Corps slang sometimes makes the action hard to follow" (24). Hasford's casual, omnipresent use of Marine Corps slang, from the opening sentence of the text, indoctrinates the reader into the rhetoric of the Corps. And as mentioned in the previous chapter, the use of nicknames in military texts is longstanding, and in the texts of the Vietnam War it is especially apparent.

In fact, Hasford sees fit to use nicknames for nearly every character, and he does not readily offer specific rank, which is a bit unusual, even in a Vietnam War text, although he does refer to hierarchical positions, especially regarding the roles in Lusthog Squad. A sample of nicknames includes but is not limited to the following: Gomer Pyle, Joker (the narrator), Cowboy, Rafter Man, Animal Mother, Alice, T.H.E. Rock, Doc Jay, Crazy Earl, New Guy, Mr. Shortround (a nickname also found in *Matterhorn*), Chili Vendor, Daytona Dave, Mr. Payback. Why the ubiquitous use of nicknames? Perhaps it has something to do with the loss of identity that begins in boot camp. One's identity is broken down so that one is no longer one but rather a component of a fire team, squad, platoon, company, battalion, regiment, and division. One is no longer an individual; one is part of a communal greater whole. As one has his identity ripped away, one is left with a vacuum; one is nameless. As such, one's behavior becomes one's name. Joker is a smart-ass; Cowboy is from Texas and wears a Stetson. Pratt is a screw-up, so he is Gomer Pyle. Rafter Man fell from some rafters while drunk in a bar—a "slop shoot." Animal Mother is an animal in a fight; the new guy is new, so he is New Guy, and on it goes. One's civilian identity and moniker is irrelevant in the Corps and in war, so that identity, and name, and person, no longer exist. And as Hasford does not ever properly name most of the characters, according to the text and its author, that pre–Marine Corps person will never exist again. Hasford's text is a compendium of Marine Corps slang; as well, the work is an almost glaringly obvious example of nicknaming in the military and in time of war. Hasford's use of slang is branch specific—"maggots" (5)/recruits; "Grunts" (5)/infantrymen; "cover" (6)/hat; "ditty-bop ... double-time ... skate ... shitbirds ... skuzzy ... hump" (11); "devil dogs" (13); "gung ho" (17); "semper fidelis" (18); "poge" (40). Thus, the rhetoric of war in *The Short-Timers* is very much war and branch specific—brutal, cynical, and Marine Corps–based.

Also Marine Corps–based is the rhetoric of war in *Matterhorn*, and what the Marlantes text offers that the other Vietnam War novels in this study do not is an extended glossary that contains general military nomenclature, Vietnam War–era fighting equipment, and Marine Corps slang—Marlantes' outstanding "Glossary of Weapons, Technical Terms, Slang, and Jargon" (569–600). It should be noted that other Vietnam War–era texts also contain paratextual glossaries, and relative to this study, Wallace Terry's *Bloods* and Mark Baker's *Nam*—among many others, fiction and nonfiction—contain useful glossaries. However, for comprehensive, branch-specific rhetoric, and as a component of a novel, Marlantes' paratextual glossary stands out. The glossary is well thought out and is pragmatic in that it benefits the unenlightened reader, and, in fact, might even be placed before the text so that non-military readers could be indoctrinated to the Marine Corps argot before entering the story. Something Marlantes' glossary has in common with Arthur Guy Empey's World War I glossary from *Over the Top* is humor, and a number of Marlantes' entries are quite funny. For example: "**A. J. Squaredaway** Marines used made-up names to personify conditions or standards. A.J. Squaredaway meant looking sharp. There were others. Joady was the guy screwing your girl [i.e., Susie Rottencrotch] back home and Joe Shit the ragpicker was the opposite of A.J. Squaredaway" (569). The author of this study, himself a former Marine, might be wrong, but one does not need to be a Marine or former Marine to see the humor in this entry, the second of the glossary. Other Marine Corps slang terms Marlantes offers, terms familiar to all Marines (even in the twenty-first century) are as follows: "the Crotch" (576)/the Marine Corps (more recently, the Suck); "humping" (581)/forced marching or hiking, with equipment, in the bush (also used by the Army infantry); "poag" (587) or pogue or poge/a useless Marine, related to a REMF (Rear Echelon Mutherfucker) and numbnuts; "shit sandwich" (592)/a very tough firefight; "skipper" (593)/a term of respect for a company commander, often a captain — see *Band of Brothers* (288); "squid" (594)/a Navy medic, usually an exceptional individual; "super-grunts" (594)/Marines assigned to Reconnaissance, also exceptional individuals; "utilities" (595)/camouflaged clothing, worn on a daily basis; "wake-up" (596)/the morning that one flies home or is discharged (for example, "I have five days and a wake-up"); and "782 gear" (600)/standard-issue combat gear — pack, poncho, entrenching tool, ammo belt with suspenders (AKA deuce gear). These ten terms are but a few of the Marine Corps–centric expressions that Marlantes offers in the glossary, words that are, of course, liberally used in the novel. The use of such branch-specific rhetoric gives the fiction the mark of truth and accuracy, something present in the Hasford text as well.

Another mark of truth and accuracy in Marlantes' glossary is the abundance of weaponry and war-related equipment listed, and the glossary offers American equipment of war as well as the equipment of war used by the Vietnamese forces (for a more thorough discussion of the equipage of war in the American novel of war, see the following chapter). First, a few of the listed tools of war used by the American forces: C-4, Ch-46, Ch-47, claymore, C-rations, Huey, K-bar, M-16, M-26, M-60, M-79, OV-10, PRC 25, .45. Next, a few of the listed tools of war used by the North Vietnamese Army and the Viet Cong: AK-47, chi-comm, DShKM .51, RPD, RPG, SKS, 82-mm mortar, 120-mm mortar. These brief and unannotated lists are incomplete, of course, but are representative of the thoroughness of Marlantes' glossary-based war equipment list, and by offering a number of tools of the North Vietnamese, tools that were Soviet-designed and Soviet-manufactured, Marlantes refers to the fact that the Soviet Union was an active participant in the Vietnam War, for if the Soviets did not provide the weaponry to the North Vietnamese Army, who then armed the Viet Cong, the war might have been shorter-lived. Marlantes' glossary is also rife with the general nomenclature of the American military, and anyone who has served in uniform would be able to define such nomenclature: ASAP, arty, battalion, battery, bird, CO, company, CP, division, DMZ, KIA, lifer, LP, LZ, MIA, NCO, NCOIC, OP, patrol, platoon, point, R&R, regiment, regular, squad, WIA, and so on. All of these terms and abbreviations are common to the U.S. military and are, as such, generalized. Thus, Marlantes' glossary offers the reader the rhetoric of war in three distinct rhetorical modes — Marine Corps–specific slang, Vietnam War–era combat equipment, and generalized military nomenclature. Marlantes' glossary is a very useful and comprehensive collection of the rhetoric of war, and readers, especially non-military readers, would do well to read the glossary before reading the novel, or even before reading any Vietnam War novel.

Tim O'Brien's highly regarded postmodern construct of the Vietnam War, *The Things They Carried*, like *The Short-Timers* and *Matterhorn*, also offers the rhetoric of war, but O'Brien's text does so in a different manner. Unlike the Hasford text, which uses Marine Corps slang on every page, and unlike the Marlantes text, which explicates its jargon and slang in a paratextual glossary, the O'Brien text, as a consciously created postmodern construct, presents the rhetoric of war metafictively and explicitly in narrator- and character-based discussions about the language of war. However, as an American novel of the Vietnam War, the O'Brien text does have rhetorical similarities with the Hasford and Marlantes texts; for example, all three texts use the expression "There it is" to designate conclusion or resignation relating to any given situation or situational outcome. Hasford uses "There it is" from the first scene set in Vietnam (42) until the next to last sentence in the text (180), and Marlantes uses "There it is" throughout his work (23, 112, 210, 367, 463, 560). O'Brien's in-text use begins on page 14 of the novel, with a discussion between two "legs" (3)—that is, grunts—on the "moral" (13) of war, which, of course, is a pun and a component of the rhetoric of war, as there is no moral of war; there is only blood and carnage: "I don't see no moral" (14), says Henry Dobbins. "There it *is*, man" (14), says Mitchell Sanders. The moral of war is that there is no moral to war, or morality to war. O'Brien's narrator later reflects on the phrase "There it is" and its peri-war use by the men: "There it is, they'd say. Over and over—there it is, my friend, there it is—as if the repetition itself were an act of poise, a balance between crazy and almost crazy, knowing without going, there it is, which meant be cool, let it ride, because Oh yeah, man, you can't change what can't be changed, there it is, there it absolutely and positively fucking well *is* [O'Brien's italics]" (21). So, "There it is" is a rhetorical absolutism. A man is killed: There it is. The company must burn a village: There it is. Another day of endless humping: There it is. Your girlfriend breaks up with you: There it is. You kill an innocent: There it is. You kill a VC: There it is; there it is; there it is: There it is. Paradoxically, the phrase is both absolute and recursive, because no matter what happens, one is still in-country, still a participant in the Vietnam War: There it is. "There it is" is part of what O'Brien's narrator labels a "hard vocabulary [of] grunt lingo" (20), language the grunts use to survive the weight that comes with the ability to kill or die on a daily basis: "They used a hard vocabulary to contain the terrible softness [i.e., fear of death]. *Greased* they'd say. *Offed, lit up, zapped while zipping*. It wasn't cruelty, just stage presence. They were actors. When someone died, it wasn't quite dying, because in a curious way it seemed scripted, and because they had their lines mostly memorized, irony mixed with tragedy, and because they called it by other names, as if to encyst and destroy the reality of death itself.... They talked grunt lingo. They told stories" (20). Thus, from the perspective of O'Brien's narrator, who is examining the perspective of the nineteen- and twenty-year-old infantrymen, the rhetoric of war, grunt lingo, the hard vocabulary, is a defense mechanism, a means to conquer and hide fear. These young men, men who were recently merely boys, American boys, are now legs, grunts, infantrymen, and as such, are playing roles radically different from high school student or university student or teenage American youth. Clearly, in *The Short-Timers*, Hasford argues that the change is manifest and forever; young recruits are evolved into "werewolves" (33, 179)—man wolves—and that the lycanthropy is an acknowledged tool of war. But O'Brien's narrator seems uncertain about the change: Is the change a role to play or a manifest evolving/devolving of each boy/man/grunt into a savage being? If so, what is the moral—the result—of war? A boy is permanently turned into an animal? O'Brien's postmodern ambiguity seems to deny the answer to this last question, and perhaps this is the true rhetoric of war in the O'Brien text—that there is no unified truth to war, of war, by war. O'Brien even includes a chapter titled, "How to Tell a True War Story" (67–85), which argues, "The truths [of war] are contradictory" (80), while it tells interpolated war stories and self-contradicts its narrator, text, chapters, and argued truths. Thus, O'Brien's text is a traditional Vietnam War novel of war in its use of grunt lingo and repetition of "There it is," but the text is also

a nontraditional Vietnam War novel of war in its structural and philosophical and metafictive approaches to the topic of the rhetoric of war in the American novel of war.

In the American novel of war, the rhetoric of war does not necessarily need to be the
rhetoric of the combatants, or even the post-combatant retrospective narrator or author.
The politicians who order and promote war have a say in the propagandizing of war(s),
and thus official propaganda and obfuscation are integral components of the rhetoric of
war. According to Peter Buitenhuis, during World War I both Great Britain and the United
States had systematic propaganda machines put in place in order to promote the war effort
in general and the necessity of the war and recruitment in particular. In the United States,
President Woodrow Wilson enlisted publisher George Creel to direct "the Committee of
Public Information" (289) — a nice, euphemistic title for a propaganda machine, no doubt —
through which Creel created "a massive publicity campaign, particularly through the press,
film" (289), and he enlisted popular writers of the day such as Owen Wister, William Dean
Howells, and Edna Ferber, "among others, to write articles about America's contribution
to the war" (289). Creel's goal was to rally the populace around the flag, so to speak, and
to promote the war (and the role of the United States as combatant nation in the war), as
a popular war, in the name of good, in the name of democracy, against a raping, pillaging,
dehumanized enemy — the Huns. A good war is easier to fight, and in such a good war, it
is easier to recruit young men to bear arms and risk their lives. Of course, George Orwell,
in his classic and timeless essay, "Politics and the English Language," has a number of things
to say about political rhetoric and its use in time of war. Under the heading "Pretentious
Diction," Orwell argues that "writing that aims at glorifying war usually takes on an archaic
color" (167) and uses words that have historic proportions such as realm, throne, sword,
shield, and so on to argue for the socially sanctioned violence of war. And on politics, in
general, Orwell argues that "politics itself is a mass of lies, evasions, folly, hatred and schiz-
ophrenia" (174) and that political language is a set of "ready-made phrases" (174), created
of "euphemism, question-begging and sheer cloudy vagueness" (173), which are "designed
to make lies sound truthful and murder respectable, and to give an appearance of solidarity
to pure wind" (177), and thus are written with the goal of giving "defence to the indefen-
sible" (173). And there is no doubt, none whatsoever, as evidenced expertly in *Johnny Got
His Gun*, that Dalton Trumbo felt the same way, and this was even prior to being called
before the House Un-American Activities Committee in 1947, before which Trumbo refused
to name names, and at which time he was subsequently found in contempt of Congress
and imprisoned for nearly a year and professionally blacklisted.

In a discussion of Evelyn Cobley's *Representing War: Form and Ideology from First World
War Narratives* (1993), Elizabeth A. Marsland notes Cobley's rhetorical starting point is the
common critical premise that writers of war texts use the war novel "as an alternative to
the official history [of the war], a challenge to the establishment's attempt to rationalize
the war and conceal what really happened" (356); thus, explicitly or implicitly, the war narratives are protest novels, whether the author sees the work as a protest or not (356). Even
a cursory reading of *Johnny Got His Gun* reveals to even the most unenlightened reader
that Dalton Trumbo explicitly created a work of protest against war. And what Trumbo is
railing against is the political rhetoric, propaganda, and obfuscation used by nations, politicos, and even common citizens to promote war and war efforts, the results of which are
death and carnage. Joe Bonham, veteran of World War I and Trumbo's narrative optic,
through whom the text is viewed, is physically devastated nearly beyond comprehension:
he is armless, legless, sightless, soundless, faceless; he cannot taste or smell or hear; he is a

thinking brain in a prison — his broken body. He is entombed. He is the result of war. He is the result of the rhetoric and the propaganda and the obfuscation; he is one who has made "the world safe for democracy" (116, 119, 121, 234, 239, 250–51). Trumbo's text seethes with anger, and the rage is directed against those who spew the political rhetoric as well as those who follow the political rhetoric. Politicians and those who promote and argue for war, including the general public, are "liars" (114, 119), and enlistees and draftees are "fools" (114). The propagandistic use of the logical fallacies that appeal to stirring symbols such as patriotism and religion are presented early in the text, as "four trainloads" (37) of enlistees and draftees — including Joe Bonham — are at the train station saying goodbye to their families (37–40), many for the last time, of course: "The whole place the station and the cars and even the locomotives were draped with bunting and the children and women mostly carried flags.... There were three bands ... and songs and the mayor giving an address" (37). The mood set is one of a celebration. People are drunk, people are laughing, and yes, the astute ones are even crying.

Trumbo then uses freestanding, single-sentence paragraphs, with and without dialogue quotation marks and end punctuation, to refer to the propagandistic rhetoric of the day; in so doing, he shows that it is not merely the politicians promoting war and patriotism; it is the common public, too: "'And their lives if necessary that democracy may not perish from the face of the earth' ... It's a long way to Tiperrary it's a long way to go ... 'As that great patriot Patrick Henry said' ... Johnny get your gun get your gun get your gun ... 'As that great patriot George Washington said' ... And we won't be back till it's over over there ... 'Step lively boy you're in the army now' ... Pack up your troubles in your old kit bag and smile smile smile ... 'As that great patriot Abraham Lincoln said' ... 'As that great patriot Theodore Roosevelt has said' ... America I love you you're like a sweetheart to me ... 'As that great patriot Woodrow Wilson has said' ... Over there over there over there over there over there" (37–39). Through song lyrics and named heroes and the repetitive use of the word "patriot," Trumbo sets the ethos and pathos of the day. Further, he conveys a sense of excitement; it is exciting and patriotic to go to war. Thus, words such as "patriot" are being used to promote war, and Trumbo is railing against the fact that men are dying for words, for symbols, for signifiers, for rhetoric sans signification; he is screaming for the dead, for "all the five million or seven million or ten million who went out and died to make the world safe for democracy to make the world safe for words without meaning" (121). The section continues: "'Let us pray.' ... 'Thy will be done on earth as it is in heaven.' ... Oh say can you see ... Whose broad stripes and bright stars ... O'er the land of the free and the home of the brave" (39–40). The rhetoric of war promotion uses religion, appeals to patriotism and heroes, and honor and duty in the name of democracy to bring the nation into the fold. As well, prayer and patriotism are married. How else would mothers and fathers allow their sons to be destroyed in war but for the name of God, of country, of democracy?

Trumbo uses a freestanding chapter — chapter X (113–23), midway through the text — to further castigate those who use rhetoric to promote war (those "high-talking murdering sonsofbitches who screamed for blood" [122]), and in so doing, Trumbo deconstructs a number of terms used persuasively — in the name of war — to appeal to the emotions of citizens and enlistees and draftees. Duty, rights, liberty, decency, honor, democracy, native land, freedom, independence, noble, heroic, flag, slogan, ideal, principle, and sacred, among others, are worked over by Trumbo and are shown to be empty, vapid, built on air, nothing, in comparison with death ... and with post-war life, especially Joe Bonham's post-war life — a life as "a side of beef" (113). First, on going to war, someone tapped Joe on the shoulder and said, "Come along son we're going to war" (113), so he had to go, but in so doing, Joe neglected his sense of "duty" (113) to himself. And as one who was drafted in such a way, he had "no rights" (114); he could not say yes or no or even ask why he had to go. As such, his life was no longer legally his own. Thus, in the land of the free, Joe was no longer so; in the name of war, he had lost his freedom and his right to manage his own life, and his duty to self no longer existed. Trumbo then attacks the concept and use of the word "liberty" in the name of war: "What kind of liberty were they fighting for anyway? How much liberty and whose idea of liberty?... What the hell does liberty mean anyhow? It's just a word like house or table or any other word. Only it's a special kind of word. A guy says house and he can point to a house to prove it. But a guy says come on let's fight for liberty and he can't show you liberty. He can't prove the thing he's talking about so how in the hell can he be telling you to fight for it?" (114). War over a concept is a corruption, argues Trumbo.

And then, Trumbo takes the idea of war over a concept as a corruption and illustrates the corruption of other patriotic rhetoric: "If they weren't fighting for liberty they were fighting for independence or democracy or freedom or decency or honor or their native land or something else that didn't mean anything.... Motherland fatherland homeland native land. It's all the same. What the hell good to you is your native land after you're dead?" (116, 117). Further, "when they couldn't hook the little guys into fighting for liberty or freedom or democracy or independence or decency or honor they tried the women" (117) — that is, you've got to save the beautiful French and Belgian girls from "the dirty Huns" (117). Of course, the "they" here are the politicians and the promoters of war, the rhetoric makers who rally the citizens around the flag so that the citizens will willingly send their children to war. And the irony is, of course, that when one is drafted, one has lost his liberty, and when one dies, the rhetoric of patriotism — "fighting for a word" (118) — is really vapid, really empty, really meaningless.

Finally, and specifically, Trumbo has a bit to say relative to the rhetoric makers, the politicos, the promoters, and the liars who argue for war: "You can always hear the people who are willing to sacrifice somebody else's life. They're plenty loud and they talk all the time. You can find them in churches and schools and newspapers and legislatures and congresses. That's their business. They sound wonderful" (119). And they live on, argue on, go on, as the rhetoricians are not in the war, are not dying, are not bleeding, are not suffering. But the dead do not get to go on, are not allowed to speak and to live and to argue, so who speaks for the dead? This is Joe Bonham's goal, to speak for the dead, as he is so nearly so. And Bonham is eventually able to communicate with the external world, through Morse code. He taps his head on a pillow, and the respondent taps his or her Morse code out on Bonham's forehead. But when he is finally able to communicate, after five or six (248) years of solitude within his own shell of a body and locked in communication only with his own mind, and when he desires to be a vehicle against war, to show the results of war, to show the "truth" (240) of war wherever statesmen "speak" (239), he is told (or rather, a government official taps it onto his forehead), "WHAT YOU ASK IS AGAINST REGULATIONS" (242). And if this denial is not devastating enough — that he would be bad for business, the business of war — the government official then taps, "WHO ARE YOU" (242–43) onto Joe's forehead. The federal officials do not even know who this man in the bed is. So, Joe Bonham is nothing but a drugged (246) side of beef lying in a bed, but he can still think, even as a side of beef, even as a brain encased in a pod, and as the text closes, he thinks of the future and of future wars and of future rhetoric and future political rhetoricians, and he warns the rhetoricians that if they point their rhetoric at the little people, then someday the guns of the little people will be pointed at them.

Clearly, then, an American novel of war must contain the rhetoric of war, and the rhetoric of war in the American novel of war is an integral and influential component of the text. The narrator and characters must continually use such era- and war-specific rhetoric — war lingo, war slang, war cliché, war abbreviations and acronyms, and, of course, official and popular war propaganda and obfuscation — to refer to war equipage, war nomenclature, and war incitation and justification. Further, the rhetoric of war outlives the war and the warriors and is appropriated and assimilated into the popular vernacular. The rhetoric of war from the era of Manifest Destiny, per *Blood Meridian*, is different from the rhetoric of war from the Civil War era, so the collation, examination, and analysis of the rhetoric of war from *Blood Meridian* to *The Red Badge of Courage* to *The Short-Timers* to *Matterhorn* to *The Things They Carried* and back to *Johnny Got His Gun* shows that while the rhetoric of war may change with the era and the particular war, the presence of the rhetoric and slang and rumor and propaganda of war during war is constant; as such, the presence of this war-centric language in the American novel of war is constant, and constantly evolving. With each new era and war come new slang, jargon, obfuscation, and language — of war, for war, born by war and in the name of war. Warriors talk about war while fighting war, and authors use war rhetoric when writing about war, and politicians talk about war while declaring and justifying war, and others "patriotically" propagandize war in the name of duty, honor, liberty, and freedom; hence, the presence of the rhetoric of war in all novels of war, each unique in its presentation of such rhetoric.

Returning to the questions central to this chapter — What is the rhetoric of war? How is the rhetoric of war both war and era specific? How does literary war rhetoric influence other rhetorics? Do different texts use war rhetoric differently? Do different authors of American novels of war use war rhetoric for different rhetorical purposes? — the responses are now clarified: The rhetoric of war is the language, first verbal and then literary, first war- and military-centric, and then popular, created at the nexus of conflict, boredom, humor, food, technology, and horror, that is born of military life and war. Additionally, the technology and tactical techniques from war to war influence the rhetoric of war, and as shown earlier, war rhetoric influences art and literature and other means of creative, cultural, and social communication. And of course, different texts use the rhetoric of war differently: *Blood Meridian*, a historicist work, uses the language of Manifest Destiny and the era of the Monroe Doctrine both allusively and referentially; *The Red Badge of Courage* uses the patois and argot of the Civil War era, as imagined by Stephen Crane in the 1890s, to promote rumor(s) in time of war; *The Short-Timers* indoctrinates the reader into the rhetoric of the Marine Corps; *Matterhorn* uses a glossary of Marine Corps–specific slang, general military nomenclature, and Vietnam War–era fighting equipment; *The Things They Carried* uses the hard language of grunt speak and the narrator's postmodernity to deal philosophically with the structural and aesthetic and metafictive approaches to the language used by men during war; and finally, *Johnny Got His Gun* catalogs the propaganda used by the political and social promoters of war in order to deconstruct the logically and morally and ethically flawed jargon of patriotism.

As each text uses the rhetoric of war differently, each author uses the rhetoric of war for a different rhetorical purpose: Cormac McCarthy is telling a tale of the violent history of the era of Manifest Destiny and the Monroe Doctrine, so the language he uses is relative to the philosophy of American and Anglo expansionism; Stephen Crane, writing of a real battle, and using the optic of one isolated modern individual, is writing retrospectively and attempting to imagine the regional and Civil War–centric language of the day so that his text is a realist excursion into the regional language of war, and with that, Henry's idealization of war and Jim Conklin's rumor(s) of war coming; Gustav Hasford's rhetorical purpose seems to be that the brutality, the savagery, and the violence of the Marine Corps rhetoric — starting from boot camp — is measured against, and is equal to, and foreshadows, the brutality, savagery, and violence of the Vietnam War; Karl Marlantes' rhetoric is that of the Vietnam War, as argued and accurately presented, paratextually, in reference text form as a glossary; Tim O'Brien, postmodern metafictional philosopher that he is, uses the rhetoric of war to examine the rhetoric of war; Dalton Trumbo is arguing against war, any war, it seems, and as Hitler was well into power and beginning his stomp through Europe at the time of the text's publication, it is easily guessed that Trumbo was arguing against involvement in another world war centrally situated in Europe. Each author uses his American novel of war differently to present the rhetoric of war. Common to all of the texts, however, is the rhetoric of war itself — subjective, of course, to the literary and philosophical needs of its author, era, and war.

V

The Equipage of War

In conjunction with the omnipresence of the rhetoric of war, the tools and equipment and weapons of war are consistently at hand in the American novel of war. The Civil War was the first war to use mass-produced weapons, which led to mass-produced death, and chronologically, from Crane's text onward, American novels of war catalog the equipage of war. Each war introduces new weapons with which and by which men can destroy one another, so as technology is created and evolved, and as new wars are fought, warriors need planes, and tanks, and ships, and artillery, and mortars, and automated weapons, and so on, to support the ground fighting, which is the systematic locus of all historical wars. As such, what is a war without the weapons of war? And what is a novel of war without the weapons of war? Responsively, of course, there is no war without weapons of war, and novels sans the weapons of war are not novels of war. By chronological order of war, *The Red Badge of Courage*, *One Man's Initiation*, *Company K*, *Through the Wheat*, *Beach Red*, *Band of Brothers*, *Hold Back the Night*, *The Things They Carried*, and *Desert Norm* each present extended registers of the weapons and equipment of war, conjunctive, of course, to each war's historical era. By presenting this system of era- and war-specific equipage of war, the authors are (without meaning to do so in some cases) juxtaposing the Civil War warrior's tools with the World War I warrior's tools with the World War II warrior's tools, and on through the Korean War to the Vietnam War to the Persian Gulf War. Each war is of a different era, and each war is fought with different tools of destruction. So, the gross artillery and the musketry and muzzle-loading riflery of the U.S. Civil War are contrasted with the massive artillery and machine-guns and grenades and gas of World War I, which thereby are contrasted with the automatic hand-held weaponry and wired radio communication of World War II, which are then contrasted with the helicopters and wireless radio communication of the Korean War, which are contrasted with the wholesale helicopter use and jungle-war equipment of the Vietnam War, which are explicitly contrasted with the early satellite imaging equipment of the Persian Gulf War, and so it goes, as goes war, which is never-ending in the history, present, or future of man. The business of war is killing, and business is booming. Further, by presenting this systemized and cumulative equipage of war, the authors of the American novel of war are juxtaposing the warrior's task with the farmer's or the carpenter's or the merchant's. The warrior's task, of course, is death and dying, and these are his tools. For example, in *Blood Meridian*, McCarthy's scalphunters are "armed with weapons of every description, revolvers of enormous weight and bowie-knives the size of claymores and short twobarreled rifles with bores you could stick your thumbs in" (78). Also mentioned in the text are horses, ammunition, powder, telescopes, lances, clubs, bows and arrows, and, not least, a howitzer. As well, food and water are present in the McCarthy text and are, necessarily, present in every novel of war, for warriors must always be fed and hydrated.

Relative to the equipage of war in the American novel of war, one must ask a set of questions. What, exactly, is the equipage of war? How is the equipage of war both war and era specific? Why is the equipage of war present in texts of war? How does the presence of the equipage of war differ from text to text? How does the presence of the equipage of war differ from era and war to era and war, and, as such, from era- and war-specific text to era- and war-specific text? What is the author's rhetorical purpose in presenting the equipage of war in an American novel of war? As examination will show, authors of American novels of war use the weapons and tools of war in different ways. Obviously, the weaponry and technology present in each war novel is shackled to the equipment and technology of the given war and era. That said, technology and weaponry do overlap from war to war, and, as Mark Grimsley notes, the U.S. Civil War "witnessed the early development and use of trench warfare, ironclad warships, rapid-fire weapons, and even airships and crude machine guns" (379), all of which are more commonly associated with World War I, of course. Further, as Philip K. Jason notes, Korean War novels "anticipate ... the themes of Vietnam War literature and include features that have been [incorrectly] singled out by Vietnam literature scholars ... as the unique, distinguishing characteristics of that war, at least as represented in literature" (122), features such as "the United States' misdirected pride in vastly superior technological capacity" (123), which is represented in *Band of Brothers* and *Hold Back the Night*, but also found in *The Things They Carried* and even *Beach Red*, a World War II tome. A belief in technical superiority can also lead to an incorrect — and often xenophobic or racist — belief in the ability to complete a war or a mission or a battle, secondary to technical superiority.

Another feature falsely attributed to one war but present in previous war(s) is napalm, the jellied gasoline found in nearly every Vietnam War novel (or film, for that matter); as Jason suggests, long before novels of the Vietnam War were published, "the largely unread novelists of the Korean War wrote of napalm and its horrors" (127). Again, the Bowman text uses weaponry created specifically for dispersing fire against humans — the flamethrower (first commonly used in World War I, actually) — and the Frank work prefaces the Vietnam War literature by using a weapon of war more commonly associated with the latter war and the literature thereof: "Worse than anything else, the Chinese feared napalm" (172). So, clearly, one must be careful when one assigns specific weaponry and equipment to specific wars. Nonetheless, wars beget technological advances, and as such, conversely, one can assign specific tools to specific wars — poison gas and World War I, or the atomic bomb and World War II, for example. Relative to the presence and use of the equipage of war in modern and postmodern American novels of war, a number of structural cum rhetorical uses can easily be identified. Some authors, such as Tim O'Brien with *The Things They Carried*, use extended catalogs that list many components of the equipment and tools of war — the things the grunts carried. Some authors, such as John Dos Passos in *One Man's Initiation*, insert war-specific equipment throughout the text, never explicitly articulating the equipment's use other than through the equipment's use in the actions of the text, yet other authors of texts of the same war, such as William March and Thomas Boyd, in *Company K* and *Through the Wheat*, focus on the use of a specific weapon of war. Ernest Frankel in *Band of Brothers* and Pat Frank in *Hold Back the Night* both use a non-lethal tool of war for rhetorical effect. Other authors, such as Terrence D. Haynes in *Desert Norm*, explicate in great detail an MOS — Military Occupational Specialty — specific piece of equipment or tool or mechanical process. As such, different authors, through different texts, which involve different wars, present the equipage of war quite differently — rhetorically and structurally — which is to be expected, of course.

In addition to being one of the first modern American novels, Stephen Crane's *The Red Badge of Courage* is the first modern American novel of war. As such, the work is the first literary presentation of the weaponry of modern war, and while the work does not explicitly catalog the weaponry used by the North during the Civil War, the text does offer glimpses of the modern, mass-produced weaponry. Rifles, muskets, artillery, ammunition, water, and food are all, if not liberally placed in the novel, readily enough present for analysis. Crane introduces the modern weaponry early in the text, as Henry Fleming's regiment is moving from their winter encampment in Washington, D.C., toward battle at Chancellorsville, Virginia: horse-bound "equipment" (15) jangles as the regiment moves, and "surly guns" (16) creak, and a man falls and reaches for his dropped "rifle" (16), and on the bodies of men "also came the tinkle of equipments" (16). In a few words, Crane clearly and specifically identifies a number of important aspects of Civil War–era equipment of war. Mounted cavalry are present, as is evidenced by the jangling equipment of the horseman, and so living equipment — the cavalryman's horse, a living tool of mobility, and here of messenger service — is obvious in its presence. Also presented are mobile guns, artillery pieces to be used in battle. The word "gun" is a very specific word, and the term usually refers to a weapon, smoothbore or rifled, most likely muzzle-loading, that has a flat trajectory, whereas a mortar has a "high, arching" ("Artillery") trajectory and a howitzer has a medium trajectory. Commonly speaking, though, the term "gun" has been generalized to refer to artillery pieces on the whole, but at the time of the Civil War, the term "gun" referred specifically to an artillery piece with a flat trajectory. As such, Crane is referring to a specific piece of equipment here.

When Crane uses the term "rifle," he likewise is referring very specifically to a certain type of weapon. Up to the Civil War, and even during such, the shoulder-mounted small arms weapon was most often a smoothbore musket, an inaccurate weapon with a non-rifled barrel. With the advent of rifling grooves, shoulder-mounted weapons became much more accurate and were able to maintain accuracy up to a half-mile ("Small Arms"), rather than the previous seventy-five yards or so. Thus, Crane's use of the word "rifle" is a very specific usage, and it refers distinctly to a certain, accurate type of war equipment, which is mass-produced and much more available to the Union troops than it is to the Confederate troops. Yet the rifles Henry and his peers are carrying are muzzle-loaders, as is seen in the first scene of battle in the text (35–39), during which "the steel ramrods clanked and clanged with incessant din as the men pounded them furiously into the hot rifle barrels" (37). Again, Crane uses the specific term "rifle" as he describes the sounds and actions of the men reloading their spent rifles, reloading from the muzzles of the rifles rather than the breeches of the rifles. Most likely, the men are using the .58 caliber Springfield rifled musket, a muzzle-loading, rifled-barrel weapon that fired an early form of a round called a Minie Ball, which was actually a bulleted projectile, and a weapon not so readily available to Confederate troops — who were victorious at Chancellorsville, incidentally. It is likely the men carry the Springfield rifled musket because, in an earlier passage, Henry's weapon is referred to as a "musket" (22). Thus, Crane uses both rifle and musket, and shows the muzzle-loading of the weapon, identifying the weapon without actually naming it.

Crane also sees fit to list general equipment the men carry going into battle, such as "thick shirts ... blankets, haversacks, canteens, and arms and ammunition" (21), and "hats"

(22), and sandwiches of "cracker and pork" (27). And the men drink and eat (38–39) before and during battle, while "guns squatted in a row like savage chiefs … [and] Batteries were speaking with thunderous oratorical effort" (39), and Henry watches as in the distance "tiny riders were beating the tiny horses" (39) they rode. So, while the Civil War saw the "employment of observation balloons and of the torpedo, the extensive use of the telegraph [and] the battle between the Monitor and the Merrimac" (Crawford, "Civil War" 91), what Crane gives the reader is a historically verifiable, land-based infantry battle, supported by artillery and cavalry, fought by men using the new but not avant-garde military equipment of the day, war, and era. Crane gives the infantryman's necessities—food, water, ammunition—and he offers the utilized and current war weapons of the day—the rifle, the gun, the bulleted projectile. In so doing, Crane offers the reader the equipage of war, circa 1863.

John Dos Passos' *One Man's Initiation* is very much a transitional text, one born of *The Red Badge of Courage*, yet very much the result of World War I. However, as an early modern text (and similar to *The Marne* in this way), the work is neither as brutal nor as explicitly cynical as are *Company K* and *Through the Wheat*. Nonetheless, Dos Passos' American novel of war is an excellent primer for the equipment of World War I —circa 1917. Dos Passos salts his text with the weapons of World War I, and as such, the reader gets a sense of the omnipresence of the weaponry unique to the First World War. In the text is a sampling of many types of war equipment, liberally presented, so that the literary effect is an argument for the always proximal equipment of war as well as the proximity of death. Paragraph one of chapter one introduces the military theme with "khaki uniforms" (9) and men and women and a band on a New York wharf, seeing the young men off to France and to roles in World War I; Martin Howe, the protagonist of the text, is among "the ambulance men" (17) who will deliver the wounded and dying of France and Belgium to aid stations so that the wounded can be saved and the dying can die. Even on the passage across the Atlantic, rumors of German gas and gas attacks are scuttlebutt: "There's nothing they can do against this new gas…. They say their skin turns green and that it takes five to seven days to die — five to seven days of slow choking" (12). Not coincidentally, German gas and the prevalence of gas attacks are present in most of the novels of World War I, and the motif of gas and the gas attack runs through the Dos Passos text. The obvious effect is that the men are afraid of the gas, more so than of other weapons of war — not without reason, of course, as the lingering, choking effects of gas upon a man are gruesome. Once in-country, however, a more relevant and more commonly deadly weapon is introduced to the ambulance men, who are on their way to their billets: "At a station where the train stopped … they could hear a faint hollow sound in the distance: guns" (22). Dos Passos introduces the artillery, and for the rest of the text, artillery and the tools thereof are a constant presence in the text, and Dos Passos seems to be arguing that World War I was a war of massive artillery bombardments, which it was, of course: "They … watched the flashes in the sky northward, where artillery along the lines kept up a continuous hammering drumbeat" (31–32). The artillery never stops.

But World War I was also a war of airplanes and aerial warfare, and these tools, new to man and new to warfare, are also introduced early in the text: "the wail of a siren woke Martin suddenly…" (23), and someone says, "It's Boche planes…. They say one of their planes chased an ambulance ten miles along a straight road the other day, trying to get it with a machine-gun" (23). As he introduces the aspect of mechanized air warfare to the text, Dos Passos, in passing, also introduces the machine-gun to the text, another piece of equipment that came into vogue during World War I. Thus, early in the text, Dos Passos pragmatically presents a number of types of war equipment commonly associated with World War I: mustard gas, artillery, airplanes, and machine-guns. As nine million soldiers were killed in World War I and twenty-one million wounded, the tools that made "such a vast number of casualties possible were advances in warfare like heavy artillery, automatic rifles, airplanes, [and] poison gas" (Miller 99), but "the weapon in World War I novels that most commonly came to symbolize the deadly mechanization of modern war was the machine gun" (Miller 99). The Dos Passos text is set among the ambulance service, so the presence of the machine-gun as a weapon of slaughter is not as obvious as it is in *Company K* and *Through the Wheat*, but clearly Dos Passos is well aware of the machine-gun: "Suddenly from the [trench] lines came a sputter of machine-guns" (35). However, the omnipresence of artillery is a more available weapon of war in the text. Artillery is everywhere and always, Dos Passos argues: "Black night. All through the woods along the road squatting mortars spit yellow flame. Constant throbbing of detonations" (83). As do most war novel authors, Dos Passos has common equipment listed, too: "helmets ... [rifle] gunbarrels ... boots ... camions ... ravitaillement ... ammunition " (26–27), and the like, as well as knives (41) and hand-grenades (54) and dressing stations (45) and ammo dumps (45) and packs (64), bayonets (96), and so on. As Martin Howe, like Dos Passos, is an ambulance man, the reader is not offered the intricate and detailed presentation of the equipage of war in *One Man's Initiation* that one finds in other World War I texts—even relative to the ambulances that the protagonists drive—which makes sense, of course, as a combatant will be more knowledgeable about the lethal equipment of war than will an ambulance driver.

However, in William March's *Company K* and Thomas Boyd's *Through the Wheat*, both of which were written by World War I Marine Corps combat infantry veterans, the exposition and cataloging of the equipage of World War I, especially the lethal equipage, is explicit, text-wide, and detailed. Further, the text-wide presence of machine-guns—on the ground and in the air—and the focus on often fortified enemy machine-gun nests clearly identifies the lethal threat of the World War I machine-gun, and the in-text repetition of the emplacements of enemy machine-guns and assaults upon those, and the devastation caused by the same, rhetorically identify the machine-gun as a psychological presence in the minds of World War I combatants long after the conclusion of the war. In addition to the motif cum thematic element of the machine-gun, and of course the common equipment carried by all troops—"packs ... boots ... ammunition, bombs, and shovels" (Boyd 20), "bayonets ... steel helmet[s] ... gas-mask[s]" (Boyd 14, 22), "rifles [and] food" (March 31, 38)—*Company K* and *Through the Wheat* introduce other equipment of war that gained wide use in World War I, such as the submarine (March 24–25) and the reconnaissance balloon (Boyd 8) and the tank (Boyd 186–89), and, of course, the airplane, here armed with machine-guns: "the planes ... came close to the road and sprayed us with machine guns.... They would swoop down suddenly and open up with machine guns and then dart up again out of range" (March 74–75, 120). And on the ground, during World War I, "the machine gun played an unexpectedly vital role in trench warfare ... and made it possible for a small number of soldiers to halt enemy offensives by inflicting massive casualties" (Heyman 28, 29). Further, "the firepower of one machine gun was the equivalent of thirty, or perhaps as many as sixty, individual riflemen" (Heyman 29), and after placing the machine-gun in a "stationary position, the machine gun's crew could calculate in advance the area the weapon was able to cover" (Heyman 29), and thus have a designated field of fire into which opposition forces would ambulate and then be destroyed: "We were returning from a wiring party that quiet night and the men were in high spirits. Then two Maxims opened a deadly, enfilading fire, and one of my companions threw his hands up and fell without a sound ... something took my breath away, and I toppled backward" (March 178).

Unlike Dos Passos, who mentions machine-gun fire but does so in passing, March introduces machine-guns early in the text (36), and he maintains the presence of machine-guns through the entirety of the work (44, 65, 75, 120, 122, 178), until the war is over on 11 November 1918 (183, 184). Machine-guns are a part of the daily life of World War I, and March explicitly sets forth this facet of the war. Even when Germans cannot be seen, machine-guns are present: "There wasn't a squarehead in sight, and except for the fact that they fired a machine gun every once in a while ... you wouldn't have known there was anybody ahead of us at all" (36). And the presence of machine-gun emplacements, "nests" (44), is a constant threat and a constant tactical objective: "Sergeant Tietjen was with me that day we took the machine gun nest in Veuilly Wood" (65); "We crept toward the machine-gun nest, each man with a grenade in his hand ready to throw ... the Germans discovered us and opened fire, shouting excitedly" (122). As a different Marine narrates each passage in the March text, it is clear that the machine-gun threat is experienced on a company-wide level and is a daily combat occurrence.

Interestingly, March, a Marine Corps infantryman, names the German machine-gun (using the generalized term Maxim — most likely an MG 08, a water-cooled, belt-fed weapon with a firing rate of 400 to 450 rounds per minute [Heyman 29]) only once in the text (178), but perhaps this non-naming is due to the 113 differently narrated vignettes that comprise the text. Would a private know the nomenclature of the German army? Perhaps, perhaps not. The only soldier who names the German weapon is the narrator of the "Unknown Soldier" passage (178–82), whose rank is not offered, of course, and who dies in the scene and is interred in the tomb of the same name. But in *Through the Wheat*, Boyd names the machine-gun used by the Germans—again the Maxim (76, 107, 113)—and the machine-gun used by the Americans—the Hotchkiss (78, 121). Boyd also refers to the devastation brought on by German airplanes equipped with machine-guns: "German bombing planes ... arrived above the advancing men and began to drop bombs and fire machine-gun bullets at them. The bombs reported as noisily as the seventy-seven-millimeter guns, but they made only a shallow hole in the ground. More devastating were the machine-gun bullets which zinged off the steel helmets of the men or bored their way through to the skull" (193). As in the March text, the machine-gun attacks by airplane come when the Marines are on the move and out of the relative safety of the trenches. As well, in a scene in which William Hicks fantastically considers going over the top of the trench and into no man's land in order to capture German prisoners so as to avoid discipline from an officer for sleeping on duty, he also refers to the danger inherent in attacking machine-gun nests: "There were plenty of heroes who could [take the emplacement]. They'd just fill their pockets with hand-grenades and blow up a machine-gun nest" (31). Of course, Hicks' fantasies of heroic deeds come to a halt when he is desensitized to the carnage of battle.

What Boyd offers that March does not is the presence of American machine-gunners. In the March text, the presence of and threat from machine-guns comes from the Germans, and much of the text is focused on attacking German machine-gun nests, but Boyd offers a brief glimpse into the American machine-gun company: "After manœuvering around for a couple of hours ... they had been joined by a section of the machine-gun company that was attached to their battalion. In a measure, this annexation was responsible for their slow progress. There were carts to be hidden, and then the men of the machine-gun detail carried their guns and their ammunition in their arms" (86–87). Positively, having a machine-gun section empowers an infantry company and equalizes the combat; however, negatively, having a weapons section means having heavy equipment that must be moved, first in wheeled vehicles and then by hand and foot, which is time consuming and cumbersome, and thus slows the infantry's movement. Further, the power of the machine-gun, even or especially the German Maxim, is evidenced when Hicks appropriates one after a fight during which the German gunners are themselves shot (107), but ironically Hicks never gets to use the machine-gun, which is destroyed in an artillery barrage. And while March's novel goes beyond the end of the war, the war is ongoing at the close of the Boyd text, and as such, the machine-guns remain present, firing and killing: "Out of the stillness of the night a Maxim sputtered.... It was not long after the platoon had arrived on the level ground that machine-guns began pouring a steady stream of lead over the field.... Then, like an express-train rattling over loose ties, machine-guns broke loose from all sides" (239, 258, 262). Explicitly, Boyd (and for that matter, March), argues that if there is the combat of World War I in the trenches, in the woods, in the fields, in the villages, there is the machine-gun, and there is machine-gun fire, primarily German machine-gun fire from the Maxim MG 08. It is obvious by the omnipresence of the machine-gun motif or thematic element in these two important and historically accurate texts of World War I that the combat equipment of the First World War that left a devastating psychological impact upon the two combat veteran authors was the machine-gun.

While Peter Bowman's World War II work *Beach Red* does contain "machine gun nests" (18) and artillery and tanks, and the other requisite equipage of war — "G.I. clothing and equipment" (4) — no one component of the equipage of war is omnipresent enough to rise to the prominence of a thematic element. What Bowman does do with the equipment of war in his text, however, is place a wide variety of common tools of war, such as "combat pack ... rifle ... steel helmet ... maps" (3), "ammunition ... field rations ... canteen ... water" (31), in conjunction with World War II era–specific items of war such as junglesuits (4) and the amphibious transports (Higgins boats, Alligators, and Buffaloes [5]), so that the reader of 1945 would gain a real sense of the tools utilized by the American jungle warriors engaging in an island assault against Japanese forces. As Bowman's work is set over a period of sixty minutes and comprises cadence lines that represent the timing of the assault, there is no traditional over-narrator to serve as a go-between or to explain actions, equipment, character motivations, and so forth. As such, there is no explication of the uses and purposes of specific tools of war, but for the functioning use of the tool or tools within the action(s) of the text. So, Bowman does not explain that naval vessels bombard the island prior to the amphibious assault in order to soften up the Japanese defenses; rather, he writes, "There is the rich, resonant cough of the Navy's guns, / as trim cruisers and destroyers clear their throats and spit" (7). This is poetic diction of a sort, a sort of quasi–Alexandrine, but what is more important here is the presence of naval vessels specific to the Second World War and the campaign in the Pacific. Also specific to the naval war in the Pacific are "battleship[s]" (3) and troop "transport" (3) ships, and "carrier-based divebombers" (7) and even the text's title, "Beach Red" (7), which is the color-designated name of the beach upon which the primary characters and "three battalions" (13) are landing.

After the landing, more weapons of war are identified, and the tools of the infantryman replace the vessels of the navy: "rifles ... machine guns ... the 4.2 mortar ... the bazooka" (13), "bullets [and] grenades" (14, 15). Some things new to the literary equipage of war are the flamethrower — a tool that offers "invitations to hell" (20), but was first regularly used by the Germans in World War I — and the "BAR" (25) — the Browning Automatic Rifle —

which was created by John Browning for World War I, but was not introduced until September 1918 and so is not found specifically or commonly in the literature of the First World War (although in the final scene of *Through the Wheat*, Hicks carries an "automatic rifle" [256, 261, 262, 265], but the weapon is not explicitly identified as a BAR). Another contemporary piece of war equipment new to the literature of war is the "CE-11" (48), a "lightweight, portable communications unit" (49) with which a reconnaissance patrol will maintain contact with its command unit. Portable communication is an excellent and useful tool of late-modern war, but what is not so excellent, especially when viewed through the prism of the postmodern era, is the fact that the device uses a spool of wire, which must be unspooled as the patrol advances in the jungle. Thus, if the Japanese forces, who are also patrolling the jungle, locate the wire on the jungle floor, the Japanese can either cut the wire and hunt the reconnaissance patrol down, while also severing the patrol from its support, or — if numbers allow — follow the wire, in either direction, to locate the main American position and also the patrol. Upon locating the wire in the text, the Japanese choose the former option, and sever the wire: "You hear a strangled distortion over the telephone and then / silence. 'Did you say something, Captain?' There is no answer / and your mind is bludgeoned with comprehension. They cut it!" (89–90). The Japanese then ambush and kill the two remaining members of the patrol (93, 122) — two more sacrifices to the "meat-chopper" (109), Bowman's term for the machine of war. Ironically, in this situation, the new equipage of war, wired communication, directly contributes to the deaths of those utilizing the technology.

Paradoxically, while new technology can contribute to the death of its users, old technology can save the lives of its users. For example, socks and gloves, while not commonly associated with the equipage of war, are war tools, and can, under certain circumstances (such as when worn by infantrymen during the hostile cold of November and December in Korea), save one's life. Further, for an infantryman, the feet are the biomechanical tools through which he practices his trade. As such, an infantryman who has foot problems cannot fulfill his role as a groundpounder, and most likely will not survive combat. Additionally, an infantryman with foot problems (in this case, frostbite secondary to the savage Korean weather) is a drain upon his peers, as he might lose his ambulatory ability, and thus need to be carried, which, of course, takes two men out of active and immediate fighting capacity. Also, one who is gloveless in the Korean elements, one whose fingers are frozen, or stiff from cold, cannot use the fine motor skills it takes to place one's index finger within the trigger-guard of a personal weapon and effectively fire that weapon, be it a pistol, a rifle, or an automatic weapon. In Ernest Frankel's *Band of Brothers* and Pat Frank's *Hold Back the Night*, in addition to the Korean War–era weaponry present in the texts (of which, there are numerous and varied examples), the presence of socks and gloves within scenes, and the importance of such items in time of warfare in the Korean cold, is a recurring motif. Thus, the low-tech equipage of war, socks and gloves, contributes to survival and facilitates success in battle. So, the casual but repetitive use of the sock and glove motif in both texts signifies the importance of socks and gloves relative to fighting effectiveness and survivability in the extreme cold of Korea.

In the Frankel text, the Korean weather is mentioned from the first line of the novel — "The marines lay on the cold ground at the crest of the ridge" (5) — and the use of the sock and glove motif is offered early in the text, as Able Company First Sergeant Wally Goober thinks to himself, in reference to company Executive Officer Lieutenant Joe Anderson, "Skipper ought to be wearing his gloves.... Damn' cold" (18). So, clearly, gloves offer protection against the cold, but heavy winter gloves, while necessary, also are cumbersome and interfere with one's work or normal range of motion: "Pat held out his hand. Huckabee started to take it, hesitated, removed his glove, and grasped the hand firmly" (22); in this case, an Anglo captain offers his hand to an African American enlisted man, who, perhaps because of politeness, degloves and shakes hands. Thus, gloves, while protective, can be social barriers. A glove can also be a useful tool, in lieu of a handkerchief: "The tip of his nose dripped, and he wiped it on his glove" (35). As the glove motif runs through the Frankel text, there is a repetition of the cumbersome nature of the gloves juxtaposed with their necessity: "He [Captain Bill Patrick] took off his gloves, rubbed furiously at his face and eyes" (109), and "His hands were freezing. He held them against his mouth, blew on them, rubbed them together. His gloves were gone" (119). Late in the text, "The first sergeant was searching his pockets ... but his hands worked clumsily, and he had to take off his gloves" (194). So, gloves, while in the way for fine motor tasks and abrasive when rubbed against the face, nonetheless save one's hands for such activities. Frankel's use of the sock half of the sock and glove motif is even more casual, but also repetitive: "Goober pulled a dry sock and continued the massage [of his feet]" (50), and Lieutenant Anderson "tugged at his socks and tightened his boots" (55), and "Lock was taking off his shoes and socks" (82) in order to warm his feet by a fire, and while cleaning weapons and maintaining equipment, "Horse changed his socks" (85). Even later, a grunt named Sanchez squeezes "the water from his sock" (241) and, sans a dry replacement, returns the sock to his foot and reboots. What is clear, then, is that the maintenance of the feet is a matter of life and death, a matter of survival to those who spend their military lives fighting on foot. To let one's feet decay or get frostbitten is to commit professional and literal suicide. Frankel does not present this rhetoric specifically, for he does not need to. A close reading of the text and an awareness of the sock and glove motif will suffice.

In *Hold Back the Night*, Frank also utilizes the sock and glove motif in conjunction with the savage Korean winter, but he does so in a more explicit and developed manner than Frankel. As the text opens, Dog Company has lost 160 men to the Chinese (10), and only sixteen men remain alive (2). Further, their jeeps are "frozen solid" (2), and the temperature "must be twenty below" (3). The cold is life threatening, and the Dog Company CO, Captain Sam Mackenzie, has had the foresight to prepare for the cold and for the maintenance of the men's feet. As the scene progresses, Mackenzie thinks about the necessities for fighting from the Chosin/Changjin Reservoir to the port of Hungnam: "[He] wondered how many things he had forgotten. The socks, of course. He reached under the back seat of the jeep and pulled out the last bundle of clean, dry socks. Two pair he took for himself, and then he tossed the bundle out into the road and shouted, 'All right, men, come and get it!'" (13). The socks are necessary equipage of war if the remaining infantrymen of Dog Company are to manage their ambulatory movement to safety. The grunts' feet must be protected and maintained, even though the men would rather remain immobile and semi-frozen: "They moaned, and swore ... but there was nothing they could do about it ... they took off their shoepacks, and the clammy socks they had worn through the night, and rubbed each other's feet for five minutes, and put on the clean socks" (13–14). Captain Mackenzie, unlike the ill-prepared Captain Patrick in *Band of Brothers*, is well aware that for an infantryman, foot safety is life, and thus, before the Chinese attack, he had "gone scrounging for extra socks. When they had fought their way out of the trap at the reservoir, Dog Company's vehicles carried five times as many socks as a company should" (14). He could accept combat casualties, if necessary, "but he'd be damned if he'd yield casualties to the weather. He'd be damned if one of his men would lose a foot to frostbite. So every morning, and every nightfall, no matter what else happened, the men changed their socks" (14). Mackenzie is a good officer, and Frank is allowing this fact, early in the text, regardless of the massive combat casualties that Dog Company has suffered. In war, combat casualties are inevitable, but in war, even a war that takes place in a frozen wasteland, weather casualties can be avoided with cogent forethought.

Later in the text, in a scene that retraces the run up to the battle at the reservoir, the sock search is articulated: Mackenzie "dispatched Sergeant Kirby to the regimental supply dump with instructions to scrounge all the extra socks he could find" (75). Part of the prelude to battle is, of course, gathering the tools of war, and obviously Frank, via Mackenzie, argues that socks are tools of war; the repetition of the scenes of scrounging for socks is evidence of such. Even the Chinese are aware of the importance of foot maintenance, and a captured lieutenant notes to himself that the Chinese fighters are "all freshly shod" (91). The sock motif, per Mackenzie's optic, runs text-wide, and the importance of socks to foot safety is never left to the reader's memory: "He counted the first-aid kits, and the bundles of socks, and the entrenching tools" (188). Note that the socks are framed by first-aid kits and e-tools, both of which are used to save men's lives; the first-aid kits are, of course, to be used on combat casualties, and the entrenching tools are used to dig fighting holes and foxholes, in which the men can be shielded from enemy small-arms fire and mortar fire. Socks, like first-aid kits and e-tools, save lives, and even when the men are completely physically and psychically exhausted, Mackenzie makes them maintain their feet: "They moved until Mackenzie's legs would move no more. The collapse of his men was immediate. He had to kick them to their feet to force them to change their sweat-soaked socks" (204). For their own good, for their feet, and for their survival, Mackenzie must compel the men to take care of themselves; this is life-saving leadership under severe duress.

While Frank develops the sock motif at length, he does not do so with the glove portion of the sock and glove motif. Nonetheless, he does briefly include the glove motif, in a scene of castigation whereby a fellow officer is labeled a traitor and coward, a bane to the company: "When Sellers came closer, the captain saw that the hands at the ends of the forearms were blackened, frozen lumps. 'I lost my gloves, sir,' Sellers said. 'You lost your gloves!' It was incomprehensible ... for if you lost your gloves there was a pretty good chance that in this cold you would lose your hands. And there were spare gloves. Mackenzie had always insisted on that, just as he insisted there be enough dry, clean socks so that every man could change morning and night" (128–29). In this brief, but telling, exchange, Frank juxtaposes an efficient, professional officer with an inefficient, unprofessional one, and in so doing, does not absolve the officer ranks from incompetence. Further, Frank continues to elevate Captain Mackenzie for his pre- and peri-battle efficiencies, and also conjoins the sock and glove motif in a scene that clearly shows the weather-related result of failing to utilize the proper equipage of war in time of severe winter weather. Comprehensively considered, *Band of Brothers* and *Hold Back the Night* are rhetorically unambiguous — socks and gloves are unequivocally life-saving equipage of war.

In the opening and title chapter of *The Things They Carried*, "The Things They Carried" (1–26), Tim O'Brien offers perhaps the most varied and most comprehensive in-text catalog(s) of the infantryman's equipage of war. Categorizing the lists by necessity, by rank and field specialty, by "whatever seemed appropriate as a means of killing or staying alive" (7), by mission, by superstition, and by individually chosen miscellania, O'Brien creates an infantryman's ethos, while he also serves to educate the reader, and, in so doing, is didactic without being pedantic. In the equipment catalogs, O'Brien also shows the physical weight of the infantryman's fighting equipment, while he offers the other weight(s) the grunts carried—the weight of the allowance to kill or be killed, and all of the power and fear thereof. O'Brien begins his calculus with the category of necessity: "Among the necessities or near-necessities were P-38 can openers, pocket knives, heat tabs, wristwatches, dog tags, mosquito repellent, chewing gum, candy, cigarettes, salt tablets, packets of Kool-Aid, lighters, matches, sewing kits ... C rations, two or three canteens of water ... steel helmets ... [with] liner and cover ... fatigue jackets and trousers ... jungle boots [on their feet] ... a steel-centered, nylon-covered flack jacket ... [a] compress bandage ... a poncho" (2–3). All of the equipment listed in this first catalog is general and non-specialized, and every grunt in Alpha Company carries this equipment, so the physical weight is evenly distributed among all members of the company. However, O'Brien's next catalog is rank and field specialty specific, and as such, shows individualization among the men. Thus, individual men carried individual burdens: The platoon leader, a first lieutenant, carried a "compass, maps, code books, binoculars ... a .45 caliber pistol [and] a strobe light" (5–6). The radioman carried a PRC-25—AKA, a Prick-25—and its battery. The medic carried "a canvas satchel filled with morphine and plasma and malaria tablets and surgical tape ... and all the things a medic must carry" (5). The machine-gunner humped the M-60 and its ammunition in belts. The "common grunts" (5) carried the M-16 and its ammunition in magazines, and some humped the M-79 grenade launcher too, and its ammunition. Again, nothing in this second catalog is too unique or personalized, so O'Brien is still preparing the reader using standard Vietnam War–era infantry equipage.

O'Brien's third catalog diverges a tad from the first two, as the grunts carried "whatever presented itself, or whatever seemed appropriate as a means of killing or staying alive" (7): "M-14s ... CAR-15s ... Swedish Ks ... grease guns ... AK-47s ... Chi-Coms ... RPGs ... Simonov[s] ... Uzis ... LAWs ... shotguns ... blackjacks ... bayonets ... C-4 ... [and] fragmentation [and] smoke [and] tear gas [and] white phosphorous grenades" (7). With the emphasis on automatic weapons and sundry types of hand grenade in this catalog, the business of killing comes forth, as well as the appropriateness of appropriation. Whatever can be used to kill effectively and quickly is utilized, regardless of whether the weapon is born of American or Russian armories. If a specific article of the equipage of war kills well, it will be well appropriated and well utilized. O'Brien then offers mission-specific equipment of war—that equipment not commonly carried, but useful contingent upon the platoon's or company's missions in the mountains, or in especially hostile areas, or on ambush and night patrol, or in tunnel searches, and so forth. For the mountains, they carried "mosquito netting, machetes, canvas tarps, and extra bug juice" (9); if an area was mined, they brought a mine detector; on ambush, they brought "claymores" (10), and on night patrol, a "starlight scope" (9), and on tunnel destruction, they carried "pentrite high explosives [and] detonators [and] clackers [and] earplugs" (10), and a handgun and a flashlight for the tunnel mole—that man who had to explore the tunnel(s) before the platoon detonated the tunnel with the pentrite.

As O'Brien adds to the catalog-by-catalog listings of the equipage of war the men carry, he juxtaposes the literal tools of war with the emotional weight the men carry so that with each list, the equipment weight the men carry grows greater, as does the psychological weight: "The things they carried were determined to some extent by superstition" (13). The tools of killing, such as they are and as effective as they may be, are not enough to offset the fear brought on by the nature of the work at hand. Thus, a grunt also will carry a (hopefully) lucky pebble, or a rabbit's foot, or a thumb taken from an enemy decedent (14); each of the three items in this mini-catalog are completely individualized, personal, focused on and specific to an individual man. But with the final catalog, O'Brien broadens the optic to complete the catalog series by again offering a generalized list of items that most, or all, of the grunts carry: "USO stationery ... pencils ... pens ... Sterno ... trip flares ... fingernail clippers ... bush hats ... empty sandbags ... Bronze Stars and Purple Hearts" (14). O'Brien's in-text series of catalogs, a sort of catalog of catalogs, is uniquely comprehensive and begins with the general, then moves to a series of specifics, then returns again to the general. The result is the education of the reader relative to the tools of war carried by the common grunt during the Vietnam War, tools that are manifest physically and are used for killing. Additionally, O'Brien adroitly juxtaposes the manifest weight the men hump with the latent weight the grunts carry, the psychologically and emotionally burdensome weight of life and death experienced daily.

However, an American novel of war need not present entire catalogs of the equipage of war to be effective in the rhetorical presentation of the equipage of war. Terrence D. Haynes' *Desert Norm* uses in-depth exposition of a single, highly technical tool of war — map-making and reproduction of satellite photographs of enemy positions in a "mobile mapping unit" (104) — to present a noncombatant's role in the effective engagement of focused combat. Haynes' narrative protagonist, Specialist Marcus Norm, is a topographer whose job is to take satellite photographs and reproduce the documents as maps and pictorial images so that the graphic replications can be disseminated to pilots for precision-bombing prior to the Persian Gulf War ground assault. As Norm says, "We map 'em; you zap 'em" (106); that is, with postmodern weaponry such as satellite imagery and nearly instant reproduction and dissemination, "to see the target is to destroy the target" (Bishop and Phillips 160), and so, "It's not just bullets and bombs that take lives in war, it's paper, too" (105). The maps and facsimiles the topographers create from the satellite photographs are to be used in "bombing sorties in which thousands and thousands of people were to be killed or wounded" (106). But Norm's goal, of course, is to reproduce the satellite graphics precisely, as an error "might mean dead civilians because some of the photos showed enemy soldiers placed in city settings" (109), and prior to starting this mission Norm prays, "Forgive me, God, for what I am about to do" (108). Then, Norm gets to work, and he takes the satellite photographs and transports the images onto printing plates, which are then developed, and which will be taken to a printing press to make hundreds of copies of the scaled photographic images (109–10). The prints will then be circulated to pilots for use in bombing sorties. The chapter closes with Norm's self-statement of culpability: "I am a soldier in the United States Army and I have done my sworn duty. I acknowledge that in a few hours I will have blood on my hands and will have to deal with it" (110–11). Specialist Norm, a highly religious individual, a technically skilled individual, pulls no trigger, lays no ambush, loads no weapon — literally, that is. But he knows that he is culpable for human death in a time of war, not through a role in the combat infantry but through his use of postmodern technology, technology used to make the killing of human beings a more effective and more efficient act.

Clearly, then, the tools and equipment and weapons of war — the equipage of war — are consistently and diversely placed in the American novel of war. Each war introduces new weapons with which and by which men can destroy one another, so ever-evolving technology is created and utilized. As such, there cannot be war without the weapons and tools of war. And there cannot be novels of war without the weapons and tools of war.

Chronologically, in order of war, *The Red Badge of Courage, One Man's Initiation, Company K, Through the Wheat, Beach Red, Band of Brothers, Hold Back the Night, The Things They Carried*, and *Desert Norm* each present extended war-relative registers of the warrior's weapons and tools of war. Every war is of a different era, even wars separated by only a few years (as in the case of World War II and the Korean War), and every war is fought with different tools of destruction. The business of war is killing, and business never slows or devolves, so the carnage continues, while the weapons and tools evolve. With each successive war, there is technological innovation, and there are more efficient ways to kill. By presenting this systemized and cumulative equipage of war, the authors of American novel(s) of war identify the warrior's task as one born of blood, and his tools are the tools of blood.

So, returning to the chapter-specific questions—What is the equipage of war? How is the equipage of war both war and era specific? Why is the equipage of war present in texts of war? How does the presence of the equipage of war differ from text to text? How does the presence of the equipage of war differ from one era and war to a subsequent era and war, and as such, from era- and war-specific text to era- and war-specific text? What is the author's rhetorical purpose in presenting the equipage of war in an American novel of war?—one can offer chapter-specific responses. Clearly, sundry authors of American novel(s) of war use the weapons and tools of sundry wars in sundry ways. The weaponry and technology present in each war novel are relative to the historical era during which the war takes place, and there is a cumulating effect upon the equipage of war as technology evolves from era to era and war to war. The equipage of war is the equipment warriors use to kill and to live, so this includes weapons as well as food and water and transport, and even socks and gloves. And of course, any novel of war must have the tools and weapons of war or it is not a novel of war, and any author of a novel of war must have a clear and comprehensive understanding of the equipage used in the war during which the work is set so that he or she can properly illustrate the equipage of war in the text, for nothing is so ersatz as a novel of war sans the proper weapons and tools of war. Thus, in *The Red Badge of Courage*, artillery and rifled musketry are liberally present, and in *One Man's Initiation*, there is a text-wide listing of the new and modern weaponry of World War I. In *Company K* and *Through the Wheat*, the machine-gun is an ever-present and deadly threat, and in *Beach Red*, peri-battle wired radio communication between Command Post and the reconnaissance patrol is offered and is a contributor to its users' deaths, while in *Band of Brothers* and *Hold Back the Night*, the pragmatic but lifesaving importance of socks and gloves is repeatedly offered. In *The Things They Carried*, the jungle warrior's equipment catalog is itemized at length, and finally, in *Desert Norm*, satellite photography and the nearly immediate dissemination of the information thereof contributes to accuracy of mass killing.

Rhetorically, the authors of these texts have different purposes, too: Crane's is the presentation of the new tools of warfare in a modern war-scape, and Dos Passos' is the exposition of the modern tools of killing, while March's and Boyd's is to argue the terrifying and effective threat of the machine-gun, and Bowman's is to show the paradox of new war technology, and Frankel's and Frank's is to demonstrate the necessity for basic articles of clothing in calamitous weather, and O'Brien's is to present a didactic primer on the tools and weapons of the Vietnam jungle-based grunt, and Haynes' is to argue that one need not pull a trigger to have blood on one's hands. Commonly, though, each of these authors, through the American novel of war, and regardless of war or era, effectively uses the equipage of war as a thematic and necessary element in their work.

VI

Death of Fighting Peers

In war—in any and every war—fighting peers die. Without fail, in the American novel of war, a significant number of allied combatants—named and unnamed, primary as well as secondary—will die, individually or *en masse*, before the close of the text. *Blood Meridian*, *Band of Brothers*, *Hold Back the Night*, *Matterhorn*, and *The Short-Timers* each has a diminishing cast of friendly characters (as does every text in this study), so one of the common thematic elements in a novel of war is this diminishing cast of fighting peers. For example, in *Blood Meridian*, a remarkable number of scalphunters, as well as filibusters, do not live until the end of the text; in fact, all are gone by the Epilogue but for Judge Holden and perhaps Tobin, the ex-priest. The filibusters and scalphunters are killed in battle; are shot, stabbed, hanged, and mortally wounded in a variety of ways; are captured and tortured and killed; are ambushed and sniped; and (occasionally) kill each other. The two Korean War texts, *Band of Brothers* and *Hold Back the Night*, contain a remarkable number of dying peers, named and unnamed, on the page and off, and in each text, American combatants die by the hundreds—or historically, the thousands—as 1st Division Marines of X Corps attempt a strategic but unbelievably brutal withdrawal through overwhelming numbers of Chinese and North Korean forces from the Chosin Reservoir to the Port of Hungnam. Conversely, the two Vietnam War texts, *Matterhorn* and *The Short-Timers*, contain a limited number of peer deaths, and the deaths concern named characters, characters with whom the reader is involved. It is not that the deaths of primary and secondary characters in *Band of Brothers* and *Hold Back the Night* are lacking in pathos, but a number of character deaths in *Matterhorn* and *The Short-Timers* are especially shocking and emotionally evocative. Thus, fighting peers die in all wars, and the American novel of war must and does present this facet of war.

A look at the numbers of combatant deaths by war reveals an obvious fact: War kills human beings, and as such, in the American novel of war, fighting peers must die. While the following numbers are approximations, the numbers include all deaths secondary to war service; thus, the comprehensive death totals include combat deaths as well as deaths caused by other means—disease, post-wound infection, vehicle crashes, accidents, heat and cold, indigenous fauna, and so on—and the numbers are stunning. In the U.S. Civil War, at least 623,000 combatants died (Linderman 125); in World War I, a war in which an average of 6,046 men died each day (Das 55), at least 112,000 American combatants died (Heyman 236), and in World War II, at least 400,000 American combatants died ("American War Deaths Through History"). In the Korean War, at least 54,000 Americans died (Ehrhart and Jason xiv), and in the Vietnam War, at least 58,000 Americans died (Ehrhart and Jason xiv). Of course, these numbers reflect only the American deaths relative to each conflict.

These numbers reflect what D.R. Sharma calls, in a discussion of *The Red Badge of Courage*, "the monstrous reality of war" (57), a reality of mass and common death, first brought forth in the Crane text by the ongoing motif of the dead soldier — both enemy and ally: "Once the line encountered the body of a dead soldier. He lay on his back staring at the sky" (24); "Under foot, there were a few ghastly forms motionless" (38); later, in the woods, skedaddler Henry "was being looked at by a dead man who was seated with his back against a columnlike tree" (49), and even later, "A dead soldier was stretched with his face hidden is his arm" (52); still later, Henry's friend Jim Conklin goes from being the tall soldier to the "doomed soldier" (60) to the dead soldier (61). According to Sarah Cole, writing in reference to the literature of World War I, "In the West, the story of war is almost always the story of males bonds" (138), because mass modern "armies seem particularly to invite an emphasis on intense masculine friendship, in part because those armies, with their enormous scale and their capacity both to inflict and to suffer extreme violence, present a challenge to the self-concept of the societies they are meant to represent and protect" (138). So, through the combat death of Jim Conklin, Henry's friend, Crane is creating a literary motif based on the reality of friendship in early modern war. The death of a fighting peer and friend is as timeless as war, and yet the scale involved with modern warfare intensifies the role of friend in both war and war literature. As Cole notes, in World War I and in the literature produced thereof, especially by war veterans, "Individual friends were killed in the ordinary course of the day, and the concept of friendship was treated with contempt by a bureaucracy that ceaselessly and arbitrarily separated friends from one another" (148). Thus, war "assaults friendship" (148) in two ways—friends are killed in combat and in war duty, and friends are separated in service. Of course, the former issue is central to this chapter and this discussion: as a matter of course, peers—friends and fighting companions—die in war and in the American novel of war.

Why and how do men and women die in the course of war? The etiology of death in war can be obvious or opaque. In the outstanding study *Daily Life During World War I*, Neil M. Heyman argues that for Americans who served in the First World War, death began at home, thanks to "America's lack of preparation for combat against the Central Powers" (23), which meant that "need to move men quickly through training and then send them abroad took precedence over actual instruction" (25). As such, many arrived in France "never having fired a rifle" (25). Battlefield tactics also contributed to the deaths of many uniformed Americans, as fighting in "closely aligned formations against German machine-gun fire" (25) led directly to "rows of corpses on the battlefield, the bodies close together in regular lines" (25). So, history and historians note that, in addition to necessary violence and battlefield casualties born of combat, inappropriate training methodology and faulty tactical praxis leads to the deaths of combatants. But how do authors of novels of war — specifically, American novels of war — use the deaths of fighting peers as a thematic device in the literature? What are the authors arguing, and how are the deaths in the literature born of the authors' military or combat experiences? For authors writing historically, such as Cormac McCarthy, how does known — albeit somewhat obscure — history influence the text of war? Can history or autobiography be separated from the fictional work or war? For example, how are Joseph Heller's World War II experiences reflected in *Catch-22*? In his fascinating and important article, "Joseph Heller's Combat Experiences in *Catch-22*," Michael C. Scoggins shows, through archival evidence, criticism, and Heller's own writings and interviews, that many of the characters (particularly those who die in the text), are based on Heller's World War II peers. The death of Snowden, a text-wide thematic element, is "a synthesis of several of his [Heller's] own combat experiences" (218), two of which resulted in American planes being shot down, and one of which resulted in the radio gunner — Snowden's flight crew role — being hit by anti-aircraft artillery — that is, flak (219); further, during another mission, a radio gunner was badly wounded in the abdomen. Heller aided the former man, who survived, but the latter man, like Snowden, died from his abdominal wounds. In a later episode in the novel, Milo Minderbinder bombs the American airbase, but historically, the event is based on a German raid that used a captured British plane as a "friendly" pathfinder to lead German bombers and fighters to Alesan Airfield, Heller's base on Corsica, which resulted in 22 Allied deaths (221–22). Additionally, a number of other peer deaths in the text (for example, that of Mudd, a pilot who never checks in and is killed on his first mission, but whose gear remains in Yossarian's tent as a reminder of the ongoing thematic element of peer death) are based on Heller's combat experiences, so obviously, the war veteran author's experiences are reflected in the American novel of war, and these experiences must, and do, include the deaths of peers in the combat zone. In war, peers die, and this facet of war is reflected on a thematic level in the American novel of war, regardless of whether the text is based on history and is retrospectively written, as is *Blood Meridian*, or if the texts are written by veterans of World War II but are of legendary combat of the Korean War, as are *Band of Brothers* and *Hold Back the Night*, or if the texts are written by veterans of the war covered, as are *Matterhorn* and *The Short-Timers*.

In *Blood Meridian*, Cormac McCarthy's masterwork of violence, history, and war, fighting peers die at a common and continual rate as first the filibusters die after an attack by the Comanche, and then the scalphunters are killed off through a variety of violent means. Necessarily, fighting peers must die, given their warring ways, and their deaths are thus inevitable but not necessarily without irony, and the thematic element of the death of fighting peers runs the length of the text (44–333). In the first scene of broad violence and peer death in the text, the kid, a wandering and violent sort, joins Captain White's band of filibusters to take the post–Mexican-American War fight into Mexico, but fighters begin to die off even before the battles begin. As 46 men enter Mexico, four are soon dead from cholera (45), so, ironically, disease kills prior to violence. And, of course, the filibusters have come to take Mexico from the Mexicans — and the Europeans — but instead are confronted with the Comanche: "A legion of horribles, hundreds in number" (52), attacks the filibusters, and in the battle, all are killed but the kid and seven others (56). So, in one scene of exquisite violence (52–52), 34 men are killed, less the four from cholera, so eight, including the kid, remain. Sproule, one of the eight, is wounded and dies from post-wound infection after suffering greatly (69), so seven remain. Captain White ends up in a jar of mescal (more specifically, his head ends up in a jar of mescal) (69–70), so he too is dead, and then there are six. The kid ends up in a jail with three other living filibusters, so four are left after it is confirmed that the Mexicans have killed "Clark and another [nameless] boy" (70). Thus, quite quickly, McCarthy has killed off 42 — mostly unnamed — souls, and in a variety of manners: pre-combat disease, combat violence, and post-combat infection, decapitation, and nonspecific murder. To survive the journey to battle is a feat in itself, and then to die in battle, against an enemy other than the planned enemy, is death by irony, and to survive the battle with wounds but then to die from infection is common for the era but agonizing for poor Sproule, and to escape massacre to die at the hands of the Mexican authorities — who are aware of the filibusters — is apt, but also ironic in that one survives a massacre, yet is killed in the "safety" of escape. Once the scalphunters — "a pack of vicious-looking humans" (78)—enter the text in their assigned duty (78), the kid, along with Toad-vine and Grannyrat—who are not filibusters—join the gang for their government-con-tracted Apache eradication mission (79). Thus, of the 46 filibusters, three filibusters are unaccounted for and are left in the jail at Chihuahua, and one moves on to continue his peregrination of war, violence, and death.

Again, though, death comes not at the hand of enemy combatants but here starts within the family of killers, which, actually, is not that surprising. In the company of scalp-hunters, there are two men named John Jackson, "one black, one white" (81), and the scal-phunters soon begin to wager upon who will kill whom. In a dispute over which campfire black Jackson should reside at—the fire with the newbies, the Delaware scouts, and the lone Mexican scalphunter, John McGill, or the fire with the Anglo veterans—white Jackson threatens to shoot black Jackson, who, in return, "bearing a bowieknife in both hands ... swapt off [white Jackson's] head" (107). Internecine violence does not end with the death of white Jackson at the hands of black Jackson. Gannyrat (AKA Granny, AKA the veteran, AKA Chambers), who has straggled from the outfit (104–5), which apparently is not allowed, is caught up with and killed by a pair of the Delaware scouts, who then return to the troop with his effects, which are mostly burned—but for his horse and rifle (112). So, as with the filibusters, even before their numbers are thinned through combat, scalphunters die. And as with the filibusters, violence is not the only means of death, as, in a scene that strains credulity, a Delaware is carried off by a bear: the animal "seized the Delaware and lifted him from the horse ... and loped horribly into the forest with his hostage and was lost among the darkening trees" (137). With the motifs of non-combat and internecine deaths that McCarthy posits in the first half of the text, the author is advancing the thesis that life in a nexus of war is a life spent in conjunction with death and that the readiness of death depends not merely upon enemy combatants but is proximal at all times and in all situations, and thus there is no safety, ever, for these men of war and massacre. In a scene in which the scalphunters slaughter an encampment of Gileños, peri-combat death finally comes to a scalphunter, and the Mexican John McGill (AKA Juan Miguel) is killed: "He had been skewered through with a lance and he held the stock of it before him" (157). Finally, nearly halfway into the text, a scalphunter dies in combat, in mission. And it is noteworthy that Miguel is the only scalphunter killed in battle under the original Chihuahuan scalphunting contract. It also bears mention that Glanton dispatches the mortally wounded Miguel (157) and has him scalped (159). However, the next peer death is another non-combat death, as a scalphunter named Grimley is stabbed in the back by a drunk in a Nacori cantina, and thus offers, "I'm killed" (178), and he is.

As such, before their contract with Governor Trias is cancelled, and they themselves become wanted (185), the total number of scalphunter deaths secondary to combat and to their contracted war mission with the Apache is one—Juan Miguel, who is mortally wounded by a Gileño but shot by Glanton. Hence, scalphunter death is not uncommon, but ironically, so far in the text, scalphunter death, secondary to hunting scalps, is. Of course, though, scalphunters continue to die violently, but not as contracted scalphunters. In a scene of bloody mayhem — is there any other sort in *Blood Meridian*?—set in the town of Jesús María, the scalphunters, now identified by the narrator as Americans, leave "six of their number behind" (194), at least four of whom are unnamed and dead, as they evacuate the town under gunfire. Later, three more members "of Glanton's party" (205) are killed in a running battle with the Sonoran cavalry, who then mass with 500 troops, with whom they will hunt down the former scalphunters. After the fight, four arrows are drawn so that each winner/loser will have to kill one of the four wounded men, as wounded men slow down running men. Two of the wounded are Delawares, so a Delaware relieves the men who had drawn the lots of their duty and dispatches the two wounded Delawares with his warclub (206); the third wounded man, an unnamed Mexican, is mortally wounded and will die anyway, so his assigned killer, Tate, leaves him to die, but the kid, who is assigned to kill the fourth, a man named Shelby, leaves him, unarmed and somewhat hidden, to live or be killed by the Mexican cavalry (207–8) — a dishonorable and irresponsible act. Pages later, Tate and the kid are attacked by a scout party under General Elias' command, and Tate, while not killed in the text, is seen no more (211–12); in the desert, four more men die (218), one named Sloat. And then four more are gone, the last two Delawares and the Vandiemenlander (AKA Bathcat) and a man named Gilchrist (227) — all of whom have been tortured and killed by the Apache. So, while the former scalphunters are still meeting violent death — at the hands of Mexican civilians, and at the hands of one another, and at the hands of the Mexican cavalry and the Apache — the number of deaths directly attributable to their originally contracted combat duties remains at one.

Their numbers continue to diminish, however, as Glanton is killed (275) in the Yuma massacre (273–76), as are Smith, Dorsey, and black Jackson (286), so, at this point in the text, and nearing the end of the adventure — but not the end of historic American violence, of course — five men of the original 21 who left Chihuahua under contract remain alive: Judge Holden; the kid; Tobin (AKA the ex-priest); and David Brown and Toadvine — both of whom are subsequently hanged on 11 June 1850 in Los Angeles (311). Then there are three, until the judge kills the man (AKA the kid) (333); then there are two, or perhaps only one, only the judge, as Tobin's whereabouts and existence are not clarified in the text. The judge, however, remains alive; of this last living combatant, this immortal metaphor for historical American violence, the reader is aware. So, in the McCarthy text, a consummate American novel of war and one that uses every defining characteristic of the American novel of war but for the oppositional dyad between officers and enlisted men, broad numbers of fighting peers die and do so comprehensively. Of the original company of 21 men — 19 men (148) plus white Jackson and Chambers — textual evidence allows that only the judge remains alive at the close of the adventure. Thus, in *Blood Meridian*, 42 of 46 filibusters die (43, if one includes the kid), and 20 of 21 scalphunters die (if one includes Tobin); that death count, numerically speaking, is a fine example of the death of fighting peers in the American novel of war.

In the American novels of the Koran War, *Band of Brothers* and *Hold Back the Night*, Ernest Frankel and Pat Frank, paradoxically, offer many more peer deaths than does McCarthy in *Blood Meridian*, but each Korean War author shows far fewer peer deaths on the page. Coincidentally, in both texts, field-important junior officers are killed in action, and not coincidentally, as each text is based upon the same historical moment — the 1st Marine Division's November-December 1950 strategic retreat from the Changjin/Chosin Reservoir to the port of Hungnam and the Sea of Japan — hundreds or even thousands of unnamed fighting peers are killed off page. Frankel begins the motif of the deaths of the unnamed early in the text, after a named character, Monk Nelson, is shot and killed by a POW named Kao Teh (36). Six days after the shooting, the company officer force — three platoon commanders and the XO, First Lieutenant Joe Anderson, and CO, Captain Bill Patrick — talk socially about their past and similar Marine Corps–related experiences, travels, and "the marines — now dead — they had known" (40). All of the men have known Marines who were killed in combat, but Frankel does not explicate the scenarios of death, nor does he name any of the dead. They are dead Marines, and all living Marines know, or knew, dead Marines; such is the business of the Marine Corps. Later in the text, just prior to the massive Chinese attack of 27 November, after an enemy mortaring, "two limp green bundles lay unmoving in the snow" (66). Frankel does not name the men; he does identify their deaths, though. Immediately thereafter, from another position, Lieutenant Allison reports over the radio: "Two dead" (67). Again, the dead peers are unnamed. Then, "A marine sat beside him [Captain Patrick], the one the men called 'Pappy.'... The man was dead" (71). In the same battle scene, a radioman is cut down; "I didn't even know his name" (71), Captain Patrick says. The man's name was Demette, but he was unnamed to the captain; as well, even though another dead Marine was nicknamed Pappy, his real name is not produced for the reader. Frankel continues this act of non-naming as the battle is concluded; two artillery rounds have fallen short and have killed Marines, men who have died anonymously. The unnamed artillery officer says, "'Short round. Nobody's fault.' But there were the bodies of the dead" (76). All told, after the battle, "eight marines lay stretched side by side" (81). And so the reader is introduced to the combat of the Korean War and to the nameless, faceless Marines who die in the Forgotten War. By not naming these dead men, Frankel is illuminating a "terse realism" (Axelsson 94) of war: men die on a gross level, and the men dying are men identified by service — Marines — and combat role — radioman — rather than by name.

As the text continues and the combat intensifies, many, many more men die — unnamed infantry Marines, of course, Marines who die while fulfilling their combat role(s): "[A Chinese tank gunner] fired a stream of tracers. The bazookaman crumpled" (100); a sniper fires, and "the wireman dropped ... he was dead" (111); Lieutenant Anderson notes, "We've got nineteen dead" (112); after the battle, Captain Patrick counts the bodies: "Nineteen.... The dead differed from each other only in the size of their protruding shoes" (114). Even when Frankel introduces the Army to the text, the motif of the unnamed dead remains: "Five miles away, across the glassy face of the reservoir, fingers of flame clawed the sky. Dead lay crumpled along the road.... A soldier lay cowering in a ditch.... Beneath him, surrounding him, were dead men.... He had dragged [the wounded] to the ditch where they died" (119). Frankel continues this motif of the unnamed dead, and while doing so, Frankel's narrator comments on the situation of being killed in uniform in a war zone: "Another death and another and another reduced the importance of death in the abstract" (176). When a company commander has 250 men (177) to direct, and is under attack by thousands of Chinese forces, that company commander must dehumanize the dead, even those with whom he was close, or else he will become distracted and will fail in his mission. Further, when a reader is introduced to a war thousands of miles away, the reader, too, cannot become distracted as the war rages; the reader, like the company commander, must stay on task and not be distracted. The safety of the company is what is important, not the individual lives of the fighting peers. As such, Frankel kills off many, many Marine grunts and not a few Army legs, who die as they lived and fought — as nameless men in uniform fighting a massive battle in the frozen Korean weather. Arne Axelsson calls to attention (94–95) the baseball team analogy used by Lieutenant Anderson in a rant against the civilians back in the United States (141–43) to note that Frankel, the author, through Anderson, argues that civilians watch a war as they do a baseball game — the warriors are a team in uniform, not individual human beings. When this point is noted, it is clear why Frankel refuses to name so many of the dead; he is doing so in protest against American civilian ambivalence.

Like Frankel, Pat Frank does not necessarily name names when most of an entire company is wiped out—by page 1 of the text, no less. While the Frankel text opens before the Chinese assault of 27 November 1950, the Frank text opens after the hasty retreat of the 1st Marine Division—as a part of X Corps—is well begun, and the men of Dog Company have already gone from the Changjin/Chosin Reservoir to Hagaru to Koto-Ri "and beyond" (2), and their company, by this time, has lost "a hundred and sixty-odd men" (10); thus, the text is set in the second week of December 1950 (Axelsson 92). Frank's text opens as Captain Sam Mackenzie awakens from a dream to find himself still in the frozen steppes of Korea; he then checks on the company wounded but finds "the three wounded were mercifully dead" (2). As with the Frankel text, the dead are unidentified by name or, at this point, even by rank or role or service. What is important to note, though, is that the men are "mercifully" dead, as if their position is better than being wounded and alive. Sadly, and pragmatically, the three dead cannot be carried out, so the remaining 17 men do not have to retain and hump the bodies, which, by the way, is against the Marine Corps credo—if possible, Marines do not leave their dead. However, one must note that severe times demand severe actions, such as leaving the dead, which is unfortunate. In a later scene, the narrator refers to the dead as "the bodies" (14), so, again, the men are not named nor are their military roles or ranks identified.

Later in the text, in a scene set before the opening scene, in a moment of reflection, Captain Mackenzie notes to himself "that everyone of [his] junior officers, without exception, was dead" (34). In so doing, Frank does something a bit unusual in a combat novel: he kills off the junior officers without first naming them—but for Lieutenant Raleigh Couzens, who is earlier (3–4) named as one of the three dead from the opening scene of the text. Not naming officers is a slight of sorts, as rank usually befits naming, but not in this case, as the dead are equal in death, but in life, leadership is needed—hence the captain's concern. Other unnamed dead in the text include a B-26 bomber crew who die when shot down at the Inchon landing (68), and sundry men who die after the Chinese attack: "two more had died" (115); "three men, dead" (117); "seventeen dead [sergeants and lieutenants]" (120); "twenty-one dead" (175). Something that Frank does that Frankel does not is specifically label a group of 17 sergeants and lieutenants among the numbered dead. To lose 17 NCOs and junior officers—who remain unnamed, of course, but for their ranking roles—is to lose the entire command structure of the company; as such, the loss leaves the company with a head—the captain—and body—the grunts—but no central nervous system to coordinate communication and movement.

Of course, while both Korean War texts utilize the unnamed dead peer motif, the authors of *Band of Brothers* and *Hold Back the Night* each identify many of the fighting peers who are killed in combat, two of whom are company-level junior officers—one a company executive officer, the other a platoon commander—and with these deaths, there is poignancy on the part of the narrator as well as tragic emotion on the part of the characters within each text. In *Band of Brothers*, the doomed executive officer of Able Company is First Lieutenant Joe Anderson, who was the interim company commander prior to Captain Patrick's arrival. Of course, this usurpation of command role creates tension between Anderson, who is a seasoned combat veteran, and Patrick, who is green to combat and to combat leadership. Under fire, of course, the men follow Anderson, who is a leader and who jeopardizes his life in battle, with cause, to motivate and lead the men. The Marines address Anderson as "Skipper," but the ranking company commander is Patrick, who, through the course of the text, must earn the moniker. As the text opens, the company first sergeant identifies Anderson as "the best skipper in the division" (6) and Patrick as a "pogue" (6).

Though resentful of Patrick's position, Anderson attempts to field-school Patrick in the ways of battle leadership. Of course, any astute reader can foretell that Lieutenant Anderson — wronged, heroic, resentful, but professional and dutiful — is as doomed as a literary character in a novel of war may be. Thus, after the inevitable fisticuffs between the two skippers (171), a brief fight during which the captain tags the lieutenant a number of times, and immediately after which a Chinese artillery barrage begins, a shocked and infuriated Lieutenant Anderson runs from the scene and toward a deserted warming-tent: "A blast ripped the snow before him, and the deserted warming-tent disappeared. Andy was down" (172). And then a second round hits. All that remains of First Lieutenant Joe Anderson, the psychological Skipper and guts of Able Company, is "a bloody parka hood and a pink glaze on the snow" (172). Ironically, even though the death of Anderson devastates the company — the company first sergeant cries — his death creates the opportunity for Patrick to lead without interference. As such, Patrick is allowed to lead, and is forced to lead, as the Marines' lives immediately depend on Patrick's leadership abilities and the results thereof. Paradoxically, while Anderson was trying to aid in Patrick's evolution as a battlefield commander, he was also, concurrently, interfering with Patrick's role as company commander and with Patrick's leadership evolution.

In *Hold Back the Night*, the relationship between Captain Sam Mackenzie, Dog Company CO, and First Lieutenant Raleigh Couzens, commanding officer of 2nd Platoon, is conjunctive rather than oppositional and built upon mutual respect rather than mutual tension. Mackenzie and Couzens are both veterans of World War II, and from the onset of the text, Mackenzie is identified as an extremely capable leader. Couzens, who is dead when the text opens but alive in back-story mode, is held briefly by Chinese forces and then released, and subsequently wonders if he has said anything treasonous to the Chinese (he has not), but his greater fear is losing the respect of Mackenzie: "He would rather lose anything than lose Mackenzie's respect and friendship. He would rather lose his life" (192). Mackenzie feels the same way about Couzens, and he personally mourns Couzens' death: "the argumentative southerner who had been his friend, and tentmate, and the reliable leader of Second Platoon" (3–4), and who, "for no good reason ... had thrown away his life" (4). Couzens, under-armed and the last man standing in a patrol of five men, assaults a house in a small village and is shot multiple times by the Chinese occupants of the house (201). Mackenzie is horrified by Couzens' actions, but only the reader knows that Couzens feels that he has betrayed his nation and his captain by saying a negative word or two about the United Nations and President Truman to his Chinese interrogator, Colonel Chu (97–107). So, as the text opens, Captain Mackenzie feels as if he unnecessarily has lost his closest friend to battle, but he has lost not merely a friend, but a battle peer, one who is also battle hardened and wizened. Thus, in both novels of the Korean War, but under very different social and command circumstances, the company at hand loses an important and skilled officer, an officer who knows combat tactics and who also is a psychological point of strength for members of the company.

In *Matterhorn*, Karl Marlantes also sees it as rhetorically fitting to kill a fighting peer who is the guts, the heart, and the soul of a fighting company. In this case, the man is a Super Grunt nicknamed Vancouver, a massive Canadian who has come south to the United States in order to join the Marines and to fight in Vietnam. Marlantes begins the fighting peer death theme with the generalized, early text motif of anonymous death: "four Marines had been killed in action" (6), and then the NVA shoots down a CH-46 and the entire crew dies (10), and then word comes that Alpha Company has had "four killed" (11), and again, there is mention of the same four dead — "four Coors" (33). So, in this way, Marlantes, whose text is very much — stylistically and structurally — a modern American novel of war written in the postmodern era, follows the Korean War texts cited above, in that the text opens with a number of deaths of unnamed peers, with the dead identified by service and MOS (Military Occupational Specialty) or role — Marine infantrymen and helicopter crew-members. Further, Marlantes includes the point that the company of focus in the text, Bravo Company, had never gone into the jungle on an extended operation "without at least three deaths" (125). So, the danger of service and the presence of death are clearly articulated in the first quarter of the text. Marines die in Vietnam, often anonymously; such is life in the Marine Corps in war. Marlantes also includes a number of non-combat deaths, as regional disease and fauna aid in peer death: possible pneumonia (145), death by tiger (158), and even "cerebral malaria" (238). Clearly, the jungle of Vietnam is a hostile environment, and the NVA are not the only life-threatening elements to be found there. So, while men, unnamed and then named, die as the text progresses (as one would expect in a novel of war), and plenty of Marines die in the larger battles in the final half of the text (also expected), there is one character's death that devastates the men of Bravo Company and serves as a rhetorical item of impact upon the reader.

That impact death, that death that devastates the characters and the reader, is the death of Vancouver, the Canadian turned Marine. According to the Canadian Broadcasting Company, in a sort of un-draft dodging, "30,000 Canadians volunteered to fight in Southeast Asia" ("Canada's Secret War"), and of the 15,000 to 18,000 who served in Vietnam — in the American armed forces — 110 were killed in action. And so it is with Vancouver, who has come south to the Marines in order to come to Vietnam, and who consistently volunteers to walk point, and who refuses leadership, and who is also the best warrior and fighter in the company (60). As Marlantes notes through the optic of Lieutenant Mellas, Vancouver, who by himself humps an M-60 plus ammo, plus 100 pounds of other grunt gear, and wears his tattered uniform and jungle rot and leech bites with pride, "was a bush Marine" (80). And Vancouver is exceptional in combat, a Super Grunt, one who could be in Force Recon if he so chose, but who likes the action of being a regular 0311 — the MOS designation for Marine Corps Infantry — on point in the jungle on search-and-destroy missions, rather than being a recon man on Snoop and Poops. What makes Vancouver an asset to the company, besides his volunteerism — to serve and to act as point on patrol — is his instinctual fighting ability. On point when the NVA are waiting in ambush (171–73), Vancouver is alert enough to notice "an oddly bent piece of bamboo" (171) and begin a rapid-rate of fire with his M-60, which saves him and the patrol. Later, on a night mission, Vancouver, on point again, as usual, first spots — senses? — NVA fighters, and fires his M-16 into the enemy patrol, once more firing first and saving his peers (252). Vancouver is, by instinct, a tremendous fighter, and he is, by action, a warrior. When Bravo Company is ordered to retake Matter-horn (366) and, once on the mountain, must fight hand-to-hand, Vancouver fights savagely, killing a number of NVA with his M-60 before being shot and having his left humerus shattered. Nonetheless, and one-armed, Vancouver pins down the oncoming NVA rein-forcements with his M-60 as Bravo Company men advance from NVA-occupied fighting hole to fighting hole. Of course, Vancouver is shot again, and eventually, he uses his "Gook sword" (63) to hack two NVA machine-gunners to death (373), and he is shot again, and again. With "his face in the mud" (373), Vancouver dies, looking "like a dog that had been run over" (375): "It was as if the company's soul had been taken away" (375). The psycho-logical toll of Vancouver's death upon the members of Bravo Company is severe. The unit feels weakened. Nonetheless, as with Able Company in *Band of Brothers* when faced with the death of Lieutenant Joe Anderson, unit cohesiveness must be maintained—especially under duress—and the mission (in this case, to abandon and then re-retake Matterhorn), must be completed. In an infantry company, no single man, not even a Super Grunt like Vancouver or an exceptional battlefield commander like Anderson, is bigger than the unit or the mission, and both Marlantes and Frankel illustrate this tactical and true rhetoric.

Death of peers in combat can and does come at the hand of the enemy, and, as occurs in *Band of Brothers*, death of fighting peers can also come by the hand of one's own allies, as is the case with the artillery that falls short and kills a number of Marines. In *The Short-Timers*, Gustav Hasford shows that death of a peer by a peer can come in a number of other ways. As previously shown, there are a number of "mercy" killings in the text—killings whereby Marines must kill mortally wounded Marines so that the wounded do not suffer more than is necessary. Additionally, there are Marine-on-Marine deaths by accident (129) and by fragging (106). In the text, Hasford is explicit: It is dangerous to be a Marine in Vietnam. In fact, it is life threatening to be a Marine in Vietnam, and the threat comes not only from the Viet Cong and NVA, but also from other Marines, who can kill their peers accidentally or on purpose. First, accidental Marine-on-Marine homicide: Rafter Man, Joker's friend and combat photographer, is run over by a tank (129), which is ironic, as in a previous scene, the same tank, led by the same blond tank commander, runs over a Vietnamese child (78–79). In the latter scene, Rafter Man and Joker are ambulating down Route One toward Phu Bai when "the deck trembles" (128) as a tank is bearing down on the pair. Through the tank's sight blocks, the driver can see the pair and swerves, but Rafter Man "pulls away" (128) from the immobile Joker, and the "tank runs over Rafter Man and crushes him beneath its steel treads" (129). Just like that, Rafter Man, a named and important character, is cut in two and wiped from the text. The suddenness of Rafter Man's accidental death is Hasford's warning against complacency—the reader's and the warrior's. Hasford sets the scene—and sets up the reader—with a lighthearted tone, as Joker and Rafter Man casually diddybop down the road. Death comes suddenly, and ironically, foreshadowed by the previous accidental tank death. Rafter Man's death is also a sudden surprise to the reader, who is reminded that, in Vietnam, death is always at hand, lurking, never resting, never sleeping.

Death can also come with malice aforethought, as is the case with the fragging death of Mr. Shortround (AKA Lieutenant Robert M. Bayer, III), 1st Platoon's commanding officer. Mr. Shortround's death, like Rafter Man's, is foreshadowed. First, a short round is a mortar or artillery round that falls short, often upon one's peers rather than on one's enemies, as is the case in *Band of Brothers*. Next, Shortround and Animal Mother—an animal sort, of course, a Vancouver sans the social friendliness—have a spat over Animal Mother's propensity to rape the indigenous adolescent civilian women (91–92). As the scene continues, and the platoon is sniped, Animal Mother says, "Lifers never get wasted. Just the ones I frag" (106). Cowboy then tells Joker, "Mr. Shortround is KIA.... The platoon radioman was down ... took a sniper round through the knee. The Skipper went out to get him. A frag got him. A frag got them both" (106). Of course, in this situation, frag means two distinct things—one, a frag is a fragmentation grenade; two, to frag someone is to kill that person, usually an allied officer, often with a fragmentation grenade. Thus, the characters—and for that matter, the reader—are aware that Animal Mother has fragged the lieutenant, as well as the radioman, who was triply unlucky, what with carrying the radio, being sniped, and then being fragged. But if the reader is not well enough aware, later in the text, in the jungle,

Cowboy tells Joker, "Never turn your back on Mother.... He fragged Mr. Shortround" (173). Never, indeed. Hasford, as one would expect, and like those before him, also uses the unnamed dead peer motif through the text, and the work is littered with the bodies of dead Marines. As Joker notes, "In Viet Nam you see corpses almost every day" (130). But the thematic death of peers, by peers, is text-wide — including in boot damp, where Private Leonard Pratt (AKA Private Pyle) shoots Senior Drill Instructor Gunnery Sergeant Gerheim (30) and then himself (31). Marines — and Marine recruits — argues Hasford, are a danger to Marines, in combat and out.

Clearly, then, in war and in the American novel of war, fighting peers die. Every text in this study possesses a diminishing cast of characters — American combatants — so one of the common thematic elements in a novel of war is this great number of fighting peers who are killed as the textual combat is ongoing. In *Blood Meridian*, of the filibusters and then scalphunters, only Judge Holden survives until the Epilogue. In *Band of Brothers* and *Hold Back the Night*, a substantial number of American combatants die by the hundreds — or thousands, historically — as 1st Division Marines of X Corps execute a combat withdrawal from the Chosin Reservoir to the Port of Hungnam. Conversely, in *Matterhorn* and *The Short-Timers*, a limited number of peer deaths take place, primarily those of named characters whose deaths are especially shocking and emotionally evocative — both to other characters and to the reader. Most obviously, fighting peers die in all wars, and the American novel of war must and does present this facet of war; otherwise, the text is inaccurate, ersatz, and lacking in verisimilitude. The death of a fighting peer and friend is as timeless as war itself, but combat and the enemy are not all that kill during combat service — disease, post-wound infection, vehicle crashes, accidents, heat and cold, indigenous fauna, and peers all can and do kill allied combatants. But why, and how, do fighting combatants die in the American novel of war? And how do authors of novels of war (American novels of war, of course), use the death(s) of fighting peers as a thematic device in the literature? What are the authors arguing, and how are the deaths in the literature born of the authors' military or combat experiences? For authors writing historically, how does known history influence the text of war? And generally, can history or autobiography be separated from the fictional work of war?

Obviously, given the subject matter, there is a need for allied combatants to die in the novel of war, and all of the authors in this chapter aptly offer this necessity of war literature. And as offered above, allied combatants die in combat. But death is always lurking, is always seeking, so dying can come secondary to a number of contributing factors — disease, infection, accident, tiger. Thematically, the authors use the necessary theme of allied peer death quite differently. Cormac McCarthy, writing a metonymous history of the history of the United States, uses a text-wide panoptic of violence and death to present the history of the United States as a history of violence and death. Writing of the same battle, Ernest Frankel and Pat Frank (both veterans of World War II), in a parallel manner, promote the knowledge of the unnamed dead; further, each author also offers a calamitous loss in battle, a loss that temporarily decenters the Marines who go on living and fighting. In the Frankel text, the loss devastates the company but offers an opportunity for the green company commander to earn his command, and in the Frank text, the loss devastates the company commander, who cannot see the act as anything but a waste, a sort of combat suicide. Karl Marlantes also offers a loss that devastates a company; this loss is not at the command level but rather a grunt, a Super Grunt, actually. All three of these veterans cum authors explicitly argue, though, that the battle — and the war — must continue, and the unit must maintain its command and fighting cohesion. Finally, Gustav Hasford, who was obviously greatly affected by his service in Vietnam, makes it clear to all that it is dangerous (even lethal), to be around a Marine — even for fellow Marines. Perhaps Hasford is arguing as well that if one takes a boy and makes him a werewolf, the boy is forever gone, but the werewolf is forever present. In war, peers die, and this facet of war is reflected on a thematic level in all American novels of war, regardless if the text is based on history and is retrospectively written, as is *Blood Meridian*, or if the texts are written by veterans of World War II but are of legendary combat of the Korean War, as are *Band of Brothers* and *Hold Back the Night*, or if the texts are written by combat veterans of the war covered, as are *Matterhorn* and *The Short-Timers*.

VII

Death of Noncombatants

In war, and in the American novel of war, warriors are not the only people who die, of course: noncombatants die, too. On purpose and through accident, men and women civilians, children, entire families, and whole populations of villages and towns are killed, regardless of combatant — ally or enemy — secondary to the war, and irrelevant to the militarized lines of battle. The death of noncombatants is a facet in all wars, and a product of all wars. Therefore, must the death of noncombatants be a facet of all novels of war, and all accurate American novels of war? A number of texts in this study — *The Red Badge of Courage, The March, The Marne, One Man's Initiation, Johnny Got His Gun, Beach Red, The Naked and the Dead, It's Cold in Pongo-Ni, MASH,* and *Matterhorn,* for example — offer no direct noncombatant death, yet each is a prime example of the American novel of war. In nearly all of the texts that do not use the noncombatant death motif or thematic element, noncombatant death is implied through omnipresent destruction of villages, towns, and cities — areas sans civilian populations but not areas sans death. And in the texts of the Pacific Campaign, enemy combatant forces — rather than noncombatants — occupy strategically held islands, so there are no civilian noncombatants to speak of in those texts. And of course, in *The Red Badge of Courage* and *Matterhorn,* the text is centered primarily on specific battle(s) and combat missions; thus, civilians are rarely present in the works. But nearly every text that has interaction between noncombatants and uniformed forces in a combat zone has noncombatant death, and a number of the texts in this study generously, textually, and rhetorically offer noncombatant death at a thematic or noteworthy level. Relative to this chapter specifically, in *Blood Meridian, I Am the Clay, The Short-Timers, The Things They Carried,* and *A Medic in Iraq,* the life of a noncombatant in a war zone is most terrifyingly presented, and the texts show that, irrespective of era or war, or location of war, or lines of combat, or friend or foe, noncombatants in war zones die.

In each and all of these texts, both allies and enemies of those who try to exist in areas overrun by battle kill local peoples who are not armed and are not active participants in the war. As such, the strong and armed kill the weak and unarmed. But how do authors, per their novels of war, present the element of noncombatant death? And why? Do warriors within war texts slay noncombatants for different reasons? What are authors arguing with the textual element of noncombatant death? And how do the in-text noncombatant deaths differ from text to text, in situation, in purpose, and in numbers slain? For example, in *Blood Meridian,* Comanche, Apache, Yumas, and, of course, contracted scalphunters kill unarmed and noncombatant Mexicans, Gileños, Tiguas, and Anglos, in and out of this order, but the scalphunters — primarily Americans, of course — slay more than the others combined. In *I Am the Clay,* it is primarily the invading Chinese forces and the uniformed

North Koreans, as well as the cold, starvation, and disease, that kill numerous rural Korean civilian peasants, and a dead noncombatant peasant in a war zone is just as dead, regardless of the uniform worn by the killer(s) or the contributing cause of death. And in *The Short-Timers* and *The Things They Carried*, American weaponry in the form of tanks, air support, and infantry kills children, women, and old men, and the characters, through their behaviors, declare such deaths to be a routine element of the war in Vietnam. Meanwhile, the narrator of *A Medic in Iraq* laments the fact that Iraqi civilians, civilians not involved in the war effort in any way, cannot even function within the parameters of daily living activities, such as going to the market, without being blown up. In a war zone, routine daily activities are deadly, life expectancy is short, and families in a war zone do not survive the war intact. The parents, grandparents, siblings, and children of the local young men who are forced or volunteer to partake in war are casualties of the war, killed through combat or violent means, or other secondary causes, but are not counted as combat casualties. Human lives become, in the current rhetoric of war, "collateral damage," and the war goes on for all but the dead, while the living are not even allowed to properly mourn their lost family members.

Even though statisticians and scholars and federal entities readily acknowledge that civilian or noncombatant deaths during war are difficult to tally, and are often in debate, actuaries and historians and governments nonetheless attempt to do so, and the numbers are staggering. Karma Nabulsi argues, "For those who seek to mitigate the effects of violent conflict, the primary difficulty is still how to best protect civilians" (9). Really? While government and military propaganda machines might articulate a care for civilians, the reality of war shows that armed conflict on a mass level begets civilian deaths, most often in the name of the greater war effort. Further, noncombatants do not die merely from violence but also from disease, famine, and genocide. That said, historically and within the context of this study, noncombatant death is a byproduct of every war. In the U.S. Civil War, common estimates posit that between 100,000 and 200,000 civilians died during the internecine conflict. In World War I, estimates range from 6 to 13 million noncombatants dead, contingent upon whether one includes the Russian Civil War and the Armenian genocide. Estimates regarding civilians killed in World War II, a war in which "the civilian was now in the enemy's sights as much as the soldier" (Roseman 255), and in which "the enormous use of air-power had brought in its train immense destruction and had meant massive civilian deaths in strategic conflict" (Misra 73–74), number around 30 million ("World War 2 Casualty Statistics"). Numerically, World War II is especially horrifying. In addition to the more than 6 million Jews killed through the Final Solution, and the millions of Roma and Sinti, and homosexuals, and religious and political prisoners, and others whom the Nazis deemed "unworthy of life," civilians within combatant and victim nations were killed by the millions: China suffered a catastrophic 10 million civilian deaths ("World War 2 Casualty Statistics"), and in the first month alone of the Japanese occupation of Nanking, approximately "350,000 Chinese civilians" (Bradley 65) were killed as "the Japanese army ... slaughtered everyone in its way, including unarmed men, women, and children" (Bradley 59); the Soviet Union suffered more than 10 million civilian deaths, while 70,000 Soviet villages and 1,710 Soviet towns were obliterated (Roseman 255); Poland lost 3 million non–Jewish civilians—including Roma and Sinti — and 3 million Jewish civilians (Roseman 256); Yugoslavia, more than 1 million ("World War 2 Casualty Statistics"); Germany at least 1.5 million (Roseman 256), and Austria more than 145,000 ("World War 2 Casualty Statistics"); France, 400,000 (Roseman 255); Belgium, the Netherlands, and Rumania all lost between 100,000 and

200,000 civilians (Bradley 65; "World War 2 Casualty Statistics"); Japan, more than 300,000 ("World War 2 Casualty Statistics"), and more than 200,000 alone in the bombings of Hiroshima and Nagasaki (Bradley 65–66). And these numbers, of course, do not include the many countries that lost less than 100,000 noncombatants.

Post–World War II "police actions" and "smaller" wars and "regional conflicts" also tally noncombatant deaths. According to Robert Hass, "More than two and a half million people died during the Korean War" (9), including more than 800,000 South Korean civilians (Hass 9). And in the Vietnam War, "body-count" (Herzog 52) policies and American combatants who had "difficulty instantaneously deciding whether Vietnamese civilians, including women and children, were friends, foes, innocent bystanders, indifferent observers, or active participants in the war" (Herzog 52) led to human beings, including Vietnamese noncombatants, being "quickly reduced to numbers on a scorecard" (Herzog 53). The result of this military policy of "body counts equals victory" and ambivalence toward who was the enemy and who was not — "if dead and Vietnamese, then the person must be VC'" (Herzog 53)— was at least 2 million Vietnamese civilians dead (Shenon). Recent wars, even in the glare of the digital and omnipresent media, also include "collateral damage" (noncombatant death). According to NPR, more than 100,000 Iraqi civilians have died since the U.S. invasion of Iraq ("The Toll of War"). And relative to the war in Afghanistan, headlines such as "Pentagon: Air Strikes Likely Killed 26 Afghan Civilians" (Winter), and "Roadside Bombs Kill 12 Afghan Civilians" (Associated Press), and "Afghanistan: Civilian Casualties Up" (United Nations Missions in Afghanistan) are a common, nearly daily, occurrence in the U.S. media, and while the numbers are quite slippery, according to the United Nations Missions in Afghanistan, from 2006 through 2010 nearly 10,000 Afghan civilians were killed secondary to the war ("Afghanistan Civilian Casualties: Year by Year").

Regardless of the lines of battle, the death of noncombatants is a facet of all wars, and in *Blood Meridian*, Cormac McCarthy ably presents this facet of war, and the novel of war, as all sides kill noncombatants. Early in the text, and after the Comanche attack the filibusters, as Sproule and the kid wander the Mexican plain, the pair comes upon "a bush that was hung with dead babies" (57). This scene begins a motif of child murder, through which many children — noncombatants, of course — die, most at the hands of the judge (118–19, 164, 191, 239, 333), but the Delawares kill children, too (156), and so do marauding Indian parties: In a "village on the plain where ... all were gone to death ... there lay a dead child with two buzzards sitting on it" (57, 61). The entire village has been slaughtered, so the children are also dead, but why does McCarthy fixate on the dead child motif? Is it because children, as a matter of course, die in combat situations? If this is so, though, why the deaths of the children at the hands of the judge? In a number of settings, in towns where one could assume that children are safe, children go missing, but while the citizens of the town(s) search, the reader knows what has happened. In the totemic warning of the dead babies, who are fixed to a tree by their heads, there is a lack of randomness, a specificity of death, an end to life before the life cycle can begin. As such, the death at infancy breaks a natural cycle whereby one is born, grows up, procreates, grows old, and dies. And to kill all the infants, and to advertise such, is to extinguish the people, the race, the family, the clan, the progeny, forever, to dust. When the Delawares kill the Gileño infants by bashing their heads against rocks, they are doing so for a different reason, though, as Glanton orders every soul in the Gileño camp killed (155); commercially, of course, every scalp is a receipt, so every scalp — man, woman, child, slave — must be taken, and even dead peer Juan Miguel's scalp is taken (159). The judge, though — a pederast and pedophile — enjoys killing, and evidently particularly enjoys killing children. Manifestly murderous, Judge Holden seems to possess a compulsion to murder children apart from his efficacy in combat. The judge objectifies and dehumanizes children, traits best identified in a brief scene in which he seems to befriend an Apache boy, a child the narrator refers to repeatedly as "it" (164), before killing and scalping the child. As the text moves on, boys and girls disappear, and the judge is always near. And while the child murder motif is text-wide, the old are readily killed, too, as in one telling scene whereby Glanton executes "a weathered old woman" (97) for her receipt. So, for the scalphunters—the "partisans" (155)—commerce is killing, of course, whether the slaughtered are young or old, as each taken scalp is a payment. But for others in the text (the judge, marauding parties, etc.) who kill children in a time of war, their motivation might or might not be relative to their work and their practice of war.

Of course, as is their way, the scalphunters excel at their practice in the scene of the slaughter of the women and children and elderly Gileños. While there are a limited number of combatant Gileños in the band of 1,000 souls, what stands out in this scene is the joy that the scalphunters take in their work and how quickly the massacre encompasses all involved: "Within that first minute the slaughter became general. Women were screaming and naked children and one old man tottered forth waving a pair of white pantaloons. The horsemen moved among them and slew them with clubs or knives" (155–56). Meanwhile, on foot, others are "hacking at the dying and decapitating those who knelt for mercy" (156). After the slaughter, the scalphunters take the scalps of the dead and dying, and in so doing, collect proof of war; noncombatant or not, all are dead and all are in receipt. On the next pass though Mexico, "they would fall upon a band of peaceful Tiguas camped on the river and slaughter them every soul" (173). Again, McCarthy emphasizes the deaths of the non-combatants: "[The women] stood dumb, barefoot.... They clutched cooking ladles, naked children. At the first fire a dozen of them crumpled and fell" (174). After the massacre, "the dead lay with their peeled skulls like polyps" (174). The scalphunters move on and soon are killing and scalping the citizenry of Mexico; in Nacori, 41 Mexicans are killed and scalped, and in some nameless town, "people ran before them like harried game [and are] slain and scalped" (181). And clearly, even though the men are merciless in their massacres, and even though there is commerce at stake in the killing, and even though the scalphunters are in the business of war, the scalphunters have exceeded their rights in war, and they run with "the blood of the citizenry for whose protection they had contracted" (185). Thus, one must assume that the scalphunters thoroughly enjoy killing, business or not, and this joy is in evidence later in the text, after the Chihuahua bounty has been rescinded, when the scalp-hunters are on the run but nonetheless sign a contract with the governor of Sonora state for Apache scalps: "A few peons waylaid and slain. Two weeks out they massacred a pueblo on the Nacozari River" (204). The tone of these two sentences evokes the randomness of daily activity. Every day, noncombatants die when encountering the scalphunters, and the scenes of noncombatant death become shorter as the text progresses. Long and detailed massacres devolve to sentence-level statements of noncombatant death, as if the narrator is bored with the redundancy of the acts, as if the killing of noncombatants becomes com-monplace, hardly worthy of narrative attention.

While Cormac McCarthy's narrator follows the scalphunters as they slaughter hun-dreds of noncombatant Indians and Mexicans, noncombatants who remain nameless and voiceless, flat and dehumanized in their deaths, Chaim Potok, in *I Am the Clay*, writes from the optic of indigenous civilian noncombatants whose lives have been usurped and disrupted by war; as such, Potok humanizes those who are the victims of the war machine (AKA "the dragon" [49]), with emphasis on three of the displaced — an old man and his wife and a wounded, orphaned boy whose life they save. Potok juxtaposes the nameless dead, littered through the text, with the three narrative protagonists, only one of whom is named: Kim Sin Gyu, the wounded 11-year-old boy the elderly pair has adopted. Constant in the text are the effects of war upon the very old and the very young; the common, repetitive result, of course, is death: "Around a curve they went by an elderly man lying on his back on the side of the road. Eyes and mouth black holes. Dead a long time" (7). As the text is a story that focuses on refugees—currently and rhetorically known as "internally displaced persons"—attempting to escape the war machine as the Chinese and North Koreans push south, and as much of the text is initially set in the brutal Korean weather, noncombatant deaths by violence are not nearly as evident as deaths produced secondary to cold, starvation, exhaustion, and so forth. So, unlike the McCarthy text, in which armed marauders slaughter noncombatants, the unnamed noncombatants in the Potok text are often killed by the elements and the situation at hand. And when someone dies, he or she is left, like the elderly man above, "on the side of the road" (7): "Here and there bodies lay along the sides of the road" (13). Racing south, ahead of the mass Chinese assault of what must initially be November-December 1950 and then early 1951, the fleeing noncombatants are on a "panicky trek" (3) and are caught between the retreating American forces and the southbound Chinese forces. Thus, when someone becomes too weak to travel, he or she is carted, if there is a cart, and when one dies, he or she is left behind. As well, even those who can travel, once exposed to the cold, often die during the night: "In the morning he [the old man] ... saw that some on the riverbank had frozen to death" (19), and later, "Many died of cold that night.... The bodies were frozen into grotesque shapes" (23), and "two old men lay very still with their eyes open to slits" (34). Repetitively, the old are identified as the weakest of the noncombatants, at risk from the severe cold, but hunger kills, too, regardless of the age of the victims: "they would probably all die of the hunger that would soon ... settle upon their lives. Many already lay dead on the beach" (61). As the three travel, they see more dead: "propped up against a low boulder [was] the badly decomposed body of a woman. Stringy black hair; empty eye sockets" (97). Dead combatants, nameless, sightless, history-less, occupy the far-reaching frozen Korean countryside.

But, of course, the cold and starvation are not unique to the deaths of noncombatants during war, and it is not merely the elderly who die. Young Kim is the only named character of the three primary characters, and one of the few named characters in the text, and as the named one, he is the only character who has a developed identity beyond his contemporary actions. Kim tells the old woman of his past and of the deaths of his friends: "they [the Chinese] killed all the children too the friends of my age and even younger" (76). Potok juxtaposes Kim's experiences, and the deaths of those around him, young and old, with the nameless deaths of the many who lie scattered on the ground throughout the text. This juxtaposition humanizes Kim and those dead from his village, and additionally emphasizes the fact that those numerous dead once had lives and human worth. But Kim's story is the root of the humanization that occurs in the text: "He saw again the killing in his village" (48), and heard "the gunfire and the screams" (51), and "it was on fire and everyone was dead" (100), including Kim's brothers (125) and sisters (168). With an 11-year old's wonder, and without melodrama or pathos or irony, he asks, "Why do they kill children?" (125). Because, of course, war is death, and noncombatants must die in war.

Later, when the fighting has cleared, and the refugees can again return to their homes, Kim returns to the locus of his former village, where he finds not a village, or even remnants of a village, but blackened earth, and the destruction is such that he cannot even locate the graves of his ancestors (199–200): "Everyone is dead" (210), he says—his grandfather, his parents, his brothers and sisters, his aunts and uncles, his friends, even his dog (211). Thus, through such comprehensive noncombatant death, as viewed through Kim's point of focalization, Potok is arguing, relative to all of the nameless dead littered through the text and the Korean War, that war destroys not merely the young, and the old, and the living, and the weak, and even the strong, but also the entirety of one's existence; one's family, one's home, one's ancestry are all destroyed in war, and every one of those nameless dead, a sack of human waste on the side of the road, placed there during an exodus of refugees, is (or was) a human being, one who had ancestors and peers and a village and an existence, all of which were collectively and comprehensively extinguished during war. As will be shown later in this study, Potok's text is very much a Holocaust text, and the exodus of the refugees, and their plight in time of war, is analogous to the plight of those who suffered in the Shoah during the Second World War and those before them whose exodus is articulated in the Torah. Here, however, noncombatants are dead, and *I Am the Clay*, even in its very title, argues the malleability of the civilian human being under the omnipotent hand of war.

In Gustav Hasford's *The Short-Timers*, the primary characters in the text—American Marines—view the civilian population as the enemy. What is more, even the deaths of noncombatants, on the page or in back-story form, are treated with nonchalance, and such nonchalance is an act of the dehumanization of the civilian populace, a populace the American armed forces are supposed to protect. Affecting the attitudes of the American combatants, of course, is the role of the Vietnamese citizen as civilian by day and enemy combatant by night. Hence, the idea that "the only good gook is a dead gook," which leads to actions that result in dead civilians, secondary to combatant ambivalence relative to whether or not any given Vietnamese civilian lives or dies. As usual in war and in the American novel of war, especially relative to the post–World War II wars in Southeast Asia and texts thereof, the unnamed very old and very young die as a common action during war. In the Hasford text, all of the up-close noncombatant death occurs in the "Body Count" section (35–140), a section built primarily around the battle for the ancient Citadel of Hue. Early in the section, the omnipresence of Vietnamese orphans is referred to as a child orphan "of undermined sex" (56) begs for candy, and one of the grunts, Chili Vendor, says, "Some of you dudes probably wasted this kid's family" (56). In response, Daytona Dave says that the kid leads an NVA rifle company, so someone needs to "blow him away" (57). While this scene is lighthearted, within context, there is an undercurrent of nastiness. The omnipresence of orphans is secondary to the ongoing war, and as the Vietnamese live in an extended family domestic model, the orphaning of a child means the loss of the entire extended family to the war. And while the indigenous combat forces of the North and the South may have conscripted a family's fighting-age men, all of the women in any given extended family—mother(s), aunts, grandmothers, sisters—are necessarily dead, or the child or children of the family would not be orphaned. Also, the conversational tone and language Daytona Dave and Chili Vendor use present the fact that killing noncombatants is an act of the current war and that the pair are nonchalant in their acceptance of this routine facet of the war.

Even the American occupational regime sees a benefit in the deaths of civilians—photographic propaganda. Joker's CO, Captain January, per the orders of corporate contributor General Motors, sends Rafter Man and Joker to Hue to photograph "indigenous civilian personnel who have been executed ... people buried alive, priests with their throats cut, dead babies— you know what I want'" (61). Naked bodies are fine, too, but only if they are mutilated. And of course, it matters not who killed the civilians; what matters is their use as propaganda for the American war effort — pics with rhetorical captions, aided by body counts and kill ratios (61). So, later in the text, Joker and Rafter Man see "corpses of Vietnamese civilians who have been buried alive" (126), and they tie up some of the dead and take the needed "atrocity photographs" (126). Of course, the body-count and kill-ratio method of war ultimately leads to the deaths of civilians, as numbers matter more than ground taken. As such, it benefits a fire team, squad, patrol, platoon, company, and others to inflate body counts and kill ratios so that the propaganda effect can take place and the popular media can be fed the numbers. And frankly, in a free fire zone, no one cares whether or not one is young or old or a noncombatant; a free fire zone is an opportunity to have fun and to kill. As Joker and Rafter Man ride a helicopter to Hue, the door gunner, with a mounted M-60, takes the opportunity to get some rounds off in the direction of a farmer in a rice paddy, a farmer who may or may not know of the free fire order, one who "knows only that his family needs some rice to eat.... He falls, and the door gunner giggles" (75). Death of the unnamed Other is funny, especially when the door gunner is lit up on dope. This brief scene highlights the broader level of American combatant nonchalance relative to the killing of the Vietnamese populace. Target practice makes target perfect, and the opportunity to take target practice at noncombatants is the opportunity to train. So, a door gunner works on his skill set, and a family patriarch dies in his paddy.

Two noncombatant deaths in the text are important to note because, taken in conjunction, the deaths illuminate the obvious— war kills the young and the old. One death is accidental, and one death is purposeful; one is a child's death, and the other is an elder's death. This is the frame of noncombatant death in war — the very young and the very old. From the LZ, Joker and Rafter Man hitch a ride on an M-48 Patton tank — part of a mechanized convoy heading into Hue — and the tank rumbles down the road. Suddenly, the tank jerks to the left, to the right, then stops. Fifty yards behind the now immobile tank, "On the deck, in the center of the road, I [Joker] see a tiny body, facedown" (78). The civilians curse and then stand in stunned silence: "Another child is dead [and] they accept it" (78). What else can they do in a situation beyond their control? They must accept the death of this child, along with the deaths of the other children — all unnamed in the text, of course. What else can they do after "their American saviors have crushed the guts" (78) of a little girl? Ironically, paradoxically, sadly, and frustratingly, the machines of American might, the apex of American combat technology, with which the United States arrogantly believes that it can win any war, serve to kill those who are supposed to be saved. This interpolated scene of the accidental death of a nameless, faceless little girl, a child unseen but in death, crushed and ground into the road, evokes an appeal to pathos unlike any other scene in the brutal text, but Hasford does not let the emotion linger, as the tank commander hops back up on the tank and continues down the road to Hue. Such is war. On the other end of the age spectrum, but still relative to noncombatant death, is Joker's first confirmed kill, a kill he makes after an anti-tank mine has exploded and killed a fat gunnery sergeant walking point one morning on Route Nine. After helping the grunts retrieve the gunny's body parts from a proximal rice paddy, into which the gunny was blown, Joker, in a rage, sees movement in the trees, "a tiny, ancient farmer" (132) preparing to go to work for the day in the paddy: "Then my M-16 was vibrating and invisible metal missiles were snapping through the ancient farmer's body.... As he fell forward into the dark water his face was tranquil" (133). As witnessed by his peers, Joker has his first confirmed kill. He is salty. But, reasonably speaking, he has killed an old man who had nothing to do with the anti-tank mine that killed the gunnery sergeant. The mine might have been placed days or weeks or months or even years prior to its detonation. And Joker has killed out of anger, rather than combat necessity, which is, perhaps, empathetically understandable under the circumstances. Joker notes, "What you do, you become" (133). Thus, Joker has become a killer because he has killed — a killer of noncombatants, no less, a killer of an unarmed old man. Hasford's text, savage as it is, nonetheless possesses some acknowledgment that the war in Vietnam was devastating to the noncombatant populace of Vietnam. Politically and philosophically, and aided by the body-count and kill-ratio method of war, the killing of civilians during the war was an accepted practice and practical act, and in *The Short-Timers*, civilians are killed for fun, by accident, and secondary to rage.

In Tim O'Brien's *The Things They Carried*, the postmodern ambiguity that runs through the text includes the death of noncombatants. O'Brien's text-wide ambiguity, relative to his wartime experiences as a leg in the Vietnam War, couch the entire text in uncertainty — rhetorically, structurally, philosophically, thematically. So, part of this thematic ambiguity, this element of uncertainty, are the feelings of the American combatants toward the Vietnamese civilians, and part of this ambiguity is the textual repetition of villages being burned and destroyed in comparison with the lack of dead noncombatants. In a 1994 piece for the *New York Times Magazine*, "The Vietnam in Me," in which O'Brien returns to Vietnam 25 years after his combat service — seeking truth, as always — a piece less postmodern than his novel-length, in-country fiction, O'Brien explicitly and repeatedly acknowledges the death(s) of noncombatants. This is the truth: American forces treated noncombatants, Vietnamese civilians, horribly, as a matter of official and unofficial course. Early in the piece, O'Brien looks at his hosts and notes, "Do not forget: our hosts are among the maimed and widowed and orphaned, the bombed and rebombed, the recipients of white phosphorus, the tenders of graves" (printed page 2 of 12). O'Brien juxtaposes scenes of his 1994 visit to Vietnam with his 1969 experiences in the country, and thus creates a dyad of then and now, with the rhetorical purpose of showing the truth — that the then still affects the now; in flashback mode: "LZ Gator's mortar rounds pounding.... Eight or nine corpses piled not 50 yards from where we now sit in friendly unison" (2 of 12). The war-born devastation brought onto the Vietnamese populace has not ended; the mourning has not ended; the dead are still known but are still dead.

O'Brien also offers a take on the Mai Lai Massacre of 16 March 1968, a massacre in which approximately 115 American forces slaughtered between 350 and 500 noncombatants: "No enemy. No incoming fire. Still, for the next four hours, Charlie Company killed whatever could be killed.... Lots of people. Women, infants, teen-agers, old men" (4 of 12). O'Brien's Alpha Company patrolled the same province — Quang Ngai — and village a year later, "knowing nothing of the homicides committed by American troops" (3 of 12). Of course, the civilians, those who were alive in 1969 and in 1994, remembered, and an old woman tells O'Brien what happened that day: "the soldiers jumped out of their helicopters and immediately began to shoot.... The Americans took us to a ditch.... Soldiers were shooting.... I lay under the dead in the ditch ... three of my four children were killed" (5 of 12). Another survivor tells O'Brien that of her 10 family members, nine died that day (6 of 12). Journalist and U.S. government estimates numbered the Vietnam War–era annual noncombatant dead in Quang Ngai Province — per annum, not cumulative — at 50,000 (7 of 12). O'Brien's article is a tale of the suffering of the civilian masses during the Vietnam War.

Noncombatants— women, the elderly, the young — suffered and died at the hands of American servicemen, men for whom "Brutality was S.O.P" (7 of 12), men who crossed "that conspicuous line between rage and homicide" (6 of 12) —à la Joker. The tone of O'Brien's article is one of sorrow — and perhaps retrospective guilt — and the reader can easily realize that O'Brien's sorrow is one of an individual and a collective experience. Clearly, too, even as the decades pass, O'Brien cannot escape the war any more than can the Vietnamese survivors, primarily noncombatants here, and the horrifying images of the war will remain in O'Brien's consciousness as well as in the consciousness of those who physically survived the war.

Conversely, in O'Brien's novel, a text that is also an attempt at truth in war and truth of war and truth after war, and is also retrospectively written, noncombatant death is not nearly so obvious an issue to O'Brien's peri-textual, peri-war, and post-war narrator, but tonal sadness is evident in the few episodes that explicitly contain noncombatant death, even while the narration is observant and mostly emotionally objective. For example, in the short chapter "Style" (135–36), a girl of 14 dances a mourning dance after her house and hamlet have been bombed and burned and wrecked beyond livability. She dances to cope, as she is the only one left alive in her village and in her family: "we found her family in the house. They were dead and badly burned. It wasn't a big family: an infant and an old woman and a woman whose age was hard to tell" (135). Again, in a repetitive action, regardless of war, and common to the novel of war, the very old and the very young are dead. The fighting-age men are gone, and those who remain are victimized. This scene lacks the conjoined tonal sadness and guilt of O'Brien's autobiographical article, but the scene conveys a sense of atrocity, while also conveying a sense of normalcy; atrocities are a normal part of war, as are the deaths of noncombatants.

A later scene (225–28) is both macabre and humorous, and contains the requisite dead old man: "Start here: a body without a name" (225) — that is, another nameless dead noncombatant, also requisite and redundant in the American novel of war, almost to the point of cliché. After taking fire from a lone sniper, sans casualties, platoon commander Lieutenant Jimmy Cross calls in an air strike on the village from which came the fire, and after 30 minutes of air support, the platoon sweeps the village and finds one decedent: "the only confirmed kill was an old man who lay face-up near a pigpen at the center of the village. His right arm was gone" (226), and his face covered by flying insects. One by one, the men of the platoon walk by the old man and "pay their respects" by shaking the old man's remaining hand and offering a word or two. The platoon toast the old man and salute his ancestors. Meanwhile, O'Brien's narrator, who at this point in the non-chronological work is a newbie, four days in Vietnam, and thus has not yet developed a cynicism and humor regarding the dead, does not partake in the "greeting" (228) of the old man, and likens the scene to a "funeral without the sadness" (227) — a funerary episode not entirely disrespectful, but one based on a noncombatant death nonetheless.

Finally, a later passage discussing the rhetoric of war refers to the noncombatant death of an infant and uses contemporary, war-specific rhetoric. O'Brien's narrator states that the verbiage one uses in war desensitizes the user, often humorously, to the horrors at hand, and, as such, makes the atrocities one sees in war less shocking; for example, a burned and dead "Vietnamese baby ... was a roasted peanut" (239) or "a crunchie munchie" (239). This act of dehumanizing a dead baby, and of using humor and rhetoric to do so, is a defense mechanism with which the grunts of Alpha Company attempt to cope with the unnatural aspects of war, such as the napalm-based immolation of children — napalm dropped by

American forces upon noncombatants, of course. So, while O'Brien uses humor and character insensitivity in these examples of textual noncombatant death, he does so ambiguously. O'Brien's narrator and the grunts of Alpha Company are not unaware of the civilian deaths produced by the American war machine; such unawareness would be reasonably and categorically impossible. Consequently, the men, like the dancing girl who has lost her entire existence but for her corporeal life, must cope in ways macabre and humorous. Indigenous noncombatant death, civilian death, faceless and nameless, is a daily fact for the infantrymen of Alpha Company during their time in Vietnam, but, as O'Brien expresses in "The Vietnam in Me," for survivors of the Vietnam War, noncombatant death devastates those whose family members died, even decades after the war. This indigenous civilian optic, this optic of the tragedy of continuous noncombatant death, contemporarily or retrospectively, is not offered in *The Things They Carried*, though. Thus, as a thematic historian, O'Brien is rhetorically unambiguous, but as a postmodern artist, O'Brien is rhetorically ambiguous.

However, in *A Medic in Iraq*, Cole "Doc" Bolchoz does offer an empathetic view of the noncombatant populace of Iraq, a populace composed of civilians who "do not have the luxury of choosing whether or not to be blown up in their markets" (Location 1595 of 1666). And this point raises an interesting observation: noncombatants do not choose to be killed; they do not choose to be proximal to war; they do not choose to be the byproducts of incendiary bombing or napalm or suicide bombers or IEDs (Improvised Explosive Devices). Nonetheless, civilians die in war, and in Ramadi, Iraq, in 2007, IEDs and suicide bombers are a constant threat, and random explosions litter Bolchoz's text: "Of course it would not be Ramadi without another *mass casualty event* [rhetoric of war in italics]. At about 8:00 last night, the shockwaves of an explosive device blew our doors open. This explosion was by far the closest to our perimeter to date ... you watch the hopelessness on innocent faces caught in the cross fire of global politics, then you dig in and try to do all you can to keep" the wounded alive (Location 305, 316 of 1666). Bolchoz's narrator, a combat medic stationed at fictional aid outpost Jazeera Station, primarily treats the uniformed, but he is also exposed to the ongoing carnage that the noncombatant Iraqi populace faces. In Ramadi, a trip to the market or to school or to the teahouse can be a fatal excursion for no other reason than one is, at that moment and on that day and at that locale, adjacent to a detonating IED or suicide bomber. And of course, while the civilian populace is often targeted uniquely, many of the IEDs and suicide bombers are used in targeted attempts to kill uniformed American personnel. So, regardless of the intended target, noncombatants often bear the ghastly brunt of the explosives.

An Iraqi interpreter with whom Bolchoz's narrator has struck up an acquaintanceship gives him a PowerPoint presentation of before-and-after photographs of Iraq War noncombatant death: "Part of me did not want to look at the faces of happy children, and then see their faces in death within seconds of each other, but the choice was not mine to make" (Location 1393 of 1666). PowerPoint becomes a weapon of photographic assault in a land of combat assault. The narrator's note of the before-and-after scenario is apropos of the contemporary combat situation. One second, a child is alive; the next second, the child is dead, and Bolchoz's narrator has no choice but to see the carnage, just as the indigenous civilians have no choice but to experience the carnage. Ironically, as the insurgents target the American military personnel, and the American military personnel have chocolates and candy and food, and the like, which they give out to children, when children crowd around the Americans who are handing out the pogey bait, they become the tertiary targets of the explosions. Thus, the children, noncombatants, are killed because they want something sweet to eat in a time of abject hopelessness and ongoing violence. And of course, civilian areas where noncombatants congregate are also specifically targeted to discourage collusion and interaction with the American forces. Thus, the very act of buying bread or some other such commodity of sustenance becomes a terminal act, an act in which one risks his or her life. Where are flour, fruit, and vegetables? At the market, of course. And as the market is a locus of civilian congregation, the market is a target of opportunity. The overall tone of Bolchoz's text is one of disgust — disgust with the U.S. government, with the military hierarchy, with the war in Iraq, and with the carnage created by what seem to be a series of random bombings, ongoing bombings that actually target uniformed and noncombatant personnel, bombings that absolutely savage the civilian populace of Ramadi, Iraq.

Clearly, then, the death of noncombatants is an important thematic element of war and of the American novel of war. Through malice, accident, planning, weather, disease, starvation, and coincidence, infants, children, women of all ages, elderly men — not of combatant age — entire families, and whole populations of villages and towns are killed regardless of ally or enemy and irrelevant to the militarized lines of battle. The death of noncombatants is a given product of all wars — a combat necessity, as it were. Therefore, most of the texts in this study offer noncombatant death, and often at a thematic level. *Blood Meridian, I Am the Clay, The Short-Timers, The Things They Carried*, and *A Medic in Iraq* each present the shortened life of the noncombatant in a war zone, and the texts show that, irrespective of era or war or location of war or lines of combat, noncombatants die in war zones, often in grand, impersonal numbers, nameless, faceless, voiceless, powerless. Relative to this chapter's specific questions — How and why do authors, per their novels of war, present the element of noncombatant death? Do warriors within war texts slay noncombatants for different reasons? What are authors arguing with the textual element of noncombatant death? How do the in-text noncombatant deaths differ by text, in situation, in purpose, and in numbers slain? — it seems that authors present noncombatant death as a needed rhetorical element in the American novel of war. When historically appropriate, civilian deaths must be noted in the text; otherwise, one writes an incomplete text.

In *Blood Meridian*, inter-racial, inter-tribal, international slaughter goes on, as it did historically, and as the text continues, the scenes of slaughter decrease in length, and thus slaughter of the unnamed becomes commonplace, the order of the day and the order of war. In *I Am the Clay*, invading and occupying forces kill numerous unnamed rural Korean civilian peasants, and those not slaughtered by violence often die by the hostile elements or by starvation or by disease, but Potok sees fit to name one of these characters so that he can humanize the faceless dead of the Korean War, each once with a life and a family and a history and a home. In *The Short-Timers*, American weaponry kills unnamed children, women, and old men, and the uniformed American characters, through their behavior, declare such deaths to be routine. And in *The Things They Carried*, the deaths of unnamed noncombatants are dealt with peri-textually through the use of ambiguity — noncombatant death, while commonplace, is tragic, but it also can be funny. Finally, in *A Medic in Iraq*, unnamed Iraqi civilians, both adults and children, cannot even function within the parameters of daily living activities without being blown up. Thus, in every text here, and according to every author, in a war zone routine daily activities became deadly, and life expectancy is short. Human lives become the "collateral damage" of war. And something else common to all of these texts, in addition to the nameless status of the noncombatant dead, are the deaths of the very young and the very old, regardless of sex. Life cycles are broken, severed.

Further, and tragically, those who kill noncombatants in these texts often exhibit a learned nonchalance relative to their actions. The byproduct of combat during war, of course, is human death, and within the spectrum of human death, noncombatants die. Consequently, war, any war, every war, in any era, in every era, in any country involved, in every country involved, is deadly to noncombatants.

VIII

Omnipresent Death and Destruction

War is death, and in addition to the peri-combat deaths of allied peers and the deaths of noncombatants, secondary to myriad means and causes, there is omnipresent death and destruction in war; and as such, in the American novel of war, there are not merely the deaths of noncombatants and combatants, but also the deaths of animals—of labor, sustenance, and domestic—and the destruction of houses, farms, churches, schools, hospitals, villages, towns, cities, roads, highways, bridges, railroad lines and railroads, cars, trucks, planes, helicopters, boats, ships, and entire nations. War is more than death alone; war is destructive in its means and methods and purpose. This destruction is a fact of every war, and omnipresent death and destruction is a defining characteristic situated in every true and accurate modern and postmodern novel of war, American or otherwise. And of course, in the works analyzed in this study, many animals are slaughtered, and sundry nameless and named towns and villages cease to exist, and wells are poisoned, and hamlets are burned into nothingness.

Each of the 23 novels in this study uses this omnipresent death and destruction defining characteristic, either at a motif or thematic level, but an examination of the rhetorical use of the element of omnipresent death and destruction in *The March*, *One Man's Initiation*, *The Marne*, *Catch-22*, *I Am the Clay*, *The Things They Carry*, and *Prayer at Rumayla*, with a brief look at *The Red Badge of Courage* and *Blood Meridian*, shows the timelessness, breadth, and scope of omnipresent death and destruction during war. In *The March*, General William Tecumseh Sherman and his Union troops ride and run through Georgia, South Carolina, and North Carolina, and devastate and destroy, and sack and burn, and collect and conquer; no town, city, countryside that faces Sherman's troops escapes the destruction and death brought by an army 60,000 strong, and the omnipresent death and destruction element is text-wide and thematic in composition. *One Man's Initiation* and *The Marne* describe repeated scenes of devastation and carnage secondary to relentless World War I artillery barrages that continue for years at a time, and Dos Passos is skilled at offering mimeography of savaged forests and gutted mules, while Wharton is especially adept at presenting imagery of destroyed villages and towns. *Catch-22* devolves ancient and beautiful Rome after four-plus years of war and aerial bombing, and the city is presented as a hellish place containing historic and recently created ruins. *I Am the Clay* offers the tools of mechanized war—jets, tanks, armored and armed personnel carriers—versus modern infrastructure and ancient villages and livestock, all of which become litter under rocket or tread or machine-gun; as well, the modern city fares no better and, like the pre-modern hamlets, lies in shambles. *The Things They Carry* and *Prayer at Rumayla* carry the theme of omnipresent death and destruction into the late postmodern era. The former text does so in an old-fashioned way, though, as American troops kill a variety of domestic and stock animals and drop the dead into village wells and burn thatched-hut villages to ashes. The latter text renders the results of the American incursion into Iraq during the Gulf War from the optic of a tanker whose mission is to destroy everything organic, mechanical, and architectural in the path of the war machine so that the combat infantry can follow. Thus, in any era, in any country, and in every war, the result of war is the same—omnipresent death and destruction, of animals, of towns, of histories, of ways of life. As such, in every American novel of war, this element is readily and rhetorically apparent.

Scholars and historians have long and commonly acknowledged this element of omnipresent death and destruction in war and in the literature of war, if not necessarily in this terminology. As well, the ethos of omnipresent death and destruction, as a method of modern and postmodern war, can be, of course, traced to the U.S. Civil War, and in "Shutting the Gates of Mercy: The American Origins of Total War, 1860–1880," Lance Janda does a fine job of defining total war, the practice of which leads to death beyond combatants and noncombatants, and destruction beyond that which is targeted relative to enemy combat capacity. Janda correctly notes, as others have done, that the Civil War "represents the first mass conflict of the industrial age" (7), and while this notation is not new, what was new at the time of the Civil War (to American militaries, at least), was the "application of force against an enemy's noncombatants and resources" (8), with the goal of total and complete subjugation—a war doctrine that was "anathema" (8) prior to the Civil War but was practiced during that war and then applied to the eradication of the Plains Indians afterward.

Janda goes on to argue that Ulysses S. Grant, William T. Sherman, and Philip H. Sheridan were "fervent and eloquent advocates" (9) of total war as well as highly successful military leaders and practitioners of the combat philosophy at hand, with emphasis here on Sherman and his march to the sea and march through the Carolinas. Further, as the war continued, Grant realized that "bringing the Southern states back into the Union required the complete subjugation of the Confederate people" (12), and thus the practice of total war came into play during the siege of Vicksburg in May-July 1863. By the autumn of 1864, Sherman, too, had "resigned himself to the necessities of total war" (16), the three tenets of which are as follows: one, military necessity; two, psychological warfare; and three, the concept of "collective responsibility" (16–17). Sherman believed that the South would not yield unless utterly and completely and thoroughly defeated, and this defeat was particular to the "destruction of civilian property and supplies" (16), which would thereby shorten the war through the deprivation of the rebel army's supply system, a system in nexus with the Confederate civilian populace. Sherman also felt that destroying the property, towns, foodstuffs, and livestock of Southerners would destroy the psychological strength and unity of the citizenry, and also quell the Southern thirst for ongoing war with the North. Finally, "there were no noncombatants in the South" (15), and this philosophy dictated that, in the Confederacy, every man, every woman, and every child contributed to the continuation of the internecine conflict; as such, all deserved what they received (17). Thus, as Sherman marched through the South, and through Georgia and the Carolinas specifically, every community item in the path was subject to destruction, and "warehouses, railroads, factories, and foodstuffs" (15) were destroyed, while thousands of head of stock were appropriated and slaughtered to feed the Union troops (17). Janda asserts that Grant, Sherman, and Sheridan tried to limit noncombatant death (18) and often evacuated noncombatants before pillaging and then destroying community and personally owned properties and items (15).

Nonetheless, the Northern commanders noted a sweet irony in the fact that the Southerners who asked for war received that which was requested (20), in totality.

But, of course, as war is death, and as war is destruction, the element of omnipresent death and destruction, in war and in the American novel of war, precedes the historical and federal practice of the concept of total war. The Plains Indians practiced total war as a matter of course, and in *Blood Meridian*, many animals are slaughtered and a number of nameless towns and villages cease to function communally. Immediately after the Comanche slaughter the filibusters, the kid and Sproule come upon an unnamed "village on the plain" (57): "They went slowly through the little mud streets. There were goats and sheep slain in their pens and pigs dead in the mud.... A dead horse lay in the square" (58). The unnamed village, littered with dead noncombatants of all ages, is also littered with the animals of the decedent residents. In this case, stock animals that cannot move in herds are slaughtered, most likely by the same Comanche raiders who decimate the filibusters, and who, when first seen, are herding horses, mules, and cattle (51). The village is pillaged, burned, and ransacked. So, unlike the "compassionate" Union generals, who — arguably — attempted to relocate noncombatants before laying waste, physically and psychologically, to all that the noncombatants possessed, the Comanche raiders leave no noncombatants alive while uniformly destroying a village and killing all the non-traveling domestic animals therein. So conceptually and in practice, omnipresent death and destruction in war — total war — is not a new thematic element, and in fact has been an aspect of war since before recorded time.

Of course, part of the destruction secondary to war, nineteenth-century war specifically, is the destruction not only of towns, villages, cities, and so on, but also of the natural world. Stephen Crane's seminal Civil War tome, *The Red Badge of Courage*, articulates this destruction of the natural world in action as well as in rhetoric: "A shell ... landed, and exploding redly flung the brown earth.... Bullets began to whistle among the branches and nip at the trees. Twigs and leaves came sailing down" (31). This motif of the destruction of the natural world, one that Crane uses in passing, is one that is prominently presented in the texts of World War I, a war in which thousands of square miles are scoured of all natural life. And as in the McCarthy work, in the Crane text, animals die and man-made equipment is destroyed at the scene of combat: "The little narrow roadway ... was choked with the bodies of horses and splintered parts of war machines" (75). In early modern war, the natural world is ravaged, animals are killed, and the equipage of war and other man-made items are destroyed. Crane even sees fit to use the word "destruction" in the text: "Destruction threatened him [Henry] from all points" (42); later, an unnamed Union combatant proclaims, "Here we are! Everybody fightin'. Blood an' destruction" (96). Thus, Crane, first through his limited omniscient narrator, uses the word "destruction" in the narration of Henry's thoughts to articulate the ethos and pathos of Henry's fears secondary to the violence of war. And then Crane, through the dialogue of an unnamed character, also uses the word "destruction" to identify, on a general level, the chaos, atmosphere and effects of combat. Early modern warfare is destruction — of the natural world, of animal and human life, and of articles made by man.

While in *The Red Badge of Courage*, Crane uses the omnipresent death and destruction element on a somewhat peripheral level, yet nonetheless acknowledges the presence of such in war, in *The March*, a text that covers Sherman's March to the Sea and through the Carolinas — a movement of total war — E.L. Doctorow fully develops war-centric omnipresent death and destruction as a text-wide thematic element, and does so in such a way that relentlessly and repetitively evokes the death-inducing, destructive power of the practice and promotion of total war: "Imagine a great segmented body moving in contractions and dilations at a rate of twelve to fifteen miles a day, a creature of a hundred thousand feet.... It consumes everything in its path. It is an immense organism, this army ... which is to move forward and consume all before it" (61–62). And part of that consumption, that comprehensive act of total movement and total war upon everything before it, is the taking of all that is useful for the war effort, and as the text opens, in a scene viewed from the perspective of a slave owner's wife, Mattie Jameson, a landed slaveholder — John Jameson — well aware of the Northern appropriation of Southern means, has his mules shot before the invading army can take the stock: "She heard a gunshot [and] saw one of the mules go down on its knees" (6). Another mule is then shot (7), and the landowner, his family, and a valued slave make their escape, while leaving seven others. Thus, even before Sherman's army is situated in the text, the death of valued animals of labor is presented, because all commodities available will be used on the march through Georgia and the Carolinas. Later, once the army has occupied the uninhabited mansion, an officer "mounted the grand staircase, and in one room after another he gutted the upholstery and the mattresses and used the butt of his sword to smash the windows and the mirrors" (12–13). Others join in and axe the furniture, tear down the curtains, and soak the place with kerosene. So while the plantation has been deserted, all the material possessions that remain, including the manse, must be "destroyed" (13), and in an act common to the march, the army proceeds to burn the place down. Later, a slave, Pearl Wilkins-Jameson, states, regarding the act, "You burned de house, took de vittles" (44), and they did.

This scene of the destruction of a single plantation and mansion is not unique in the text, and Doctorow takes pains to show that other architectural entities (in Milledgeville, Georgia, for example) meet the same fate as the common mansion: "St. Thomas had been vandalized.... They tore out the pews for their campfires. They befouled the altar.... The penitentiary had been set afire. Muffled explosions came from the city arsenal. Milledgeville was devastated — windows broken, gardens stomped on, stores stripped of their goods" (30). The town is in ruins; the social institutions of heaven and hell and armed protection have been dismantled, and personal space and property has been trod upon and, if useful, usurped, yet a young officer states, "General Sherman does not war against women and children" (25). Nonetheless, Janda's aspects of total war are in effect: one, military necessity; two, psychological warfare; and three, the concept of "collective responsibility." Sherman argues it is a military necessity that the civilian population of the South be thoroughly defeated, crushed to the point of submission, or the South will never surrender. Thus, Sherman allows systematic destruction of all in the way of the Union army, which leads to the psychological and emotional collapse of the will of the Southern populace, who are, it is argued, collectively responsible for the secession from the Union and the call to civil war. So, while the population of Milledgeville watches, the town is decimated, and even the trees that line the streets are forsaken to the cause: "Black pioneers with two-man saws felled the trees. Other black men stripped off the branches, and still others loaded trunks and limbs aboard drays.... It was all very efficient, a matter seemingly of moments in which to flatten a city" (32). Of note here is a huge refugee presence — former slaves who now are following and, in many cases, working for the Union army. So, Union utilization and appropriation of Southern "property," even post–Emancipation Proclamation (effective 1 January 1863), includes former slaves. The result of Sherman's march through Milledgeville is, as understated, "dishevelment" (33) of the town, which is left "empty and quiet" (33) once the Union army has moved on.

Mansions and towns are not unique in their common result of destruction, and the Union masses have a similar effect on the rural areas, smaller villages, and houses that they encounter, and domestic animals and stock fare none too well either: "the countryside looked flattened and scorched, as if a hot clothes iron had been taken to it. It was no longer the natural world God had made" (51). So, as in the Crane text, war is devastating to the natural world, and the secondary effects of the passing of an army are the leveling and the destruction of the natural flora upon which the army moves. Unnamed whistle-stops meet the same fate born of total war: "The depot had been burned to the ground. The village behind it was destroyed" (52), and "the stench from the dead cattle lying beside the road was intolerable" (53), while the road was littered with dead dogs, "every hound to be seen was shot through the head" (54). Sherman's total war is destroying everything in its wake, with an emphasis on the material possessions of the Southern populace, and even the animals that cannot be used as labor or consumed are, as such, killed and left to rot in the sun. Plantations, mansions, farms, towns and cities, villages, houses, railroad depots, churches, prisons, armories, and the trees and flowers and fields of the natural world all fall before Sherman's mighty centipede of more than 100,000 legs. And as the "Georgia" (1–133) section closes, Sherman notes, "I have gutted Johnny Reb's railroads. I have burned his cities, his forges, his armories, his machine shops, his cotton gins. I have eaten out his crops, I have consumed his livestock and appropriated ten thousand of his horses and mules. He is left ravaged and destitute" (119–20). In other words, Sherman has practiced total war against the populace, the land, the property, the means, and the army of the South. He has broken the noncombatants materially and psychologically, and he has gathered from them and theirs that which his army needs, that which was once the South's, including acreage — the Confederate state of Georgia is now the North's— and what remains of the insurgent army will fall concurrent to the destruction of the Carolinas. Doctorow adroitly and continually and systematically uses the theme of omnipresent death and destruction, via Sherman's practice of total war, through the entirety of the text; as such, *The March* is a very effective American novel of the Civil War and is, pragmatically speaking, a textbook on the rhetorical use of the defining characteristic of omnipresent death and destruction in the American novel of war.

Moving forward five decades to the wholesale devastation of the First World War, John Dos Passos' *One Man's Initiation* and Edith Wharton's *The Marne* each offer omnipresent death and destruction through the presentation and devastation of the natural and man-made world. Relentless, years-long artillery barrages obliterated animals, thousands of square miles of countryside, and hundreds of European villages and towns, and photographs of the era offer a bleak portrait of mile after mile of mud and dirt, the horizon broken up occasionally by a stick of a stripped tree trunk fingering out of the ground. And nearly all World War I novels of war have an artillery motif in the text, whereby the sound and effects of artillery are constantly presented. Dos Passos' text is no different, and the effects of artillery are readily found in the narration of Martin Howe's initiation into warfare, and the wreckage is situated in populated areas, in the country, and in the trenches: "At Epernay the [train] station was wrecked" (22), and after shelling, "the woods became broken and jagged, stumps and split boughs littering the ground, trees snapped off halfway up" (73), while "artillery along the lines kept up a continuous hammering drumbeat. [And a] shell burst into a house on the crest of the hill opposite" (31–32). Dos Passos places destruction randomly and often, and in so doing, the omnipresence of ruination of the European landscape becomes an offhand matter of fact. And while Dos Passos, like Wharton, offers destroyed villages and man-made structures, unlike Wharton, Dos Passos also offers a number of scenes that incorporate the destruction of the natural world, and thus shows that when man's goal is to slaughter man, the secondary effect is the ruination of the natural. At dawn, after a night of shelling, "Everything was lost in mist that filled the shellholes as with water and wreathed itself fantastically about the shattered trunks of trees.... Dawn in a wilderness of jagged stumps and ploughed earth" (81). For repetitive effect, Dos Passos offers another eerie dawn in another area, but the destruction is similar: "Against a red glare of the dawn the wilderness of shattered trees stands out purple, hidden by grey mist in the hollows" (92). By placing a similar dawn in another geographical area, Dos Passos is arguing, appropriately and accurately, that the rural landscape of Europe, not merely France or Belgium, is in ruins. And before the text closes, a reminder to the reader: "The woods all about [Martin Howe] were a vast rubbish-heap; the jagged splintered boles of leafless trees rose in every direction from heaps of brass shell-cases, of tin cans, of bits of uniform and equipment.... And this was what all the centuries of civilization had struggled for" (103). Note how Dos Passos bitterly conjoins the litter of man, the refuse, the garbage of war, with the destruction of the natural world, and note how he castigates twentieth-century man — the civilized animal. This is the wreckage of civilized, evolved modern man, argues Dos Passos, the destruction of the natural world.

As well, Dos Passos calls attention to the omnipresence of dead mules in the theater of war, and thus adds animal death to the text-wide omnipresent destruction of the natural world. During an artillery barrage, and in a vehicle convoy, "Martin remembers the beating legs of a mule rolling on its back on the side of the road and, steaming in the fresh morning air, the purple and yellow and red of its ripped belly" (74–75). The eviscerated mule is suffering before dying, and the pathos involved in the scene is quick, but nonetheless is present and effective. Later, on another road, in another scene of carnage, "Along the roads camions overturned, dead mules tangled in their traces beside shattered caissons" (82), and finally, another road, but merely another locus of destruction: "On the other side of the road a fallen mule feebly wags its head from side to side, a mass of purple froth hanging from its mouth and wide-stretched scarlet nostrils" (92). Dos Passos does a fine job of snapshoting the suffering of the mules, animals of burden that serve the whim of man, and mules die in the Doctorow and McCarthy (194–95) texts as well. Overwhelmingly, though, in *One Man's Initiation*, while the brief scenes of mule suffering and death are readily noticed and emotionally inductive, it is the omnipresent destruction of the natural world, secondary to relentless artillery bombardment, that is thematically and rhetorically important. Dos Passos argues that man, civilized man, evolved man, modern man, is responsible for destroying the natural world.

Conversely, Wharton's text, often castigated by critics as both a romantically tinged propaganda — which is fair, of course — and a text that switches genres from realist to fantasy when Troy Belknap is wounded and then saved by the "ghost" of childhood friend Paul Gantier (135–37) — which is debatable — is more readily situated in the war-born destruction of man-made entities such as French villages and towns and the loss of history and culture resultant of the ruination. Wharton's propaganda piece — an effective screed against World War I–era American ambivalence, materialism and pacifism, not unlike Willa Cather's *One of Ours* (1922) and Dorothy Canfield Fisher's collection *Home Fires in France* (1918) — laments the savagery brought forth by the barbarian Huns against the civilized French through the optic of Troy Belknap, a moneyed American who has spent the summers of his childhood in France, and who, upon reaching adulthood, volunteers to be an ambulance

man in France. And while Wharton's text is not nearly so brutal as is Dos Passos' work—
with its eviscerated mules and disfigured veterans (20)—the omnipresent destruction of
war is nonetheless easily situated in the short novel. Early on, Wharton shows the nation-
wide destruction of France and of French villages secondary to the war, as Belknap reads
the news of "the names of the ruined villages" (14), including "that of the little town where
they had all lunched with the Gantiers" (14), and the report offers "not a house standing"
(15). The village has been destroyed, and with it, its culture, its history, and, of course, any
number of its inhabitants. Wharton, somewhat melodramatically, repeats this element of
the destruction of French culture and history through the destruction of the villages and
towns of France: "It was a fateful week, and every name in the bulletins— Amiens, Com-
piègne, Rheims, Meaux, Senlis— evoked in Troy Belknap's tortured imagination visions of
ancient beauty and stability ... and the thought of the great stretch of desolation spreading
and spreading like a leprosy over a land so full of poetry of the past, and so rich in a happy
prosperous present, was added to the crueler vision of the tragic and magnificent armies
that had failed to defend it" (19). In a few short lines, Wharton lists a number of French
towns and villages destroyed and then overrun by the Germans, and she also labels the
French army weak and incompetent and unable to defend its history or its people or its
land.

As the text continues, Wharton angrily argues— through Troy's optic— that war, war
in the specific, this war, in this locale, "devastate[s] regions" (27): "This is what war did!
... it killed houses and lands as well as men" (28), and resulted in "wan ruins ... gutted
houses and sterile fields" (29). Again, Wharton is particular to France, its culture, its history,
and its losses secondary to the destruction of its villages and towns. When Troy returns to
France three years after the start of the war — after coming of age — and is six months in-
country, he is sent to the "exposed sectors" (68), "the desolated country" (68) of his youth,
and what he finds when he returns to the village of his childhood is omnipresent destruction:
but for a terrace wall, "Everything else was in ruins: pale weather-bleached ruins over which
the rains and suns of three years had passed effacingly. The church, once so firm and four-
square on the hill, was now a mere tracery against the clouds; the hospice roofless, the
houses all gutted and bulging, with black smears of smoke on their inner walls" (69). War
has come to town, but not recently, and with the passage of time, that which was destroyed
in 1914 is now being worn away, erased but for skeletal structures, under the sun and the
weather. So, metonymously, this little village, destroyed in the opening days of the First
World War, has lost its history, its culture, its place in France, just as France, through the
omnipresent destruction born of World War I, and the destruction of villages such as this
one, has lost much of its history, its culture, its place in world.

In *Catch-22*, Joseph Heller also offers the ancient destroyed by the modern, but the
city is Rome, the villages are Italian, and the war is World War II. And in "The Eternal
City" (415–30) chapter, a chapter in which bombardier Captain John Yossarian wanders
the anarchic city at night, Rome is a horrifying, terrifying locus of violence, death, and the
destruction of war. Gary W. Davis argues that, in a text built upon discontinuity, "violence
never appears to be neatly confined within the [American] Air Corps or any other military
or economic organization" (68), and thus the peri-war capitalist tendencies brought forth
in the text by characters such as Milo Minderbinder lead to, ironically, "the needless bombing
of undefended villages" (68) and the corporeal and material mutilation of Italian towns
and cities and citizens "by those who have come to liberate" (68). So, the destruction of
great and ancient Rome, by forces American and otherwise, is symbolic of the greater

destruction created during the Second World War. As such, Yossarian's wandering through the horror of the Roman streets after dark "demonstrates ... the distorted violence of experience, the completeness of the physical and spiritual destruction which have been brought about by human imagination and institutions" (Davis 69). Consequently, the "Eternal City" chapter is a reminder that it is man who has created the omnipresent death and destruction of war, and it is man upon whom responsibility rests. Further, there is a conjunction between the ancient city of Rome and the Roman state (built upon violence, of course) and World War II (and the violence therein). Violence is timeless, as are death and destruction secondary to the propagation of war, and as Michael Bibby notes, "mutilation *is* the war experience [italics Bibby]" (37) — mutilation of human beings, of animals, of architectural institutions, of villages, cities, and states.

Interestingly, Heller creates Rome, ancient and modern, historical and grand, military and civilian, as hellish and in tatters, secondary to the omnipresent death and destruction of war: "Rome was in ruins, he saw.... The airdrome had been bombed eight months before, and knobby slabs of white stone rubble had been bulldozed into flat-topped heaps on both sides of the entrance through the wire fence surrounding the field. The Colosseum was a dilapidated shell, and the Arch of Constantine had fallen. Nately's whore's apartment was a shambles" (416). In an effort to evince the destruction of war, Heller frames the destruction of the ancient — the Colosseum and the Arch of Constantine — with the modern — the airdrome and the apartment. The destruction of war — random perhaps, inaccurate perhaps, purposeful perhaps — uses no filter when destroying, and thus the modern, the military, the ancient, and the civilian are all fodder for bombardment and wastage. And of course, there is symbolic value to these destroyed architectural items. The airdrome is a locus of war, and more specifically, a locus of aerial war and, the destruction in the text is the destruction secondary to aerial bombardment. Ironically, air warfare destroys the proximal locus of air warfare, yet does not end the air warfare. The apartment (a brothel, a place of sexual release and carnality and even sensuality) falls under military might, too, so the noncombatant's home — ideally, a safe zone — is no different than the military target. The impersonal destruction of the noncombatant and her or his home, or village, or town, or city, is nearly universal in war and in war literature. And such destruction is so commonplace, in war in general and in this text specifically, that the old woman who remains in the apartment says, "They [military occupiers of any nation] have a right to do anything we can't stop them from doing" (417).

Symbolically, the Colosseum — the Flavian Amphitheater — represents imperial Rome, and its blood sport, and the citizenry's thirst for blood, so possibly Heller is making the analogy that humans — in the first century or the twentieth — seek blood, and war is nothing more than blood sport. In showing the Colosseum as dilapidated, Heller is arguing against the destruction of war — that is, blood sport; conversely, he is also arguing that the destruction of war, through man, is nothing new, and therefore arguing against war and the destruction secondary to war is a futile act. Finally, the "fallen" Arch of Constantine (symbolically rather historically fallen), a triumphal arch, an arch celebrating fourth-century military victory, represents a lack of victory on any country's part. There is no victory secondary to the omnipresent death and destruction of the Second World War, or any war, even a "necessary" war. Modern war destroys the ancient, the historical, the modern: "Everything breakable had been broken. The destruction was total" (418). Heller uses the rhetorical trope of war to conjoin man's history and man's present, a present defined by the death and destruction secondary to humanity's promotion and practice of catastrophic violence.

In *I Am the Clay*, however, Chaim Potok situates the omnipresent death and destruction of war in a matter-of-fact tone and obviousness that belies the horror of such calamitous peri-war events. Potok offers dead animals, ruined roads, and destroyed villages and towns and cities to convey the omnipresence of material destruction born of mobile mechanized war. As the narrative follows the trio of peasants south and then north, death and destruction are as visible as the three primary characters. So, in this way, omnipresent death and destruction in time of war becomes characterized in the text: "An ox lay dead in the ditch, still harnessed to its ruined cart.... The once frozen road had been ground to powder by the steel-cleated tracked vehicles" (4, 5). Here is the standard peasant-issue beast of burden, dead, as is the norm in novels of the Korean and Vietnam Wars. A dead ox (or, as in *The Things They Carry*, a dead water buffalo), is a dead tool of sustenance, as one cannot farm or move one's goods or carry a sick or wounded family member sans the beast, so the death of the ox destroys a family's ability to work, to feed itself, to relocate, and to transport family goods. In other words, the death of a family ox is a catastrophic event. And the destruction of the road secondary to the movement of armored personnel carriers and tanks and the like is almost a throwaway sentence; nonetheless, the sentence is quite important, as it clarifies the nonchalance with which military personnel destroy indigenous, man-made civil infrastructures. Mechanized militaries move along created roadways, destroying such as they relocate — the "mutilations in the road caused by the war machines of the foreigners" (10) — without any forethought or care; thus the insensitivity to the inherent needs of the indigenous populace — during and after the war — leads to a dislocation between the occupying forces and the regional populace — see Chapter X.

Of course, as the people flee, Potok offers images of villages and towns under war: "torn earth, wrecked houses, broken sewage lines, rotting flesh" (13). Houses and buildings have been devolved into "shattered beams and broken boards" (21), and even "stone buildings" (45) are "charred and battered" (45), with smashed windows, doors, and walls. Notice in these images of war-centric death and destruction that particular villages and towns (and ox owners, for that matter) are not named. There is a depersonalization motif occurring in the text, and Potok is arguing that the omnipresent death and destruction born of this war — the Korean War — is a depersonalized brutalization of a civilian and peasant populace that does not have the means to off-put the mechanized war of the American and Chinese war machines. The combatants are irrelevant; North Koreans, Chinese, and Americans are all dehumanizing tools of death and destruction whose machines and methods of war lead to cataclysmic events that disrupt the human rights of the noncombatant Korean populace. It is not just that domestic animals — such as Kim's dog Badooki (211) — and stock animals are being killed randomly and by choice; roads, villages, cemeteries, towns, and cities are all being decimated secondary to the war. Meanwhile, familial histories are being erased as well, as entire populations are relocated and then, after the war, return to find whole villages gone. And so Potok is arguing that, once gone, some things are forever gone, and in the destruction of war, some acts of destruction can never be taken back, so permanent is the destruction. Obviously, once dead, the ox or the dog is dead forever, yet destroyed roads and urban buildings can be rebuilt eventually, but more troubling is that, once destroyed, once erased, the village, its history, it familial linage, is forever effaced from the earth; as Kim says, referring to his home village, "everything is gone" (211). This is what war destroys. Not merely the material, but also the historical and the familial. War is an act of omnipresent death and destruction that is both manifest and latent. Explicitly and obviously, war kills all manner of animals — stock, domestic, feral, wild — and war destroys natural and man-made elements, but implicitly, and not so obviously, war destroys common histories and cumulative bodies of knowledge, and this omnipresent destruction of war is that which Potok laments in his work.

In *The Things They Carried*, Tim O'Brien offers the requisite Vietnam War novel destruction of rural villages, but he is more rhetorically forceful in his presentation of the killing of indigenous animals than he is in the matter-of-fact references to the destruction of villages. As former U.S. Army psychiatrist William Barry Gault notes, "During the actual waging of war, especially a war like that in Viet Nam, standard civilized conventions and prohibitions are widely suspended. Trust, decency, restraint, and gentleness are of little use in the face of relentless pressure to kill or be killed" (452), and thus psychopathology is an asset, and the destruction of "relatively innocuous village[s]" is commonplace (Gault 452). Included in this destruction is the slaughter of animals and, as O'Brien notes in "The Vietnam in Me," during the My Lai massacre, in addition to the hundreds of noncombatants who were butchered, domestic and stock animals were killed as well: "Charlie company killed whatever could be killed. They killed chickens. They killed dogs and cattle" (4 of 12). This action is repeated in the novel as well; after a grunt named Ted Lavender is sniped, Alpha Company destroys the village of Than Khe: after burning everything that would burn, "They shot chickens and dogs, they trashed the village well" (17), and then they finished off with artillery strikes. Psychopathic retribution for the loss of a peer is not uncommon in the novels of the Vietnam War, nor is this type of action uncommon in written or oral histories of the war, and O'Brien's matter-of-fact tone evinces the argument that this type of village destruction is, in fact, a common occurrence in the practice of the Vietnam War. Thus, after watching the artillery strikes, the company humps to its next point of patrol. O'Brien also asserts that the psychopathology of the war need not be born secondary to the loss of a peer. In a telling scene in which Lavender adopts a puppy and feeds it and humps it around through the bush, the puppy is killed one day when "Azar strapped it to a Claymore antipersonnel mine" (37) and detonated the device. So, the animal death goes from the random and vague unnamed "they" killing miscellaneous village animals—also unnamed or individually identified—to a named animal killer who blows up a specific, adopted puppy.

O'Brien further elevates the grotesque pathos of animal slaughter with the torture and killing of a baby "VC water buffalo" (78); again, this action occurs after a peer is killed. This time, a grunt named Curt Lemmon, who was not even particularly well liked, is blown up after stepping on a booby-trapped howitzer round (78). After placing a rope around the animal's neck, the company medic Rat Kiley, Lemmon's friend, shoots the baby water buffalo in the right front knee; he then shoots an ear off, and subsequently, shoots the animal in the "hindquarters" (78) and then in its back hump, and then a couple of times in its "flanks" (78)—not to kill the animal, says the narrator, but "to hurt" (79) the animal, to torture the animal. Kiley then shoots off the animal's mouth, and the narrator notes that the witnesses to this death secondary to destruction are feeling all types of emotions watching this act, but pity is not one of the emotions (79). Kiley continues to fire, and he shoots off the tail, and "chunks of meat" (79) from the beast; he then switches his weapon to full automatic and continues to "the belly and butt" (79), to the left front knee, to the nose, the throat. The narrator notes, "We had witnessed something ... profound" (79). Yet the baby water buffalo is still alive. Finally, two grunts take the water buffalo and dump it into the village well. In closing, a grunt named Mitchell Sanders offers this philosophical summation: "Well, that's Nam ... Garden of Evil ... every sin's real fresh and original" (80). This scene is as violent and destructive and wrenching as any scene of human death in any war novel. The baby water buffalo really suffers at the hands of Rat Kiley, and O'Brien stretches out the systematic death and destruction of the water buffalo over three pages of mostly narrated text. By compartmentalizing each sub-act of violence, each shot and each body part, O'Brien is articulating the reactionary psychopathology that the grunts experienced in the Vietnam War. Peer deaths secondary to sniping and booby traps were psychologically devastating, and the masochistic reactions by those affected by such guerrilla acts of violence were manifestly exponential relative to the individual killings of a peer at a time. And of course, poisoning a village well — chemically or by dropping an animal carcass down the mouth of the well — and killing the village stock has the effect of destroying a village's ability to continue to function, and thus to exist, as the stock are needed for sustenance and farming and the well for water. But the masochistic psychopathology present in the VC water buffalo scene is a unique rhetorical act of the omnipresent death and destruction in war, even within a text that also offers the destruction of named and unnamed villages and the deaths of dogs and cattle and chickens, and O'Brien explicitly details the actions of Rat Kiley so that each shot is a microcosm of death and destruction and the act is one of profound devastation.

Also capable of a profound devastation, especially in the face of a lesser-armed enemy, is the M1A1 Abrams tank, the tanker's tool of the Persian Gulf War, and in *Prayer at Rumayla*, Charles Sheehan-Miles, a former M1 tankloader in the First Gulf War, creates a narrator, Chet Brown, who seems to be overwhelmed by the omnipresent death and destruction created by the M1 tank, and possesses a memory built of inescapable, tank-specific horrors: "We charged across Iraq and killed everything in our goddamn path, we left a trail of burning vehicles and broken bodies hundreds of miles long. If it moved, then it was the enemy, and we killed our fair share of civilians too" (98). Clearly, in the pre-infantry race across the country, the devastating destructive power of the M1 tanks does not differentiate among the Iraqi populace, and who is enemy and who is friendly, combatant and noncombatant, is irrelevant. In a major tank assault, the tanker's duty is to clear the way so that the mechanized and ambulatory infantry can take and occupy acreage. So, the tanks are mobile and hostile, and the tankers have neither the time nor the inclination to differentiate between friend and foe. This is war, and this is the scenario of omnipresent death and destruction at the onset of a major mechanized offensive assault. After the war, Sheehan-Miles' narrator is horrified by the undifferentiated death and destruction secondary to these acts, but during the war, he is participating in the death and destruction and has no time to ponder that which he sees. Later in the text, on a highway near An-Nasariya, Iraq, there is more death and destruction: "The scene on the highway was one of total devastation ... literally hundreds, possibly thousands of bodies stretched all the way to Basra.... An army truck that had been destroyed. A dead man was kneeling, leaning against it in an attitude of prayer ... body parts [were scattered] indiscriminately around the area" (145). Sheehan-Miles' scenes of the immediate post-assault carnage born of offensive mechanized warfare are suitably and graphically bloody in detail and serve the peri-textual rhetorical purpose of illuminating the narrator's post-combat psychological trauma(s). Through participation and practical observation of the death and destruction produced by tank warfare, Chet Brown is effectively scarred by his war experiences and traumatized by what he has done and what he has seen — the nexus of action and observation and memorization. Brown exists in a post-war rage, secondary to the omnipresent death and destruction of tank combat and the butchery thereof, and Sheehan-Miles' rhetorical purpose is to articulate this tank-bred horror and the post-combat effects upon the practitioners of the carnage.

Clearly then, war is death, and in addition to the peri-combat deaths of allied peers and the deaths of noncombatants, secondary to myriad means and causes, there is omnipresent death and destruction in war, and as such, in the American novel of war. Animals of labor, of sustenance, and domestic, die, are killed, and are tortured and slaughtered, and the destruction of architectural entities and man-made constructs—ancient and modern—includes the demolishment of houses, farms, churches, schools, hospitals, roads, highways, bridges, railroad lines and railroads, villages, towns, cities, and entire nations. Also, included in this war-born destruction is the desecration and devastation of the natural world. War is more than death alone, and war is destructive in its means and methods and purpose; this destruction is a facet of every war, and omnipresent death and destruction is a defining characteristic situated in every true and accurate modern and postmodern novel of war, American or otherwise, and in the works utilized in this study, many animals are exterminated, and the flora of the natural world and sundry nameless and named towns and villages and man-made entities cease to exist or are catastrophically ruined; wells are poisoned, hamlets are bombed into nothingness, and sacrosanct icons are despoiled. An analysis of the thematic and rhetorical use of the element of omnipresent death and destruction in *The March*, *One Man's Initiation*, *The Marne*, *Catch-22*, *I Am the Clay*, *The Things They Carry*, and *Prayer at Rumayla*, including a brief and situating look at *The Red Badge of Courage* and *Blood Meridian*, shows the timelessness, breadth, and scope of omnipresent death and destruction during war—war, early modern, high modern, or postmodern. In *The March*, Sherman and his Union troops ride and run and tromp through Georgia and the Carolinas, and devastate and destroy, and sack and burn, and collect and conquer; no town, nor city, nor countryside that faces Sherman's centipede escapes the destruction borne of an army 60,000 strong, and the element of total war is text-wide and thematic in composition and plays a major rhetorical and situational role in the sections on Georgia, South Carolina, and North Carolina. *One Man's Initiation* and *The Marne* offer and describe repeated scenes of devastation and carnage secondary to relentless World War I artillery barrages that continue on for years at a time, and Dos Passos is skilled at offering mimeography of savaged forests and gutted mules, while Wharton is especially adept at presenting imagery of destroyed villages and towns. *Catch-22* devolves and deconstructs ancient and beautiful Rome after four-plus years of war and aerial bombing, and the city is presented as a hellish place containing historic and recently created ruins. *I Am the Clay* offers the tools of mechanized war versus ancient villages and livestock, both of which become litter under rocket or tread or machine-gun; as well, the modern city and infrastructure fare no better, and like the pre-modern hamlets, lie in ruins. *The Things They Carry* and *Prayer at Rumayla* carry the theme of omnipresent death and destruction into the late-postmodern era. The former text does so in an old-fashion way, though, as American troops kill a variety of domestic and stock animals and exquisitely torture a VC water buffalo, and poison village wells, and bomb and immolate thatched-hut villages to ashes. The latter text renders the results of the American incursion into Iraq during the Gulf War, from the optic of a tanker whose mission is to destroy everything organic, mechanical, and architectural in the path of the war machine so that the combat infantry can follow. Thus, in any era, in any country, in any war, in every war, era, and country, the result of war is one, the result of war is unified, the result of war is common—omnipresent death and destruction, of animals, of the natural world, of towns, of histories, of ways of life. As such, and while sundry authors use the theme in sundry ways, to argue sundry literary philosophies, the rhetorical element of the omnipresent death and destruction of war is situated in every American novel of war.

IX

Displacement of Locals to Refugees

Logically, local noncombatants who are not killed secondary to battle are quite often displaced from their regions or homes secondary to the omnipresent death and destruction born of the propagation of the war machine and are thus forced to become refugees in their own nation or land. Noncombatant death and regionalized devastation secondary to modern and postmodern warfare inevitably leads to large-scale relocation of those in the way of the war's progress, and in the American novel of war, if noncombatants are present — and remain alive before, during, or after combat manifestations — the displacement of locals to refugees takes place in the text. One must move his or her family, or they will die; this is the reality of war, and this thematic element of war and the novel of war is timeless, trans-war, transnational, trans-ethnic, and trans-religious. *The March*, *The Marne*, *Hold Back the Night*, *I Am the Clay*, *The Short-Timers*, and *Prayer at Rumayla* present a fairly comprehensive portrait of this enduring war theme, while a number of other texts in this study offer the refugee element in passing or in detail, but commonly, in war and in the novel of war, the child of the confluence of war and civilian is the refugee. *The March* and *I Am the Clay* show — in the mid–nineteenth and twentieth centuries, respectively, and in the United States and Korea — the steamrolling effect of the early modern and early postmodern war machine upon the local population; the former, from a limited optic as well as an optic broad and deep and sweeping, and the latter, from the finite and localized viewpoint of a makeshift refugee family of three. In each text, the plight and travel and displacement of refugees is elemental to the rhetorical purpose of the text, is thematic, and is text-wide. Further, the theme of the war-born refugee occurs in wars great and limited; *The Marne* and *Prayer at Rumayla* present the theme of the Christian and Muslim war refugee in the early and late twentieth century, in Europe and the Middle East, in World War I and the Persian Gulf War. Finally, *Hold Back the Night* and *The Short-Timers* illustrate the effects of internecine war among the local population as Chinese and American invader/occupiers ally with indigenous national political comrades in arms to oppose disjunctive political combatants in arms. What all of these texts have in common is the argument that war begets refugees, and so does the American novel of war.

In war and in an American novel of war, becoming a refugee might be an event that is immediate or foreseen. When one's house or village or town is destroyed through acute combat, one is out of a home, suddenly displaced — a refugee of sudden violence. For example, in *Blood Meridian*, immediately upon the start of the scalphunter slaughter of the Gileños, a hasty exodus begins: "a whole enfilade of refugees had begun streaming north along the shore wailing crazily..." (156). However, in the McCarthy text, the refugee's life is only worth the refugee's receipt, and even those who flee are killed nearly immediately, so their role as refugees is short-lived. Regardless of war, this immediacy of refugee status is found in other war texts. In *Company K*, Private Jesse Bogan narrates, "Below us the Germans were shelling Marigny, a small town. We could see people running out of the houses, making funny gestures, and down the narrow streets, until they joined the line that filled the highway" (48). Again, noncombatants are immediately transformed into refugees, and the reader sees this urgent status change. One moment, one is at home, one has a home; the next, one's home is a target and one is displaced — a refugee. Refugees can also be produced secondary to their "rescuers," as in *Catch-22*, whereby the American Military Police violently evict the prostitutes from their apartment — their residence and place of sanctuary: "The M.P.s busted the whole apartment up and drove the whores right out.... They flushed them right out into the street" (414), says a zealous Captain Black. Thus, absurdly, and in conjunction with the American bombing of Italy (post-occupation), the rescuers are displacing those they are supposed to rescue. The apartment/brothel has no strategic or military bearing, yet falls under the attack of the American war machine.

The presence of refugees in war can also be situated in the text as, logically enough, visibly displaced peoples, carrying their remaining or important possessions; in *Company K*, per the narrative of Corporal Frederick Willcoxen, "all day we saw French civilians, mostly old men and women, trudging to the rear, loaded down with their personal property" (171). Here, the presence of refugees in time of war is signaled by their very presence in the text of war: this is war; war begets refugees. In *Through the Wheat*, Thomas Boyd, as does William March, presents the French citizenry: "the streets were crowded with wagons, carts, domestic animals, and people. Comforters were thrown over the hard pavement, and families were lying on them, resting" (64). Interestingly, Boyd suggests that the refugees always have mirrors with them: "Mirrors in ornate frames apparently had a special significance for the refugees" (65), as if seeing one's reflection, even sans a home or former civilian and material existence, equals a state of human existence — a quasi–Cartesian, "I see myself; therefore, I am."

Ironically, refugee status in a novel of war is often evident secondary to the lack of civilians in deserted, semi-destroyed villages, towns, and cities through which the war machine rolls or has rolled. So, the absence of civilians means the presence of refugees, even though those seeking refuge are not situated in the scenic actions of the text. For example, in *The Red Badge of Courage*, during a battle, a house sits alone in the path of the war machine: "Over some foliage they could see the roof of a house. One window, glowing a deep murder red, shone squarely through the leaves" (104). The house, deserted, and having been artilleried, is on fire, and the absence of occupants indicates the presence of refugees. And in *Through the Wheat*, there is "a deserted village.... It was a very small town and had been evacuated two days before" (67–68). When possible, and time and tactical issues permitting, prior to the war coming to town, citizens are evacuated, and refugees are created. Finally, in *It's Cold in Pongo-Ni*, the village of Pongo-Ni "is close enough to the Chinese positions to catch stray incoming rounds every time The Claw is bombarded. ['The lieutenant'] sees no one among the shell-shattered ruins" (86). In this case, one must relocate or die. So, clearly, the issue of refugees is a component both of war and of the novel of war. War produces refugees in a number of different manners — acute violence, chronic violence, malicious violence, random violence, foreseen violence.

Thus, war engenders refugees; regardless of continent or war, this is true. Refugee status in war and in war novels is ever-present, and, of course, the root word of "refugee" is "refuge," and what refugees are seeking is refuge from the chaos, danger, and violence of war. Western readers are most aware, logically, of the wars fought by Western nations that have produced the war literature written by Western authors, and thus have read war literature from the Western perspective. Nonetheless, wars fought on other continents, by indigenous combatants, have also produced war literature and, topically, have produced refugees. For example, post-colonial Africa has been a locus of war for a century or more, but as the continent has imploded, the implosion has been largely ignored by the American and pan-European reader. For example, according to Maxine Sample, during the Nigerian Civil War (July 1967–January 1970), "hundreds of thousands of civilians, many of them children, perished in the thirty months of its duration" (445), and the war produced millions and millions of refugees, who fled ethnic-based genocidal violence—for example, at least "two million Ibos" (446) from the Northern Region alone. The war also produced the literature of war, and writers such as Chinua Achebe, Cyprian Ekwenski, Gabrial Okara, Flora Nwapa, and Christopher Okigbo would heed the call to write of the civil war of the day (Sample 447). According to Achebe, the best known to Western readers, "The involvement of the Biafran writer today [1969] in the cause for which his people are fighting and dying is not different from the involvement of many African writers—past and present—in the big issues of Africa. The fact of war merely puts the matter in sharper focus" (qtd. in Sample 447). Thus, the writer, according to Achebe, a person of "heightened sensibilities," must write of the atrocities of war, and one of the atrocities of war is the displacement of people from their native homes—the creation of refugees. Sample argues that "the Nigerian writer's treatment of [the Nigerian Civil] war" uses "the refugee phenomenon ... as a focal point in the literature" (448). For example, Flora Nwapa, in *Never Again* (1975), "emphasizes the psychic trauma of refugees in the process of fleeing from one town to the next, the federal troops at their heels. [And the] novel captures the simultaneous hysteria and the weariness of a people fleeing for their lives, leaving behind the security and memories of past lives" (449). Thus, regardless of continent or race or ethnicity, the refugee's life is a traumatic one—one of psychological, social, physical, cultural, and material loss and displacement and decentering.

Of course, and this is important to note, as it severely contrasts with the perspective of the American war author, Nwapa's text—as well as the texts written by other contemporary Nigerian writers of the civil war—is written from an internal perspective, a perspective of one who not only participates in the war experience from an indigenous experiential point of view, but also empathizes, rather than sympathizes, with the refugees of the war, as the refugees are the self-same citizens as the authors. Thus, the Nigerian-authored works of the Nigerian Civil War utilize insider, participatory optics, while the American works of war most often utilize observational, non-indigenous optics; so the insider optic allows the Nigerian authors the opportunity to create conjunctive, collectivist works, while the American-authored, observational texts allow only for disjunctive, separatist works. So, the American-authored text of war is written by an American author who is observing the refugees—one who watches and identifies the refugees—and is most often written from a narrative perspective that is nationally allied with the American combatants in the work. Consequently, the American works of war that do present the war refugee peritextually lack empathy for the war refugee. This lack of empathy even (or especially) includes—secondary to journalistic objectivity—the reports filed by American journalists during recent wars in Iraq and Afghanistan-Pakistan. For example, this note from the *Washington Post*, titled "War in Iraq Propelling a Massive Migration": "Nearly 2 million Iraqis—about 8 percent of the prewar population—have embarked on a desperate migration, mostly to Jordan, Syria, and Lebanon, according to the U.N. High Commissioner for Refugees.... Another 1.7 million have been forced to move to safer towns and villages inside Iraq, and as many as 50,000 Iraqis a month flee their homes" (Raghavan). And this recent refugee-centric blurb from *Newsweek*, titled "Pakistan Uprooted": "Pakistan surpassed war-torn African nations such as Sudan in the number of newly displaced people last year, according to a recent United Nations Study.... Islamic insurgents who seized large swaths of territory along the Afghanistan-Pakistan border — and the military offense to weaken them — drove some 3 million Pakistanis from their homes in 2009" (Moreau and Yousafzai 5). Common to both these citations and situations, in addition to the millions of refugees born of war, is the citation of the United Nations; as such, these news reports are less than observational — the reports are tertiary, far removed from the plight of the refugees. The result, then, is that the refugees, a total of more than six million displaced victims of war, are completely and absolutely dehumanized — nothing more than vague numbers on a page. Thus, the human toll of the refugees born of the Iraq and Afghanistan-Pakistan wars is irrelevant, a catastrophe of nothingness that encompasses six million human lives. Nonetheless, authors of the American novel of war do present the displacement of locals to refugees in their works, albeit at widely contrasting thematic and rhetorical levels, and most often — but not always—from an observational perspective.

A deeper and more thorough examination and analysis of the presence of refugees in *The March, The Marne, Hold Back the Night, I Am the Clay, The Short-Timers,* and *Prayer at Rumayla* shows that, on a gross level, all of the texts (except for *I Am the Clay* and, in places, *The March*) present the refugee element as observational and objective. In E.L. Doctorow's *The March*, the refugees— thousands of whom are recently emancipated slaves— are peripherally observed, but for a very limited number of characters. A number of Southern former slave-owner refugees are situated in the text, but again, those refugees born of the war, whose towns sit silent, destroyed, and deserted, lack any development in the text. However, on the first page of the text, in a foreshadowing of the Anglo-American and African American refugee theme, Doctorow offers the reader one Letitia Pettibone, of McDonough, Georgia, a displaced Southerner whose home and town have already been overrun by General Sherman's army of total war. Pettibone rails at Mattie and John Jameson, her niece and her nephew by marriage, to escape before the Union pillagers arrive: "Get out, get out, take what you can and leave" (4). The Jamesons do as advised and leave a number of (immediately) former slaves in their wake, one of whom, a young woman named Pearl, the offspring of John Jameson and a deceased slave named Nancy Wilkins, will evolve into a developed, primary character — a subjective refugee.

Doctorow likewise develops the observational refugee status of the freed slaves who follow Sherman's army as it runs through Georgia, then South Carolina, then North Carolina. Before the first chapter is complete, "About a thousand blacks were following the army" (13). One must remember that these immediately freed slaves have had their lives decentered in such a way that they have no homes, no owners, no place to go, and thus have no choice but to follow the Union army as it completes its course. Left behind, what would the slaves do? What *could* the slaves do? As noted in the narration, rebel guerrillas roam the country, and if such angered (also displaced) individuals found the refugee former slaves, the result would be horrifying for the freedmen and women (13). Consequently, the former slaves cum refugees are allowed to trail the Northern forces. In Milledgeville, to the southeast, and in the path of Sherman's ever-growing centipede, "raised voices and the rattle of carriage wheels.... One carriage after another" (17) rolls out of town, loaded with persons and material goods. So, early in the text, Doctorow effectively creates the theme of the war-born refugee, and he subjectively shows the refugee as landed Anglo Southerner as well as immediately freed former slave, while he also objectively notes that the body of refugees who are former slaves is huge and growing with every plantation or town taken. Thus, Doctorow has created a text-wide theme, on a number of different rhetorical levels, of the Displacement of Locals—former landowners, former townies, and former slaves— to Refugees.

By contrasting the Anglo refugees, immediately deprived of their land, homes, and lives, with the African American refugees, immediately freed and displaced of their status as slaves, Doctorow is contrasting the emotional space occupied by each caste. The Anglo refugees, who have lost all their landed and worldly possessions, are psychologically and emotionally devastated, lost: Emily Thompson (through whose optic much of the Anglo refugee's perspective is subjectively presented), upon seeing the Union army enter Milledgeville, is aghast: "A deep misgiving arose in her" (26). Conversely—collectively and objectively— the former slaves, who also have lost what little they knew, but are nonetheless, no longer owned peoples, are not so devastated, and the "parade of black folks" (33) who follow the army creates a "festive sound ... a celebratory chatter ... like birds" (33) who sing and laugh. Note the language and diction: A "parade" follows the army; by connotation and denotation, a parade is a ceremonial procession, an evocation of happiness, a gathering to celebrate an occasion. In this situation, of course, the occasion is freedom. Also, Doctorow compares the members of the parade to birds. Birds, of course, are free to fly, and in long-held literary tradition, the presence of birds in the text symbolizes freedom. Further, birds flock together for social interaction and safety. So, tonally and socially and behaviorally, Anglo refugees are filled with dread, while African American refugees are filled with happiness. As the chapter closes, Emily Thompson rides out of Milledgeville, crying (35): she, too, a newly minted refugee, and the narrator, notes, "Everyone from the Governor on down was gone" (36). Doctorow thoroughly evacuates the town of Milledgeville and, in so doing, bespeaks the theme of the war-born refugee. Everyone, at all levels of society, from every caste—free and formerly enslaved— is displaced in time of war. The war machine does such a thing, and one and all must move.

Concurrently, the mass of freed slaves grows, and the Union army groans under the load; according to one young officer, "They are too many mouths to feed" (44). As is usual in time of war, the old and the young will suffer, for the young men can be enlisted, but what purpose in war do the very old, the very young, and the women serve? (44). Regardless, as the army moves southeast to Savannah, the freed slaves "trailed the columns" (116), and Savannah becomes a temporary refugee camp cum army base, a locus where the population grows "with whites [too] who'd fled" (116) the Union machine of total war. So, generally speaking, much of the "Georgia" (1–133) section of the text is, typical of American novels of war, an objective and observational presentation of the war-born refugee, and while the subjective optics of a small number of Anglo and African American refugees are offered, the mass of freed slaves that follows Sherman's army is very much a focal point of the refugee theme.

At the close of the "Georgia" section, Sherman, through Field Order Number 15 (120), which grants 40 acres of land to the head of every African American family, manages to separate many of the multitude from his army, but regardless, with the taking of South Carolina, "at least a thousand blacks had assembled" (197) to march behind the Union forces. Additionally, Southern Anglos sympathetic to the Union cause (not safe, of course) also follow. So, in the "South Carolina" (135–210) section of the text, the objective refugee element is still offered, but it is even more peripheral and less personal than in the first section of the text. Developmentally, what the second section of the text does (other than give the reader an account of Sherman's devastating push through South Carolina and the destruction, in detail, of Columbia, South Carolina) is align the paths and subjective characterizations of three refugees (two Anglo and one African American)—Mattie Jameson, Emily Thompson, and Pearl Wilkins-Jameson—each of whom is an "encumbrance, a Southern refugee" (143) among the "crowd of the newly homeless" (190), and each of whom serves a role in a nursing capacity of sorts in Dr. Wrede Sartorius' field hospital, a mobile medical residence never short of business. All three women refugees have suffered tremendous losses—of family, of home, of every social identifier—and each deals differently with the losses: Mattie, the senior most of the three, loses her mind slowly; Emily, though young, grows into a matronly role and attaches herself to an "orphan asylum" (210) in Columbia; and Pearl, Mattie's former slave and "step-daughter," also evolves and takes a role as caretaker to Mattie.

As the "North Carolina" (211–363) section opens, the objective observation of refugees returns again, as an "uprooted civilization" (239) follows Sherman, and the freed slaves alone are "twenty-five thousand" (248) in number. The masses also include increasing numbers of "fugitive whites" (247) from the South. Sherman orders the freed slaves separated from the Union army (248, 256) so that he can continue his march unencumbered, an order and rhetorical act further objectifying the thousands of war-born African American refugees, leaves the unnamed, faceless refugees in a state of "wretched disillusionment" (256). In a number of melodramatic pathos-centric rhetorical movements that strain the credulity of the text, refugee Mattie Jameson is reunited with her only living relative (290), her son Jaime, a Confederate prisoner of war, whom Pearl and a Union soldier named Stephen Walsh have freed (289), and she and Jaime are then redirected by Pearl back to now-unoccupied Georgia by way of Columbia. As the text closes, and the war ends, refugee and—light-skinned—freed slave Pearl is headed to New York City with Walsh so that they can marry, he can study law, and she medicine (361–62).

Referring to Edith Wharton's final scene in *The Marne*, John J. Murphy asserts that "Wharton's ending is symptomatic of an ongoing failure of confidence in verisimilitude to contribute to closure" (158), and this criticism could, indeed, be applied to Doctorow's melodramatic wrapping up of the situations of all three subjective refugees in *The March*: Emily Thompson leaves the medical service in order to angelically manage an orphanage filled with African American war refugee children; Mattie Jameson is to be returned to Georgia with her remaining son, a freed Confederate prisoner of war; and Pearl Wilkins-Jameson is to go to New York, marry a future lawyer, and become a doctor. The only realistic refugee portrayal at the close of the text is the portrayal of the masses of freed slave refugees whom Sherman severs from his army, who may or may not get a bit of land out of the deal. That said, when considered as a thematic and rhetorical element in the text, the use of the displacement of locals to refugees element in *The March*, both subjectively and objectively presented, is well developed and text-wide and thorough enough to bear attention on its own rhetorical merits and, more specifically, its merits as a defining characteristic of the American novel of war.

War creates refugees irrespective of religion, and in *The March* and Edith Wharton's propaganda novel, *The Marne*, the refugees are, obviously, primarily Christian. That said, the major wars in this study are based in politics and geography rather than religiosity.

Nonetheless, one must be aware that war begets refugees of all religions, and the First World War, of course, is not an exception. Neil N. Heyman notes, "Floods of civilians fled the assault of the German armies on the western front in 1914. [And from] the war's start, observers were struck by the sight of pitiable families, hauling possessions selected in a moment of panic, racing to escape advancing Germans" (181–82). Wharton's text is aware of this exodus of refugees and the refugee motif runs the length of the text. From the onset of the war, refugees are mentioned or are placed directly in the text; first, at the start of the war in 1914, Troy Belknap's former French tutor, Madame Lebuc (now out of work, of course), is aided by Mr. and Mrs. Belknap in locating a job in "a refugee bureau" (13). The use here of an indefinite article rather than a definite article implies that refugee bureaus are immediately common in France and that there exists a sudden need for such bureaus in the face of war. As Heyman notes, at the onset of the war, approximately 1.4 million Belgian refugees were forced to evacuate as the German push began (181), so France was flooded with external refugees in addition to local refugees, and France was not alone among countries producing and receiving refugees, as Lady Kennard attests in *A Roumanian Diary, 1915, 1916, 1917* when viewing a train accident in which a train full of women and children refugees from Bucharest are horribly killed: "No one knows how many hundreds died there by the roadside, some in the flames of the engine's exploded petrol tank, the greater number crushed into one huge formless mass of flesh and horse-hair, splintered bones and wood" (qtd. in Higonnet 98). This horrible scene of refugee death is not repeated in the Wharton text, but the urgency of the refugees in the face of war is evident, as the streets of Paris are filled: "With trains of farm-waggons, drawn by slow country horses, and heaped with furniture and household utensils; and beside the carts walked lines of haggard people, old men and women with vacant faces, mothers hugging hungry babies, and children limping after them with heavy bundles. The fugitives of the Marne were pouring into Paris" (22). The refugees are fleeing the First Battle of the Marne (6–12 September 1914), a battle that produced approximately 500,000 casualties and subsequently the stalemate that gave rise to four years of trench warfare.

In the refugee scene, Wharton is offering melodrama, yet doing so does not negate the truth of the scene and the misery and suffering experienced by the refugees. While Wharton's text is an emotional appeal and an argument against "self-centered" (Murphy 161) American materialism and materialists, the text is nonetheless effectively accurate in the presentation of the ethos of the war-born refugees. And after introducing the refugee motif in general through the nameless, faceless train of refugees wandering through the streets of Paris, Wharton later personalizes the motif with a reference to Madame Gantier, the matriarch of the family with whom the Belknaps once socialized; as an ambulance man stationed in France who coincidentally travels through the village once occupied by the Gantiers, Troy is trying to locate those he once knew, and "before a Y.M.C.A. hut" (70) — a Christian organization, of course, readily present all through Europe during World War I — asks the locals of the whereabouts of the Gantier family, and one man replies, "The old lady? Ah, she and her sister went away ... some charitable people took them, I don't know where ... I've got an address somewhere" (71). Troy, coincidentally again, locates Madame Gantier in a Paris refugee bureau (74), the same one in which Madame Lebuc still works (72). This series of coincidences, among others in the text, "breaks whatever realism survives" (Murphy 164) in the remaining prose, but does not destroy the rhetorical effect of the plight of the families "of foot-sore refugees" (83). And even though Wharton does use coincidence in a nearly haphazard way, one must remember that Wharton's text is a propaganda piece, an argument against American material, social, and military selfishness, and if some of her platitudes are clumsy, so be it.

Wharton's refugee motif runs the chronological length of the war, from 1914 to 1918, from the First Battle of the Marne to the Second Battle of the Marne (15 July–6 August 1918), and refugees are situated in the text from the open to the close of the work — and the war — as "hay-carts packed with refugees" (109) are concomitant components of "the usual dense traffic of the front" (109), so as Troy travels toward the Marne, he watches "women crouched sobbing on their piled-up baggage" (110). The build-up to battle is ongoing, and the refugees exist in fear — homeless, lifeless, lost once again in the face of the machine and carnage of war. The Second Battle of the Marne has begun, and "a stream of haggard country people was pouring from the direction of the Marne. This time only a few were in their carts: the greater number were flying on their feet" (115). Once again, the war has come to the Marne, and the citizenry, country folk, are in hasty flight and newly felt fear. Note how Wharton specifically identifies the refugees as rural people and, in so doing, simplifies and idealizes those in flight: these fair agrarian people, with their rabbits and their horses and their simple pastoral lives, deserve not to be placed in such dire circumstances at the will of mighty governments and violent armies. Nonetheless, the war comes and the refugees go. Through the length of *The Marne*, Wharton does not ignore the plight of the refugees of World War I; in fact, she adroitly uses the presence of the refugees in war-destroyed France to effectively enhance and build pathos, regardless of the segues into melodrama.

In the war texts of the Korean War, specifically *Hold Back the Night* and *I Am the Clay*, refugees are also commonly situated, especially in the latter text, which is entirely a refugee-filled tale of exodus and return; as a rule, the texts born of the Korean War that are set early in the conflict offer significant numbers of combat-fleeing refugees, peoples displaced secondary to Chinese and North Korean pushes southward and subsequent American and South Korean pushes northward. Pat Frank's *Hold Back the Night* presents refugees through their absence from towns and villages, and thus the issue of war-displaced noncombatants is one of negativity: the towns are not occupied; as such, the civilians are displaced refugees. Lieutenant Raleigh Couzens, after being captured, interrogated, and then freed by the Chinese forces, is released before the Korean town of Ko-Bong, a town situated between the advancing Chinese forces and the American line of defense. Couzens asks his Chinese guard which force occupies the town, and the guard replies that the Chinese do not. Couzens enters the town, and listens, and he hears that Ko-Bong "was not deserted by all its sorrowing people" (110). There are a number of implications in this short passage: Ko-Bong sits between the Chinese and American forces; as such, Ko-Bong is in the path of the Chinese war machine, so Chinese troops will occupy Ko-Bong sooner rather than later, and Ko-Bong will fall. The civilian citizenry are aware of the impending Chinese occupation, and as a result, most, but for perhaps a lone woman and her infant, have deserted the town — Frank's "sorrowing people" (Ko-Bong's newly displaced locals— Ko-Bong's refugees). And as is often the case with American-authored perspectives of war, the point of view is observational and objective, rather than participatory and subjective. Typically, in an occupied country, the American military man — or narrator — notes the absence of indigenous civilians, and this absence is not surprising, for this is war, and war breeds refugees.

Later in the text, when Dog Company pulls out of Koto-Ri, the absence of civilian personnel on the road unsettles Captain Mackenzie: "All the people, the people that armies call 'indigenous personnel,' seemed to have disappeared. That disturbed Mackenzie" (166), and he asks, "Where are the people?" (166). The locals, aware that the Chinese own the country, are either in flight or in hiding, conspicuous through their absence. The war has come to the countryside, and those civilians who remain or expose themselves will be killed. Mackenzie likens the civilians to "small game" (167) and the Chinese to "tigers" (167) — prey and predators in the jungle of war. So, again, refugees are present in the war because they are absent from the text, and this presence through absence motif continues as the men of Dog Company race to the Sea of Japan. In the village of Sinsong-Ni, an old man remains, and he tells Mackenzie what has happened to the people who once occupied the village: first, Chinese and North Korean invaders appropriated the village and took with them the young women of Sinsong-Ni; then the American forces bombed the Chinese-occupied village; then the village elders decided, logically enough, that "the village should move" (182), and so "the older men, and the older women, and the children who were left, they moved to another place" (182). Again, and so typical of war ancient, modern, and postmodern, the very old and the very young are the victims of combat, and it is they who must become refugees or die. The young women who once lived in the village have been taken as sexual chattel, and the young men who once occupied the village have been conscripted: the "normalcy" of war. Thus, the village, as it once existed, is dead, at least until after the war, and perhaps for all time.

Unlike the Frank text, which primarily situates the refugees' presence by the refugees' absence, Chaim Potok's *I Am the Clay* follows three refugees as they embark on an exodus south, spend time in a cave and a refugee camp, and then return north in an attempt to repatriate what remains of their village. Similar to Doctorow in *The March*, Potok places the focus of the text on three refugees, while he also imparts the mass number of refugees for effect. In so doing, Potok presents the acute misery of three specific refugees and also acknowledges the chronic suffering of thousands and thousands of other, unnamed refugees. The thematic trope of the displacement of Buddhist Korean locals to refugees — and their exodus and suffering — is the central element of the text, which is very much analogous to the exodus and suffering of the ancient Jews in the Torah, and from the first sentence of the text, the refugee theme is presented: "[W]hen the Chinese and the army from the North swept down into the South, an old man and his wife fled from their village ... and embarked on a panicky trek ... with other refugees" (3). The pair is forced into a ditch so as not to be run over by a column of American military vehicles, and they happen upon a boy. So, in the first sentence and in the first paragraph of the text, Potok subjectifies and personalizes the plight of the refugees by introducing the three primary characters, and he also objectifies and depersonalizes the mass of refugees by showing that the three are but three among many "townspeople and farmers and villagers ... [a]ll begrimed, terrified" (4). Counterintuitively, Potok litters the text with unnamed, undeveloped refugees, and in so doing, he dehumanizes the displaced human beings in a rhetorical effort to promote the plight of those who die and suffer and are displaced secondary to the actions and effects of the war machine. Rare for an American novel of war, the refugees who are subjectified are neither American nor Christian, because, in most cases, the American novel of war observes refugees while focusing on the rhetorical situations of the uniformed American characters. In the Potok text, the refugees are, generally, poorly treated by the American military, who make the refugees walk off the thoroughfare(s) so that mechanized and ambulatory military personnel can utilize the causeway(s): "Military police kept the refugees off the road" (40). Again, Potok presents the broad and the specific; the optic of the unnamed woman is often the optic through which the reader observes the mass of refugees: "So many. The woman had not thought the war had undone so many. Each with eyes fixed to the ground" (67).

Interestingly, and actually not surprising at all, the refugees keep to themselves, each an island of suffering and self-preservation. The roads are populated with the corpses of refugees whose bodies have given out, but the masses keep moving, keep placing one foot in front of the other. Even children left alive on the side of the road are ignored: "A grimy-faced little girl squatted alone on a pile of rubble, crying" (13), but no one, no refugee, comforts or helps the child. And unlike the mass of post-slavery, African American refugees in the Doctorow text, who were excited to be finally free from bondage, these refugees, displaced from their homes but trapped within the dynamism of ongoing war, exist in abject misery. The refugees are sick; they are starving; they are wounded; they are wandering without a homeland. Potok's three focal characters, after recovering in a cave — quite biblical, of course — seek and locate a refugee camp on a "vast plain dotted with shanties and firepits" (114), but instead of respite, the camp is a locus of death, and refugees continue to die, secondary to the cold and to disease, as "new refugees entered the plain" (133). When spring comes, and the Americans have again pushed north, the refugees leave the refugee camp and begin the trek home; this time, and in a rare optimistic — and symbolic — note, the refugees are on the road rather than in the ditch or on a road-side trail: "Straggles of refugees on one side of the road" (167), and soldiers on the other, and ambulances in great numbers. Of course, as detailed previously, Kim's village has been destroyed and his family is dead, so he remains with the unnamed couple. *I Am the Clay* is a work of staggering emotional and psychological depth, sans melodrama and explicit pathos. This subjective and objective study of the plight of the Korean peasant refugees displaced by the Korean War humanizes the faceless and nameless refugees found in so many novels of war. And by humanizing the refugees of the Korean War, Potok takes non-descriptive "locally displaced persons" and returns developed human beings.

Vietnam War texts in general, and Gustav Hasford's *The Short-Timers* in particular, return the indigenous refugees to the status of persons of observation, and in the Hasford effort, but for one scene set in the ancient Citadel of Hue, refugees are mostly ignored by Hasford, the author, and Joker, the narrator. In the scene that does present refugees, however, Hasford, through Joker's observational optic, seems to empathize with the "locally displaced persons." In an interesting point, the refugees are situated at the University of Hue, a locus of learning. Ironically, man, inherently violent, ever waging war and slaughtering warriors and noncombatants alike, is incapable of learning from previous wars, so a university, whose mission is, of course, higher education and enlightenment, is useless during a war. Thus, a university's mission is set aside so that the acreage and buildings can situate those refugees traumatically displaced by war. Thus, Hasford is proclaiming the uselessness of rational, cogent thought and elevated intellectual education in a time of war; war supersedes intellect, and so man does not learn by or from war. Upon entering Hue, Joker and Rafter Man exit their tank taxi and observe the scene: The university "is now a collection point for refugees.... Whole families with all of their possessions have occupied the classrooms and corridors since the battle began. The refugees are too tired to run anymore. The refugees look cold and drained the way you look after death sits on your face and smothers you for so long that you get tired of screaming" (80–81). The university no longer collects scholars and students; now, the role of the university is to collect the displaced, the lost — the victims of war. Consequently, the primary mission of the university is void; no one, not the civilians, not the military members, not the governmental entities, is learning here. And these refugees are extant as extended families, or so Joker believes. Inferred here is the fact that the families are multigenerational, and thus are composed of the very old, the very young, and most likely women of childbearing age with children. Young men, of course, are not mentioned, as most or all are conscripted or have volunteered to fight—for either side.

In a rare moment of less-than-cynical commentary, Joker notes that the refugees are exhausted, "too tired to run anymore." These refugees, nameless, but not role-less, have run and run and run, from death, from destruction, from war; yet they remain exhausted but alive. And historically, relative to the centuries-long symbiotic practice of Buddhism and Taoism in what is now called Vietnam, to leave one's ancestral home — and one's familial burial grounds— is to, in effect, reject the spirits of one's ancestors and their sacred place in both familial history and cosmic present. Thus—and this was an issue the American administrators of the Vietnam War somehow, astoundingly, failed to comprehend, even after more than a decade of occupation — to leave one's home is a severe act, a transhistorical, trans-cosmic act. So, civilian refugees in Vietnam are not merely physically displaced from their homes and familial lands, and psychically and emotionally displaced — as are all war refugees— but also cosmically and spiritually and ancestrally displaced. Accordingly, the indigenous refugees of the Vietnam War are suffering beyond the mere physical and emotional; they are in a spiritual crisis, too, brought on by the severing of the people from their familial lands and their ancestors' spirits. Hasford is aware of this psychic and cosmic fracture, of course, and in a very rare moment, Hasford admits and acknowledges the suffering of the Vietnamese people.

In Charles Sheehan-Miles' *Prayer at Rumayla*, the war-born refugees of the Persian Gulf War are Sunni and Shia Muslims, even though, with the minority Sunnis comprising much of the Ba'ath Party under Saddam Hussein, as well as the majority of the army (especially the officer and non-commissioned officer classes), most of the combatants killed through tank assaults in the text are Sunni. However, during the massive armored assault of 26–27 February 1991, along Highway 80 and Highway Eight, outside the city of Basra, thousands of Iraqi army members deserted and fled into Basra, so, under the threat of imminent destruction and death, thousands of civilians fled the city and, through displacement, became war refugees. The horrors of war live with Chet Brown, Sheehan-Miles' war veteran narrator, and he cannot replace the ghastly images that reside in his post-war mind: "it would always be right there, right behind my eyes, all I have to do is close my damn eyes to see the burning man ... the exploding tanks ... the dismembered bodies ... the refugees fleeing Basra" (82). While the first three images are explicitly of death—a man on fire; exploding, crew-filled tanks; fragmented corpses— the last image — that of nameless, faceless refugees in flight — is important because of the association with the deceased. In a massive mechanized ground and air war, today's refugees might very well be tomorrow's corpses. Thus, Sheehan-Miles conjoins the dead with the living and, in so doing, foreshadows the potential death(s) of the refugees. This connection of the dead to the living dehumanizes the refugees to the point that they, even while living, are worth no more humanistically than the dead. The refugees are not described as men or women or children; they are merely and abjectly refugees, and are not characterized or humanized at any level.

Later in the text, Sheehan-Miles again refers to refugees, but this time Brown's vision is post-assault, post-war, yet still on Highway Eight; in this instance, Sheehan-Miles humanizes the refuges, even though, narratively, the optic is observational: "I remember the day we left Iraq. We were back on highway eight, lined up in battalions and brigades for the road march back to Saudi Arabia ... and hundreds, maybe thousands of refugees were streaming out of Basra into the interior of Iraq. I don't know what condition the city was in, where they were going. Families, women, children, deserting soldiers, all of them in this slow exodus past us.... And the kids— all those kids, so many of them had lost their fathers, and they were hungry, hungry" (99). In this second — post-combat — reference to refugees, there is some level of compassion on the part of Chet Brown. Conversely, in the first — peri-battle — reference to refugees, Brown is apathetic. One might argue that, in combat mode, the combatant is not allowed, or cannot allow, him- or herself to feel emotionally attached to the human beings caught under the tracks of the war machine, but after the combat is complete, the combatant, now out of a life-threatening situation, can allow him- or herself to examine those suffering the horrors of war. As a result of this peri-combat and post-combat dyad, Brown's description of the refugees, and the tone and diction with which he describes them, is radically different. An interesting word that Sheehan-Miles uses to describe the train of Muslim refugees in the latter description is "exodus," a word commonly applied to the second book of the Old Testament and to the Israelites going out from Egypt. Sheehan-Miles could not have used "exodus" accidentally, and he must be using the word analogously to allude to the Iraqis' travels in the quest for safety, perhaps even safety from dictatorial rule under Saddam Hussein. Nonetheless, the narrative transformation of Chet Brown's two descriptions of Sunni and Shia refugees manifestly identifies the narrator's dehumanization and then humanization of those seeking refuge with the dehumanization coming during war and the humanization coming after.

Clearly, then, war begets refugees, local noncombatants who are not killed but are displaced from their homes secondary to the omnipresent death and destruction of war. Forced to become refugees in their own land, these displaced peoples are the litter of war. And in the American novel of war, if noncombatants are present — those lucky enough to remain alive before, during, or after combat manifestations— the displacement of locals to refugees takes place in the text. It does not matter if one is American Indian, African American, Anglo, Franco, Asian, or Arab; it does not matter if one is Pantheistic, Christian, Buddhist, Taoist, or Muslim; it does not matter if one resides in North America, Western Europe, Southeast Asia, or the Middle East; it does not matter if the conflict is the War of Eradication against the Native Americans, the U.S. Civil War, World War I, World War II, the Korean War, the Vietnam War, the Persian Gulf War, the Iraq War, or the Afghanistan-Pakistan War — or any and all wars before, between, or after. What matters is this: war breeds refugees. Collectively, *The March, The Marne, Hold Back the Night, I Am the Clay, The Short-Timers*, and *Prayer at Rumayla* present a fairly comprehensive and varied presentation of this enduring war theme, a theme situated in most of the texts in this study, either in passing or in detail. *The March* and *I Am the Clay* both show the steamrolling effect of the early modern and early postmodern war machine upon the local people. The former text demonstrates that while becoming a war refugee is a life-changing and decentering event, it does not necessarily have to be a negative experience, as the freed slaves in the text are given their opportunity to escape bondage. The latter text offers the finite and localized point of view of a makeshift refugee family of three; however, their refugee status is one of misery and common suffering, and the three are metonymously representative of the peasant Korean populace, which suffers greatly secondary to the brutalities of invading armies and mechanized warfare. *The Marne* and *Prayer at Rumayla* likewise present war great and small and show the military entering noncombatant areas while refugees flee in the opposite direction, so as war enters an area, civilians cum refugees must, under the threat of death, exit the area. Finally, *Hold Back the Night* and *The Short-Timers* illustrate the effects of internecine war among the locals as invader/occupiers ally with indigenous national political-military comrades in arms to oppose disjunctive political-military combatants in arms. The former text indicates the presence of refugees through the absence of noncombatants in deserted villages; hence, a lack of civilians means a populace of refugees—somewhere, but not at home. The latter text evinces the catastrophe of forced refugee status upon Buddhist-Taoist peasants who are forced to commit metaphysical betrayal or face annihilation; further, a university is redesigned as a refugee pivot-point, so the role of intellect in war is secondary to more practical aspects of war, such as brutality and survival. What all of these texts have in common, though, is the argument that war produces refugees, and so does the American novel of war.

X

The Oppositional Dyad Between
Occupying/Invading Forces
and Indigenous/Local Peoples

Even without the war-born deaths of noncombatants, and the omnipresent death and destruction of local geographies, animals, and habitations, and the displacement of locals to refugees, the presence of non-native, non-national armed forces during war is a cause of great social, cultural, political, racial, and religious enmity between the occupier/invaders and the local/indigenous peoples. So, naturally, in both war and the American novel of war, there is an oppositional dyad between the occupying/invading forces and the indigenous/local peoples. The inherent sense of mistrust between those who have come and those who have been invaded or occupied also enters the socio-cultural fray and leads to a supposition that no one — on either side — can be trusted by the other. *The Red Badge of Courage, Company K, Band of Brothers, The Short-Timers, Desert Norm,* and *A Medic in Iraq* each show that this oppositional dyad between invader/occupiers and the locals is one that runs from the nineteenth century to the twenty-first century and occurs wherever war occurs. A brief passage in *The Red Badge of Courage* sets a corpulent Union soldier against a civilian "young girl" (17) as the soldier arrogantly attempts to steal the woman's horse, and multiple sketches in *Company K* posit war-exhausted French civilians against new-to-war American Marines. And so, even when allied, occupiers and the indigenous do not seem to want one another, as the uniformed occupiers are merely reminders (often unpleasant) of the war at hand. *Band of Brothers, The Short-Timers,* and *Desert Norm* show that the locals and the occupiers, even when invited by the government of the occupied, in the Far East or in the Middle East, in the middle or late twentieth century, tend not to get along, often to the point that the occupied physically attack or kill the occupier. And finally, *A Medic in Iraq* offers the explicit hatred of the local population toward the uninvited American invaders whose quid pro quo toppled a dictator but invited the insurgent and the terrorist. Obviously, then, invited or invading armed occupiers are resented to the point of hatred by the indigenous occupied. Further, the civilian deaths, the destruction of native land and property, and the subsequent displacement of locals during time of war cumulatively and exponentially affect the resentment of the locals toward the non-native uniformed forces.

Historically, and in the literature of war, this oppositional dyad is a fact of all wars, as racial, cultural, political, theological, linguistic, and social differences between occupiers or invaders and the locals contribute to the tension, and a mutually felt lack of trust of the Other creates a (sometimes deadly) fracture between allied occupier and occupied, as is the case in *Blood Meridian*, whereby the fine citizenry of Chihuahua cannot trust those with whom they have contracted — the marauding American scalphunters, who seem to revel in the destruction of the lovely Mexican city (170–71), and who eventually are escorted from Chihuahua for the final time by 100 or so motley indigenous soldiers (176). McCarthy astutely points out that in war, those who occupy (or, in this case, those who are hired) often hold the local residents in contempt, possibly secondary to the inability of the locals to defend their land, property, and people. This lack of local self-defense breeds a latent condescension within the occupier-protectors that proceeds to evolve from emotion to thought to action. The result is situational abuse of the locals, which then grows progressively in violence and scope. In the McCarthy text, the governor of Chihuahua, Angel Trias, acknowledges that neither the Mexican forces nor the locals are able to defend the regional citizenry from raiding Apache and Comanche, and thus are forced to contract with Glanton's gang of hired militants. The act of contracting with the gang weakens the Chihuahuans in the eyes and minds of the mercenaries, and inevitably the gang acts out against those under whom they are employed. In the excellent study *Acts and Shadows: The Vietnam War in American Literary Culture*, Philip K. Jason identifies a similar derision for the local peoples, one that was pejoratively labeled "the gook syndrome" (125), whereby (as seen in the Vietnam War and in the resultant literature, but born of the Korean War, a previous war in which American occupiers supported and fought for an indigenous Other) "Negative attitudes toward those we [American uniformed forces] are supposedly helping are based, according to several Vietnam [literary] portraits, on misunderstanding due to cultural difference" (124). As well, "Vietnam War literature often concerns itself with racist attitudes toward both enemies and friends" (124), and "cruelties toward South Vietnamese abound, as do representations of the impossibility of distinguishing friend from enemy in an absurd war" (124). So, comparatively, and away from the geographical boundaries of the United States, when dealing with an allied Other, be that Other, Mexican or Vietnamese — or Korean, for that matter — the American response is one based upon an ignorance of cultural understanding and one that is inherently racist. As such, in 1849 or in 1969, in Mexico or in Vietnam, in the Western Hemisphere or the Eastern, abhorrent treatment of locals by allied Americans is not uncommon. Yet, at differing levels to be sure, the oppositional dyad between — in this case and in this study — American occupiers and invaders and the occupied or invaded local peoples exists in all wars.

Naturally, this oppositional dyad exists between the Northern invaders cum occupiers and the Southern invaded cum occupied. E.L. Doctorow's *The March* contains a number of scenes presenting this dyad, and in a subjective scene set in Savannah and narrated by former landed slave-owner Mattie Jameson, the practices of Sherman's total war are in effect and are realized by the Jamesons and their cotton broker, Mr. Feinstein: "Two Union soldiers stood guard at the [cotton] warehouse doors with their rifles held in front of them.... John, [Mr. Feinstein] said, my business has been taken from me. I have this paper with the order signed by General Sherman. He says my warehouse and all the cotton it holds is the property of the Union army" (110). Of course, appropriating the buildings and agricultural commodities of the Southerners was a facet of total war, even though a warehouse full of cotton might not be of immediate use to Sherman's army. The idea was to take the cotton out of the Confederate supply line, and as no Southerners were considered civilians, no Southern property or commodity was considered civilian property or civilian commodity. Regardless of the fact that the South asked for war via secession, the taking of all that was owned by the civilian populace was an act that promoted decades- or centuries-long oppositional feelings between the invaded/occupied Southern citizens and the invading/occupy-ing Northern army. Returning to the text, as the household property of the Jamesons is being stored in Mr. Feinstein's warehouse, Mr. Jameson is, at this point, according to his wife, "beyond reason" (111), and thus he confronts and threatens the Union guards, one of whom, in return, "raised his rifle [and] brought the rifle butt down" (111) upon the head of John Jameson, mortally wounding the irate former plantation owner. This act of violence, an act against an unarmed, but apoplectic, noncombatant, one who has lost his entire psy-chic and physical and social and commercial estate, is an act of lasting residue, an act couched in a hierarchical status whereby the invader/occupier has the means — and the free-dom and allowance — to commit an action that summarily condemns a non-uniformed noncombatant to a slow and miserable death. Thus, acts such as this one, though rare in the Doctorow text (but not necessarily rare in times of broad and deep war, war that con-joins national resentment with military need), stigmatize the occupier/invader and victim-ize the occupied/invaded, regardless of the historical necessity and correctness of the war effort.

Looking at the First World War and the oppositional dyad between occupying forces and local peoples relative to the texts in this study, Edith Wharton's *The Marne* and John Dos Passos' *One Man's Initiation* rarely offer this thematic element but for occasional ref-erences to the German invasions into France (Wharton 70) and military actions of the "Boches" (Dos Passos 22) and as such, both texts are fairly benign in the presentation of the American forces and the individual actions of those in uniform. The Americans in these texts observe the French, but rarely do they interact with the local people. However, in Thomas Boyd's *Through the Wheat*, in a scene reminiscent and perhaps derivative of a sim-ilar scene in Willa Cather's *One of Ours* (a scene that also includes a character named Hicks — Cather's Sergeant Hicks — in which the sergeant and his men offer the characteristic "ugly American" behavior stereotypical of U.S. tourists abroad through "the consumerist gutting" [Cohen, "Culture" 192] of a French cheese shop [Cather 240–42], Boyd's William Hicks deals with a "wizened little French clerk who regarded him with suspicion through the window of" a canteen in a village in northern France (2). The clerk is hostile to Boyd's Hicks because, as Hicks ponders after the fact, "He had, he realized, made an ass of himself by pointing to ambiguously labeled cans piled on the shelves inside the canteen and saying, 'la, combine?' [how much?]" (2–3). The clerk shuts the window dividing the two and leaves Hicks with his money and his goods, and "in the morning the platoon would find the canteen and buy the last can, the last bottle" (3). This somewhat amusing scene, the first in the text, is one that identifies the Americans, rather than the French, as the invasive Other — bad tourists in a country not their own (Cohen, "Culture" 190–91); the scene also foreshadows later oppositional dyads situated in the text. A scene a few pages after the first, in which the men of Company C participate in drill in order to maintain discipline and to kill time, uses the optic of the narrator to present the oppositional dyad: "Stupid-looking old Frenchmen, a few thick-waisted women, and a scattering of ragged children dully watched the company march down the street" (13–14). This time, and amusingly so, Boyd castigates the French, and men, women, and children are swathed in the narrator's brush-stroke. The men are not stupid, but rather, "stupid-looking"; the women are not beautiful, but "thick-waisted," and the children are not well kempt, but "ragged." Thus, the entire French citizenry are condemned as, against type, homely and unattractive. This humorous description also identifies the entire group as slow-witted — dull. So, in one condescending sentence, Boyd metonymously labels the French as stupid and ugly. Of course, and obviously,

Boyd is using a bit of humor and light tone and diction to lull the reader into a sense of complacency, as the violence that follows is, for the day, quite brutal and graphic.

The texts of the Second World War also offer the oppositional dyad between occupiers and local peoples, and in Joseph Heller's *Catch-22*, the element of sexualized violence perpetrated by the occupiers against the local allied peoples — most obviously and often against women, of course — is presented in a number of different manners and scenes, two of which are situated in the hellish chapter titled "The Eternal City." In the first scene, which takes place in the chapter set as Yossarian wanders the Roman night, an intoxicated woman is raped by a group of American military men: "At the Ministry of Public Affairs ... a drunken lady was backed up against one of the fluted Corinthian columns by a drunken young soldier, while three drunken comrades in arms sat watching nearby.... 'Pleeshe don't,' begged the drunken lady.... 'Come on, baby,' [Yossarian] heard the drunken soldier urge determinedly. 'It's my turn now.' ... 'Pleeshe don't,' begged the drunken lady. 'Pleeshe don't'" (424). Note the language that Heller repeats: "Pleeshe don't," "begged," and "drunken lady." The woman obviously does not want to participate carnally with the American soldier, and even highly intoxicated, the woman is still, while slurring her words, attempting to maintain politeness, most likely based in fear. And by having the woman slurring her "s" in "please," Heller is explicitly presenting the woman as acutely inebriated, incapacitated, defenseless. Also, note that the narrator identifies the woman as a (or the) "lady." In so doing, Heller's narrator is contrasting the woman with the "whores" in the text, and thus is socially elevating the woman while also allowing that the "whores" choose carnality, but this woman is not choosing and exists as a victim of sexual violence. Finally, it is evident — per the man's "It's my turn now" — that the other members in the soldier's group have already assaulted the victimized woman. Obviously, of course, group sexual assault of allied women by those who are their liberators is a way to create a long-lasting oppositional dyad between the liberators and the occupied, and the destructive psychological and emotional effects of group sexual assault will forever affect the victim. Accusingly, Heller places the sexual assault in front of the Ministry of Public Affairs, as if the sexualizing of the local women and the violence directed toward them is a public affair, and as such, is commonly and publicly known — by occupiers and occupied — and what is worse, is commonly and publicly (and socially) accepted — "The night was filled with horrors" (425).

A later scene of sexual violence, this one resulting in the death of the victim and an act perpetrated by a named character, and an ally of Yossarian, occurs at the officers' now-prostitute-free apartment. Unlike the scene above, this scene of sexual violence involves a named character — Aarfy — and a named victim — Michaela, the apartment maid. By naming the victimizer and the victim, after the scene in which neither the victimizers nor the victim are named, Heller dehumanizes the Us and humanizes the Other: "Her name was Michaela, but the men called her filthy things in dulcet, ingratiating voices" (427). None of the officers wanted to sleep with her except for "Aarfy, who had raped her once that same evening and had then taken her prisoner in a clothes closet for almost two hours with his hand over her mouth.... Then he threw her out the window" (427, 428). Note that Heller names the woman in the pre-assault description, but he then dehumanizes and de-names her, using the personal pronoun "her" repetitively when narrating the assault and murder. Aarfy still has a name, but Michaela is a "her," almost an inanimate object, who then, per the Latin *anima*, is inanimate, as her life force is taken from her when she is defenestrated. Sexual violence against the women of an occupied or invaded country or locale is not a new element in war, and for millennia, invaders and occupiers have appropriated the women of invaded and occupied nations and states, but Heller's presentation of such, and the evo-lution and devolution thereof—from unnamed victim and victimizers to named victim and victimizer, to the de-naming of victim — identifies American uniformed personnel not as liberators but as sexual predators who take advantage (as predators do) of prey in a weakened state, be that weakened state acute intoxication or the social hierarchy of the ten-ant-maid relationship, or the even physical hierarchy of man to woman. The oppositional dyad created when liberator/occupiers sexually assault intoxicated local women is clear, of course, but the exponentializing of the dyad through post-sexual assault hostage-taking and murder furthers the hatred between the occupied and the occupiers, and the nihilism exhibited, especially by Aarfy, negates all moral foregrounding in the act of peri-war lib-eration of the Italian people. Therefore, Heller creates an oppositional dyad between the uniformed male American occupiers and the non-uniformed female Italian occupied that is based entirely upon sexual violence and the dehumanization of the Italian women.

Uniquely, Chaim Potok, in *I Am the Clay*, creates oppositional dyads among the indig-enous Koreans and all occupying/invading foreigners, regardless of nationality or combat loyalty, and this includes the military representing the "Northern" Korean forces. Potok's text, narrated omnisciently as well as from the perspective(s) of three Korean refugees, bas-tardizes the invader/occupier of the past and present, and the characters express hatred for the Japanese, the Chinese, and the American and United Nations forces, each of whom has, at one time in the past or contemporary to the action in the text, occupied or invaded Korea; thinks the old man, "Chinese, Japanese, Americans. Foreign devils" (36). Regardless of nationality or ethnicity, what conjoins these non–Koreans is that each group falls under the auspices of the nationalized military uniform and the might allowed secondary to national and military power (that is, might makes right), and further, these uniformed invaders and occupiers are recipients of the hatred felt by the Korean civilians, regardless of military role or nation of origin. So, collectively, soldiers from Japan, China, the United States, the United Nations, and even North Korea are hated by the Korean noncombatants, and individually, according to country, each military's combatants are hated uniquely, too. For example, the Japanese are "savages, hopeless barbarians" (43), "uncivilized" (44) behaviorally and cultur-ally, invaders who suspended men "head-down over open firepits" (14). Universally in the text, the Japanese, who invaded and occupied Korea from 1910 until 1945, are loathed for their brutal treatment of the indigenous Koreans, and beyond being loathed, the Japanese are routinely identified as lacking in civilized behavior—"barbarous" (143). Conversely, the Chinese invaders cum occupiers, the current non-indigenous, non–Korean invaders, are also identified as brutal, but compared with the Japanese, they are acknowledged as civ-ilized; thus, the Japanese are uncultured and "unacquainted with Chinese ways, the wisdom of Chinese writing, the beauty of Chinese characters" (43). So, even though the Chinese are the invasive enemy, an invader who "looted everything" (7) and burned the rest, and thus are hated, the Chinese are, nonetheless, perceived by the old man to be mannered and cultured in a way that the Japanese are not. The old man also castigates the "soldiers from the North" (23)—indigenous Koreans, of course, but Koreans who force men, women, and children to "dig their own graves" (23) prior to being executed. During a civil war, obviously, nationality is bifurcated, and the peer—civilian and uniformed, man, woman, and child—becomes the enemy, and the role of the Korean soldiers from the North is conjoined with the role of the Chinese: "Blame the North and the Chinese" (30) for the state of the refugees, says one unnamed man. In a trope repeated through the text, Potok is explicit in his iden-tification of the soldiers from the North as Korean, and he is also explicit in his conjunction of the Northern soldiers with the Chinese. Thus, the soldiers from the North are labeled as renegade "fiends" (91) who are in league with non–Korean nationals rather than their own countrymen. In military practice with the Korean citizenry — and military — are the United Nations forces, represented textually, and repeatedly, as "foreigners" (22, 143, 184, 234, etc.). These foreign fighters, of course, are primarily American military personnel who bring the mechanized war — tanks, jeeps, planes, helicopters— to the peasantry and to the rural lands of Korea: "The machines of the foreigners" (22). To the Korean civilians, the American are the Other —"giants of pale skin" (22)— so in a contrast to most American novels of war, the narrative optic, viewed through the perception of the indigenous and invaded peoples, identifies the outsiders— the Americans— as the ethnic and physical and racial Other. As such, Potok places the American forces clearly in the column of occupier/invader cum enemy to the indigenous people. Consequently, the Americans are linked with the North Koreans, the Chinese, and the Japanese, all of whom are loathed by the contemporary Korean citizenry.

Returning to the nineteenth century, and in contrast to Doctorow's work, Stephen Crane's *The Red Badge of Courage* places in opposition a civilian noncombatant and a Union soldier, or, more accurately, a "young girl" (17) and one "rather fat" (17) Union infantryman. While Doctorow places the Southern noncombatants in opposition to the Union invaders cum occupiers, Crane uses the oppositional dyad to lighten the pre-combat mood of the textual participants, who are ambulating from bivouac at Washington, D.C., to wage war at what will be known historically as the Battle of Chancellorsville. While on the march, the fat soldier "attempted to pilfer a horse from a dooryard" (17), and in so doing, creates an oppositional dyad where none before existed. The thief "was escaping with his prize when a young girl rushed from the house and grabbed her animal's mane" (17). This oppositional dyad between a transient and uniformed male occupier and a landed and civilian female noncombatant is, of course, grounded in the subservient social and legal role of the nineteenth-century woman. As well, the physical dominance of man over woman is indirectly alluded to, as is the role of combatant over noncombatant. Crane, socially and physically and rhetorically, creates a dyad in which the man should be able to overcome the physical defiance of the young woman. Yet it is the "young girl" (note the adjective and noun) who wins this battle for the horse: "There followed a wrangle. The young girl ... stood like a dauntless statue.... There were crows and catcalls [from the regiment] showered upon him when he retreated without the horse" (17), and "the maiden ... stood panting and regarding the troops with defiance" (17). Through the physical description of each character, Crane idealizes the young woman while he de-idealizes the "fat" soldier. Physically, and truthfully, the soldier, even while fat and slovenly, should be able to take a horse from a young woman. But in an escape from verisimilitude and to rhetorically lighten the mood and tone of the text, Crane creates a comic scene in which a young girl defeats a uniformed occupier. Contrast this light scene with Doctorow's scenes of Southern whites who fear and loathe the Union invader/occupier. Also, note that Crane identifies the young girl as a "dauntless statue" and "a maiden" and "defiant." This language elevates her among the characters in the text, very few of whom, but for Henry's mother, are women. Thus, this unnamed young woman, one who stands up to the unnamed uniformed soldier, is, for the era, atypically drawn; she is a strong woman character in a time of war, and she is relentless in her desire to keep her horse and then in her defiance of, not merely the fat soldier, but the entire regiment, who take her side, of course, in the tug-of-war over the horse, and who "rejoiced at [the fat soldier's] downfall" (17) and subsequent humiliation.

Rhetorically and structurally, Crane places this gynocentric scene early in the otherwise androcentric text, before any combat has taken place, and thus Crane lulls the nineteenth-century reader into a state of complacency. Crane's scenes of battle, though imagistically detailed, nonetheless are realistic enough to be, for the day, violent and brutal relative to then contemporary presentations of the Civil War violence. Preemptively, as the regiment is traveling to war, Crane, as manipulator of the reader, inserts a comic scene — a scene in which a woman uniquely and physically and heroically defeats a slovenly soldier — in order to tranquilize the consumer of the text. For the war, and the violence therein, is coming. So, as is often the case with Crane's work, the text is seminal in a number of ways. The text, rather than presenting a woman as a weakened victim, as is typical of the Civil War texts of the day, presents a young woman, a "young girl," really — as a strong and dignified character, and Crane's proto-feministic creation of the young woman is unique to the genre and the literature of the era. As well, Crane villainizes a military character, one who chooses to steal a horse — an animal of subsistence, transportation, and property — from an unarmed and occupied female noncombatant. So, rather than drawing the young woman as an innocent and weak victim, and the Union forces all as idealized heroes, Crane creates characters either strengthened or flawed, human beings not caricatures of human beings. Conveniently, too, Crane clearly creates an oppositional dyad between an occupying combatant and an occupied local noncombatant.

Unlike Thomas Boyd, who, in *Through the Wheat*, uses humor and stereotyping to present the oppositional dyad between occupiers and the occupied, William March, in *Company K*, presents the oppositional dyad seriously and often portrays the American soldiers as ignorant of the devastating peri-war hardships experienced by the French citizenry. As a different American combatant narrates each scene in the March text, Americans who cannot or do not or will not sympathize or empathize with the French civilian victims of war run the length of the work; as such, March, as the author, castigates the behaviors of the insensitive Americans. Four sketches effectively offer the oppositional dyad between the American occupiers and the French occupied: those of Private Samuel Updike (26–27), Private Thomas Stahl (42–43), Private Harry Waddell (86–87), and Private Robert Nalls (144–45). Interestingly, each of the four is narrated by an American private — the lowest and perhaps most culturally unenlightened enlisted rank. The Updike sketch takes place immediately after the company has disembarked from their Atlantic passage, and the Americans, unschooled in the French suffering, are overjoyed to be off the transport ship and are laughing and clowning around. The French present "stood there looking at us, with their mouths open, a surprised expression on their faces.... They just looked at us ... and turned their heads away" (26). Another soldier, Private Stahl, accusingly inquires, "What's the matter with these people?" (26). In return, a woman replies in English: "'The people ... are in mourning,' she said, as if she were speaking to a child. 'We're having a war, you know'" (26). The sketch closes with Updike's admission of embarrassment at their behavior in front of the French mourners. Of course, by the time the Americans arrive, the French have been at war, invaded and occupied, for three years, but the Americans, 92 of whom in the text are privates, rarely acknowledge this fact. So, the dyad here is one of youthful ignorance and wizened maturity, and the woman speaks to the private as if "speaking to a child."

The Stahl sketch also identifies American ignorance of the French situation, this time through the haphazard loss of a well bucket, a commodity of tremendous use-value in time of war. In this sketch, privates Stahl and Halsey are taking water from a village well when the bucket separates from the rope, and the bucket falls into the well, irretrievable. Halsey says, "I'll go inside and tell the old lady, and get another bucket from her'" (42). Obviously, Stahl and Halsey fail to see the seriousness and gravity of their accident, and the elderly Frenchwoman comes running out of her cottage "tearing her hair and beating her breasts" (42), and Stahl notes, "it was all Wilbur and I could do to keep her from jumping after the bucket" (42). After Stahl, as Americans typically seem to do, offers to pay for the bucket, the woman knocks the money from his hand and throws herself onto the ground, disheartened. The rest of the village is similarly shaken, and by the next day, "everybody in town had come to look down the well" (43). Still, Stahl and Halsey do not realize the catastrophe that has occurred, and upon leaving the village, Halsey says, "Everybody here is nuts" (43). It is not by accident, of course, that war texts set in and among small villages and towns have well motifs, for the well is water, and water is life. And it is no accident that in war texts, especially those of the Vietnam War, when a unit wants to kill a village, it kills the village's well, chemically or by throwing an animal carcass down the well. So, losing a bucket, a use-value commodity, in time of war is a catastrophic event because the loss of the bucket means the inability to access water from the well. Nonetheless, for some unfathomable reason (other than American ignorance coupled with American arrogance), Stahl and Halsey seem to be unable to realize that losing the bucket down the well is a life-changing event for the old woman and the town's residents. In a country that has been at war for three years, buckets, like all man-made objects, are scarce.

The next sketch of opposition between occupier and occupied is one that begins and ends with a plea for belief that "This is the way it really happened" (86). In this sketch, one Private Harry Waddell has possibly committed an attempted sexual assault of a young French woman, but there is a certain ambiguity in the narrative, and the ambiguity is tinged by the fact that the accused assailant is the only one narrating. The private, who was AWOL — absent without leave — at the time of the incident, states that he came upon a young woman in a field who was tending a cow, and who immediately began seductive behavior toward him — "grind[ing] coffee" (86) with her hips — but then, upon seeing a man — possibly her father? — watching them, acted as if she had been accosted and began to hit Waddell with a branch. Waddell ran from the area and was chased down by a village mob-esque group of locals who then cornered and caught him — a Frankenstein's monster of sorts, the creation of Dr. Frankenstein, er, Uncle Sam. The passage ends with Waddell's repeated claim of truth. As previously noted, sexual assault of indigenous women is a common motif in novels of war, and historically, a motif of war itself, as occupiers and invaders sexualize and appropriate the women situated in locales of war. And in this instance, Waddell is not helped at all by being AWOL when the incident occurred. At the very least, this sketch identifies a sexualization of the local women, which would create resentment among the locals, of course, and while there is ambiguity in Waddell's version of the events, there is no ambiguity in the oppositional dyad that exists in the scene, for any scene in which a village mob corners a foreign serviceman is explicitly oppositional in its theme and action.

Finally, in a sketch that admonishes another American private, Private Bernie Glass, for stealing a family heirloom, but elevates and humanizes the narrator of the sketch, March conjoins castigation and humanization in the same scene, and he argues, forcefully, that not *all* Americans are ignorant clods. In this illustration, Private Nalls tells of a French family in Blenod in whose house Nalls and Glass are temporarily billeted. The couple's son was killed early in the war, and the French government sent the parents a "small copper plaque" (144) engraved with a relief of a heroic-looking woman and the words "Slain on the Field of Honor" (144). The plaque is not fancy, nor is it personalized, but rather "the sort of thing that a Government would send to the next of kin of all men killed in action" (144), and yet the parents of the slain boy hold the plaque in great value. Weeks after moving out and moving on, Nalls notices the plaque when it falls out of Glass' kit bag. Nalls, the good American, is shocked, and asks Glass, the bad American, why, would, and how he could steal such a treasured object from a family that had treated them so well — an object, of course, that symbolized their dead son. Glass replies, "I thought it would make a good souvenir to take home" (145). Nalls closes the sketch in a somewhat — but appropriately — melodramatically fashion: "I wish they [the old couple] knew that I am ashamed of the whole human race" (145). So, even though March closes this sketch on a positive note, that of an empathetic and sympathetic American, the broader blame in the text for the oppositional dyad between the American occupiers and the French occupied falls cleanly and clearly upon the Americans, who, out of youthful ignorance and cultural and social indifference, behave boorishly toward the French people.

In Ernest Frankel's *Band of Brothers*, which is, like Potok's *I Am the Clay*, set early in the Korean War (November-December 1950), the oppositional dyad between occupiers and occupied is best evidenced through the behaviors of two Korean characters — one nicknamed You-all, who serves as a subservient gofer for the American Marines, but is actually a traitor, and one named Won Cook Choy, who serves as Able Company translator — both of whom are forced to choose between the "colonial domination" (81) of the Americans or the "Communist enslavement" (81) of the Chinese. Choy, formerly a philosophy, literature, and history student, formerly a man of intellect and debate rather than action, sees the Americans as "foolish" and "given to bragging. Children, eager to be liked" (80). Choy's family, all dead now (except perhaps for a younger brother suffering post-traumatic dementia), "had trusted the Americans — although the Americans had not trusted [the Koreans]" (80). And while Choy's family, as well as his teacher, might once have trusted the Americans, the trust did not, and does not, include respect — mutually or exclusively. As Choy says to an American lieutenant who has just referred to the indigenous Koreans as "gooks," "We should not delude ourselves there is respect for Americans. It would be as foolish as to say there is respect on your part for these people you call gooks" (38). So, the Korean populace is given a devil's choice; they can serve under the Chinese Communists, who will enslave them, or they can serve under the American imperialists, who are racists but less brutal than the Chinese. In fact, according to Choy, "the average Korean sees little or no difference between you [the Americans] and the Chinese" (39). Choy has made his choice, of course, yet he sees the American officer class as "brash, unschooled, intolerant ... dull, colorless, dependent ... without sensitivity, culture, vision, or purpose. [And finally] ... weak" (81). Clearly and obviously, Choy, an ally, resents and dislikes the Americans; perhaps more telling is the lack of respect Choy has for the uniformed Americans in general and the individual officers of Able Company in particular. In contrast to the peasant refugees in the Potok text, Choy is well educated, well read, and well able to articulate his feelings — philosophically, emotionally, and intellectually — toward the Americans. While Choy is an ally, he is more allied with Korean unification than he is with American militarism; thus, he serves alongside the Americans not out of respect but out of pragmatism.

You-all, on the other hand, is a traitor in the guise of an ally, but the reader does not know this until after reading Choy's autobiographical optic (77–81) and "hearing" Choy's anti–American dogma (38–39), which is, in fact, merely the indigenous perspective translated to English. In fact, Lieutenant Cagle, to whom Choy's social theories of invasion and occupation are being directed, says to the interpreter, "I'm starting to wonder whose side you're on!" (38). To which Choy replies, "I am on the side of Korea" (38). Thus, the reader, too, must wonder, as Choy lies in wait for a certain someone to ambush (77–87). When Choy's "quarry" (87) appears, and he fires his carbine, You-all is the recipient of the sniping. You-all, playing the lackey, has been serving the Chinese by stealing American equipment — weapons, maps, and the like — from the American forces and delivering the weaponry (and more importantly, related intelligence) to the Communist forces, and thus has been directly responsible for a number of American deaths. You-all also stole Captain Patrick's .45 caliber ACP and gave it to the Chinese POW Kao Teh, who then killed Radioman Monk Nelson. But it was only Choy who figured out the identity of the traitor, and rather than report the traitor, Choy, formerly a thinker but now a sniper, chooses to kill You-all rather than have him arrested. Choy's sniping merely wounds You-all, who then is a prisoner among former allies. Choy's attempted assassination is an act of internal and external self-loathing, of course, as Choy sees You-all's alliance with the Chinese as self-destructive, an act contrary to Korean propagation and self-rule. Given a devil's deal, a life under imperialism or a life under Communism, there is no promise under the latter, but some exists under the former. As Choy tells You-all when the pair is left alone in a first-aid hut, "These Americans you hate, they are your only hope" (95). Of course, Choy is speaking in the present, and he is referring to the American belief that You-all be taken prisoner rather than summarily executed, but in the greater philosophical and political sense, Choy is speaking in terms of the war and the future of Korea. Nonetheless, Choy then — after some hesitation and self-debate — executes You-all with a saber (96). Symbolically, in the text, and in this scene, as written, American ideology, while imperialistic, has triumphed over Chinese Communism. Choy, regardless of his hatred and lack of respect for the Americans, hates a Korean traitor more, and thus manifestly practices that hatred. This scene also argues for intellect over blind adherence to political doctrine sans thought. Choy is a thinking man, and even though he does not respect or like the American imperialists, he is still able to see the benefit of their presence over the insatiable Chinese. So while there exists a great oppositional dyad between the occupied Koreans and the occupying Americans, in this case at least, Choy's choice is to serve and exist under imperial occupiers rather than Communist invaders. Symbolically, of course, Choy's ability to kill You-all is Frankel's rhetorical cum political argument for republican-imperialist governance over Communist rule.

The noted scholar of war literature Stanley Cooperman argues that the Vietnam War offered the combatant cum author an "opportunity for [war] fiction to go beyond protest, and beyond mere technology or reporting; indeed it offer[ed] an opportunity for fiction to examine the metaphysical darkness of the human condition itself" ("American War Novels" 520). Historically, according to Cooperman, the American soldier has been taught that he is "neither master race nor killer, but *liberator* [italics Cooperman]" ("American War Novels" 522). And of course, during the post–World War II era, the stated political and military goal of the United States was, as in *Band of Brothers*, liberation from Communism. But when "the liberated are themselves the enemy, the result of this is a process of exasperation leading to incomprehensibility, leading to a nightmare of total nihilism" (Cooperman, "American War Novels" 522), leading to Philip K. Jason's "gook syndrome" (125). And Jason, of course, argues that "gook syndrome" was born in the Korean War, rather than the Vietnam War, but is, nonetheless, readily present as an identifying characteristic in the Vietnam literature of the Vietnam War (125, 121–29). As shown above in the Frankel text, American servicemen use the pejorative label "gook" liberally when referring to those indigenous

Koreans who are the object of American — and United Nations—liberation policy. But in Gustav Hasford's *The Short-Timers*, Hasford shows that the oppositional dyad between liberator and liberated does not have to be deadly, and can even be a source of humor — a cynical humor, of course, but humor nonetheless. For example, in a scene in which Daytona Dave and Chili Vendor are using a rubber Hershey bar to stage propaganda photographs with Vietnamese orphans — see the Marine giving chocolate to the poor, but liberated, orphans (55–57) — a little kid tries to eat the rubber candy bar and is a bit put off. Later, Daytona Dave says to Joker, "Remember that gook kid that tried to eat the candy bar? It bit me ... that little Victor Charlie ambushed me. Ran up and bit the shit out of my hand.... I bet I get rabies" (66). Ah, the agony of the liberator via the little teeth of the liberated. In a text as brutally violent as Hasford's, comic relief is a rhetorical necessity, or the reader will become exhausted and overwhelmed. Also, in keeping with the cynicism and nihilism of the Vietnam era, a bit of humor alleviates the gross philosophical realities with which the author is dealing. This light scene is serious, though, in that it explicates the tensions between liberator and liberated, tensions that are not so humorous when the dyad exists between adults. And note that the child is identified as an "it" and also is labeled a Viet Cong who "ambushes" Daytona Dave, and thus is a participant in the war. In a later snapshot of the oppositional dyad, Joker and Rafter Man are waiting to hitch a ride into Hue, and they buy five-dollar Cokes from a "*mamasan*" (76) who bows to the pair when they speak to her and who smiles at them constantly. Joker, astute cynic and nihilist liberator, notes that he and Rafter Man do not comprehend the woman's "magpie chatter, but [do comprehend] the hatred in the smile frozen on her face" (76). The hatred is immobile, non-moving, not to be relieved but for the removal of the Americans from Vietnam. Regardless, though, and cynically and practically, the woman takes the Americans' money, an act that has its own cost, of course. Acknowledged hatred between occupier and occupied, in the Korean War and in the Vietnam War, is not a reason to cease capitalist or political or military business; as such, the hatred need not be hidden away, and thus is readily evident and readily practiced by occupiers and by occupied.

Of course, the oppositional dyad between invitees and the indigenous can be treacherous and tricky to manage. During the Persian Gulf War, as evidenced by Terrence D. Haynes in *Desert Norm*, and regardless of the fact the American forces, among others, were invited to encamp in Saudi Arabia for the preparation and practice of war, Arab/Muslim resentment was created secondary to the presence of armed Western forces in the land of Mecca. As one security officer states, "Hussein is NOT our only foe ... by the way!! There are many Arab groups who are p.o.'ed that so many Americans are on their home soil!... The bottom line is this: we are all sitting ducks in the Arab world" (74). So, of course, at this point in the text, during the run-up to war, the Americans are confined to the safety of their base, but after the war is completed, the Americans, as Americans are wont to do, go to the mall: The Riyadh Mall. But the women soldiers, as is the custom in Saudi Arabia, must wear an *abaya* and a *niqāb*, a body-length cloak and face veil, or else they will face the wrath of the local religious police, regardless of their invitee or military status — or perhaps because of this status. At the mall, narrator Specialist Marcus Norm comes across a number of American military women in the local dress, and the reader is told of what happens to a woman who does not follow the regional, gendered religious rules of dress: "Ma'am, are you dressed this way because of the way Lieutenant Smith was paddled by the local religious police a few days ago?" Norm asks (209). And, for the reader's sake, of course, the story of the public corporal punishment of an American officer is recounted: "Smith was out in her black thing [*abaya* and *niqāb*]. Guess she thought being an American military officer made her exempt.... A van pulled up from nowhere ... and out pops these religious zealots. They start yelling and the next thing, she's getting her buttocks beat, right there in public" (210). According to one unnamed *abaya*- and *niqāb*-clad woman officer, Brigade has hushed up the incident, lest it become internationally known that the religious police of the protected are beating their women protectors in public. The assault of a female American officer would be bad television rhetoric, especially during a televised war, but regardless of whether the incident went public, the war, at this time (March 1991), is over, and the invitation into the Kingdom of Saudi Arabia has nearly expired. Kuwait has been liberated, Saddam Hussein's military has been thoroughly thrashed, and the characters in Haynes' text are nearly finished with their mission in Saudi Arabia. However, there is a disturbing aspect to the practice of beating one's female guests, and Haynes associates the institutional sexism — misogynistic practices, really — with the institutionalized racism of the early and mid–twentieth-century United States. Of course, there may be a resentment felt among the religious police toward the uniformed American military women. Such religious "zealots" are not used to seeing women in positions as uniformed defenders, and this must surely be emasculating to the religious police, who then, when the opportunity arises, beat Lieutenant Smith. So, in this situation, the oppositional dyad between invitee and inviter is misogynistic but is allowed from a cultural, social, and legal aspect. Thus, the religious police can, and do, beat a female American officer in public. Even in a situation whereby the invited uniformed military members are in place to protect the indigenous peoples (such as with the case of the American military present in Saudi Arabia prior to and during and immediately after the Persian Gulf War), social, cultural, linguistic, and sexual, and religious resentments exist, and thus there is an oppositional dyad between the inviters and the invitees.

"'What I did was a natural response to the occupation.' Iraqi Journalist Muntadar al-Zaidi, after throwing his shoes at President [George W.] Bush" on 14 December 2008 (al-Zaidi 25). Al-Zaidi was originally sentenced to three years in prison for this anti-occupation act of protest, but he served less than a year in prison. What al-Zaidi's individual act shows is that, even when displacing a hostile dictator, those who first invade and then occupy (and subsequently invite a mass campaign of terrorist slaughter of innocents) are loathed by those the invader/occupiers have attempted to "save." So, regardless of the original mission and its purposes and goals and rationalities, what lasts is the hatred of the Iraqis for the Americans, and in Cole Bolchoz's *A Medic in Iraq*, even a critic lacking in astuteness can easily see, as the "boots on the ground plainly see," the oppositional dyad that exists between the occupied Iraqi civilians and the invader cum occupier American military: "Youngsters and older men walked by our sector, watching us like spies. Some of these same people want us dead or alive — preferably dead. They can make $7,000 to $10,000 for each soldier they capture or kill for the insurgents. No wonder I feel like a target" (Location 403 of 1666). What is scary in this brief passage is that the civilians are sub-contracting for the insurgents, and so no one can be trusted. The civilians know the insurgents, but the American military knows only that the civilians need money and can make money at the expense of American lives. What is more, the Iraqis can openly observe the scheduled movements of the American forces, and then they can sell or give this intelligence to the insurgents, who, of course, can use the information to act out violently against the Americans. This is a very dirty situation, and later in the text, a peer of Bolchoz's narrator says, matter of factly, "Most of the Iraqis do not like us" (location 401 of 1666). Such is the life of an invader/occupier and the hatred felt by the invaded/occupied.

Bolchoz's narrator feels and argues that the insurgents attacking the Americans are primarily Iraqi and that, in general, "The people over here do not want change" (location 1000 of 1666); that is, the people do not want representative democracy, and so "We are all becoming complacent about the idea that these people are not on our side" (location 1096 of 1666). Of course, complacency in a locus of war, and in the face of a non-uniformed enemy, leads to death. As well, complacency in war leads to atrocities in which uniformed personnel kill indigenous noncombatants, either by choice or through apathy. All through the text, Bolchoz's narrator repeats these lines of distrust and complacency and explicates the Iraqi dislike for the Americans: "We know the people don't like us. This inhospitality has been demonstrated on various occasions" (location 1183 of 1666) and in various ways, from the mundane (being overcharged for needed items such as paint and tape) to the deadly (being blown up by an IED while on patrol) (location 1067 of 1666). As the text closes, and the tour of Bolchoz's narrator comes to an end, the static rhetorical element of the work is the oppositional dyad between the occupier and the occupied, and with each day of occupation, the hatred for the occupiers grows, regardless of the official efforts "to win hearts and minds": "No matter how many good will gestures we provide or envoys of democracy to the Middle East, they will always hate and despise us" (Location 1576 of 1666). And of course, Bolchoz's narrator is speaking not only of the Iraqi populace, but also of the entire pan–Arabic world, a world (perhaps) illogically tied to the Western world through petrochemicals. There is no doubt that Bolchoz's narrator argues that the oppositional dyad between Middle Eastern Muslim and Western Christian is not born merely of the American invasion of Iraq, but is cultural, social, religious, and ethnic, and is, as such, ongoing, and irreparable, and timeless.

Clearly, then, the presence of non-native, non-national armed forces during war is a cause of enmity between the occupier/invaders and the local/indigenous peoples. As such, in war, and in the American novel of war, there exists an oppositional dyad between the occupying/invading Forces and the indigenous/local peoples. Among the texts in this study, *The Red Badge of Courage*, *Company K*, *Band of Brothers*, *The Short-Timers*, *Desert Norm*, and *A Medic in Iraq* demonstrate that this oppositional dyad between invader/occupiers and the locals is one that occurs wherever war occurs. A brief passage in *The Red Badge of Courage* sets a corpulent Union soldier against a noncombatant "young girl," and multiple sketches in *Company K* contrast war-exhausted French civilians with immature, culturally unenlightened, and new-to-war American Marines. Post–world war texts *Band of Brothers*, *The Short-Timers*, and *Desert Norm* show that the locals and the occupiers, even when invited by the government of the occupied, tend not to get along, to the point of murdering each other, and when one includes Communism, racism, and religious zealotry and factionalism, along with indigenous resentment toward the occupying other, a certain exquisite loathing of the occupiers takes place. And finally, *A Medic in Iraq* offers the explicit hatred of the locals toward the uninvited American invaders who evicted Saddam Hussein but unintentionally invited internal and external terrorism. Obviously, whether invited or invading, armed uniformed occupiers are despised by the indigenous occupied. This facet of war, a war within a war, is neither unique nor uncommon and is part of all wars in which Americans have participated, and, of course, is common to the American novel of war. Add perceived and real mistreatment of the locals by the occupiers, and the oppositional dyad between the occupying/invading forces and the indigenous/local peoples is manifested in explicit violence and implicit acts of subversion.

XI

The Oppositional Dyad Between Officers and Enlisted Men

Another oppositional dyad that exists in the American novel of war is an oppositional dyad between officers and enlisted men. This dyad between officers and enlisted goes back hundreds, if not thousands, of years and is time-honored in the literature of war, American and otherwise. The conflict between the officers and the enlisted men is complex and historical and involves tensions related to education level, command level, military experience and service in relation to rank, combat experience in relation to battlefield command, pay scale, and food and housing discrepancies, and can be seen explicitly in *The Red Badge of Courage, Company K, One Man's Initiation, Through the Wheat, The Naked and the Dead,* and *The Short-Timers.* In the American novel of war, the result of this tension between the officers and the enlisted entities within a fighting unit can be catastrophic, as well as comedic, contingent upon the novel, and the conflict can be violent, even murderous. *Company K, The Naked and the Dead,* and *The Short-Timers* show the catastrophic, the act of "fragging" an officer — the killing of the offending officer — while *One Man's Initiation* and *Through the Wheat* offer the oppositional dyad in a lighter tone, as, among sundry scenes of this oppositional dyad (most of which show the officer in a less than flattering light), the former presents a decorated officer as other than an honorable warrior, and the latter shows a major general as a narcissistic buffoon. *The Red Badge of Courage,* the seminal American text containing this thematic element, uses a number of scenes of a low-ranking officer — a company lieutenant in particular — beating the enlisted ranks, including Henry Fleming, and as well as scenes of hapless, confused generals, to pillory the officer class (from the perspective of Henry's limited optic, of course). And as officers are often drawn as incompetent and clownish in novels of war, enlisted men are just as often drawn as murderous and vengeful. Time and battle — and text — tested, the oppositional dyad between officers and enlisted men is a ready literary device in the American novel of war.

In the locus of war, a time and place and situation in which violence and the capacity for such is celebrated, honored, and decorated, is it any surprise, any at all, that there exists violence between the officer class and the enlisted class? When men are taught, and practice, and are encouraged to be violent, is it any wonder that these men will use violence in situations other than against the uniformed or identified enemy? Most obviously, the answer to both questions is a forthright no, and when one considers that man, as an animal, is inherently and instinctively and aggressively violent, the allowances relative to violence afforded in wartime are not easily controlled. Thus, in war, violence as a means of reaction becomes commonplace — and even encouraged — but those who are encouraged to act violently occasionally do so against their hierarchical superiors, often as the result of some actual or perceived injustice. As such, in the American novel of war, the most common violence between officer and enlisted man is violence perpetrated by an enlisted man against an officer, and in the novels of the twentieth century, this act of violence is often a murderous act and therefore leads directly to the death of the officer. Interestingly, though, the perpetrator of the murderous action is often unpunished, and the decedent goes un-mourned. Not coincidentally, and not un-ironically, the authors of these novels of war are frequently former enlisted men, men who are taking the literary opportunity to skewer the officer class in general and, no doubt, particular officers of derision. As such, officers are drawn in caricature, but not comedic caricature, as their behaviors in war lead to the deaths of the enlisted; these officers are incompetent, ignorant, poorly trained, inexperienced in battle, malicious, cowardly, mean, shortsighted, narcissistic, egotistical, tyrannical, ineffective, sloppy, goofy, clumsy, and even (albeit rarely) cared for, respected, and honored. Overwhelmingly, while texts may contain officers of competence, the literary projection of the officer class in the American novel of war is bleak, and frankly, were one to read nothing but American novels of war, especially those written by former enlisted men, one would wonder how the United States won any war.

In *The Red Badge of Courage*, Stephen Crane pillories the officer class, from lieutenant to general—"The generals were stupids" (25), thinks Henry Fleming prior to battle—which is not a surprise as the text is primarily experienced through Henry's optic, the optic of a new enlistee and a private in rank, and one who, as the cited passage attests, is emotionally immature. However, relative to the novels of the twentieth century, the violence between officer and enlisted man in the Crane text is, perhaps secondary to the day, of course, initiated by the officer and directed toward the enlisted. Immediately following Henry's castigation of the generals, and while he is daydreaming, moping, and lollygagging toward battle—his first, of course—Henry is beaten by a lieutenant for his malaise: "He was surprised presently by the young lieutenant of his company, who began heartily to beat him with a sword" (25). Later, as the battle rages on, the lieutenant again makes a violent appearance, this time as he beats a man who has fled the battle, and he "seized [the man] by the collar and was pummeling him ... with many blows" (37). The repetition of this violence—of a line officer beating a malingering enlisted man, for the purpose of getting the man into combat—evinces the contemporary commonality of this action. No one in the text, not even Henry, is surprised that the lieutenant is beating his men. Henry may hate the lieutenant and see him as brutish (25), but Henry is not shocked that the lieutenant resorts to violence in order to get the enlisted to enter the fray.

Andrew Lawson notes the oppositional dyad between officers and enlisted in *The Red Badge of Courage* is born of era-specific class conflict and that the officer hierarchy in the text "parallels the managerial hierarchy of the modern [nineteenth-century] industrial corporation with its layers of top, middle, and lower managers" (62), with the officer classes as the managers, the lower of which are the company lieutenants (Crane's "shepherds" [97]), who must control and direct the enlisted men, the "sheep" (97)—animals to be beaten and herded and sacrificed and slaughtered. Of course, controlling one's animals through fear and violence is nothing new, historically and in literature—see the Old Testament, for example—but the analogy of the modern industrial corporate hierarchy is one born of the American Industrial Revolution, and is important because, at the time, management viewed workers as expendable animals of labor, animals to be used and sacrificed, just as the officers in the Crane text view the enlisted men as fodder for battle. The "savage-minded lieutenant"

(97) also refers to the men as "hens [and] jackasses" (97), which serves to dehumanize the troops, and thus make each of them less valuable as a human being. So, in *The Red Badge of Courage*, there is a parallel dehumanization of the enlisted men; first, there is a corporate hierarchy at play, a hierarchy born of the Industrial Revolution–era roles of management and labor; next, there is a hierarchy whereby the officers are shepherds and the enlisted are sheep — or lesser animals of sustenance and burden. These dual dehumanizations, the former corporate and capitalist, and the latter rural and agricultural, allow for the officers to beat the enlisted men and assign the function of lamb upon those to be sacrificed in the abattoir of battle.

By the twentieth century and the First World War, there is less overt physical abuse of the enlisted in the texts, but the officers are still drawn as vicious or cowardly, or, generally speaking, an impediment to the survival of the enlisted. In John Dos Passos' *One Man's Initiation*, while Martin Howe and Tom Randolph are ambulance men, and thus are not true enlisted combatants, the presence of the oppositional dyad between officers and enlisted men is contained, repeatedly, in the text, and officers (as seen through the perspectives of the combatants) are guides into hell —cruel, liars, and cowards. Midway through the text, Martin Howe asserts, "I want to be initiated in all the circles of hell" (69), and a combatant named Merrier responds, "I suppose Virgil was a staff officer" (69). A number of rhetorics are at play in this brief interchange. Of course, there is the allusion to Dante's *Inferno*, and the role of Virgil as guide through the circles of hell. War is a hellish experience, and the men led into battle are led by staff officers, those who are assigned to commanding staff. And war is fire, as is the Christian interpretation of hell — thanks to John Milton, of course, and *Paradise Lost*. So, officers, specifically staff-level officers, are guides into hell, and the enlisted men are those who are guided, those who are led, into the pyre of war. Most obviously in war, officers lead enlisted men to their deaths; such is war, but in the Dos Passos work, even those officers in a medical capacity are cruel to the enlisted men, and in one particularly telling scene, during an extended gas attack, a medical doctor orders a number of enlisted men — men who are fleeing the poison gas and seeking refuge in a covered medical dugout — out of the protection of the dugout and back into the gas-filled atmosphere: "Suddenly, as three soldiers came in, drawing the curtain aside, [the doctor] shouted in a shrill, high-pitched voice: 'Keep the curtain closed! Do you want to asphyxiate us?'" (78–79). The doctor then verbally attacks the men, demanding, "Are you wounded?... You can't stay here. There's not enough room for the wounded.... Get the hell out of here, d'you hear?" (79). One of the men repeatedly replies and pleads, "But, my lieutenant..." (79). Nonetheless, the men are ordered out of the dugout and back into the poison gas-filled night: "The men began stumbling out into the darkness, tightening the adjustments of their masks behind their heads" (79). Ironically, the men are re-entering the poison, and might therefore soon earn the right to be situated in the medical dugout. Further, and absurdly, contingent upon the severity and amount of gas in the attack and external atmosphere, and the quality of the men's gas masks, the doctor might be condemning the men to a slow and agonizing death. There is a certain bitterness to the narrative irony that a medical doctor (an officer, of course) is ordering the men, who are enlisted in rank, to their potential deaths rather than letting the men rest out the gas attack in the dugout.

Dos Passos further castigates the officer class, metonymously, but cumulatively, in two other scenes, one brief — a mere sentence (88) — and one diffuse — an interpolated narrative aside (85–87). First, the longer, the tale of how a lieutenant earned the Croix de Guerre. Martin Howe and another American, a combatant named Will, are sitting at a crossroads, taking a break from the war, drinking champagne and discussing life and battle, and Will tells Martin of a lieutenant named Duval, who spells his name "duVal"—pretentious, of course. It seems that Duval desires a Croix de Guerre, the French medal commonly awarded for combat heroism to foreign combatants who are fighting in assistance of France, and Will tells Howe, "[Duval has] been wanting a Croix de Guerre for a hell of a time" (86), because a number of men in the company had already—rightfully—earned the commendation, and Duval is jealous. Thus, Duval had attempted to earn the medal by sucking up to the General Staff, but that had not worked, so, as a matter of course, the only option was "to get wounded" (86) on purpose, so Duval "took to going to the front posts" (86) of the combat sector, but this did not work either, as the sector was a quiet one. However, as luck would have it, one day a shell landed proximal to Duval's "staff car" (86), and he, being the astute officer, "showed the most marvelous presence of mind ... clapped his hand over his eye and sank back in the seat with a groan" (86). Duval then heroically ignored a doctor's assistance and self-bandaged the "wound" and went about his duties. Subsequently, Duval was awarded the Croix de Guerre for "for assuring the evacuation of the wounded under fire" (87). The story of Duval's manipulation of the commendation process, and the dishonor thereof, is brought to a close by Howe, who says, "He'll probably get to be a general before the war's over" (87). This interpolated story is a long example in a short text of the common enlisted man's distaste for the officer class. An identifying factor in this scene is the presence of the "staff car" and the immediate condemnation that comes of being a rank that travels in a staff automobile. The common enlisted men travel by foot—during battle—and by camion—when moving to battle. The staff car motif is repeated, for effect, immediately after Will's narrative of Lieutenant Duval, as artillery starts falling in the area: "There was an explosion and a vicious whine of shrapnel bullets among the trees. On the road a staff-car turned round hastily and speeded back" (88). The 11-word sentence that follows the narrated announcement of the presence of artillery and shrapnel castigates, condemns, vilifies, denounces, and censures the entire "staff car"–riding officer class. Dos Passos offers neither rebuke by Howe and Will nor narrative condemnational commentary. The rapidity of action of the officer(s) in the staff car, who flee afraid and under (indirect) fire, needs no further explanation, nor clarification; the officer, or officers, are cowards.

Other texts of the First World War also contain the oppositional dyad between officers and enlisted men, and Thomas Boyd's *Through the Wheat* manifestly lambasts officers while it shows that carelessness on the part of the officer class leads directly to the deaths of enlisted men. After more than six weeks in the trenches (during which a corporal named Olin is killed by friendly fire, secondary to a company commander forgetting that a patrol from the Intelligence section is out in no man's land, directing automatic fire toward the patrol, having mistaken them for Germans [32–38]), 3rd Platoon and the rest of Company C are allowed relief and respite in a "vermin-infested" (44) bunkhouse in the Bois La Vec valley. Hours after arriving at the bunkhouse and collapsing secondary to absolute physical and psychological exhaustion, the men are awakened by a "touring-car"–riding lieutenant who informs the platoon sergeant and company commander that Major General Bumble will inspect the troops in two hours (44–46). Of course, as the reader is well aware, any officer riding in a "touring-car" (Dos Passos' staff car) is a member of upper echelons of the officer class, and is thus an enemy of the combatants, especially the allied enlisted. And obviously, even to the most uninitiated reader, there is a certain absurdity, bordering on stupidity, in holding a company inspection mere hours after the company has been relieved after weeks at the front. Unshaven, filthy, hungry, the men are mentally, emotionally, psychologically, and physically broken down, knackered. Yet, for reasons unknown to the enlisted men — possibly General Staff–level boredom — the major general demands a company inspection. So, a company inspection is to take place, and a couple of hours after the men have formed in ranks, a "huge touring-car rounded the road and stopped" (49–50). Major General Bumble and his immediate staff "walked pompously along the line of the front rank ... climbed in [the car] and the car spurted away" (50). There is a certain military-centric silliness in this scene that anyone who has been in the military, regardless of branch or era, will understand. The officer says hop, and the enlisted masses hop. Of course, the silliness is enhanced by Boyd's moniker for the general — Bumble, as in bumbling buffoon.

Boyd also includes a brief scene between Hicks and an unnamed company-level lieutenant (in the vernacular, a "mail-order shavetail" [41]), reminiscent of other war texts in its construct — the power-driving officer, usually a non-combatant sort, dressing down the front-line enlisted man for his non-standard, non-military issue appearance. In fact, in this study, Gustav Hasford's *The Short-Timers* also has an excellent and biting scene of this sort (135–39). Boyd's narrator notes that this lieutenant had "offered to remain out of the [current] attack in order that, should the company be annihilated" (203), he would be able to reform a new company with non-combat personnel — orderlies, kitchen assistants, and so forth. In other words, this lieutenant is not exactly a warrior. The lieutenant notices Hicks, who has replaced much of his standard-issue gear with battlefield salmagundi, and demands to know why Hicks is out of uniform. Hicks replies, earnestly, that he does not know. The officer, "who had received at least ninety days training [is] horror-stricken" (204), and asks why Hicks has not saluted — one does not salute at the front, of course, as doing so alerts enemy snipers of officers, who are then shot — and places Hicks under arrest. Hicks, though, is off to battle, so the arrest is meaningless, a feeble attempt at a hierarchy of rank by a petulant lieutenant.

Finally, in the text, not all scenes of the oppositional dyad between officers and enlisted men are so humorous. Foolish officers directly cause the deaths of enlisted combatants under their charge in vain attempts at glory, and Boyd illustrates such actions. During a large, forest-set battle fought by French and American troops against Germans, Hicks and a platoon-mate named Ryan discuss the battle-field situation, and Ryan notes, "Some poor fool is making our regiment attack without a barrage. Did you see the outfit over on the right ... that was the third battalion, and I'll bet there's not a third of the men left" (83–84). Hicks replies that such an act, to assault a hill without artillery, is murder, and "What can these fool officers be thinking of?" (84). The answer, of course, is "Glory" (84), says Ryan. Boyd demands to know what such unnecessary, narcissistic glory is good for; it cannot bring the dead back. In *Through the Wheat*, Boyd scripts the oppositional dyad between officers and enlisted men a bit more broadly than Dos Passos in *One Man's Initiation* or Crane in *The Red Badge of Courage*; Boyd uses comic absurdity and the tragic to create the dyad. What none of the three authors do, however, is allow an enlisted man to kill an officer; this act is clearly a dividing line over which most early modern authors are not willing or eager to cross. In *Company K*, though, William March goes a-fragging.

The act of "fragging" an officer is an extreme one, yet a number of texts in this study have scenes in which an enlisted man's actions — or inaction — lead to the death of an officer. *Company K*, *The Short-Timers*, and *The Naked and the Dead* each offer the oppositional dyad between officer and enlisted man differently, though each text contains an enlisted man who feels so radically disjunctive relative to his relationship with an officer that the officer's life becomes unnecessary to the war at hand. William March's *Company K* is a work with a text-wide thematic element of anti-officer sentiment, and nearly universally, officers are presented as selfish, incompetent louts who care very little or not at all about the enlisted class of men. For example, early in the text, in a sketch narrated by company CO Captain Terence L. Matlock (31–33), 50 men have been granted a day's liberty, but Matlock calls for an equipment inspection prior to the liberty. Of course, living outdoors for weeks, in the rain and the mud and the muck, leads to permanently soiled and mildewed clothing, but Matlock nonetheless dresses down a private who has been unable to clean his underwear to a satisfactory sheen, after which someone in the ranks gives Matlock "the raspberry" (32); when Matlock demands to know the provocateur, no one answers forth. Matlock then, in an act of pure childish petulance that does nothing but destroy any extant respect between the CO and the enlisted, throws each man's clean clothing in the mud and, in a final tantrum, takes the liberty passes and tears all 50 up and scatters the pieces on a pile of manure. Thus Captain Matlock is symbolically identifying the men, his men, with shit. Their worth is equated with the waste of an animal, and this act of equation dehumanizes the men, putting them on a level with beasts of burden — horses and mules. Matlock ends the episode with a brief lecture on respect, of which he has earned none and lost much, if any existed at all. Later in the text, Captain Matlock, whom the men have nicknamed "Fishmouth Terry" (157) and "Nit-wit Terry" (34), is shot in the head and mortally wounded, an act that literally blows particles of the captain's brain out of his skull. A private recounts that about a "teaspoonful" (158) of Fishmouth Terry's brain exited his head as he was loaded onto a stretcher, and another man says, "If that many brains ran out, it couldn't possibly have been *our* Terry!" (158). Cue the laughter, which March is astute enough not to include in the scene.

But March is also brutally serious in his presentation of this oppositional dyad, as he presents two sketches that narrate a private's act of murdering a lieutenant. As is not uncommon in the text, a dead man narrates a sketch, and March places the lieutenant's narrative before the private's. What is also interesting, and not uncommon (at least in the texts in this study), is that the murdering enlisted man gets away with the murder. All three "fragging" texts here allow the murderer to continue his role within the fighting unit. In the March text, Lieutenant Archibald Smith narrates his own murder (91–92), and then Private Edward Carter narrates his act of murder (93–95). By placing the lieutenant's narration first, March humanizes the officer and dehumanizes the killer, and thus creates a victim of a murder. However, once March presents the private's perspective, the lieutenant is villainized, and is perhaps even — contextually — worthy of murder. Smith's narrative reads as a victim's, one in which the lieutenant is cornered in a trench by an armed assailant, one who emits "a piglike grunting noise in his throat" (91). The attacker is an animal, and the victim is a human being. The attacker is presented as unstable, and March uses exclamation points when the attacker speaks — "You know you got it in for me!" (91) — but Smith presents himself as calm: "'What do you want, Carter?' I asked ... quietly" (91). The private's accusations toward Smith are of the "You got it in for me!" sort, but the lieutenant's retorts are of the "You are a good soldier, so I choose you a lot" sort. Thus, Carter's military competency is Smith's undoing. Carter repeats the "You got it in for me!" line through the scene, as if in some manic haze, and he finally bayonets Smith to death (92). Smith — cogent, rational — is dead, and Carter — piglike, manic — has murdered him. However, in the following sketch — Carter's narration — the reader is offered an articulate, although murderous, human being. According to Private Carter, on at least four successive days and nights, without allowing for break or rest or sleep, Lieutenant Smith has asked for or ordered Carter to take part in patrols, guard duty, galley duty, sentry duty, wiring parties, work parties, and the like, and then, after finally being allowed to sleep, Carter is personally awakened by Smith, who informs him that there is an all-night patrol taking place, to which Carter is invited. It is at this point that Carter thinks to himself, "I sat there for a minute before making up my mind" (94). Of course, Carter has decided to kill Smith. Carter then goes to the unoccupied communication trench to intercept Smith, the point at which the lieutenant's sketch takes place. Ironically, when Smith comes upon Carter in the trench, Smith is humming "La Paloma [The Pidgeon]" (94): "He tried to talk me out of it, but I pinned him to the side of the trench and stuck my bayonet in him until he quit breathing" (95). Carter runs back to his bunk and returns to sleep before being missed, a successful murderer. While Smith argues to Carter that competence is the reason behind the constant duty, the actual duties Carter undertakes — sentry duty, galley duty, guard duty, work parties — can be manned by any man whose turn is up. And even though wiring parties and patrols in no man's land do take skill, any infantryman should be able to take his turn at such patrols. Thus, Smith's rationalization for continually choosing Carter for duty seems a bit disingenuous, the immediate rhetoric of a man attempting to prolong his life. And while Carter may not be excused for murdering his own platoon lieutenant, one must allow that Lieutenant Smith lacked some leadership sense. A fatigued man, an ally, does not think clearly, and Carter does not, but a military machine can still act mechanically, and Carter does so.

When Private Carter murders Lieutenant Smith, he "frags" the lieutenant, and apparently Carter gets away with the murder. Frag, of course, is a Vietnam War–era word that means to kill an unpopular fighting ally, most often an officer. And both reference text author/editor Paul Dickson and novelist Karl Marlantes include definitions of "Frag" (271)/"Fragging" (578) in their texts. As well, both writers note that the word "frag" and the act of "fragging" are born of the fragmentation grenade — the handy and effective tool with which to frag. In Gustav Hasford's *The Short-Timers*, as has been previously discussed, Animal Mother frags Lieutenant Shortround (106); and in so doing, he kills not an unrespected and hated officer, but a respected and liked officer, a Mustang, in fact — a former enlisted man (87) who has evolved or has been promoted into the officer class. Further, and contrary to the Carter/Smith fragging (in which no one but the reader is aware of the situation), Animal Mother frags Mr. Shortround, and the platoon is aware of this, yet Animal Mother is not punished. Why is Animal Mother allowed to continue on, even though he has murdered a respected leader and officer, one who has been promoted from corporal to lieutenant (87), one who is often addressed honorably and respectfully as Skipper? Perhaps the truth lies in the practical aspects of infantry combat. Animal Mother is a Super Grunt, and thus is a needed and necessary element in the platoon. Lieutenant Shortround, however, even though well respected and well liked — a former snuffy, a grunt in body and soul, a Mustang even, and one who is addressed as Skipper — is, frankly, expendable. The platoon moves on, the war moves on, the grunts move on, but for the dead, who are left as lumps in body bags (107–8). Animal Mother moves on, too, because he is needed in combat. As well, there is perhaps an element of fear. Who wants to be the next man fragged by Animal Mother? When Animal Mother frags Mr. Shortround, he also kills the unnamed platoon radioman (106), without remorse or cause. Animal Mother is afforded the opportunity to frag the lieutenant because of the combat situation — the platoon is under sniper fire — and he does so. Thus, even to the stupidest member of the platoon, Animal Mother is a dangerous SOB, one to fear, regardless of uniform or rank. So, because of this unique combat calculus, one built at the nexus of fear and necessity, Animal Mother gets away with double murder. And perhaps out of pure meanness, Animal Mother survives the text, although many other named — nicknamed — primary characters do not. Even as he is dying, Cowboy tells Joker to never trust Animal Mother, for he is not merely a killer in war, he is a murderer. Hasford is excellent at highlighting the dangers of the war zone, and one of the ongoing thematic elements in *The Short-Timers* is the obvious dangerous nature of the Marines, who prove lethal even to other Marines. And Animal Mother, murderer among killers, is an exceptionally brutal character, even when measured beside and beyond his peers, and his obvious and unjustifiable act of fragging Lieutenant Shortround is astounding in its arrogance, yet, for all its explicit criminality, it is an act that goes unpunished. Animal Mother is neither arrested nor killed in battle, and so perhaps Hasford's dominant rhetorical argument is that animals survive.

In *The Naked and the Dead*, through the character of Staff Sergeant Sam Croft, commanding non-commissioned officer of Intelligence and Reconnaissance Platoon (I and R) and existential nihilist, Norman Mailer also offers the enlisted man as animal, as killer, as predator among his peers; as well, Mailer offers a lieutenant, Lieutenant Robert Hearn, as prey. Unlike Lieutenant Shortround, a mustang cum Skipper, who is known and respected and well liked by those under his command, Hearn is neither known nor respected, nor particularly well liked, by the men of Intelligence and Reconnaissance Platoon, over whom he is spitefully thrust into command by Brigadier General Edward Cummings, commanding general of American forces on Anopopei Island, a fictional Japanese-occupied island in the Pacific Campaign of World War II. A "bourgeois intellectual" (343), a child of capitalist privilege, one who is a liberal in political leaning but "independent of economic considerations" (343), and thus "without [the] fear" (343) needed to comprehend class structure and schism produced through the capitalist hegemony, one who is a quasi-unionist, a quasi-Communist, a man sans true passion, one who is not an infantry officer in psyche or in training, Hearn is forced — in an act of humiliation by the general — into command of a specialized platoon, a platoon that has no officer in charge, a platoon sent on a mission to "reconnoiter the trails in the Japanese rear" (400), in order to see if a company-size element could possibly make it through the jungle and safely attack the Japanese from behind their own lines. Interestingly, Mailer noted in a 1948 interview titled "*The Naked* Are Fanatics *and the Dead* Don't Care," "To this day I don't like officers" (3), and enlisted men "operate" (10) on hatred of officers, and that as a GI during World War II, "I hated officers" (11). Mailer's dislike for the officer class is not unique in the enlisted classes, or among authors of World War II tomes, and as John T. Frederick notes, one of the "themes all but universally present in the fiction of the Second World War [is] the antagonism between the ranks and all but a few commissioned officers" (198). Specifically referring to *The Naked and the Dead*, John M. Kinder posits that "Mailer seems to revel in the failures of the officer class" (199) and argues that the oppositional dyad between the officers and enlisted men in the text is one created by "class antagonisms between officers and enlisted men" (188), the "brutality of combat and the physical and mental abuse suffered by 'common soldiers' throughout the war" (191), and the peri-textual role of the "officer-class as antidemocratic, anti–American — even fascist" (194). According to Kinder, the officers in the text lead through fear and intimidation, while the men exist as "cogs in the military machine" (198). Thus, from the Crane text to the March text to the Mailer text, enlisted men have evolved from sheep to be slaughtered, to pigs that grunt, to gears to be ground down in the war machine, but they are not yet human beings.

But in general, Kinder is correct; General Cummings is fascistic — "the embodiment of military fascism" (Aldridge 136) — though he is not the only character who leads through a philosophy of force, fear, and intimidation. I and R Platoon Commander Staff Sergeant Sam Croft is, as others have noted, "the enlisted counterpart of Cummings" (Aldridge 138), a "brutal man of force" (Hoffman 237) who holds the men of I and R Platoon "together only by their common fear" (Palm 105) of his violent retribution. Croft is the near-perfect, ever-evolving (or, as it were, ever-devolving) existential nihilist — "I HATE EVERYTHING WHICH IS NOT IN MYSELF" (164) — and he is hardly the idealized non-commissioned officer offered in many novels of war, modern or postmodern. Croft's murderous impulses are on display in the "Time Machine" (156–64) section, subtitled "Sam Croft The Hunter" (156), in which Croft, scion of West Texas, while serving in the National Guard, snipes an "oil field" (161) striker, and enjoys the act. Croft believes in nothing, and exists in "an endless hatred" (164); as the text opens, Croft is in charge of I and R Platoon, and as the text closes, Croft is in charge of I and R Platoon. But it is what happens when Hearn is in charge of I and R Platoon, when the platoon is on its reconnaissance mission, that Croft's savagery is explicitly manifested. When Cummings assigns Hearn to I and R Platoon, Hearn involuntarily usurps Croft's command position; of course, Hearn is instantly loathed by the former commander of the platoon, and further, Hearn's mortality rests upon Croft's cold, hard bearing, but Hearn does not even realize it. What is interesting is that Hearn is excited to be out of the General Staff and out from under General Cummings' thumb. Hearn has had only a day to prepare for the recon mission, yet he exhibits a certain and specific "pleasure" (433) at his newly assigned role, even though Mailer's narrator foreshadows the journey by noting that the men of I and R "prepared for a miserable trip" (433); further, there are an unlucky 13 members of I and R on the mission. Hearn is not unaware of his newbie role in the platoon, nor is he unaware that "Croft resented him" (435). Hearn is even astute enough to understand that "Croft knew more than he did" (435) and that his and Croft's would be "a difficult relationship to handle" (435). Croft, correctly described by Eric Homberger as "highly competent and vicious" (189), does indeed resent Hearn, and at this point in the text, the reader is acutely aware that Croft must resent Hearn, has to resent Hearn. However, what the reader does not assume, as Croft is a professional soldier and a leader of men, is that Croft will willingly allow Hearn to be murdered because of the desire to re-assume command of I and R. As Homberger notes, Croft is "too instinctive and inarticulate to engage in a dialogue with Hearn; all he can do is kill him" (189), so he does, if not by his own hand, then by his own means.

As the men circumnavigate half of the island on their landing craft, and before the mission commences, the enemies seen and unseen are known — the terrain, the Japanese — and for Croft, "Hearn was his foe" (440). Yet, Croft thinks to himself, "To resent an order, to be unwilling to carry it out, was immoral" (440). Clearly, Croft is at odds with the situation and with himself; while clearly existential and nihilistic, Croft does adhere to the military chain of command and possesses a self-assigned scale of morality. Croft instinctually hates and resents Hearn because Hearn has replaced him as ranking hierarchical leader of I and R Platoon, a role at which Croft excels militarily, but opposing Hearn's orders and rank would be to oppose his own rules of honor and character. However, inevitably, and paradoxically, Croft must betray himself and his self-defined sense of honor in order to re-assume command of that which he sees as his— Intelligence and Reconnaissance Platoon. As the platoon grinds through the jungle toward the Japanese position, antipathy builds between Hearn and Croft, and each man, as well as the reader, can feel the tension. Hearn is aware that the men look to Croft as their leader and, ironically, Hearn is cogitating how he can enforce upon the men that he is to be their permanent commander. In so doing, Hearn shows that he is, at this point, not yet fit to lead. Of course, as war novel tropes go, to think of the future is to doom oneself, so the reader must be aware that Hearn is fated to die; there can be no other way. Hearn is a character out of his element; he is in the jungle and he is aware that Croft resents him, but he does not instinctively know that Croft is his mortal enemy, and thus Hearn makes the fatal mistake of trusting Croft. As the men enter a grove that lies before an intermountain pass through which the platoon must travel, Japanese forces, who, of course, occupy and patrol the area, attack the platoon with small arms fire (510). This is Hearn's first time under fire, and he is taken with fear, but gathers himself and assumes a leadership role and, with Croft, directs the platoon to safety. After retrieving a wounded man, a scene occurs in which Croft kills a small bird that had been found by another member of the platoon. Hearn makes Croft apologize to the man, and the "unaccustomed words dropped leadenly from his tongue" (532). While John W. Aldridge argues that "it is Croft's fear that Hearn will usurp his command that causes him to bring about Hearn's death" (139), it is this scene, this forced and ordered apology, that motivates Croft to kill Hearn, or, better, allows Croft to let Hearn be killed: "If Croft had been holding a rifle in his hand, he might have shot Hearn at this instant" (532). Even up to this point in the patrol, while there exists mutually acknowledged, though unsaid, animosity between Croft and Hearn, Croft has not explicitly or instinctually desired to murder Hearn, as he still exists under the Croft Code of Honor, such as it is. But being forced to apologize to a lower-ranking member of the platoon is a forced humiliation that Croft cannot forgive.

One cannot forget that Croft is indeed capable of fratricide, as in the case with the oil field striker, whereby Croft took advantage of situation and circumstance and allowed himself to kill another American merely for the opportunity and experience of doing so. Thus, given the opportunity, like a wounded animal existing on instinct, Croft is deadly dangerous, because here he is wounded secondary to being undercut twice in a matter of days; Hearn has taken charge of I & R Platoon, and he has also made Croft apologize to a lower-ranking member. And when Hearn, correctly, decides to abort the mission — their cover is blown, obviously, so their ability to reconnaissance the Japanese rear is negated — Croft is taken aback, yet he is able to convince Hearn to allow a one-man reconnaissance mission to slide up the mountain pass to see if the pass is guarded, so Sergeant Martinez is sent up the mountain, but before he goes, Croft tells him, "'When you get back, don't say anything to anybody till you see me. If the Lootenant is up, you just say to him nothing happened, do you understand?' Croft ... felt the powerful anxiety of disobeying an order" (583). By not waking Hearn upon Martinez's return, as ordered, and by intercepting Martinez's recon report, Croft is, of course, usurping Hearn's command. Croft wants to complete the mission, regardless of the fact that the original reconnaissance purpose is now corrupted. As he is on the recon up the mountain pass, Martinez discovers a Japanese machine-gun emplacement, and in his terror and haste, he kills the man occupying the gun (595); realizing his mistake (for if another Japanese soldier sees the dead guard, there will be an alarm sounded), Martinez returns down the pass, and he tells Croft about the machine-gun emplacement, but Croft does not tell Hearn, demanding of Martinez, "Don't say a damn word to the Lootenant. You went clear through the pass without seeing a damn thing, y' understand?" (598). At dawn, Croft, "with a nervous flush" (600), reports to Hearn that Martinez said, "The pass is empty as far as he went" (601), an obvious lie, known to Croft, to Martinez, and even to the reader, but not to Hearn. The pair discuss the situation, and Hearn says, ignorant of the machine-gun emplacement, "We'll try it through the pass" (601). Upon hearing this, Croft "felt a curious mixture of satisfaction and fear. The thing was committed" (601).

Hearn tells the men of the situation, and in so doing, exposes Martinez and Croft to themselves, and thus makes the here-to-fore honorable Martinez a participant in Hearn's death: "Quite naturally he [Hearn] assumed the point and led the platoon toward the pass" (602). In so doing, and a bit coincidentally, Hearn allows himself to be shot in ambush, and thus Hearn fulfills Croft's wish and will: "A half hour [after taking point], Lieutenant Hearn was killed by a machine-gun bullet which passed through his chest" (602). That is the end of Hearn, and so "Croft felt a deep release; at that moment his body was light" (603). Croft, as one would assume, immediately takes control of the platoon, and (personal mission accomplished), organizes a hasty retreat back down the pass. This example of the oppositional dyad between officer and enlisted man is the literary example *par excellence*. Mailer takes 200 pages to create and build rising action, and then climax this oppositional dyad of rank. And while the reader knows that Lieutenant Hearn is doomed, the abruptness of the killing is shocking — a one-sentence paragraph is the immediate end of Hearn. What is interesting is that by the time Croft decides to let Hearn die, Croft has betrayed himself and his finite sense of honor, and therefore has devolved into a genuine existential nihilist, a true postmodern literary character. As Jeffrey Walsh correctly, but not completely, notes, "Hearn is pointlessly killed, ostensibly because he threatens Croft's dominance of command over the platoon" (*American War Literature* 117). While Hearn is indeed a threat to Croft's command, Hearn is fated to die because he embarrasses and humiliates Croft by forcing him to apologize for killing a bird. This ordered act is Hearn's capital sin against Croft.

In war and in the American novel of war, the oppositional dyad between officers and enlisted men is time- and text-honored, and the conflict between officers and enlisted can be seen implicitly and explicitly in *The Red Badge of Courage, Company K, One Man's Initiation, Through the Wheat, The Naked and the Dead,* and *The Short-Timers. Company K, The Naked and the Dead,* and *The Short-Timers* show the act of fragging an officer, with the chosen actions of enlisted men leading directly to the deaths of various officers, while *One Man's Initiation* and *Through the Wheat* offer the oppositional dyad in a lighter tone. Also included in the Boyd text are more serious scenes in which officer incompetence leads to the deaths of enlisted men, a common motif in many novels of war. *The Red Badge of Courage* uses a number of scenes of a low-ranking officer — a company lieutenant in particular — beating the enlisted ranks, including Henry Fleming, and more then of hapless, confused generals, to rebuke the officer class—from the respective of Henry's limited optic, of course, an optic created through Crane's noncombatant authorial role. And as officers are often drawn as incompetent, useless, dangerous, and clownish in novels of war, enlisted men, with emphasis here on the works of the twentieth century, are often drawn as murderous and vengeful. Is it any surprise, then, that in time of war when violence is celebrated, there exists violence between the officer class and the enlisted class? When men are encouraged to be violent, and are allowed to kill, is it any wonder that these men will turn violent toward someone other than the enemy? Violence gets easier when practiced. Thus, violence as a means of reaction becomes commonplace in war, but those who are encouraged to act violently occasionally turn against their superiors. In the American novel of war, the most common violence between officer and enlisted man comes from the enlisted side; however, the perpetrator of the (often murderous) action often goes unpunished. Regardless of right or wrong, the oppositional dyad between officers and enlisted appears destined to continue as a theme in the American novel of war.

XII

The Terrain/Weather as Enemy

As war, and the American novel of war, most often includes the deployment of American forces on foreign soils, the foreign terrain and/or weather becomes an enemy or a battlefield opponent, and even in texts set in the Americas, terrain and weather are hostile to the fighting men. As legendary battle tactician and philosopher Carl von Clausewitz observes, "combat uninfluenced by its surroundings and the nature of the ground is hardly conceivable" (142), while Mary A. Favret asserts that, in reality (and thus in literature), war is "a vast impersonal system whose agents include clouds, mists, thunder, drought, and snow" (535). Therefore, extreme heat, extreme cold, jungles, mountains, deserts, rain, ice, sleet, snow, wind, dust, rivers, oceans, and lakes each adversely affect the warrior's mission and life and combat conditions, as do indigenous flora, fauna, and disease; collectively and individually, all add misery to the daily existence of the warrior, no matter the rank, age, land in question, service branch, century, or war. As such, nearly universally, war texts must include such external factors and forces. *Blood Meridian* explores the hostilities of the Chihuahuan desert, while *The Red Badge of Courage* is framed by the weather's effects upon the combatants, as the text opens while Henry Fleming's regiment fights only the cold as it waits out the months of the harsh winter in Washington, D.C., and closes as rain pours over the tapped-out soldiers. Further, novels written about specific wars and eras share the intertextuality of the locus of the war, and therefore utilize the same motifs and thematic tropes relative to the indigenous flora, fauna, terrain, and weather. Novels set in Europe during World War I, such as *One Man's Initiation, Company K*, and *Through the Wheat*, offer the related natural elements of that war — rain, mud, lice — while novels set in the Pacific theater during World War II, such as *Beach Red, Ceremony*, and *The Naked and the Dead*, possess the hostile elements of Pacific jungle warfare, such as rain, heat, humidity, and disease-ridden insects — "Jungle law" (57), as Bowman's narrator labels the situation. Novels set during the brutal winter campaigns of the Korean War, such as *Band of Brothers, Hold Back the Night, I Am the Clay*, and *It's Cold in Pongo-Ni*, utilize the thematic element of the Korean winter, and in each text, the hostile winter weather — death-inducing weather — becomes a character in the text as the works clearly illustrate how the severe cold can kill warriors as quickly and decisively and heartlessly as can an enemy combatant. Jungle law returns through the novels of the Vietnam War, as evidenced in *Matterhorn* and *The Things They Carried* — novels in which animals and insects and triple-canopy jungle and monsoon rains are unarmed, uncombatable enemies in war. This motif of the terrain or weather or both as enemy, hostile to the point of being murderous, is one that is found in all of the American novels of war in this study because it is one that is found in all American wars; truth finds its way into art, verisimilitude into artifice, fact into fiction.

For example, in *Blood Meridian*, early in the text and long before he has aligned himself with the scalphunters, the kid, accompanied by Sproule (as filibusters under Captain White), survives the Comanche assault but endures a post-massacre ordeal and exodus in the Mexican desert: "They struggled all day across a terra damnata of smoking slag, passing from time to time the bloated shapes of dead mules or horses ... and went on and they walked the cinderland till they were near fainting" (61). The "terra damnata" (the damned ground, or cursed ground or condemned ground) easily kills four-legged animals, which is a warning, as the endurance and strength of the beast of burden — the mule or the horse — is such that when contrasted with the endurance and strength of man, it clearly shows man as the weaker of the beasts. Also note the rhetoric of fire, of Purgatory, or of Hell. The slag, the scoria of metallic earthen elements, smokes, as if on fire in the desert heat, and the pair walk in a "cinderland," a locus of the dross born of a furnace, or even (in association with the smoking slag) the locus of an active volcano. The savage heat also has the power of physical and optical and psychic distortion, as dead animals bloat into grotesque caricatures of their previous, living, selves, and heat waves radiate from the ground, and the pair of wanderers becomes the walking unconscious. For these former filibusters, the heat, the desert, the dehydration, and the incoherence that comes of such are the enemy. Eventually, Sproule dies (69), but not before being bitten by a bat (66). And even before the kid and Sproule wander the desert, and even prior to being massacred by the Comanche (51–54), four filibusters die from cholera (44–45). So McCarthy, in a few brief pages of a text epic in scope and in war violence, clearly acknowledges the non-combat hazards of war in a foreign land, even a land proximal to the newly established American border — those of the hostile terrain, the searing desert weather, the hungry local fauna, and the deadly disease born of travel in a non-native location. In so doing, McCarthy accurately includes in his American novel of war the deadly peri-war enemy that is the weather and terrain, and local fauna, of a nation unwisely invaded.

In *The Red Badge of Courage*, Stephen Crane frames his short and seminal American novel of war with inclement weather, while he also shows the weather to be an enemy in war, even in a war fought within the borders of one's own nation. Thus, Crane allows that in time of war, weather at home is a factor in the conditions of the fighting; in fact, in the nineteenth century, war had to break for the winter weather and months to pass, and so Henry's regiment, while bivouacked near Washington, D.C., for the winter, do little but drill and "try to keep warm" (8). So, before combat commences, before battle is set, before violence rages and Henry flees into the forest, Henry and his peers must face the weather, the winter, the cold; and as such, the weather, not Johnny Reb, is Henry's first foe. And after the Battle of Chancellorsville is nearing completion, and the Union forces are executing an organized retreat, the spring rains fall upon the vanquished: "It rained. The procession of weary soldiers became a bedraggled train, despondent and muttering, marching with churning effort in a trough of liquid brown mud under a low, wretched sky" (139). Ironically, Crane sees fit to use a battle in which the Union forces were defeated, and the battles in *Red Badge* mirror events that took place on 2 May and 3 May 1863 (Hungerford 105–15). Crane furthers the text-wide irony of Henry Fleming's evolution into manhood (139) through defeat in battle by placing a symbolic and literal rain shower upon the bleary and beaten warriors, and thus reminds the reader that while there is battle against man in war, in war there is also battle against the natural world.

In addition to framing the work with scenes of inclement weather (first the winter cold and then the spring rain), Crane personifies the natural world, and in so doing, creates a wilderness of threat, a wilderness in which (and prior to battle) the "landscape threatened" (24) and the "woods were formidable" (24) foes—woods into which Henry absconds (42), where "brambles formed chains and tried to hold him [and trees] forbade him to pass" (52). Obviously, the psychological impact of Henry's subjective fear of combat is conjoined with Crane's anthropomorphizing of the natural world, which is viewed, of course, through Henry's optic. It is not enough that Henry's terror is driven by battle fear and accentuated by viewing corpses prior to combat. Henry's fear is exponentially elevated by the hostility of the natural world, which is subjectified with every tug of every branch or bramble upon Henry's gear or clothing. Thus, the terrain is—if not a stated enemy—Henry's felt and perceived enemy. Further, the Confederate forces are distant to Henry, seen in miniature, yet the trees, the brambles, the woods, are proximal to Henry, tactilely immediate, and thus are more of a perceived threat than the rebel forces. Tactically, too, the woods must be beaten, overrun, passed through, in order for the Union forces to gain ground, and so, collectively, to take ground is to defeat the natural enemy as a means of defeating the armed combat enemy. Finally, of course, as Henry absconds and runs through the forest, the forest fights Henry's flight, unwilling to allow easy passage to safety and away from armed conflict. So in *The Red Badge of Courage*, Crane, that seminal modernist, that man of the modern literature of the modern war, who had not yet seen war, uses the thematic element of the terrain and the weather as enemy in different ways. Crane frames the text with inclement weather to produce pre-combat and post-combat misery in and for the characters, and he personifies the wilderness to manifest a subjective, formidable, active and threatening enemy for Henry. In so doing, Crane creates a precedent for the use of the terrain and/or the weather as enemy in the American novel of war.

Moving forward chronologically to the twentieth century and combatively to the First World War, it is no coincidence that American novels of war written by those who participated in the war effort, either in the ambulance service — John Dos Passos—or as uniformed combatants—Thomas Boyd and William March—individually and collectively offer the same peri-textual motifs born of experiencing continental European weather and terrain as an enemy force while existing and enduring in the trenches and conditions born of trench warfare—mud, lice, rats, rain, and so forth. Conversely, Edith Wharton's work, *The Marne*, written by a noncombatant who is using the text as a propaganda piece, mentions the weather as an oppositional force only one time, and in passing, as American combatants complainingly inquire "whether it rained every day all the year round" (85). By placing the French weather in the form of an American complaint, Wharton creates the American soldier as whiner, one who cannot see the cultural and historical benefits and beauty present in the nation he has come to save. Thus, Wharton produces an unenlightened, ignorant American, a stereotype created to juxtapose with the idealized Troy Belknap. Dos Passos' *One Man's Initiation*, though, most probably because of its authorship by a member of the ambulance service, illustrates the adversarial weather throughout the entirety of the text, and thus offers the reader a more realistic view of the harshness of trench life and war in seemingly endless inclement weather. And the aspects of weather that are nearly omnipresent in the text are the rain (23–26, 35–39, 66, 71, 95) and the mud born of day after day after day of rain (26, 39, 46, 56, 65–66, 69, 72–74, 77–78, 82, 93, 95, 100–102, 125), as the rain falls "with unfaltering determination" (23) and creates mud that lasts long after the rains have subsided. This twin motif of rain and mud is text-wide in Dos Passos' work and is therefore a thematic element, central to the propagation of the text and the war effort within. One must fight the rain and the child of the rain—the mud—in order to fight the war. And while the "Huns" might be defeated through savage combat, the weather never will be, as the weather is greater than the mighty war efforts of man. Therefore, this idea of the weather as an enemy that cannot be defeated, that will not be defeated, is both new — a new century, a new war, a new locus of war — and old, as per the Crane text. Man can defeat, can slaughter, and can destroy other men and other man-made elements, but man cannot defeat, slaughter, or destroy the weather. As Neil M. Heyman notes, during the First World War, there were "factors beyond leaders' decision-making. One was the mud that came ... each year with the spring and late summer rains" (57). Additionally, Heyman notes that men "unfortunate enough to be wounded in such circumstances drowned — and sometimes disappeared — in the mud" (69).

When one adds trench life to the rain and the mud, secondary effects such as vermin and disease are produced, and are therefore experienced and endured by the combatants. Not surprisingly, World War I texts written by those who served and fought in the trenches prominently feature trench life and the unsanitary, brutal conditions thereof. In *Through the Wheat* and *Company K*, Thomas Boyd and William March make an effort to offer the abject and dangerous existence of life in the trenches, life filled with rats and lice and rain and mud, and sniper and mortar and artillery attacks, as well as the dead from previous engagements. As the trenches were geographically static for months or even years at a time, the area "was pounded by artillery shells for years to the point where it resembled a huge mud pit" (Schweitzer), in which, in conjunction with seasonal and out-of-season rains, daily life in the trenches "was something of a wet nightmare [as] the trenches were usually wet and sometimes flooded" (Schweitzer). A secondary effect of the constant rain and mud and flooding was the collapse of trench walls (Heyman 44), which "necessitated constant repair and rebuilding" (Heyman 44–45) and which could lead to the entombment and suffocation of those who were caught under the earthen slurry. To combat the boot-level mud, "wooden duckboards" (Heyman 48) were placed on the trench walkways, but often became dangerously slippery, as Boyd notes when introducing the mud and trench conjunction early in the text; while men are maneuvering the trenches, they slip "off the slimy duck boards which had been placed in the bottom of the trench to prevent traffic from being buried in the mud" (20). So, paradoxically, the duckboards both hamper the men and serve the men. However, to fall is to fall into mud that can eat a man alive, and Heyman recounts the story of a man who was sucked into the mud while still alive (69–70), all the while begging to be shot. Boyd, too, notes the danger of falling off the duckboards when, after sentry duty, men slosh through the mud, "with now and again a man slipping off the boards and floundering hip-deep in the mud" (40). March likewise includes the nexus of mud and trench life in his tome, as Lieutenant Archibald Smith narrates that after being stabbed, he "fell to the duckboards and lay there in the mud" (92), wet and cold and dying. Thus, the calculus of life in the trenches and the rain-produced and omnipresent mud offer a unique and threatening danger to the participants in the war.

The mud is a threatening foe, but the mud is not the only opponent trench occupants face; there are "cooties," too. Heyman notes, dryly, "To live in an unsterile, outdoor environment brought an inevitable infestation of lice" (49) to the trenches, and in fact, the presence of insects in war is neither a new literary or war motif nor an obsolete aspect of war, as currently the U.S. "Deployed Warfighter Protection Research Program dispenses $5 million a year to find new ways to combat disease carrying insects that threaten [American combat] troops" (McConnaughey A7). So, the presence of insect vermin in war and in the literature of war is ongoing. In *Company K*, Private Sylvester Wendell, tasked with the duty of writing letters to the parents of young men killed in action, creates a hypothetical letter, one that tells the truth of a combatant's death rather than lionizing the decedent: "at the time of his death he was crawling with vermin and weak from diarrhea" (101). Here is the simple truth of a private's life in the trenches: it is a lice-infested, diarrhea-producing life of germ, disease, and pestilence, and there is the combat, too, which kills the already infested and ill. But higher-ups are aware of the vermin in the trenches—hence the presence of delousing excursions. Private Byron Long describes one such excursion, whereby the men are sent through a "delousing plant" (104), while their clothes are placed "in an oven to bake for an hour or so" (104). After the men are sprayed with insecticide and the extant lice are baked, the men gather their uniforms and return to the war. Of course, and most obviously to all involved, the lice remain in the trenches, awaiting the return of the deloused men. So, the delousing, while temporarily effective, is a short-term measure in the war against the critters. Lice appear in the Boyd text, too, as men, when bored, "sat around ... their shirts off, hunting lice in the seams" (20). Even when not killing men, the combatants continue to kill foes—insect foes, of course. Boyd's narrator even describes a louse—a creature "small, carnivorous [and] yellow ... with a large black speck" (60) on its back. The presence of lice in both trench-based texts attests to the presence of lice in the World War I trenches. Interestingly, though, not situated in either text are rats, which were, according to scholars, readily present in and about the trenches (Heyman 49), the result of an endless food supply of dead soldiers, the corpses of whom often went uncollected and unburied. Nonetheless, *Through the Wheat*, *Company K*, and *One Man's Initiation* effectively present the weather and terrain as enemy in the American novel of World War I. Rain, mud, and lice were foes to be dealt with on a daily basis, regardless of combat situation on any given day.

A different sort of natural foe presents itself in the American novels of World War II. In the novels of the Pacific Campaign, "Jungle law" (Bowman 57) is the order of the day, and in Peter Bowman's important but nearly forgotten postmodern effort, *Beach Red*, jungle law includes an entomological list of insect types, a catalog of infectious diseases, and sundry combative indigenous flora. Minutes 27 and 28 (55–56, 57–58) catalog the jungle as enemy motif, correctly, effectively, and succinctly. Minute 27 identifies an entomologist's dream of various biting and stinging insects and arachnids: "Here in the rank growth, they welcome you" (55). There are "tactical mosquitoes ... the Anopheles, Aedes, and Culex types" (55), each with a different set of markings, but common to all is the hunger for blood. As well, "The ticks are present, too, with their flat, oval bodies" (55), also disease-ridden and hungry for human blood. And "All manner of flies are zooming about.... Small sand flies [and] buffalo great flies" (55). "Then there are the endless varieties of kissing or assassin bugs, colonies of fleas, mandated gnats and whole republics of mites.... Leeches ... sweatbee[s] ... large and hairy spiders ... little, unnoticeable spiders ... scorpions and land crabs and centipedes ... chiggers and cone-nosed bugs ... midges and flying bedbugs" (55–56). Further, there are ants "everywhere. Large, small, medium—red, black and white. Some bite and some sting and some bite and sting. [Some] attack in swarms" (56). And, of course, there is "the universally uninvited parasite, the louse" (56). This wonderful catalog of insects and arachnids, and crabs and segmented arthropods, presented over less than two pages of text, has the rhetorical effect of evincing the hostility of the indigenous insect and arachnid life toward the occupying combatants. The bugs are omnipresent and inescapable, even during the brief periods of non-combat downtime. The insects and arachnids and arthropods never sleep, never rest, never give quarter, and thus are perfect foes.

The passage closes with this explicit identification of the nonhuman life in the island jungle as enemy combatant: "All the insects seem to sting with a Japanese accent" (56).

In Minute 28, Bowman continues the barrage of insect life through the conjunction of insect contact and infectious disease: "By continued exposure to insects you may manage to contract malaria, filariasis, yellow fever, dengue fever, relapsing fever, pappataci, espundia, oriental sore, typhus, trench fever, bubonic plague, tularemia, dumdum fever or loaloa" (57). These fourteen insect-born diseases individually can lead to incapacitation or death, but when considered collectively — each man can, of course, contract more than one disease — the diseases can produce a pandemic effect upon a landing force that has no natural defense against the indigenous insects and their island-based diseases. Further, the local water supply brings forth "an impending attack of dysentery, cholera, typhoid fever, helminthic infection or undulant fever" (57), while the local fungi brings forth skin diseases such as "pinta ... trichosporosis ... dhobie itch" (58) and the better-known athlete's foot. So, common to the island are diseases of the blood, the brain and the skin. Of course, the indigenous flora have even more to offer: "The thorns and spines of poisonous or irritant trees and vines and shrubs and miscellaneous plants may cause severe blisters. The sap of ... tree[s] will occasion painful rashes and sores which heal with difficulty, while nuts of ... palms are covered with needles which penetrate and irritate the skin" (58). Other plants emit poisonous juice, contain barbs, cause blindness, or even kill if their oil enters an open wound (58), and there are also "coral snakes, moccasins, and vipers as well as wild hogs, bats, alligators and swamp lizards" (58). Clearly, then, the indigenous flora and fauna on Bowman's Pacific isle are lethally threatening to the occupying combatants. Every bug or plant or life form, it seems, will sting, stick, stab, bite, swarm, infect, poison, or kill outright. Yet, Bowman's narrator notes, "your greatest danger is from your fellow human beings" (58). This outstanding understatement, after four pages of death- and disease-inducing indigenous flora and fauna and fungi and disease, reawakens the reader from the stultifying — but effective — journey into indigenes by reminding the reader of what is at stake in the text — human life though the combat of world war.

As Eric Homberger notes, the "jungle warfare of the Pacific seemed to American writers particularly terrifying because it lacked clear demarcations and sides" (178), so unlike the static combat of World War I, the dynamic, borderless, trenchless, jungle fighting of the Second World War was very much a psychological — and physical — battle against the elements of the jungle. And in Norman Mailer's *The Naked and the Dead*, an epic-length text with very little actual combat, there are a number of passages and scenes (extended, of course, as this is Mailer) that include this element of the American combatant against the jungle elements, primarily the terrain and the indigenous fauna. The first scene (129–38) is one in which the men of I and R Platoon grind through the hilly, rain-soaked, and muddy jungle, as they push and pull and coax two wheeled antitank guns to the locus of emplacement. As the men begin to lug the guns, "their feet sank into the deep mud and, after a few yards, their boots were covered with great slabs of muck" (130). And so it begins, this fight against the mud and the muck: "Every ten yards a gun would bog down and the three men assigned to it would have to tug until their strength seeped from their fingers" (130). The men drag the guns down the muddy, rutted trail, inches at a time, while "huge roots continually tripped the men, and their faces and hands became scratched and bleeding from the branches and thorns.... By the time an hour had passed, nothing existed for them" (131). The task has come immediately to dominate the very existence of the men pulling and pushing and dragging the guns through the jungle mire. Mailer is astute enough a writer to inform readers that, on level ground, a single man could pull each gun, but, of course, this ground is neither level nor dry. The men grind forward a few yards at a time, throwing away gear, while "the air was unbearably hot under the canopy of the jungle, and the darkness gave no relief from the heat of the day" (132). The men cannot speak or breathe normally, are exhausted, are abandoning their weighted gear, yet they have completed only half of the trek (one mile), but "in the darkness, distance had no meaning, nor did time" (133) and "they stank [and] their clothing was plastered with the foul muck of the jungle mud" (133), and "each turning in the trail [presented] only another ribbon of mud and darkness" (134). After nearly reaching battalion, their locus of relief, the men must, naturally, cross a stream fit with slimy clay banks, which are situated at an incline. As one team of men gets its gun nearly to the top of the opposite bank, the end of the journey, "perhaps four feet from the crest" (135), the gun, thanks to gravity, slipperiness, and the men's absolute physical exhaustion, "began to slip" (135), and slide, and fall away: "The gun struck some rocks at the bottom, and one of its wheels was knocked completely away" (136). After his customary reaming out of the team that lost the gun, Croft, in a succinct understatement, observes, "Well, that's one gun they ain't going to rescue for a little while" (138). This ten-page scene of man against jungle terrain is absolutely excruciating in its attention to the terrain-based suffering of the men lugging the antitank guns.

Mailer also offers other scenes of the men of I and R Platoon versus the terrain of Anopopei Island. Among these, the men have to drag a wounded man through the jungle, and analogous to the antitank gun passage, the wounded man is dead weight, a tragic reminder of the cost of combat, as well as a burden to those who attempt, but fail, to keep him alive (678); later, while trying to ford a stream, the men lose their load—the dead man's body (680–81): "One moment they had been carrying Wilson, and now he had disappeared" (681), washed away in the rapids. The irony here is very interesting because it shows the terrain as enemy, yet the terrain also washes away the men's burden, similar to the antitank gun scene, in which the bank takes away the gun and, therefore, the burden. Yet there is a punishment for each loss, of course, so the loss of one sort of physical burden is the offering and acceptance of another, heavier burden—the burden of failure when facing the natural world.

There are other human failures present in the text, too. Croft is obsessed with the summit of Mount Anaka, the highest peak on the island; in fact, "Croft's mad drive to conquer the mountain" (276), as Randall H. Waldron puts it, is one of the reasons Croft does not want to turn the reconnaissance team back, even after their cover is blown when they come across the Japanese patrol, and even after he allows Hearn to be killed (see Chapter XI). Nonetheless, in a great selfish act and tactical failure, under the threat of death, Croft pushes the remaining members of the platoon to attempt to summit the mountain, and in so doing, Croft loses the platoon, but, though intimidation, forces the men to keep attempting the summit (692–98). And as luck, or Mailer, would have it, just when the men are nearing the summit, as the men are retching and "even Croft was exhausted" (699), as their futile and non-tactical mission is nearing completion, Croft, in a fit of fatigue-based clumsiness, falls into a hornet nest, "and in a few seconds they raced down the line of men like a burning fuse.... For the platoon this was the final unbearable distress" (700). The men flee down the slope, down the mountain, down to the valley below. The climb is over; the summit untouched, unreached, unpassed, unbeaten. Croft has been defeated—by nature, of course, and then by his own men. He has killed, threatened, and contributed to the deaths of those under and above him, all in a desperate effort to defeat the terrain, his foe, his enemy. Croft has failed; the natural world has won again, as it always does (at least up to the point at which man splits the atom).

The terrain and weather is also the enemy in Leslie Marmon Silko's masterwork, *Ceremony*, a postmodern Vietnam War–era text cloaked in World War II garb. Much commented upon is the issue of Tayo's belief that his cursing the torrential jungle rains—"He damned the rains until the words were a chant" (12)—while captive to the Japanese causes the drought that the Laguna Pueblo suffer: "the monsoon rains are so suffocating and harmful to Rocky that Tayo curses the rain ... [and] later concludes that his doing so caused the drought at Laguna" (Beidler, "Bloody Mud" 27, 28); "Tayo ... curses the rain ... [and] he is broken by grief and guilt ... for the years of drought he believes his curse of the rain has brought" (Getz 134). It is also argued that the drought begins "about the time the Manhattan Project was authorized, thus bringing even this remote patch of [Laguna Pueblo] land into the pattern of nuclear holocaust" (Nelson 310). But whether Tayo or the Anglo uranium miners and atomic scientists cause the drought — and both do, for nothing is all good or all bad — what is not in doubt in the text is that the weather is an adversarial character, an enemy force, and within the jungles of the Pacific Campaign, the rain is the overwhelming oppositional natural element: "Jungle rain had no beginning and no end; it grew like foliage from the sky, branching and arching to the earth, sometimes in solid thickets entangling the islands, and, other times, in tendrils of blue mist curling out of coastal clouds" (11). Silko describes a beautiful liquid jungle, growing downward to meet the earth, to meet the plant life in a nexus of glimmering wetness and life force: "The jungle breathed an eternal green that fevered the men until they dripped sweat the way rubbery jungle leaves dripped the monsoon rain" (11). At the convergence of the blue liquid jungle, falling downward, and the green floral jungle, growing upward, are the men, Tayo and Rocky, men out of their desert element: "Jungle rain lay suspended in the air, choking their lungs as they marched; it soaked their boots until the skin on their toes peeled away dead and wounds turned green" (11). The rain chokes and soaks and rots the men's skin, and it "filled the tire ruts and made the mud so deep" (11) that men slip and slide and fall, and the corporal, who (along with Tayo) carries the wounded Rocky, cannot keep his feet. The rain is ceaseless, threatening, hostile, nearly personified. There is even a certain arrogance to the rain, as if it is mocking Tayo, daring him to drop Rocky: "The sound of the rain got louder, pounding on the leaves, splashing into the ruts; it splattered on his head, and the sound echoed inside his skull. It streamed down his face and neck like jungle flies with crawling feet. He wanted to turn loose the blanket [that supported Rocky] to wipe the rain away; he wanted to let go for only a moment" (12). Clearly, the rain has a personality, if even that of an irritating insect. So, the rain, an element of relentless, powerful beauty when introduced, evolves (or devolves) into an element of hostile intent and threat, and as the text moves on, the rain is explicitly a carrier of death: "jungle clouds raining down filthy water that smelled ripe with death" (56). In the peri-war scenes, Silko takes a component of "jungle law,"— jungle rain — and she creates a character that is paradoxically malevolent and beautiful, a character that rapidly grows more malevolent and less beautiful as the work progresses. Within the novel-wide thematic element of drought and responsibility, she identifies Tayo and the Anglo participants of the Manhattan Project as "Destroyers," contributors to the drought, those who curse nature—verbally or through splitting the atom. Relative to this study, Silko, through the use of a particular facet of "jungle law," furthers Mailer's and Bowman's theses that the jungle is, generally speaking, an exceptionally hostile element of war, and thus should be aptly presented in the American novel of the Pacific Campaign.

The dominant, the overriding, the overwhelming element of the weather as enemy in the texts of the Korean War is the Korean cold. Severe, brutal, and life-threatening, the cold becomes a character in the American Novels of the Korean War. And every author of a Korean War text in this study pays particular attention to the Korean cold. In order of publication, Pat Frank's *Hold Back the Night*, Ernest Frankel's *Band of Brothers*, Edward Franklin's *It's Cold in Pongo-Ni*, Richard Hooker's *MASH*, and Chaim Potok's *I Am the Clay* each effectively stage the Korean War as not only a war against a combatant enemy, but a war in which the United Nations forces (primarily Americans here, of course) have to combat the cold and its devastating effects upon indigenous and non-indigenous personnel. As Philip K. Jason notes, "Frank's *Hold Back the Night* stresses extreme hardship caused not only by an unusual enemy force but also by difficult terrain and climatic conditions" (123), and the hostility of the cold relative to immediate combat readiness is immediately introduced as the first page of narration allows that the Marines of Dog Company must sleep with their weapons so that the devices "would not freeze and jam" (1), as a frozen weapon is, of course, useless in combat. Also useless to the seventeen remaining men of Dog Company are their means of transportation — Jeeps — that are "frozen solid" (2) after a night in the elements: "Must be twenty below" (3), says Communications Sergeant Ekland to Captain Sam Mackenzie, who has "icicles growing from his beard" (2). So, in the first three pages of the text, Frank identifies the frozen and hostile Korean weather as an elemental and oppositional combatant, one that the Marines must face, if not overcome, in order to survive. And common to all of the Korean War novels in this study is this nearly immediate identification of the Korean winter — fall really, for all three of these first texts are set only in November and early December — as characteristically malicious.

Band of Brothers also opens with the cold: "The marines lay on the cold ground at the crest of the ridge" (5). Frankel goes further, though, and explicitly identifies the enemy: "There was no contact with the enemy.... The battle was against the piercing winds that blew down across the mountains from Manchuria, drove the thermometer to eighteen below zero, slowed movement, dulled reaction" (37). Like Frank, Frankel identifies the temperature by number, and number below zero, to emphasize to the reader that this cold is not the cold of the continental United States; this cold is "kill-you cold." And Frankel also describes the route of the cold, the wind, and thus makes the wind and weather a traveler of sorts, a journeyman who has come to fight. Edward Franklin likewise uses a route system to tell the travel — and oppositional nature — of the wind: "It's not on our side, the wind. It comes down from the steppes of Russian Siberia, from the snows of Russian Mongolia, and it gains its bitterness coming over Chinese Manchuria and finally through the gaps in the sawtooth mountains" (12). Of course, there is an analogy in all three texts here: The Chinese combatants and the Russian comrades thereof — furnishers of weapons, if not men, with their participation and their arming of the Korean Communist fighters — also come from the north, and also come to combat the American and United Nations forces. So the wind, the cold, the Chinese, and the Soviets are all against the Americans. Franklin continues the motif of the hostile wind: "There is nothing else to do at the foot of the hill so they sit up and suffer the full force of the wind. There is a message in the wind after all, isn't there? The wind comes down from the steppes and over the battered land and skims the dark trench of The Claw and through the ruins of Pongo-Ni and into our faces and the wind says, 'Beware'" (79). Like Frank and Frankel, Franklin specifically identifies the ever-present and ongoing hostility of the wind and weather; even when the combat is at a lull, the weather is still antagonistic, lethal.

Like the previous three texts, Richard Hooker's *MASH* begins in November, as on either side of a muddy road, there reside "rice paddies skimmed now with November ice" (13) and "a cold steel rain started to fall, almost obscuring the jagged, bare hills on either side of the valley" (13); "the cold, slanting rain was mixed with flat wet flakes of snow" (14). As the scene continues, "The rain had changed to wet snow ... and off the muddy road the ground was white" (15). So, while Hooker (actually the *nom de plume* of former Army MASH surgeon H. Richard Hornberger and journalist W.C. Heinz) does not evince the immediate and life-threatening hostility of the Korean November, as do Frank, Frankel, Franklin, and Potok (see below), Hooker does immediately introduce the Korean cold. And of course, the perspective of the Hooker text is that of a uniformed noncombatant in a safe area, while the previous three texts are narrated through the optic of unprotected combat Marines, Marines present in the fields of fire, as it were — so Hooker's text allows for the cold, but does not present the cold as an enemy force. Nonetheless, the text does note the prominence of the Korean winter, which is not unique to Korean War texts, of course, as well as the heat of the Korean summer, which is unique to Korean War texts: "The temperature at noon, day after day, was between 95° and 100°. The temperature at midnight, night after night, was between 90° and 95°" (136). Most obviously, then, the Korean weather is antagonistic in both the winter and the summer. Of course, the only reason the Frank, Frankel, and Franklin texts do not allow for the Korean summer is because the texts each are set within a very finite chronology, whereas the Hooker text is set from November 1951 through the year of 1952 and into 1953.

Also set over a period of more than a year, but analogous chronologically to the Frank and Frankel texts (November-December 1950), is Chaim Potok's *I Am the Clay*, which, of course, follows the flight south and then north of three peasant refugees during the Chinese advance into Korea during the early stages of the war. Like the Hooker text, the Potok text opens on a muddy road with snow all about, and like all of the Korean War text authors here, Potok uses the cold as an active participant in the peri-textual action and outcomes. Many unnamed characters are felled by the cold, and such death is commonplace through the entire text, so while the characters are noncombatants, they are, regardless, at war with the elements. The characters cannot hide from the cold or the wind, and later, with the changing seasons, come heat, dust, and drought. In this way, the Potok text is similar to the Hooker text, as it presents in full view the cold but acknowledges the heat. Taken as a comprehensive whole, though, these five American Novels of the Korean War overwhelmingly present the Korean cold as the most hostile weather element, the most hostile non-human element, at work during the war.

"Jungle law" returns in the American novel of the Vietnam War, and in the texts in this study, jungle law is a leech or a tiger or a mosquito or the rain. In "Alienation and Environment in the Fiction of Vietnam," Pilar Marín argues that "what sets the Vietnam War apart from others is also that which differentiates its literature from the literature of previous wars. One of these differentiating characteristics is its pervading sense of alienation which is fostered by, projected on and expressed through the physical environment [of Vietnam]" (25). While Philip K. Jason correctly notes that many elements of the Vietnam War and the literature thereof are present in the Korean War and its fiction (121–29), the element of the jungle as a living, breathing, menacing foe is more akin to the work of Peter Bowman than it is to the literature of the Korean War, in which the predominant elemental enemy is the cold and the wind rather than the flora and fauna of the jungle. Marín also posits, correctly, that the land in the literature of the Vietnam War is "alien and surreal ... a living presence with an identity of its own ... a contented organism living in self-contained isolation ... something monstrously alive, dangerous and terrible ... [a] voracious presence" (28, 29). This living presence, this presence composed of living things, is manifested in sundry ways in Karl Marlantes' *Matterhorn* and Tim O'Brien's *The Things They Carried*. In the O'Brien text, monsoon rains play a determining character, one that is a foe to the men of Alpha Company: "The rain was the war and you had to fight it" (163). A natural enemy, and relentless, the rain cannot be killed, cannot be overrun, cannot be isolated and bombed, cannot be napalmed, cannot be defeated: "For a solid week, the rains never stopped, not once ... the land turned into a deep, thick muck" (142). The Vietnamese ground is a literally man-eating monster, for in a chapter titled "In the Field" (162–78), a grunt named Kiowa is sucked into the mire during a mortar attack, never to be seen alive again (171). So, in this situation, the Vietnamese weather — through the monsoon rains— and the Vietnamese terrain — through the flooded lands— work in unison with the Viet Cong, who are directing the mortar attack on Alpha Company. Thus, the weather and terrain of Vietnam are contributory and culpable, relative to Kiowa's death.

In the Marlantes text, from the opening chapter, the Vietnamese fauna are actively attacking and killing the Marines of Bravo Company. In the first chapter, in a cringe-inducing scene, a leech enters a man's penis and, gorging on blood and perhaps urine, becomes lodged in the poor fellow's urethra (8). Of course, when the man must void, there is an immediate urgency as the man's discomfort soon grows into crippling agony. In the boonies, and away from a hospital, the "Senior Squid," the medic of highest rank, must perform field surgery. While the man is held down by his peers, sans anesthetic, the Senior Squid pushes a knife blade into the man's penis, above the leech, letting loose a shower of blood and urine (38) but not lacerating the leech; he then punctures the man's penis a second time, and this time gets the leech (39). This scene merely introduces the reader to the hostile animal life of Vietnam. Later in the text, creatures great and small kill Marines as effectively and efficiently as the North Vietnamese Army. First, a Marine dies of "pneumonia" (145)— a cause of death commonly known to the Americans, but not necessarily bacterially or virally or diagnostically accurate, as "something" (some indigenous disease) killed the young man, but a field autopsy, of course, is not possible, so a commonly known disease — to the Americans, at least — is applied to the man. Still later, a man in Lieutenant Mellas' platoon named Parker contracts a similar disease, and he is taken with convulsions and a temperature at "one hundred and six" (235); Parker dies (238), and Mellas is informed over the comm that Parker died of "cerebral malaria" (238), "which was carried by an isolated species of mosquito found only in the mountains [of Vietnam and the proximal geographic area]" (238). So, even the local insects and germs are against the American forces. But it is not merely the indigenous insects and leeches and germs that fell the Marines; tigers, too, roam the jungle, and in a short, shocking scene of immediate death, a Marine named Williams, who is on security post duty in the jungle, in the sightless blackness of the night, is attacked and killed and dragged off and eaten by a tiger (158). The tiger crunches Williams' skull, and Williams is gone into the darkness. What all these instances of hostile indigenous fauna have in common is the inability of the attacked American to defend himself. When a man is in combat, and he is fighting, he knows the enemy combatant, and fights within the given situation. But when a man is attacked by a leech that falls from a tree or sidles up one's trousers, what can be done in defense? Or when a man is bitten by a disease-carrying mosquito, a mosquito carrying a disease that no American is able to ward off, what can the American combatant do? Or when a tiger crunches one's skull, well, there is no defense —

for the tiger, the mosquito, the germ, or the leech. There is futility, there is agony, and there is death, but there is not combat, yet this is war — war against the indigenous terrain and weather, and elements thereof and therein.

So, conclusively and clearly, as war, and the American novel of war, most often includes the deployment of American forces on foreign soils, the foreign terrain or weather, or both, become an enemy or a battlefield opponent, and even in texts set in the Americas, terrain and weather are hostile to the fighting men. Extreme heat, extreme cold, jungles, mountains, deserts, rain, ice, sleet, snow, wind, dust, rivers, oceans, lakes, each and all, adversely affect the warrior's mission and life and combat conditions, as do indigenous flora, fauna, and disease. So, regardless of rank, age, land in question, service branch, century, or war, hostile terrain, inclement weather, indigenous flora, and antagonistic fauna add misery to the daily existence of the warrior, and in modern and postmodern American novels of war, the belligerent nature of the natural world is explicitly presented and characterized in the texts, and without exception, every work in this study —from those set in the nineteenth century to those set in the twenty-first — uses a truculent natural world as a motif or thematic element. *Blood Meridian* explores the hostilities of a hellish Chihuahuan desert, which offers "a terra damnata of smoking slag" (61), dead men, and dead animals, while *The Red Badge of Courage* is framed by the effects of the cold and the rain upon the Union combatants, as the text opens with Henry Fleming's regiment fighting only the cold as it waits out the months of the harsh winter in Washington, D.C., and as the text closes with saturating rain pouring over the weary and defeated soldiers. Further, novels written about specific wars and eras utilize the intertextuality common to the locus of the war, and therefore, share the same motifs and thematic tropes relative to the indigenous flora, fauna, and weather. Novels set in Europe during World War I, such as *One Man's Initiation, Company K*, and *Through the Wheat*, possess the related natural elements of that war — rain, mud, and lice, while novels set in the Pacific theater during World War II, such as *Beach Red, Ceremony*, and *The Naked and the Dead*, offer the hostile elements of Pacific jungle warfare — rain, heat, humidity, disease-ridden insects—"Jungle law." Novels set during the brutal winter campaigns of the Korean War, such as *Band of Brothers, Hold Back the Night, I Am the Clay*, and *It's Cold in Pongo-Ni*, fixate on the thematic and meteorological elements of the cruel, harsh Korean winter, and in each text, the hostile winter weather — death-inducing weather — becomes characterized and personified as the works clearly illustrate how the severe cold can kill warriors — and noncombatants, too — as effectively and efficiently and heartlessly as can an armed enemy. Jungle law returns through the novels of the Vietnam War, as evidenced in *Matterhorn* and *The Things They Carried*— novels in which animals and insects and leeches and triple-canopy jungle and monsoon rains are unarmed, yet deadly and uncombatable, enemies in war. And of course, and incidentally, novels of the Persian Gulf War and the War in Iraq, Terrence D. Haynes' *Desert Norm*, Charles Sheehan-Miles' *Prayer at Rumayla*, and Cole Bolchoz's *A Medic in Iraq*, as one would presume, for each is a desert-situated work, refer often to heat and blowing sand. Nearly universally then, this motif or thematic element of the terrain or weather as enemy, or of the terrain and weather as enemy, hostile to the point of being murderous even, is one that is found so commonly in American Novels of War because it is one that is found so commonly in American wars. Consequently, truth finds its way into art, verisimilitude into artifice, nature into fiction.

XIII

The Burning/Fire Motif

Another truth found in war and in the American novel of war is the burning or fire motif. Modern and postmodern war machines run on fuel (and fuel burns and explodes), and modern and postmodern war machines run on explosives (and, of course, explosives explode), and all this fire and all these explosions lead to the collateral burning of humans, vehicles, buildings, towns, cities, regions, states, and nations. War and burning are conjoined, shackled, and bonded to one another, and war and fire exist in a destructive and symbiotic relationship. However, even though the burning or fire motif is elemental to texts of war, the presence of fire and explosions and burning objects and beings rarely reaches the level of thematic element in the texts. Nonetheless, nearly all well-thought-out novels of war contain this motif of fire, and especially shocking are scenes of humans burning and burned. *Prayer at Rumayla* shows what postmodern incendiary weapons can do when such weapons are unleashed upon human flesh, while *I Am the Clay*, with a recurrent and explicit burning motif, seems to be a panegyric to the Holocaust and to all those who lost their lives in the fires of World War II and the Korean War. Conversely, *The March* seems to be aware that, yes, fire is indeed a physical and psychological component of the new modern concept and philosophy and practice of total war; in this way, Doctorow's historicist text is a harbinger of the fiery peri-war terrors to come. Yet, obviously, fire as a tactic to terrorize and destroy is not a new war tactic, and many cities and places and people have burned in ancient, pre-modern, and early modern times, as a glance at the Old Testament or extant Greco-Roman writings attest. Therefore, the fire or burning motif is liberally present in the nineteenth-century settings of *Blood Meridian* and *The Red Badge of Courage*. But what makes the fire or burning motif elemental in modern and postmodern warfare (and the modern and postmodern American novel of war) are the tools used to conduct fire- and burning-specific warfare. *Through the Wheat* shows how World War I mustard ("poison") gas leads to severe, debilitating, excruciating — and often fatal — burns after it comes into contact with the victim-combatant's skin. *Beach Red* offers the results of what happens when a man meets a flame thrower, and *It's Cold in Pongo-Ni* introduces the chemical effectiveness of white phosphorus hand grenades and napalm. In war, and in the American novel of war, fire (chemically enhanced or not) beats, and burns, and immolates man, and places, and things.

In *Blood Meridian*, Cormac McCarthy uses fire quite liberally, and McCarthy's burning and fire motif runs text-wide and includes Toadvine, David Brown, the Comanche, the Apache, the Yumas, and the scalphunters — and other Anglos — using fire to kill, terrorize, and destroy, but the scenes of humans burning and burned — with specific reference to Brown's case here — are especially unnerving and gruesome. However, McCarthy first introduces the fire and burning motif in a brief scene (12–14) in which Toadvine, accompanied by the kid, and aided by oil-based varnish, burns a hotel down, along with at least two men who are beaten into unconsciousness before the arsonist and his accomplice flee the burning building. This brief sketch introduces fire as a weapon, and thus offers the reader the first glimpse of the conjunction of fire and intended human death. Analyzed previously are the Comanche and their habit of burning the Mexican villages that they pillage (57–58), while Anglos massacre and burn other Anglo travelers to make the work appear Indianesque (152–53), and the scalphunters burn the huts of the Gileños in order to get the residents into the open for slaughter (156). Later still, at the hands of the Apache, the remaining two Delaware scouts are hanged by their pierced Achilles tendons and are burned alive and into death (226–27), and finally, at the hands of the justifiably disgruntled Yumas, Glanton's body and his still-alive dog (and Dr. Lincoln's body, and his living dog, as well as the corpses of eight others) are immolated in a post-massacre, ritualistic, cathartic bonfire (275–76). But perhaps it is the scene in which David Brown catches a man on fire that is the most horrifying and rhetorically effective; after a day of drinking in a San Diego slopshoot, and after an altercation with some soldiers, Brown pours a pitcher of aguardiente — literally, fiery water — over a soldier and uses his lit cigar to catch the fated man afire: "The man ran outside mute save for the whoosh of the flames and the flames were pale blue and then invisible in the sunlight and he fought them in the street like a man beset with bees or madness and then he fell over in the road and burned up. By the time they got to him with a bucket of water he had blackened and shriveled in the mud like an enormous spider" (268). What is a tad shocking in this episode, other than the garishness of the man's manner of death, is the immediacy involved. In a non-war zone, the scalphunters still practice war, as is their preference, and the young soldier is alive and then immolated, a burned and blackened spider. And, ironically, while the decedent is in uniform, he is not at war, but nonetheless is a victim of the fire of war. Clearly, then, in the text, the characters, of all races and nationalities and loyalties, use fire as a weapon of war, as a weapon with which one can kill and torture and terrorize oppositional combatants and noncombatants alike. In this way, McCarthy's text — written by an author who has seen the birth and practice of the atomic era and its tools — as historically set, seems an acknowledgment of the war-manifested holocausts to come.

In Stephen Crane's *The Red Badge of Courage*, fire is presented liberally, as is the rhetoric of fire and Hell, and therefore, Crane creates a rhetorical and peri-textual conjunction at which war and fire come together. Early in the text, Henry "burned" (5) to enlist, and combat is referred to as "the blaze" (13) — a fire into which the youth must enter in order to prove himself a man. And as the text is a coming-of-age work, in which the crucible is duty and honor in combat, the rhetoric and the presence of fire are repeated as the text unfolds. Later, while camping prior to battle, the camp fires and the men surrounding them are hellish in their appearance; the fires are "peculiar blossoms" (17) and the men are "implike" (18), and the effect, interpreted through Henry's optic, is "satanic" (18). And this demonic imagery, this fiery rhetoric, this carnivalesque scene, occurs prior to battle, prior to the fire of war. The symbolism here is strongly evocative of the evil inherent in the practitioners of war. War is a hellish experience, while the men who practice the violence of war are demons themselves residing in Hell. And of course, those demons who reside in Hell serve the demon-master, Satan — hence, the "satanic" effects. Interestingly, the hell-like scene is presented before battle. As such, the men/imps/demons are of Hell, so the men go from Hell into battle, rather than into the hell of battle. Unique in war writing, this pre-battle Hell assigns the men a particular evil during their preparations for war, a pre-combat evil rather than a peri- or post-combat evil. As the text progresses, this analogy of war and Hell continues, as the youth observes combat from afar; the word "fire" is used as a verb and adjective to modify the actions of battle and weapons (28), and Henry says, "What the devil" (29), in response to another man's (non-combat) request of him. So, indirectly, Crane is arguing that war is by and of the "devil." Man may practice war, but the act is the devil's, as no mass violence and destruction such as this could ever be manmade. And still later, after having tasted battle, and after having fled battle, and after having deserted the tattered man, Henry comes upon the "furnace roar" (66) of battle again; of course, in the literature, a mass roaring furnace can easily symbolize Hell, the hell of battle—fire, and flame, and noise, and demons all. Crane takes a neophyte warrior, a boy, and thrusts him into the hell of war, and as an imagist, Crane offers the reader the colors, the sounds, the tactile sensations and symbols of Hell for consummation.

As E.L. Doctorow's *The March* opens, through the practice of total war and (perhaps occasionally by accident), General William Tecumseh Sherman, according to one character, "burns where he has ridden to lunch [and] fires the city [Atlanta]" (4) in which he once socialized. This accurate accusation begins a text-wide thematic element of fire and burning as an act of terror and war against an enemy that possesses no civilian populace; everyone in the South is an active combatant, except the slaves, and therefore everyone's possessions and person are at stake. In actions and scenes similar to (and derivative and reminiscent of) William Faulkner's *The Unvanquished*, Doctorow uses the firing of the South theme through the text, with the theme reaching its apogee in the burning of Columbia, South Carolina (176–87), a burning that Sherman blames on retreating rebel forces who are burning extant bales of cotton as they flee (197), which then spreads to the wooden buildings in the town (176). Historically, of course, there is both primary and secondary evidence of the use of fire as a device of terror, destruction, and war during the Civil War; General Ulysses S. Grant, who would later become Commanding General of the Union Army, in a letter to his father dated 8 November 1861, tells of a raid on a Confederate camp at Belmont, Missouri, after which they "burned everything possible" (591), so as to destroy Confederate supplies and equipment and to prevent the re-use thereof. While this burning is early in the war, and these acts of peri-war arson are directed toward uniformed personnel, the acts, nonetheless, are testimony of the use of fire as a weapon in and during the Civil War. Scholarship, too, supports the historical use of this war device, but in this example from Gerald F. Linderman's *Embattled Courage*, the cited material supports Doctorow's cum Sherman's claim that the Confederate forces used fire as a defensive tactic when in retreat: "Union soldiers in North Carolina watched a Confederate soldier cover a retreat by burning a bridge under their fire; later they were appalled to find him, with a leg shot off, 'writhing in terrible agony,' frying in his incendiary materials, tar and turpentine" (125–26). So, this passage indeed supports Doctorow's literary rhetoric. Or does it?

Another passage in the Linderman text notes that Union forces regularly burned Southern homes in order to remove sharpshooter positions (193), but, before and after doing so, they looted the homes and then proximal towns (193), and as antipathy toward noncombatants grew during the war, Union soldiers "became intent on foraging, fence-burning, and house-burning" (195): "We burn the country and go on" (Doctorow 13), notes one Union officer, whose role is to lead a "foraging party" (10). Thus, in the Doctorow text, first, one forages; then, one burns. The arson also takes place in cities and towns along Sherman's March to the Sea, and Atlanta "is burned" (19), then Milledgeville, then "Sandersonville [*sic*]" (46, 47, 79), and Waynesboro and Millen — where the "Yankees were burning down everything with the name of Millen" (67) — to Savannah, at which time there is a Christmas respite from the firing of the South. The firing begins anew in South Carolina, and the undefended town of Barnwell, a town filled with "only women and children" (163), is burned after being pillaged: "Thin tongues of fire shot skyward as the lovely late afternoon turned to dusk" (163). General Kil Kilpatrick enjoys the victory, the burning, the pyre, and he argues that the scene is better than the Fourth of July (163), and the next morning, there remains nothing but a "gutted village" (164), which Kilpatrick renames "Burnwell" (164). All of these scenes of the firing of houses and manses and towns and cities are leading, of course, to the burning of Columbia, the state capital of secessionist South Carolina, a burning that begins "on a side street of commercial buildings [with] a stacked row of cotton bales" (176) on fire, and ends with the decimation of the city. While the initial fire seems extinguished, a tiny heat resides in the bales, and the night wind lights the fires again, and Columbia becomes "an inferno [with] whole streets aflame" (178), with even the sky on fire. Ironically, this great scene of fire, this scene born of the cotton of the Confederacy, that commodity upon which the South thrived, is Doctorow's symbolic fall of the South, a funerary pyre produced by that which, along with slavery, gave rise to the Confederacy and its economic model. Whether or not this cotton bale story holds up — recent scholarship both supports and refutes Sherman's claims that the retreating rebels started the fire(s) — the city did indeed burn on 17–18 February 1865, and Doctorow does indeed act as an apologist for the burning, per his narration and Sherman's optic (197).

Thomas Boyd's *Through the Wheat* shows how World War I mustard gas led to horrendous burns after it came into contact with the victim's skin. In his outstanding study, *Daily Life During World War I*, Neil M. Heyman notes that in "April 1915, German forces [first] used a chlorine gas attack against the Allied defenses at Ypres" (102), followed by the "growing use of more deadly phosgene gas in 1916 ... and 1917 saw the introduction of mustard gas" (103); mustard gas, of course, "caused the skin to burn and blister" (Heyman 72), while phosgene and chlorine gases radically affected the eyes and respiratory systems. In fact, during their 19-month presence in the war, "70,000 Americans had to be hospitalized following gas attacks" (Heyman 103). Boyd, in fact, was a victim of a gas attack on 3 October 1918, and was incapacitated through the final month of the war (Simmons xii); subsequently, he was in and out of hospitals for the next six months because of pulmonary and respiratory effects, secondary to the gas inhalation, and tragically he died at the age of thirty-seven, secondary to a cerebral hemorrhage (Simmons xiv). Speculation, rather than contemporary medical science, must infer that the gas wounds adversely contributed to Boyd's untimely death. Boyd's protagonist, William Hicks, is aware of the mortal — and awful — danger of the German gas attacks, as is his mother, who writes in a letter, "Those frightful Germans have liquid fire and deadly gasses" (101), and then offers to mail Hicks "a quantity of cyanide of potassium" (101) so that he may commit suicide upon being gassed. He declines, but not without thought and regret, as he does not want to visit Purgatory upon the act. Later, in a scene foreshadowed through the occasional reference to gas attacks, Hicks is gassed while serving as a litter bearer during a German attack. As Heyman observes, "One of the particular horrors of mustard gas was its propensity to remain on the surface of the ground for long periods of time" (72–73), and Boyd, who has experienced such, is aware of this facet of mustard gas, as during the attack, "the thick yellow gas clung to the ground" (158–59). And what the gas touches, the gas burns: "Wherever the gas had touched the skin of the men dark, flaming blisters appeared. Like acid, the yellow gas ate into the flesh" (159).

Hicks has been gas-burned upon the legs (159–60), and he is sent to the hospital and relieved of duty, then returned to duty (168), relieved again because the burns have not healed (171), and finally returned again to duty (172). The specter of gas attack haunts the novel, and the gruesome effectiveness of the chlorine gas upon the skin is evinced through Hicks' burns and suffering and incapacitation. So while, traditionally, one might not consider gas burns as a component of the burning or fire motif(s) in the American novel of war, the burns produced by contact with mustard gas are nonetheless devastating and incapacitating and even lethal to the combatant-victims involved.

Peter Bowman's *Beach Red* offers devastation and lethality through the results of what happens when a man meets a flame thrower. Bowman's version of the fire and burning motif in the American novel of World War II is seminal in its graphic description of the catastrophic effects of propelled, fueled fire spent against a human target. And while the Germans were the first to use flame throwers during World War I, with the other belligerents on the Western Front following (Heyman 34), the casualty effect was statistically minor, relative to conventional weaponry and warfare. The more common use of the weapon was initiated during the Pacific Campaign, and Bowman, as a participant in that campaign incorporates the weapon and its ghastliness into his text, so, as the American forces assault Beach Red, and the Japanese defense lines are breached, "the men with flame throwers dart though the opening and inscribe their invitations to hell on ignited sheets" (20). Again, as is seen in many other American novels of war, the rhetoric of Hell is conjoined with the rhetoric of war, and the eternal flames of Hell are shackled to the mortal flames of combat. Bowman also uses a rhetoric of burning and fire through the text, starting with the opening pages, as wardroom lights on troop transport ships "burned" (3) through the night, and an officer says prior to the beach landing, "All right, men, twenty-five seconds to hell!" (4). Once the beach landing commences, carrier-based divebombers drop ordnance that produces "lashes of flame" (7), while "towers of orange flame spring up in their footprints" (9). As the battle goes on, the rhetoric of fire and burning continues but becomes more focused, more finite, more gruesome, more personal, as high-pressure fueled and directed jellied-fire consumes and kills on an individual basis: "A Jap runs out of the ruins, his uniform ablaze, and cartridges popping from the ammo belt around his waist. The engineer wheels and aims his nozzle and presses the trigger plate on the top of the barrel of his M1-A1 apparatus. A stream of livid fuel spurts like a fiery rod and describes a trajectory as cleancut as a tracer bullet, searing the Nip till his entrails ooze pink" (20). Fire, exponentialized by chemically fed combustion, devours the Japanese combatant until he is nothing but immolated tissue and wet, scorched guts. Interesting to note is that Bowman's narrator specifically refers to the accuracy of the fire stream, "cleancut as a tracer bullet." As such, this flame thrower is not a sloppy weapon but an accurate and grotesquely lethal weapon, one that results in "a macabre pot of flesh" (20) and air "sticky with smoke and flame" (20) and the odors thereof. Bowman does his rhetorical best to evince and narrate the horror of the nexus of flame thrower and human flesh, but, were that not enough, Bowman even offers a postmortem comment from the perspective of the unnamed grunt: "The Jap bastard went up in flames, like tissue paper. Christ, Jimmy, did you ever see a human body burn? Everything goes poof except the skull and the knee caps. But the insides don't burn. They just pop and sizzle" (36). Hence, the entrails that "ooze pink" after the directed immolation.

Later, lest the Americans be unjustly identified alone as military pyromaniacs, as Bowman's protagonist is on a reconnaissance patrol, he spots Japanese forces readying a beach assault of their own, which will take place behind the American forces, and he notes that there are "about twenty men assigned to every [landing] boat, and at least one of them has a flame thrower" (89). Interestingly, the Japanese assault troops are disguised as Americans so that they will not be fired upon immediately upon landing behind the American forces, so one must ask, are the flame throwers the Japanese carry their own, or are they mimicking the Americans? History notes that the Japanese did indeed use flame throwers during the Pacific Campaign, so perhaps the correct answer is yes, the Japanese do use their own flame throwers, and yes, the Japanese are attempting to look like the Americans. Bowman closes the fire and burning motif with another conjunction of war and Hell, and in so doing, he creates a nicely recursive rhetorical and peri-textual motif: War is "an intimate hell where a corpse dances on a firelit wall" (102). As with so many other effective texts written by war veterans, Bowman's text is a catalog of the horrors of combat, and especially haunting are his metonymous images of the awful results born of the use of the individual flame thrower against the individual human being.

Already articulated in previous chapters is Philip K. Jason's cogent and correct argument ("Vietnam War Themes in Korean War Fiction" 121–29) that many social and literary motifs considered by critics and popular readers to be of the Vietnam War and literature thereof are actually first situated in the Korean War and the literature thereof. Relative to the burning or fire motif and the combat and literature of the Korean War, Jason notes that napalm, the jellied gasoline situated in seemingly every novel of the Vietnam War, "was nothing new" (126) during the Vietnam War, having been invented in 1943 and used during the latter days of the Second World War (127). Napalm, Jason notes, "was a staple of America's arsenal in Korea" (127), but the 1950s American public, sans the immediate photojournalism and television of the Vietnam War, did not get to see the use of napalm on the evening news, and thus "had little, if any, awareness of the consequences of napalm bombing during the Korean War" (127). However, those on the ground knew of napalm, and in Pat Frank's *Hold Back the Night* and Edward Franklin's *It's Cold in Pongo-Ni*, one sees literary precedence of the napalm motif, which perhaps is preceded in the literature by Bowman's passages of unnamed World War II–era incendiaries. However, Frank and Franklin expressly identify napalm as the incendiary device used to instill fear and immolation ("Worse than anything else, the Chinese feared napalm" [Frank 172]), and in a scene in *Hold Back the Night* as short as it is brutal, a number of Chinese forces are saturated with Corsair-based aerial napalm and are immediately incinerated: "Where there had been [Chinese combatants], there was a wall of fire. It was a wall of fire that did not subside, for napalm is tenacious. It sticks and clings to whatever it burns, until it has burned everything entirely. Out on the plain, a wave of men was burning. It was the most frightening spectacle of war..." (173). Frank's narrator intrudes a bit to comment on the efficiency and effectiveness of the jellied gasoline, and in so doing, provides an account and commentary that is obviously based on eyewitness experience filtered through the writer's optic. Napalm is frightening, horrifying, even to those who view it and use it.

In the Franklin text, the protagonist (ironically labeled the "peace officer," and, like all officers in the work, identified usually by rank sans last name—"the lieutenant") cannot even watch as napalm is utilized on Chinese forces who are firing upon the escaping reconnaissance team: "Now the planes are coming down, the first one coming from the southwest, a Marine Corsair.... There's a dull explosion behind him but Richard [the lieutenant] doesn't turn to see the black-and-yellow ball of flaming napalm pour across the valley; he simply shakes his head. Too much. All of the planes drop napalm, and ... he feels the heat at his back" (153–54). The lieutenant knows the result of the napalm —fiery death and incinerated human beings, oppositional combatants or not. As such, the "too much" is meant to mean too ghastly, too gruesome, too horrifying to witness again. Nonetheless, the scene is not yet over, as, once the Corsairs fly off, "the engine noise of the Corsairs fades away and there remains only the sound of the morning wind and the light crackling of the fires burning in the field above Pongo-Ni" (154). The remaining fires bespeak Chinese death, and the lack of enemy fire evinces the effectiveness of the napalm run; these Chinese forces are now, and forever, incapacitated.

Franklin also introduces another incendiary weapon of war into the action — white phosphorous, in the form of the white phosphorous hand grenade. It must be noted that white phosphorous is a very special, very scary tool of war, and in "Why Men Love War," William Broyles, Jr., compares white phosphorus to napalm: "Many men loved napalm, loved its silent power, the way it could make tree lines or houses explode as if by spontaneous combustion.... I preferred white phosphorous, which exploded with a fulsome elegance ... throwing out glowing red comets ... I loved it more — not less — because of its function: to destroy, to kill" (6 of 7). Prior to the napalm bombing, the lieutenant's team is pinned down in Pongo-Ni, attempting to escape the enemy small-arms fire, and one of the men produces a "blue cylinder, a white phosphorous grenade" (151). The man "pulls the pin, rises up to a crouch, and flings the grenade into the paddy" (152) — the source of the small-arms fire. White phosphorous, once ignited, continues to burn unless deprived of oxygen, and white phosphorous burns through that with which it comes in contact. Thus, white phosphorous is especially nasty — a lethal chemical reaction in a can. Franklin's narrator describes the action of the white phosphorous grenade, and the accompanying results, in a short freestanding paragraph: "*Piff* it goes, and the silvery white plumes arc out in all directions. Someone in the paddy begins to scream hysterically, gets himself under control, and then merely moans, a half muffled sound, as if his face is to the ground or hidden behind a sleeve. 'Oh, oh, ummm'" (152). Fragments of the grenade have pierced his body, and chunks and particles of white phosphorous are burning through the mortally wounded man. Unlike a fragmentation grenade, from which shrapnel flies outward and into all that it contacts, and then stops, the white phosphorous from a WP grenade, even after its physical propulsion has ceased, continues to burn and penetrate. So, the damage — and agonizing effects — continues, even after the explosive force has abated. Franklin's narrator notifies the reader of the Chinese soldier's death in a pithy sentence: "The moaning has stopped" (153). The irony of a long death is a short sentence, and death from burning, is immediately followed by the napalm scene — more death from burning, on a greater scale, of course — and the reconnaissance team continues on, eventually reaching safety, medical care, and support forces (155). In a few pages, in two short interpolated scenes of the fire and burning motif, on a petite and grand scale, Franklin adroitly shows the grotesque — and effective — lethality of chemically produced fire. Fire, whether mechanically or man directed, is a great and terrible weapon in war, argues Franklin, the author and Korean War veteran.

In *I Am the Clay*, Chaim Potok also uses fire and burning, but does so at a thematic level, as the text — consciously or unconsciously — is written as a Holocaust analog. In interviews published before and after the publication of *I Am the Clay* (1992), Potok repeatedly referred to his time in service as an Army chaplain in South Korea as a life-altering experience, an experience for which rabbinical seminary and life growing up in the United States left him ill prepared: "When I left the Seminary and went to Korea [1955–1957], I brought with me a very lovely cultural package; what my Americanism was all about and what my Judaism was all about. It was very tidy, and it fell all to pieces in Korea" ("An

Interview with Chaim Potok" 316–17). In another interview, he states, "It was a transforming experience. I was not the same person coming out of the army and Korea as I was going in…. The Korean experience, the entire encounter with the world of Asia, was absolutely extraordinary in my life — as a writer, as an American, and as a Jew " ("A *MELUS* Interview" 153). Obviously, spending fifteen months in a nation devastated by decades of invasion, occupation, and war radically altered Potok's worldview and, according to Marcia Zoslaw Siegal, "Potok says [*I Am the Clay*] confronts, for the first time, the Asian experience that irrevocably changed his life" (93). What is fascinating, though, is that critics have failed to make the discovery or argument that *I Am the Clay* is a Holocaust analog; in fact, in post-publication interviews, Potok himself does not seem to make the connection, nor does he explicitly argue the connection, even though "the entire European branch of the Potok family was destroyed by the Nazis" (Siegal 94), and Potok suffered "recurring nightmares" (Siegal 95) secondary to the horrors born of the Holocaust. Nonetheless, and regardless of a text-wide thematic element of burning and human immolation, there exists very little, if any, scholarship arguing the connection between the human immolation in *I Am the Clay* and the Shoah. How can this be? Clearly, the text is an analog between the religious cum ethnic-based suffering of the European Jewry under the Nazis during World War II and the national cum ethnic-based suffering of the Korean people under the occupation of the Japa-nese, and then the Chinese, during World War II, and then the Korean War. During the Japanese occupation (1910–1945), "living men suspended head-down from chains over open firepits" (14). This mental image from the old man's past is an introduction to the old man's, and the occupied Koreans', present, but the contemporary occupation is that of the Chinese, rather than the Japanese, yet the human immolation continues: "Burning? He smelled it in the dark frigid air. Wood and rubber. Flesh too?" (35). The old man knows this smell. One does not forget what a burning human smells like. During the flight south, ahead of the Chinese invasion, hundreds of thousands of refugees exist in the November-December cold, dying by roadsides, freezing to death at night, an exodus from war and from home. All the while, the refugees search for a camp, a rumored "refugee camp" (66). Note the lan-guage — a camp, a locus of a concentration of displaced peoples — and relative to the Holo-caust, of course, camps were the locus of mass human death and burning. Paradoxically, in the text, fire is a life-saving element, and Potok litters the work with the rhetoric of fire, with scenes in which fire is used to warm cold refugees. Yet repeatedly juxtaposed with the life-saving heat from fire are fevers that "burn" and memories of villages alight.

Once the refugee trio arrives at the refugee camp (115), Potok elevates the rhetoric of fire, and he — consciously or not — creates the Holocaust analog. Repeatedly, in the refugee camp chapters, chapters five and six (115–64), the motifs of unnatural earthen mounds, unnatural smells, and unnatural black clouds occur, and the reader is aware that something bizarre is going on in the text, but Potok feeds the reader slowly and builds rhetorical tension until the truth is revealed — the mounds are burial mounds, dirt piled upon rotting corpses; the smells are those of human corpses being immolated, and the black clouds are the products of the immolation fires. The opening paragraph of the first of the two refugee camp chapters introduces the olfactory motif but does so in a subversive way, as it appears that Potok's narrator is referring to oil drum fires when he mentions that the "air was thick with the hot acrid stench of the smoking fires" (115). After passing the entry checkpoint, the trio is incorporated into a shantytown of thousands of displaced peoples, all situated on a vast plain, which bizarrely, in the Korean cold, is "not frozen to stone" (120); the old woman wonders why, as does the astute reader, and even the boy thinks to himself, "There is something strange about this place" (124). The old man, too, is aware of non-natural goings-on, small events that are contrary to the Korean weather: "Melted snow around the fire, the ground oozing water and mud. Raw brown seeping earth. Strange" (128). Yes, it is strange indeed for the ground, which should be frozen solid, to ooze liquid; further, heat comes up from the ground, and it melts the snow around the fire. The old man moves away from the area and feels the ground, and it is solid. Something is amiss. Something is in the ground, and is chemically heating the ground; the old man looks around and notices that the soft, wet earth has been "recently turned" (128). Yes, something is amiss; something is wrong; something unnatural is occurring on this plain.

After a night of sleep, the woman examines the scene for the first time in the daylight: "She saw the mounds immediately. Two low snow-covered mounds: each roughly circular and about fifty feet in diameter" (130). The man-made mounds contrast with the natural landscape of the plain and are radically conspicuous. The woman observes the trio's situation, relative to the other refugees, and notices that the three are encamped at the edge of a "huge mound" that "rose irregularly" on the plain (131). The trio is the only group situated upon the mound, the only group apparently unaware of that which the mound contains. And it is that which the mound contains that warms the ground and melts the snow and produces sludgy mud where such things are unnatural. As more refugees enter the camp, more are forced to reside upon the mounds; all the while, the old woman thinks to herself, "This is a terrible place" (133), and the boy wonders why birds constantly circle overhead (133). What the mounds contain is offered through the old woman's optic, as she prays for those who permanently reside in the mounds: "for the soldiers who lie in these mounds, a kindness" (134). The combat dead are from a previous battle, and it is these war dead, these decomposing bodies, that produce the chemical reactions that warm the frozen ground and melt the snow and produce the mud where none should be.

However, the combat dead are not the only humans dying, and each night brings more dead refugees. Ominously, and transitionally, a "column of black smoke" (142) rises from the plain, a smoke that produces a fetidness not of nature and black clouds not of the weather: "An odd smell hung in the air [and a] dense jet-black greasy cloud" (144, 145) rose up from the plain at a distance. The newer refugees, including Potok's trio, stare with wonder and lack of comprehension, and the cloud and smell spread over the plain, particulate falling as some dirty, fetid rain, "leaving behind a coating that could be tasted" (146). After the black cloud dissipates, the stench remains, clinging to all that it touches, and soon enough, the old woman and the old man "knew what had been burning" (146). Each morning, those who have died during the hostile night are taken away, and then the "black cloud boil[s] up again" (147) and the "stench of iodine and roasting meat" (147) returns. The old man spits and spits, but the "smell of the black cloud" (148) remains a taste present in his mouth, and even when there is no black cloud, the rancid biochemical taste remains in the refugees' noses and tongues and throats (155). Finally, the reader, through the optic of the boy, who with the old man is taking a peasant corpse to the locus of corpses, is allowed to view the birthplace of the greasy black cloud and the rank, sticky, tactile smell: "A large length of charred earth lay before him, black against the snow. Heaps of scorched twisted shapes darkened grotesquely the frozen ground" (161). Soldiers order the refugees away once they are unburdened of their load, and the black cloud returns later in the day (162). As the section closes, the American forces move out, the spring breaks, and the cloud and its stench are gone. But for the refugees, those who saw the cloud, those who knew of its origin, those who smelled and tasted its ghastly biochemical composition, the memory of the pyre and the immolation of the noncombatant dead will forever remain. Both the old man (181, 226) and the old woman (206) carry the images of the cloud and the smell and the pyre with them, but the boy, in a counterintuitive and paradoxically hopeful note, fixates on the burning of his home village, which is, symbolically and literally, a starting point for his post-war life. So, there is hope, there is life, there is a future after a holocaust, but there is memory, too, and it is the duty of the survivors to remember, but also to go on, to live. Responsively, then, how can the reader, the critic, not see the analog Potok creates? How can one not call *I Am the Clay* a Holocaust text? Obviously, one must identify *I Am the Clay* as such an analog.

Finally, in this examination of the fire or burning motif in the American novel of war, Charles Sheehan-Miles' novel of the Persian Gulf War, *Prayer at Rumayla*, is worthy of attention, as it readily presents the immediate and catastrophic results of postmodern tank weaponry when direct toward enemy combatants in human form. Sheehan-Miles' narrator repeats through the text a horrific scene of fire and explosion and the human carnage thereof, and as in the Potok text, the narrator, a tank loader during the Persian Gulf War, articulates the malodorous scent that comes from burning human flesh. In a scene set mere weeks after the end of the war, Sheehan-Miles uses a burning building in Atlanta, Georgia, as a trigger to return Chet Brown to the war, as the smoke from the burning building is similar in composition and color — black — to the smoke created from burning Iraqi tanks and vehicles. The scene flashes back to the war: "I stared, long and hard at the body of the tank commander, half propped in the hatch by the butt of the 12.7 machine gun, his body engulfed in flames ... overwhelmed by the near overpowering smell of burning flesh ... the heat, the stench" (11). But it is not merely images of the enemy combatants who have been captured in their vehicles and killed, nor the stench of burning flesh, that haunts Brown. Haunting Brown are the men who fled the burning vehicles while also on fire, and one burning man in particular, whom Brown shot: "all I have to do is close my damn eyes to see the burning man as I shot him down" (82). The man on fire motif begins on page 1 and is repeated through the entire text (1, 9, 19, 62, 81, 94, 107, 112, 130, 137, 141, 144, 145, 149, 155, 157), as Brown never properly assimilates back to the post-war United States. Further, arson, as a motif, is also present in the text (7, 10, 11), as if Brown unconsciously feels himself to be an arsonist. After all, in combat, he did directly light many fires and produce much destruction and death secondary to incendiary and explosive ordnance. Further, symbolically, the post-war, post-combat Chet Brown is a man on fire, one who burns and seethes with anger, one who cannot express himself except through violence and rage; not ironically, Brown is intelligent enough to realize the rage he carries, but he is powerless to combat it effectively. Thus, Sheehan-Miles creates a metaphor in which Brown kills the burning man, the man on fire, in time of war, yet becomes the burning man, the man on fire, after the war. So, as the post-war Chet Brown self-destructs and murders a man and is sentenced to prison at Fort Leavenworth — where he dies of pancreatic cancer (170), perhaps secondary to Gulf War Syndrome — Brown effectively kills himself, the man on fire.

Clearly then, an omnipresent truth found in war is the presence of fire and explosions and burning, and as such, in the American novel of war, there is the burning or fire motif. All manner of objects and animals and people and places burn and are burned, and modern and postmodern war machines run on fuel, and fuel burns and explodes, and modern and postmodern war machines run on explosives, and of course, explosives explode, and all this fire and all these explosions, in war and in novels of war, lead to the directed and collateral burning of humans, vehicles, buildings, towns, cities, regions, states, and nations.

War and burning are a nexus—conjoined, shackled, and bonded, intersected — and war, and fire and burning and immolation, exist in a destructive and symbiotic relationship, and even though the burning or fire motif, or the burning and fire motif, are elemental to texts of war, the presence of fire and explosions and burning objects and beings rarely reaches the level of thematic element in most works of war, present texts excluded, of course. Nonetheless, nearly all well-thought-out novels of war contain this motif of an ancient Classical element evolved into a modern and postmodern tool of war, and of course, especially shocking, and readily present, are scenes of humans burning and burned, and relative to this study, *Prayer at Rumayla* shows what postmodern incendiary weapons can do to the operator and the receiver when such weapons are unleashed upon human flesh, while *I Am the Clay*, with a recurrent and explicit burning motif, is a panegyric to The Holocaust and to all those who have lost their lives in the fires of World War II and the Korean War. Conversely, *The March*, contextually, argues that fire is indeed a physical and psychological component of the new modern concept and philosophy and practice of total war, and in this way, Doctorow's text is a harbinger of the war-manifested pyromania to come, while the text also seems to defend Sherman and the burning of Columbia — accidental or not. Most obviously, though, the use of fire as a tactic to terrorize and to destroy is not a recent tactic of war, of course, and many nations and states and cities and people have burned in ancient, premodern, and early-modern times, as a glance at the Old Testament or extant Greco-Roman writings attest. Thus historically, and specific to the practice of war, fire is not a twentieth or twenty-first century weapon, so the fire or burning motif is liberally offered in the nineteenth century settings of *Blood Meridian* and *The Red Badge of Courage*, as in the former text, fire is used as a weapon to burn and torture and kill, and in the latter, the rhetoric of Hell is used to evince war as a hellish experience and its participants as devilish beings. What makes the fire or burning motif essential in modern and postmodern warfare and the modern and postmodern American novel of war, though, are the tools used to conduct fire- and burning-specific warfare. *Through the Wheat* shows how World War I Mustard ["Poison"] Gas leads to severe, debilitating, excruciating — and often fatal — burns after it comes into contact with the victim-combatant's skin. *Beach Red* offers the results of what happens when a man meets a flame thrower, and *It's Cold in Pongo-Ni* introduces the ghastly chemical effectiveness of white phosphorus hand grenades and napalm. In war, and in the American novel of war, fire, chemically enhanced or not, beats, and burns, and immolates, man, and places, and things.

XIV

Prostitution

Along with fire and burning and explosions, and catastrophes thereof, can there be war and warriors—and American novels of war—without prostitution? Prostitution is nearly always present in the novel of war, and in this study, most of the texts offer prostitution in passing or at the motif level (or even thematically), but interestingly, especially when considered with the *Maggie: A Girl of the Streets*, which was published two years prior in 1893, *The Red Badge of Courage* does not explicitly mention prostitution in any way (although one scene does warrant attention, analysis, and perhaps a bit of speculation). Of course, the woman's body as commodity is a motif or thematic element in literature that can be easily traced to pre-classical eras and texts, as is the motif of the woman prostitute in time of war. When a woman is a refugee and has no money, or home, or food, or possessions, or anything else materially or socially, she still has one commodity, her sexualized body, and male warriors—on all sides of every war—seek sexual release from the life and death pressures of war. As such, prostitution thrives in times of war. Of importance here, *MASH* and *Catch-22* show thriving and organized prostitution operations that are text-wide and fully realized and thematic in nature. *MASH* shows that organized prostitution activities befit organizational names—in Korea, The Famous Curb Service Whorehouse, and in Japan, Dr. Yamamoto's Finest Kind Pediatric Hospital and Whorehouse (the former of which operates "regardless of the [brutal] Korean weather" [14]), and the latter of which, with philanthropy in mind, is an idealized presentation written from the perspective of an American war participant, after the fact and sans the prostitutes' perspective). Prostitution is so omnipresent in *Catch-22*, in fact, and the American airmen spend so much time with Italian prostitutes, that the trope of the man in love with the whore occurs (repeatedly) and is then reversed, as the character of Nately's whore falls in love with Nately, who is subsequently killed on a bombing run; Nately's unnamed whore then spends the rest of the text trying to murder Yossarian, who breaks to her the news of Nately's death. Regardless of the text's comic absurdity, *Catch-22*'s prostitution theme is sad and enlightening. *Company K* likewise presents prostitution as sad and enlightening, as a young, sexually immature member of Company K is introduced to carnality by a diseased prostitute—as a joke played upon him by his company peers—and is later court-martialed for failing to "report for a [medicinal, post-coital] prophylactic" (107) at the hospital dressing station. *I Am the Clay* also presents the dismal role of wartime prostitute, as women who have nothing in a time of war are rarely far from the compounds of American soldiers. As these and numerous American novels of war show, thriving and organized wartime prostitution operations are situated where men of war are situated.

An examination of scholarly and informative sources shows that prostitution in time of war is an ongoing non-novel literary topic, as war itself is seemingly eternal and ever-lasting. In the history of man, war never ceases, and therefore prostitution in time of war never ceases. Even relative to contemporary wars in Muslim nations, such as the War in Iraq, prostitution, secondary to the desperation of women in the war zone, thrives, and thus "there are thousands of women ... working in the sex trade in Iraq. Most of whom ... enter this life because they have no support systems and no way to make a living" (Jamjoon). So, even in the twenty-first century, even in an extremely socially conservative Muslim culture, in time of war, in time of desperation, "thousands of women" use their sexualized commodity, their bodies, for sustenance through paid sexual services. Clearly, these women—many of whom are war widows or war orphans—are desperate to feed their families and themselves, and selling one's body for sex in this peri-war situation can hardly be labeled "voluntary." In her qualitatively and quantitatively excellent work, *Sex Among Allies: Military Prostitution in U.S.–Korea Relations*, Katharine H.S. Moon notes that contemporary feminist scholars such as Cynthia Enloe and others "have asserted that the very maintenance of the military establishment depends on promoting gendered notions of femininity and masculinity, weakness and strength, conquered and conqueror" (10), and among these "gendered notions" and defined roles are peri-war prostitute and warrior. Further, and tragically, imperial and occupying powers often make it official military policy to force women into prostitution to service the uniformed members of the invading or occupying military. In fact, the numbers can be staggering, even in a small chronological window: "Between 1932 and 1945, the Japanese military forced anywhere from 80,000 to 200,000 Asian women to serve as their prostitutes" (Berndt 177), and from 1955 to 1995, "over one million Korean women have served as sex providers for the U.S. military" (Moon 1).

With such numbers at hand, one must ask, what is the official or unofficial government policy regarding indigenous prostitution services and non-indigenous uniformed personnel? According to the late Iris Chang, in her powerful and stunning and tragic *The Rape of Nanking: The Forgotten Holocaust of World War II*, "the Japanese high command [created] a giant underground system of military prostitution" (52), the "comfort women" system, whereby women were enslaved and forced to serve Japanese invader-occupiers during the length of the invasion-occupation. Further, Margaret Hillenbrand notes that there is an "age-old linkage between imperialism, fraternization, and prostitution" (403–4), and that, further, there is an "age-old linkage between the conquest of empires and the conquest of local women" (406). Interestingly, Hillenbrand, unlike Chang, is not arguing relative to the Empire of Japan and its overtaking of Asia in the first four decades of the twentieth century; Hillenbrand is referring to the empire of the United States and its presence in Asia in the last six decades of the twentieth century. As Hillenbrand notes, in time of war and occupation, "the services of flesh-and-blood local women are essential for keeping the occupying presence happy" (407), and thus "it is undeniable that the sex industry that sprang up to cater to the extensive American military presence throughout East Asia during the post–World War II era" (409), while not of the forced violence of the Japanese comfort women system of World War II, was nonetheless the result of official and economic policies between and among occupied and occupying governments. In an occupied nation, organized prostitution keeps occupying soldiers happy, while it is also an ongoing economic engine; therefore, after an occupier or invader or imperial military post is created, organized prostitution follows nearly immediately (Hillenbrand 408). And according to Moon, during and after the Korean War, "military-oriented prostitution in Korea" (1) was not merely happenstance but was and is a "system that is sponsored and regulated by two governments, Korean and

American (through the U.S. military)" (1–2). So, in concurrence with Hillenbrand (or vice versa, actually, as it is Hillenbrand who cites Moon), Moon argues that "military-oriented prostitution" is an official mandate used to keep uniformed soldiers "happy" (2). So, disturbingly, in time of war, and in times after war, the allies as well as the enemies, the occupiers as well as the invaders, the rescuers as well as the rescued, are all complicit — all promote prostitution. And therefore, in the American novel of war, there is the taken-for-granted presence of prostitution and the prostitute in time of war, but rarely, if ever, is the character of the prostitute created as a tragic or sympathetic or empathetic or victimized figure.

Cormac McCarthy's *Blood Meridian* is an American novel of war, of course, and prostitution — while not explicit — is present all through the text. McCarthy introduces prostitutes first in Galveston (5) in 1849, and he then offers them in a number of cities or towns throughout the text. In Chihuahua city, prostitutes infiltrate Governor Trias' banquet hall while the scalphunters dine and drink (170), and the town becomes a locus of mobile bordellos (171); in Ures, Sonora, Irving rounds up twenty to thirty prostitutes of sundry age and composition (201). Then, much later, sometime between 1851 and 1861, the kid — now "he"— sees men kill one another over two-dollar whores (313). And, of course, the text-closing scene at Fort Griffin, Texas, set in 1878, is brimming with prostitutes of all sorts and sizes and aspects (325, 326, 332). As the man —formerly "the kid"; formerly "he"— spends time with a dwarf of a prostitute (332–33), he seems to be rendered impotent and unable to have intercourse. This impotence, of course — in the only scene in which a scalphunter is presented specifically with a prostitute — is symbolic of the man's inability to ward off the judge as the judge rapes and murders the man in the jakes (333). The judge, a bisexual pedophilic sociopath, culminates his decades-long attraction for the man through the sexual violence of sodomy and a lethal bear hug. This homoerotic element and the physical attractiveness of the kid cum man are also foreshadowed in a brief passage in which the kid is mistaken for a male prostitute (311). Thus, *Blood Meridian*, as novel of war, shows thriving and organized prostitution operations situated where men of war are situated.

In Stephen Crane's *The Red Badge of Courage*, the other American novel of war in this study situated in the nineteenth century, women rarely enter the text; but for Henry's mother (6–8)— present as the text opens and Henry idealistically enlists (6)— and a pair of young school-mates (8), only one other woman is to be found in the work. And while Crane does not explicitly identify this unnamed woman as a prostitute, there is enough evidence in the text for hypothetical speculation. The woman — a "young girl," actually, per Crane's narration — is, of course, the young woman who tussles with the fat soldier attempting to steal her horse (17). What bears speculation is that this young woman, apparently alone, and apparently residing in a homestead on a roadway commonly traveled by uniformed forces moving to battle, at least situationally, fits the "prostitute in time of war and locus of war" model offered in scholarly, historical, and fictive texts. Further, by 1895, Crane, with *Maggie: A Girl of the Streets*, had already written and published a novel with the explicit use of prostitution as a thematic element. So, one must ask, is the young woman in *The Red Badge of Courage* a prostitute? One can certainly consider the potentiality of such a role for the young woman, but one must also acknowledge that Crane does not legibly identify the young woman as a prostitute. Nonetheless, of course, such speculation is intriguing, although proof either way is not supported by the text.

In William March's *Company K*, the prostitution motif is introduced early in the text and returns a number of times, but the most telling scene is a sketch in which a young private, Private Philip Wadsworth, is court-martialed for failing to take a post-coital prophylactic at the battalion dressing station (105–7). In the text, the standard operating procedure of taking a post-coital prophylactic, which is administered forthrightly and openly at unit medical facilities, is introduced after a pair of privates, Wilbur Halsey and Herb Merriam, visit "Rue Serpentine" (84) in a brief sketch that serves as notice of in-country unofficial official American policy. Conversely, though, official U.S. military policy during the First World War unsuccessfully attempted to address "prostitution and venereal disease as a moral crusade" (Moon 37), from thousands of miles away, of course, in Washington, D.C. Actual practice, as dictated in prose by combat veteran March, however, seems to be more realistic and pragmatic: treat the potentially infected immediately with prophylactic medicine, and do so under the threat of court-martial. This is illustrated in the sketch in which Halsey and Merriam seek prostitutes, locate prostitution, and participate in paid acts of carnality, and then are forthright enough to admit it through, if not their words, their blushes, when asked about Rue Serpentine. After confessing, as it were, the men are told by the day nurse to "go downstairs and take a prophylactic" (85). So obviously, whether the powers in Washington are aware or not, those in the field are attempting to prevent sexually transmitted diseases, as incapacitation secondary to an STD is still incapacitation, and an incapacitated Marine cannot fight. As such, avoiding the prophylactic is a punishable offense, as Private Wadsworth learns.

Wadsworth — a name pun if ever there was one — is a virgin as the sketch opens and is on a work detail as the sketch closes. In between, Wadsworth is set up by his peers, who pay a diseased prostitute to seduce him by telling tales of her deceased former fiancé — who was killed early in the war, of course (105–6). Wadsworth, who has sworn loyalty to his girl back home, rationalizes, "My morals are absurd. I may get killed next week" (106), so he accompanies the prostitute to her room, and he sacrifices his virginity — and his oath — in time of war. After the act, Wadsworth attempts to pay the girl, who refuses — she has already been paid by Wadsworth's peers — and who, according to Wadsworth, "all the time knew she had diseased me" (107). As a sexual neophyte, Wadsworth, it seems, is unaware that he needs to seek prophylactic medical protection, and apparently none of his allied peers are kind enough to tell him to do so. Thus, he continues: "Later I became alarmed and went to the dressing station. The doctor looked me over, laughed [and] I was court-martialed for failing to report for a prophylactic and sent to this labor battalion" (107). So, official and public propaganda and policy is one thing, but in-country practicality in a time and locus of war is another. Washington fights a moral crusade against prostitution by advocating chastity (Moon 38), but on the ground, and in reality, when given the opportunity, fighting men are going to frequent prostitutes. And of course, prostitutes carry diseases. So, prophylactic medicine becomes a post-requisite, secondary to a visit to the brothel — unofficial official policy, up to the point at which a man can be court-martialed for ignoring the policy. Obviously, poor Wadsworth is punished — by his peers, by the prostitute, and by the Marine Corps — for his chastity, as well as his ignorance and his gullibility. Regardless, March draws Wadsworth as a bit of a fop and whiner rather than as a victim, and as the sketch closes, Wadsworth mopes about, wondering "what there is about male chastity that is humorous, or why it repels and offends" (107). Unstated here, of course, is the idea that a man can kill or die for his country, yet he can remain a virgin while doing so, which, apparently, is an irony and a paradox the androcentric hegemony of the warrior cannot accept, and will not accept.

In Joseph Heller's masterwork, *Catch-22*, the prostitution theme is bifurcated into the syndicated and the personal through the presence of Nately's whore and Luciana — the former a professional associated with a thriving prostitution organization, and the latter the object of Yossarian's short-lived, self-destructive, and failed obsession. Conversely, Nately's whore sells sex for money, and Yossarian's "whore" sells sex for fine food. Easily acknowledged by readers and critics and characters in the text is the role of Nately's whore as professional prostitute, but not so easily acknowledged is Luciana's role as prostitute. Early in the text, as characters are being introduced, Nately and Nately's unnamed whore are identified as he is in "Rome courting the sleepy whore who was bored with her work and bored with him too" (27). Nately's whore works and lives in an apartment that serves as a "brothel with its multitudinous bedrooms on facing sides of the narrow hallways going off in opposite directions" (34) from a main living and socializing area. So, it is readily apparent to all involved with the text that Nately's whore is a prostitute who earns her war-time living through the selling of sex to uniformed occupiers. Luciana's role as whore is not so clear, though, as she meets Yossarian not at the brothel but at the "Allied officers night club" (163) in Rome. Luciana immediately tells Yossarian, "I'll dance with you.... But I won't let you sleep with me" (163). Later, Luciana tells Yossarian, "I will let you buy me dinner. But I won't let you sleep with me" (163). Further, Luciana lives with her "mamma" (164), rather than with other working girls. Finally, Luciana has a job; she works at a "French office" (164) in Rome. So, if Luciana's word is to be trusted, she is not a professional prostitute. Nonetheless, she does indeed sell her sexualized body. Yossarian takes Luciana to a high-end "black-market restaurant" (163), where the food is "elegant and expensive" (164), and she eats "like a horse" (164), and then tells Yossarian, "Now I will let you sleep with me" (164). So, it is clear that, while not a professional prostitute, Luciana's sexual favors can be purchased.

Luciana — who perhaps is poor, who is working a subsistence living in a country that has been at war, under dictatorship, occupied, bombed, and even invaded, a country of rich, delicious foods now unavailable to the common woman — is hungry. As such, she sells sex for fine food. In fact, Luciana even tells Yossarian that her mother does not like her dancing with soldiers or letting them take her to dinner (164). Why? Because of the postprandial sexual obligation involved with the meal. Thus, in order to appease her mother, and to maintain calm in the home, no doubt, Luciana does not sleep with Yossarian that night, but instead goes to him in the morning, before she must go to her legitimate employment. Nonetheless, Luciana is selling her sexualized body for material gain. In this case, however, the gain is caloric rather than financial. And further, scholars and Heller identify Luciana as a prostitute — one who sells sex for material gain. Michael C. Scoggins, in "Joseph Heller's Combat Experiences in *Catch-22*," identifies Luciana as an "Italian prostitute" (223), while he quotes Heller — from a well-known and oft-cited 1975 Sam Merrill *Playboy* interview — who identifies Luciana as "the Roman whore" (qtd. in Scoggins 223) with whom Yossarian has an abortive encounter. Consequently and subsequently, as evidenced in the text, as argued in scholarship, and even as articulated by Heller, one can readily posit Luciana's role as prostitute or (in the vernacular) "whore." But Luciana, in all probability, does not see herself as a whore. She readily repeats "I won't let you sleep with me," but regardless, does allow Yossarian to possess her sexually (168) — if only one time, and at the officers' apartment rather than the brothel. Additionally, Luciana's decision to forgo any future encounters with Yossarian supports her role as prostitute. Her willingness to give Yossarian her home address, and her refusal of his offer of money, seem to contradict this argument, unless one rightly considers that Luciana foretells Yossarian's act of ripping up the address (172–73), which he does once Luciana walks away from him after their sexual encounter. So, paradoxically, Luciana, by refusing money and by accepting a one-night (or, in this case, a one-morning) stand with Yossarian — a sexual encounter he paid for with food rather than money — sees herself as a woman coping with life in a war zone, rather than a woman who sells her sexualized body for material gain. However, Luciana is, sadly, a prostitute in time of war, whether she admits such or not.

Conversely, Nately's whore, a member of a thriving organized prostitution cabal, a carnal syndicate situated in a multi-bedroom brothel, has no qualms relative to her self-identification. She is a whore, and she makes a living selling her body. She accepts this, and easily severs her love for Nately from her professional role and wants to promote and practice both concurrently. The love is emotional and personal, and the work is impassive and professional. In fact, before Nately rescues her (362–67) from the clutches of the field and general officers who have picked her up off of the street (260) and who then hold her hostage in their apartment, she is identified by the narrator as "the apathetic whore" (171) and "an indifferent girl" (259) with whom Nately is in love. But there are practical aspects to her role as prostitute: she makes a living; she has a place to live — a "wonderful and resplendent tenement apartment" (251); she has a place for her younger sister — appropriately named Nately's whore's kid sister — to live; she has a peer group with whom to socialize — "an infinite and proliferating flow of supple young naked girls" (251); and as the old man who occupies the bordello notes, "Prostitution gives her an opportunity to meet people. It provides fresh air and wholesome exercise, and it keeps her out of trouble" (369). Although, it must be noted, more seriously, that a woman who works on the streets and in a brothel, a woman who sells sex for survival in a war-torn nation, "occupies a doubly subordinate position as a woman of a conquered people and a prostitute" (Pollard 116), and thus is a victim of war exponentially. Further, the fact that Nately's whore remains unnamed in the text is an explicit act of dehumanization. However, and conversely, there is an aspect of power involved with the woman's possession of her sexuality and sexualized self, but there is, again, an ongoing act of victimization with the penetration of the woman's body secondary to the act of coitus.

Juxtapositionally, Nately's whore, professional though she is, and professionally ongoing, nonetheless loves Nately — her rescuer — and she "missed Nately when he was away" (370) and is angry when Yossarian punches Nately and breaks his nose (372) — the accidental result of a drunken practical joke. This anger toward Yossarian, and the fact that she misses Nately when he is not in Rome — he has to fly combat missions, after all — show that Nately's whore, indeed, loves Nately, although she still resides in the brothel and continues to earn a living. When Nately, along with 11 others, is killed on a mission over Spezia (387), Yossarian is left to break the news to Nately's whore, and in so doing, and in accordance with his smashing Nately in the face, earns the everlasting wrath of Nately's whore, who, in an act of penetrative empowerment, repeatedly attempts to stab Yossarian — with a potato peeler, with a bread knife, with a steak knife, with a carving knife, and finally (and successfully) with a "bone-handled kitchen knife" (439). Ironically, the penetrated becomes the penetrator, as Nately's whore uses a knife (a phallic device) to stab Yossarian, and the penetrator becomes the penetrated. The dominant and subordinate socio-sexual roles have been subverted, and it is Nately's whore who is the penetrative aggressor to Yossarian's punctured and passive victim. Fascinating, too, are the implements Nately's whore uses in her serial attempts to stab Yossarian, bladed kitchen utensils all. So, in an implicit or explicit act of rhetorical recursiveness — who knows with *Catch-22* — Heller returns to the prostitution cum food motif. In so doing, he readily conjoins Luciana's role to Nately's whore's role — both women are, indeed, prostitutes.

In Chaim Potok's *I Am the Clay*, prostitution is a peripheral element in the text, and prostitutes are present primarily through their association with uniformed American forces. Potok's prostitutes are explicit examples of Moon's "camp followers" (3), prostitutes who followed "troops during the Korean War; they did laundry, cooked, and tended to the soldiers' sexual demands. Some had been widowed by the war, others orphaned or lost during a family's flight from bombs and grenades" (3). Sad cases all, these prostitutes differ radically in their circumstances when compared to Heller's "Roman whores." These are disenfranchised women, expatriates at home — desperate, alone, nameless, faceless, pastless, and futureless. But for their sexualized bodies, many or all would likely be dead, lost and frozen to death on the Korean plain. Potok does not present the prostitution motif until well into the text — after the refugee trio has traveled south, bivouacked in the cave, and then, finally, located the refugee camp. It is at this camp, a camp populated by thousands of displaced and living and dying Koreans, and managed by the American forces, that prostitutes are first presented. Hence, an observer who has spent time in uniform in Korea — former Army chaplain and author Potok — readily articulates and supports Moon's conjunction of the camp follower prostitute and the American soldier. Potok first identifies the locus of American troops as a "military compound" (114), but he then gets more specific and repeats the locus of the troops as the "American compound" (126, 139, 141, 142, 153); Potok then identifies the Korean camp–following prostitutes with the American camp or compound (142) by placing a small but silent group of young Korean women proximally to the entrance gate of the American camp. Potok further conjoins the women to the American forces, more explicitly this time, by having the women proposition the American soldiers in English and by having one woman flash her breasts at the Americans (153). This latter scene is viewed through the optic of the boy, but the women's words are not directly cited, as the boy does not understand English; still later, another, older boy mentions to the boy that girls can make money and get food (154). At this point in the text, even if the boy is somewhat slow to grasp the situation, the reader is well aware of the professional sexualized role which the young women have taken on. The specific identification of the women as camp-following prostitutes is further delineated as the refugee camp chapters close, and the occupying American forces exit, accompanied by the current group of prostitutes. Then, as new American forces arrive, a new group of camp-following prostitutes enters this location, relative to the repopulated American compound (163). It seems as if each group of Americans has its own group of prostitutes, a group that relocates as the American forces relocate (Moon's "camp followers"). And of course, as the American troops move north and repel the Chinese advance, and the refugees follow and return to their villages, the presence of the prostitutes and prostitution remains in the text, if peripherally, but nonetheless proximal to the American military (185, 197, 200, 233–36, 240). Clearly, Potok argues that these ongoing and evolving and growing prostitution enterprises, which by the end of the text are permanently situated in ready-built houses as the American forces are building long-standing occupational compounds, thrive for no reason other than the presence of the uniformed American forces. So, while the prostitution motif in *I Am the Clay* appears as a peripheral motif, it is nonetheless a rhetorically effective example of the obvious and explicit conjugation of American warrior and camp-following prostitute during the Korean War.

Richard Hooker's *MASH* is also an American novel of the Korean War, but the Hooker text is a comedic work that borders on the idiotic, and the prostitution element in the text is comically presented, regardless of the peri-war tragedies involved (even the authors' pseudonym is pun on prostitution). As the text opens, the prostitution element (for it is

neither as brief as a mere motif nor as fully developed as a true theme) is immediately introduced, along with the November Korean weather, as on the outskirts of the shanty town of
Ouijongbu, the "most prominent ... tourist attraction" (13) is "The Famous Curb Service
Whorehouse" (13). This brothel, most obviously, is an organized and thriving business, as
it is "advantageously placed ... on the only major highway between Seoul and the front lines
[and] had the reputation of being very good because all the truck drivers stopped there"
(13). And of course, as one well knows, if the truck drivers frequent a roadside business, it
is for some reason other than proximity. Further, the bordello is "unique for its methods
of merchandising and outstanding for its contribution to the venereal disease problem faced
by the U.S. Army Medical Corps" (13). So, like any good capitalist enterprise, the bordello
actively advertises its wares, and of course, its business is women and sex, so the tools of
the advertisements are the women — "beckoning personnel, clad in the most colorful ensembles available through the Sears Roebuck catalogue [who] lined the highway regardless of
the weather" (14). In keeping with the greater text, "author" Hooker — former MASH surgeon H. Richard Hornberger and journalist W.C. Heinz — juxtaposes the comic with the
tragic, which is fine when done so artistically, as evidenced in the Heller text, but Hooker
allows the comic to overwhelm the more serious aspects of the work. The tragic aspects of
wartime prostitutes — women selling themselves as a means to peri-war survival, women
who live in "mud and thatch huts" (13–14) and who sleep and work on "dirty straw and
soiled mattresses" (14), who carry with them the ever-present and thriving "venereal diseases" propagated through their coupling and trade — are hardly the stuff of comedy, unless
adroitly presented. Further, the prostitution element is created as a base consumer activity,
as one doctor says to another, "I shopped in Seoul last night" (14); thus, he does not need
to "shop' that day at the roadside bordello. And unlike the Potok text, also written by a former Army officer who served in Korea, in the Hooker text, no aspect of empathy is given
to the indigenous personnel who sell their bodies for the sake of survival and the sexual
release of the men in uniform. The women are dehumanized to the point at which they are
nothing more than sexual capital for purchase. They do not have names, or personalities,
or emotions, or anything else other than their sexualized bodies.

In a later scene, set in Kokura, Japan, another working establishment is offered, Dr.
Yamamoto's Finest Kind Pediatric Hospital and Whorehouse (88–101), and a sick child —
born to an unseen, unnamed Japanese prostitute — is operated upon and subsequently
adopted and sent to the United States. In this scene, too, as in the text-opening scene,
Hooker dehumanizes the prostitute and humanizes the Americans. The manager of the
brothel-hospital says, "One of our girls got careless" (95). The pregnancy is the woman's
fault, although, of course, one does not conceive alone, and when the child is post-operative,
the child is sent to the United States, while the woman who carried and gave birth to him
is nowhere in the text. So, unlike Heller, who in *Catch-22* creates a thriving prostitution
organization, complete with living, breathing, emoting human prostitutes, Hooker creates
two organized prostitution enterprises, but he fails to offer any prostitutes. Later in the
text, Hooker does have a sketch involving an "epileptic whore" (144–53), a prostitute who
has a "hysterical convulsion" (151) each time she "services" a client. But, in keeping with the
andro- and ethnocentricism of the work, the convulsive prostitute is not seen in the
text, although the narrator notes that "the epileptic whore was in popular demand" (151).
So, in three freestanding and focused passages, posited early, middle, and late in the work,
Hooker presents prostitution in time and locus of war, yet he utterly ignores the humanity
of the prostitutes involved. The prostitutes have use-value as sexual devices, but the pros-

titutes have no human value, and are drawn as nothing more than sexual objects—less than that, even, as the prostitutes do not exist as characters in these scenes other than in narrative description or the dialogue of male characters (American, of course).

And thus, and clearly so, in the American novel of war, prostitution is nearly always present, and most of the texts in this study offer prostitution in passing or at the motif level, or even thematically. *The Red Badge of Courage*, while not explicitly mentioning prostitution in any way, does offer one scene worthy of attention, analysis, and a bit of speculation. And while, in literature, the motif or thematic element of the woman's body as sexualized commodity can be easily traced to pre–Classical eras and texts, so can the motif of the woman prostitute in time of war. When a woman is a refugee, when a woman has no money, or home, or food, or possessions, or anything else materially or socially or familially, a woman still has one commodity, her sexualized body, and male warriors—on all sides of every war, in the past, in the present, in the future—seek sexual release from the life and death pressures of war. As such, in times of war, prostitution thrives, and nearly every novel of war researched and read for this study, American and otherwise, contains the presence of prostitutes and prostitution. Of importance here, *MASH* and *Catch-22* show thriving and organized prostitution operations that are text-wide and fully realized and are ultimately quasi-thematic or thematic in nature—although the presentation of the prostitutes in either text is radically different. *MASH* shows that organized prostitution activities befit organizational names—in Korea, The Famous Curb Service Whorehouse, and in Japan, Dr. Yamamoto's Finest Kind Pediatric Hospital and Whorehouse—the former of which, operates "regardless of the [brutal] Korean weather" (14). The latter of which, with philanthropy in mind—is an idealized presentation, of course, written from the perspective of an American war participant, after the fact, and sans the prostitutes' perspective. In *Catch-22*, in fact, prostitution is so omni-present, and the American airmen spend so much time with Italian prostitutes, that the trope of the man in love with the whore occurs repeatedly—see Yossarian and Luciana, and Nately and Nately's whore—and is then reversed, as Nately's whore falls in love with Nately, who, thereafter, is killed on a bombing run. Nately's unnamed whore then spends the rest of the text trying to kill Yossarian, who has broken to her the news of Nately's death, and previously, had broken Nately's nose. So, regardless of the text's comic absurdity, *Catch-22*'s theme of prostitution in time and locus of war is sad and enlightening. *Company K* presents prostitution as sad and enlightening, too, as a young, sexually immature member of Company K is introduced to carnality by a diseased prostitute—as a joke played upon him by his company peers—and is later court-martialed for failing to "report for a [medicinal, post-coital] prophylactic" (107) at the hospital dressing station. *I Am the Clay* also presents the sadder, necessary role of wartime prostitute, as women who have nothing in a time of war are rarely far from the compounds of American soldiers. And so, while prostitution might not be necessary for the combat of war, prostitution is indeed a necessary by-product of the situation of war. As these and numerous American novels of war show, thriving and organized wartime Prostitution operations are situated where men of war are situated.

XV

The Absurdity of War

In the American novel of war, the absurdity of war is presented, often generously or with savage irony, with comic absurdity or with abject tragedy. While the absurdity of war is found in many American novels of war, the absurd situations are frequently so seriously presented that one may not notice the absurdity of the given scene and situation because of the life and death nature of the events in the text. In some war texts, the absurdity is laughable, but, as the locus is war, in many instances the comic absurdity leads to the death or deaths of the allied combatants, so the reader does not readily notice the absurd. While *Catch-22* and *MASH* immediately come to mind when one thinks absurdity of war and war texts, *Company K*, *Johnny Got His Gun*, *It's Cold in Pongo-Ni*, and *Desert Norm* all deal overtly with the absurdity of war, both comic and tragic. Of course, *Catch-22*'s title reflects, among other things, the ever-increasing number of bombing missions that Yossarian and his peers must undertake before being transferred to a non-combat billet, while the comedic absurdity in *MASH* is nearly overwhelming and rhetorically counterproductive. Less humorous, though, is the fact that the in-theatre surgical hospitals in *MASH* exist to mend battered warriors so they can return to battle, and in *Catch-22*, each increase in flight count leads to the deaths of more pilots, co-pilots, and flight-crew members, so beneath each comic text lies rage, an incipient anger at war and its deathly absurdity. *Company K* and *Johnny Got His Gun* are also texts that howl with fury. The former, a very serious text, is littered with vignettes of comic and seriocomic absurdity; for example, officers get morphine sulfate for pain, while enlisted men do not; some prostitutes service officers only; and a man with sniping skills taunts an enemy sniper — and endangers his own life — by altering his gait and attitude as he moves about the trenches. *Johnny Got His Gun* presents a narrative protagonist who is so maimed from war that he cannot even commit suicide; this situation is absurd, but not untrue, nor unrealistic. Like *MASH*, *It's Cold in Pongo-Ni* uses the motif of inter-unit American football to present the comically absurd; in the latter text, a starting fullback is sent on a combat reconnaissance mission, so it is imperative that he survive the mission, for he has a football game to play — no doubt that in each text there is present the absurdity in the rhetorical and over-used analogy between the game of football and the "game" of war. Closer to the end of the twentieth century, and in the Middle East, *Desert Norm*'s narrator refers to the Persian Gulf War as a television war, one offered to the public and to the warriors by cable and satellite news feeds; this television-ization of war makes celebrities of those on TV, especially the commanding generals. These examples show that one should not necessarily conjoin the absurdity of war with the humor of war. The absurdity of war can be tragic, of course, and it often is, yet the absurdity can also be comic. But while humor is often present in war novels—literary and pulp—many serious American novels of war do not contain humor; that said, most, if not all, do contain the serious absurdity of war.

As Harmon and Holman note, Absurd is "a term applied to the sense that human beings, cut off from their roots, live in meaningless isolation in an alien universe ... its philosophical base is a form of EXISTENTIALISM, which views human beings as moving from the nothingness from which they came to the nothingness in which they will end through an existence marked by anguish and absurdity." Thus, the absurd is different from Satire, in that Satire, according to Harmon and Holman, "blends a censorious attitude with humor and wit for improving human institutions or humanity." And the absurd is different from Parody, in that Parody, "a potent instrument of satire and ridicule," according to Harmon and Holman, is a "composition imitating another, usually serious, piece ... designed to ridicule a work or its style or author." So, for example, while *Catch-22* is indeed satirical, it is not Satire, as no human institutions — or humans — are improved. And while it is indeed parodic, it is not Parody, as it ridicules no previous work or author; even when considered as an anti-war text, *Catch-22* is hardly imitative. Peter Aichinger, in *The American Soldier in Fiction: A History of Attitudes Toward Warfare and the Military Establishment*, in the chapter titled, "The Absurd" (81–88), notes, "The relationship between warfare and the literature of the absurd ... found its origin and greatest impetus in the horrors of World War I" (81), and "the treatment of warfare in terms of the absurd derives also from the loss of a sense of the ennobling aspect of combat, an effect which had been growing in the public mind ever since the holocaust of World War I and was reinforced by events like the firebombing of Dresden and Hamburg in World War II" (84). Further, and finally, Aichinger argues that "the sense of absurdity of further conflict derived from a national realization that none of the wars in which the nation had engaged [with emphasis on the Korean War and the Vietnam War] had ultimately achieved their long-term purpose" (84). So, according to Aichinger, the nexus of the absurd and the twentieth century American novel of war was created secondary to the "horrors" of the First World War, which were themselves exponentialized by the carnage of the Second World War, which were then fed by the cynicism born of the results of the Korean and Vietnam Wars. The thematic literary effect is, indeed, villainized military institutions, villainized proponents and practitioners of war, and war itself as the true enemy. Thus, the rhetorical purpose of these novels of war is the destruction of the myths that glorify war and warriors and the proponents of war (Aichinger 85). That said, modern and postmodern American novels of war are also rife with scenic examples of the absurd situations born of military life — small but effective absurdities created secondary to military rules and regulations, the hierarchies of rank, tactical and combat issues, and even boredom. Thus, an American novel of war that utilizes the absurd can be scenically absurd, as is *Company K*, or it can be situationally absurd, as is *Johnny Got His Gun*, or it can be a novel of the absurd (per Aichinger) as is *Catch-22*, or it can be comically absurd, as is *MASH*, or it can be analogously absurd, as are *MASH* and *It's Cold in Pongo-Ni*, or it can even be absurd secondary to technological advances, as is *Desert Norm*. So, even within the definition of the literature of the absurd, sub-categorized within the American novel of war, there are sub-categories of the American war novel of the absurd.

In "Christ in Khaki: Religion and the Post–World War I Literary Protest," war literature scholar Stanley Cooperman, writing about absurd situations in war and in the American novel of World War I, notes that "the association of religion and patriotism has been part of modern nationalism itself" (361), and that, during the First World War, "ten million corpses were produced in the combatant armies alone, and not since the days of the Crusades or Islamic expansion had slaughter been so blessed by God" (361). Cooperman asserts that in Great Britain and the United States, the war effort as "political cause was rapidly subordinated to Holy Cause" (362), and for evidence of this absurd socio-political cum religiosity in the literature of the First World War, Cooperman references a number of scenes in William March's *Company K*: a sketch in which a mortally wounded private is threatened with Hell's fires eternal unless he accepts Christ (234–35) — he does, according to the narrator, Private Colin Wiltsee; a sketch in which a private, Private Charles Gordon, under orders, executes a number of German prisoners and thus refutes the Christian concept — man-made, thinks he — that God is love (130–32); and, finally, a brief sketch, that of Private Howard Nettleton, in which Captain "Fish-mouth" Matlock orders the company, under threat of military justice, to attend church ... and to like it (138–39). These examples of absurdity in *Company K* evince March's ability to insert the absurd among the tragic, and further, March offers other peri-war absurdities in the text. For example, officers are privy to that which is held from enlisted men, and while this fracture between the officer class and the enlisted is nothing new or unique, the class allowances are even allowed in the medical treatment of the wounded: Private William Anderson (66–67), who is wounded in the foot and is informed at the dressing station that he must endure suturing sans anesthetic or pain relief (due to a shortage of morphine sulfate, the remains of which are being held for wounded officers), and who is then threatened with being dumped in the snow because of his protestations, objects vociferously until a doctor allows the anesthetic to be administered, not out of compassion, but just to shut the private up. And the class allowances do not occur merely on the battlefield, as prostitutes are choosy, too; according to Private Alex Marro (108–9), some houses of commercial carnal enjoyment reject enlisted men, even though the men have the ability to pay for the services of the prostitutes. But March's absurdities are not limited to religion or battlefield treatment of the enlisted or elitist prostitutes — battlefield absurdity is likewise present in the text, and perhaps the most absurd example is the sketch of Private Leo Hastings (149), who, with sniping skills of his own, and out of boredom it seems, teases a German sniper to pass the time. Hastings walks around the trenches, varying his gait, moving about awkwardly, laughing all the while, as the German sniper misses shot after shot. Of course, while acknowledging tactical assurance, Hastings ignores luck, his or the German's, but nonetheless, survives the scene. March's text is littered with small examples of absurdity in war, and those offered here are but a few of the absurd events in the work.

March's ability to place the absurd in the catastrophic in not unique to the American Novels of World War I, and Dalton Trumbo's *Johnny Got His Gun* is entirely created of the absurdity of Joe Bonham's post-war situation. Bonham, devastatingly wounded during the war, the result of an artillery shell's created purpose, has no arms, no legs, no face, no eyes, no ears, no mouth, no tongue, no nose, no sight, no hearing, no taste, no smell; he is a bodily stump with a brain attached. Conversely, and absurdly, Bonham is a miracle of modern combat medicine, which has evolved — through much opportunity to experiment — to a point at which it possesses the ability to keep a bodily stump alive (85–87), regardless of what the wounded man would choose, of course. And the brutal, absurd irony is that Bonham is so maimed that he cannot even kill himself (64), and as his brain stills functions cognitively, he is aware of this absurdity. Further, Bonham thinks, he is not alone; there are perhaps thousands and thousands of Joe Bonhams, men so wounded they cannot die, no matter how much they desire to do so (88): men savaged by the violence of combat and saved by the science of modern medicine. As Neil M. Heyman notes, during the First World

War, the concept of triage was practiced by the French medical corps, through which the wounded were separated into three groups: the first, those who would die anyway, were left to die; the second, those who could be saved but would never fight again, were treated — but only after the third group; the third, the most important group, those who could be treated to fight again, were treated immediately (108). So, while the French triage system might have left Bonham to die from his catastrophic injuries, the American medical system saved him. And to add to the irony, as Bonham was injured during a relative lull in combat, there was more time and more medical staff able to treat his injuries, and as a "challenging case," Bonham was a victory for the doctors who "saved" him (85–86). Hence, Bonham is a "lucky guy" (89), the beneficiary of medical advances, but a lottery loser (89). In the text's final and perhaps most outrageous absurdity, once Bonham makes contact with the world external to his mind through Morse code, the powers that be, the federal entities, will not allow him to "speak" publicly because doing so would be "against regulations" (242), especially since the federals entities do not even know the identity of the communicating stump (242–43). So while March's absurdity in war, and of war, contains the comic among the tragic, Trumbo's contains no comic absurdity at all. None.

Joseph Heller's *Catch-22*, though, as is well known, contains comic absurdity as well as tragic absurdity. The most obvious examples of the absurd in the text are squadron mess officer Milo Minderbinder's capitalist syndicate, M&M Enterprises, and Colonel Cathcart's mission creep, through which he steadily increases the number of missions the pilots must fly — most obviously, as Yossarian nears each completion number; thus, the men never achieve their go-home number, and never get to leave the war. Milo, while completely devoid of a conscience, according to Jamie Granger, "is not the ultimate evil force in the novel" (81), even though his actions do lead to the suffering and deaths of fliers. Pragmatically and numerically speaking, Colonel Cathcart is a more ready villain, as Cathcart personifies, in uniform and in action, "the Army's camouflage of absurd rules and regulations" (84), of which the flight mission creep is the most deadly representation. According to Leon F. Seltzer, the World War II universe inhabited by Yossarian, Minderbinder, and Cathcart "is an irrational, sometimes nightmarish world in which one's superior ... officers constitute a greater threat to one's life and sanity than the enemy" (75). Thus, while Milo is a metonymous symbol of wartime industrial capitalism run amuck, whose "absurd laissez-faire attitude ... derives not from any political ideals but from purely economic concerns. War *is* profitable to [Milo's] private industry, and Milo has no desire to see it end" (Seltzer 81) — as the end of the war, obviously, would severely cut into the syndicate's profit margins — it is Cathcart who is a more literal and ready threat to the lives of the fliers, for as the metonymous face of the Army, Cathcart is proof that "the system controlling the military is morally mad" (Seltzer 75). Rather than protect his men in time of war, Cathcart, "who wanted to be a general [and who] was impervious to absolutes" (Heller 197), directly and specifically endangers the lives of his men by summarily raising the number of combat flight missions the fliers must complete before being rotated out of combat. As the war in occupied Italy portends to be winding down, this mission creep is recognizably absurd, but not that funny; as Yossarian thinks to himself, "strangers he didn't know shot at him with cannons every time he flew up into the air to drop bombs on them, and it wasn't funny at all" (26).

As the text opens, with Yossarian having flown forty-four missions, the number of combat flight missions required of the fliers is then identified as fifty: "The colonel wants fifty missions" (30), says Doc Daneeka to Yossarian. And for the reader, while this number seems arbitrary at this point, Yossarian's tone seems to indicate that this is not the original number of required combat missions: "But I've only got forty-four!" (30). So, it seems as if the mission number is increasing already, from that which it once was, to that which it is, to that which it will be. And as the text is told in a fractured, non-sequential, non-linear chronology, a later passage evidences Colonel Cathcart's ongoing mission creep: "'Forty missions,' Hungry Joe announced.... 'The colonel raised them again.' Yossarian was stunned. 'But I've got thirty-two, goddammit! Three more and I would have been through'" (174). And the fliers know "from bitter experience that Colonel Cathcart might raise the number of missions again at any time" (36), and he does, as has been his habit, for the original mission number was twenty-five missions, which Cathcart changed to thirty missions (62). Thus, the true mission count has gone from twenty-five to thirty to thirty-five to forty to fifty to ... well, why stop at fifty missions? Doc Daneeka informs Yossarian "the colonel now wants all of you to fly" (68) fifty-five missions. And Colonel Cathcart, who "wanted to be a general so desperately" (199), later raises the mission number to sixty, and then to sixty-five (350) and then to seventy (351), and after Yossarian has flown seventy-one missions (411) and as his peers are dying through the text, secondary to mission creep, Cathcart ultimately raises the number to eighty missions (385, 386, 415, 416). Cathcart's mission creep is murderous, and secondary to "Heller's vision of the horrifying absurdity of service life in World War II" (Kennard 75), and the text is "Heller's illustration of the irrational nature of the world" (Kennard 75), best evidenced through Colonel Cathcart's mission creep. Cathcart's desire to be a general negates any ability he has—if he has any—to consider the plight of the men whose lives he is effectively extinguishing. The psychological toll of the mission creep devastates the psyches of the men, who must fulfill the missions or choose to be traitors to their nation. Man, according to Heller, is an irrational, selfish, homicidal beast, and this identification is intra-ally rather than ally to enemy—thus, in this situation, one's allies are a greater threat to one's existence than are one's enemies.

Edward Franklin's *It's Cold in Pongo-Ni* offers the absurdity of war in a couple of different but related ways as the motif of an inter-unit American football game is used to present the comically absurd—a starting fullback is sent on a combat reconnaissance and prisoner snatch mission. And further, and comically, the members of the reconnaissance team are not exactly Super Grunts: "All good men, hand-picked by their platoon leaders" (27), says the company commander, "the Captain," to "the Lieutenant," the officer assigned to lead the mission; the lieutenant replies, "[Hand-picked] for mess duty" (27). Arne Axelsson notes that *It's Cold in Pongo-Ni* "captures the madcap, absurd qualities of modern war" (103) and that Franklin "demonstrates the superior efficiency of his satire" (101)—satire that mocks the institution of post–World War II regional warfare, and the futility thereof, as represented by a reconnaissance mission that is completely meaningless relative to the outcome of the war, for, as Axelsson declares, "the war cannot and will not be won [and thus the lieutenant] and his messmen will be risking their lives to achieve absolutely nothing" (103). So, again, as in the Heller text, American combatants are ordered to risk their lives in futile combat situations. When the captain and the lieutenant go to meet the team, Franklin first identifies the motley group *en masse*: "The messmen slowly get to their feet and form into line. All wear field jackets with armored vests underneath. They have no helmets or weapons. Their dungarees bear the stains of their work" (28). Of course, when one thinks of the twentieth-century warrior, one envisions a man with a rifle and a steel helmet on his head, but for rhetorical, comic, and absurdist effect, Franklin denies these Marines their tools of war—at this point, at least. And note, the men's trousers are stained with food and other such work-related markings—not blood, not mud, but gravy and the like.

The men are introduced to the reader, and the officer pair comes to the fullback: "'This is Jarvinen,' says the Captain, indicating the first man. 'Jarvinen here is our star athlete,' and, as one does with athletes, he socks the man's arm. 'He's going to play in the I Corps championship game'" (29–30). The lieutenant replies, "Tennis?" (30), to which the captain — unnecessarily — responds, "No, no, football" (30).

Before taking off on their raid, the assembled team is put through a rehearsal at the behest of the unnamed colonel who has ordered the mission (41–44), and the image of the men "standing on a barren hill playing pretend games" (44) is a comic respite from the serious absurdity of the raiders' deadly mission. After the rehearsal, the captain informs the lieutenant that "Due to the possibility of bad weather, the I Corps championship football game has been moved up. It's going to be played tomorrow afternoon" (51). So, obviously, Jarvinen should not go on the mission, as he has a football game to play, but the colonel, in his wisdom, sees fit to send Jarvinen on the mission regardless: "Jarvinen is vital to both teams ... he can make first string on both clubs" (53). With this absurd and stupid statement, the analogy has been fixed: war is analogous to football; only, and one must remember this slightly important difference between the two, on reconnaissance raids, men kill and men die. As explicated in previous chapters, the team completes its mission, of a sort, but fails to collect a prisoner to take back for interrogation, although Corporal Ford and the lieutenant do consider returning with a Chinese corpse (109–10) to please the colonel. So, essentially, the mission is a failure, yet paradoxically, the mission is a success, as at the conclusion of the deadly mission, and after the deaths of the squad leader Ford and another Marine named Haverstick, Jarvinen is readily available, despite a "slight" hand wound, to fulfill his true regimental role, that of ball-carrying football player. And as the scene and the text close, Jarvinen, as per his essential role — and in a closing frame that references the initial unarmed-messmen scene — hands over his tools of war, his "submachine gun" (157) and its ammunition clips, and moves off to play a football game. Thus, the absurd analogy between football and war is complete.

Axelsson correctly argues that, with *It's Cold in Pongo-Ni*, "Franklin succeeds so well in his particular blend of Korean War horror and humor that his novel definitely deserves to be better known and more widely read" (99). One cannot say such a thing about Richard Hooker's *MASH*, a text widely read, widely praised, and widely disseminated. But, one must ask, deservedly so? Problematically, the comedic absurdity in *MASH* is rhetorically counterproductive in its exponentially explicit and less-than-subtle nature. And while *MASH*, like *It's Cold in Pongo-Ni*, does offer a football and war analogy (Chapters 12 and 13), the Hooker text fails to take advantage of two of the more common absurdities of war — that of the advancements made in medicine, secondary to battlefield trauma and injury, and that of the irony of treating wounded combatants with the goal of returning them to the field of combat, which is contrary to the Hippocratic ideal of "Do No Harm." And while field surgeons assigned to combat zones may practice their surgical techniques to the best of their abilities, there must exist, consciously and unconsciously, an ethos of remorse and futility, as one must know that one is helping to heal in order to return the wounded patient to battle. As such, the philanthropic and human nature of the doctor helping the patient ceases to exist.

Relative to ongoing medical advances during the Korean War, Jane Colihan and Robert J.T. Joy note that during the Korean War, there was a "formal recognition of war's role as a laboratory of science" (75) and that MASH medical professionals "studied wound infection, dehydration, and kidney problems [and] new ways of repairing arterial wounds, [thus] reducing the need for amputation" (75), and further, "Korea's cold led to advances in the prevention and treatment of frostbite" (75). Yet, while the Hooker text does indeed mention the Korean cold, and while wounded patients do succumb to death, the greater and more serious, and morally treacherous, aspect of the absurdity of treating wounded combatants in order to return the men to the field of battle is rarely addressed in the text. The greater goal of the MASH surgeons, relative to the treatment of the catastrophically wounded, is indeed noble — as Captain Hawkeye Pierce tells a new surgeon, "We are not concerned with the ultimate reconstruction of the patient. We are concerned only with getting the kid out of here alive enough for someone else to reconstruct him" (195) — but it cannot make up for the missing moral conundrum. And while the novel devotes two full chapters to the Thanksgiving football game, Hornberger and Heinz — AKA Richard Hooker — do not adequately address the dilemma faced by each combat surgeon. Of course, MASH is nearly clownishly comedic in nature, ridiculously absurd at points, and even as its authors attempt seriousness, most often through brief references to combat casualties and the post-combat surgery rush, a critic must ask why the inner workings or external angst of the surgeons, relative to the moral dilemma of healing combat casualties so that the ambulatory post-operative wounded can be returned to battle, is not offered, at least in passing, for it seems only natural that a surgeon, a doctor, a healer, would experience some conflict relative to his role as contributor to battlefield excess. And in an absurd American novel of war, a novel pregnant with absurd scenes and situations, this element, this crucial absurdity of war, is absent, and that is absurd.

Closing the twentieth century, in Terrence D. Haynes' *Desert Norm*, the narrator refers to the Persian Gulf War as a television war, one offered to the public — and to the participants, the warriors — by "CNG" — "Cable News Group" (102) — and cable and satellite television feeds; this instant television-ization of war makes celebrities of those on the TV, especially the commanding generals, one of whom is fawned over, not merely by the members of the professional media, but also by those whom he leads — the uniformed members of the American military. Thus, when an opportunity comes to meet a TV general, the troops line up for said general's autograph, as they would when meeting a television star such as Bob Hope or any other celebrated entertainer. Further, when a war is viewed through the optic of a television screen and the war is fought using high technology — often from a distance — to the viewers of the televised feed, who are consumers now, and even to those participating on the periphery of the conflict, who also consume the televised war, the war becomes not a catastrophic human event, but a video-game war, no more than two-dimensional images on a screen.

Haynes presents both absurdities early in the text, prior to the combat engagement, in a section set in December 1990, in Tulte Village, Saudi Arabia, appropriately titled "We Were Trying to Get on TV..." (21–34). In the passage, Army Specialist Marcus Norm and another enlisted man named Johnson are attending the Bob Hope Christmas show for the troops, and the pair, knowing the show "would be recorded on post ... and broadcast in the United States at a later date" (21), want to "*land some media time* [italics Haynes]" (20) — that is, they want to appear on TV in the United States. When Norm and Johnson arrive at the taping site, "Several hundred soldiers already were on the premises, jockeying for prime places near the TV cameras. A number of soldiers had signs that they hoped would be seen at home during the telecast" (23). So at this point in the cable-television era, even the common uniformed service member is well aware of the power — and immediacy — of television, but this awareness is not necessarily new to the participants and consumers of the Persian

Gulf War, as the participants and consumers of Vietnam War USO shows exhibited a similar awareness, sans the immediacy of satellite and cable technology, of course. Johnson pleads, nearly obsessively, but with savvy, "We *have* to get on TV!... We should have brought a sign. People with signs always get on TV!" (23). And as any consumer of live television knows, Johnson is correct in his assertion; people with signs do get on TV. The pair then discuss collecting celebrity autographs, and the media-philic Johnson expresses a desire to get Bob Hope's autograph, as the legendary comedian and entertainer is, of course, the biggest celebrity present (24). Norm replies, "I'd much rather get one from General Norman Schwarzkopf" (24). As the commanding general of the American ground forces, and a telegenic and astute — and common — media presence, the general has achieved celebrity status in the eyes of Specialist Norm, who, like Johnson, Schwarzkopf, and the other members of the American uniformed forces, is himself media savvy. Johnson responds, "What would you want with some Army General's signature, anyway?" (24), to which Norm replies, "He'll be huge in the future" (24). Of course, Norm is correct, as after the war, Schwarzkopf does become a television celebrity, one who over-saturated the airwaves.

Absurdly, and in an explicit presentation of the general's celebrity status, when Schwarzkopf's motorcade arrives, and Norm attempts to get access to the general, he is readily threatened by one of the general's bodyguards, who motions for his .45-caliber semi-automatic handgun and says to Norm, "Put your hands where I can see them, Soldier — and go" (25). Norm is — understandably — shaken and says, "That SP was thinking about shooting me over an autograph — an *autograph!*" (25). And thus, and absurdly so, the general as media-celebrity is in full postmodern effect. Later, after welcoming the troops to the show, "Schwarzkopf paused to wave to the audience and sign a few autographs for the lucky soldiers standing near the left side of the stage. He then was led off stage by a group of husky SPs" (31). The bitterness present in this scene is the bitterness born of the fragmentation of the Army hierarchy, secondary to the general's celebrity status; according to the narrator, the Special Police will kill a person who wears the same uniform rather than allow the uniformed service member access to the general — who is, of course, no longer a mere general, but one who now occupies the rarified air of media celebrity. The culture of and access to television, obviously, has made narcissists, egoists, and fawning sycophants of everyone involved, regardless of rank or military role, and in chapter 21, titled "Watching The War" (101–3), one might understand the power of the televising box over all involved: "*Technology is such a wonderful thing! The war is being brought to the world's living rooms like a daily soap opera! Just tune in and there it is in real time! The war is packaged, analyzed, and served up for all, in a nice little media snack* [italics Haynes]" (101). To use a Vietnam-era, Marine Corps–relative summation (albeit in a different context from Haynes' use above): There it is. There is the sum total of the absurdity of the postmodern, instantly televised war. The warriors are watching the war, as they are, of course, fighting the war — war as meta-war. And what differentiates these TV warriors from their counterparts of the Vietnam War is that these combatants are watching themselves — in real time — as they fight the war, as is the world public; thus, these combatants are consumers of the war as well as participants in the war, whereas the combatants in Vietnam were the observed participants of that war, whose actions were consumed by the American viewing public. Thus, bizarrely — past the point of absurdity — and meta-observationally, the viewers are themselves the viewed, as well as the participants and promoters of the actions being observed.

Certainly then, in the American novel of war, the absurdity of war is often presented, liberally, generously, generally, ironically, and commonly, with comic absurdity and with abject tragedy. While the absurdity of war is found in most American novels of war, frequently, the absurd situations are so seriously presented that one may not notice the absurdity of the given scene and situation because of the life and death nature of the actions within the work. In some war novels, the absurdity is laughable, but however, as the locus is war, in many instances, the comic absurdity leads to the death or deaths of the allied combatants, so the reader does not readily notice the absurd. While *Catch-22* and *MASH* immediately come to mind when readers and critics think absurdity of war and war text, *Company K*, *Johnny Got His Gun*, *It's Cold in Pongo-Ni*, and *Desert Norm* each deal overtly, explicitly, and rhetorically with the absurdity of war, comic and tragic. Of course, while Milo Minderbinder's syndicate, M&M Enterprises, signifies the capitalist industrialization of war, and the express absurdity thereof, *Catch-22*'s true combat-related absurdity is relative to the ever-increasing number of bombing missions that Yossarian and his peers must undertake before being transferred to a safe, non-combat billet — if this safety is ever available. And while the comedic absurdity in *MASH* is nearly overwhelming and rhetorically counterproductive in its exponentially explicit and less-than-subtle nature, the text's true absurdity is that which is not present in the work — the moral dilemma of treating the wounded so that they may return to battle. Also less than humorous but absurd, and in *Catch-22*, each increase in flight count leads to the deaths of more pilots, co-pilots, and flight-crew members, so beneath each comic text lies a rage, an incipient anger at war and its deathly absurdity. *Company K* and *Johnny Got His Gun* are texts that howl with fury, too. The former, a very serious text, is salted with sketches of comic and seriocomic absurdity; for example, morphine sulfate for pain is administered only to officers if supplies are low, while wounded enlisted men are treated sans narcotic pain reliever; uppity prostitutes service officers only, and a man skilled in sniping practices taunts an enemy sniper, as he endangers his own life, of course, by staggering his gait and attitude as he moves about the allied trenches. *Johnny Got His Gun*, a text absolutely seething with rage, presents a narrative protagonist who is so maimed from war that he cannot even commit suicide; this situation is absurd, but not untrue, nor unrealistic, nor uncommon, frankly. Like *MASH*, *It's Cold in Pongo-Ni* uses the motif of inter-unit American football to present the comically absurd; in the latter text, a football-playing ringer is sent on a combat reconnaissance mission, so it is imperative that he survive the mission, as he has an important game to play. At the conclusion of the deadly mission, and even though wounded, the man is called upon to fulfill his true uniformed role, and there is no doubt nor denial that in each text there is present the unstated but obvious absurdity in the rhetorical and over-used analogy between the game of football and the "game" of war. At the end of the twentieth century, and in Saudi Arabia rather than Korea, in *Desert Norm*, narrative guide Specialist Marcus Norm refers to the Persian Gulf War as a television war, one offered to the public and to the warriors by world-wide cable and satellite television networks, and this instant and ubiquitous television-ization of war makes celebrities of those on TV, especially one commanding general, who is fawned over by the troops and is closely guarded by specialized military police — SPs. Consequently, the troops line up for said general's autograph, even though doing so is less than dignified, as they would when meeting television star Bob Hope or any other celebrity. These examples show that one must not conjoin the absurdity of war with the humor of war, for the absurdity of war can be tragic, of course, and it often is, and the absurdity can be comic, too, and it often is. So, while humor is often and readily present in American war novels — literary and pulp, many serious American novels of war do not contain humor; that said, most, if not all, do contain the serious absurdity of war.

Epilogue

Traditionally, in a broad study such as this one, the author can close the work with either a summary conclusion or a forward-looking epilogue. After 15 chapters explicating and analyzing the defining characteristics of the modern and postmodern American novel of war, the optimum choice is to look forward rather than repeat — to the point of redundancy — that which has already been offered and argued. Thus, a brief examination of a number of motifs and thematic elements from the American novel of war — motifs and thematic elements that are worthy of study, of course but that were not presented here — is in order. Like the preceding motifs and thematic elements, these are also definitive and are found in many, if not most, modern and postmodern American novels of war.

Drugs and alcohol, in the forms of beer, wine, booze, medical drugs (narcotic pain relievers and antibiotics), tobacco, and, in later texts, street drugs (marijuana, primarily) are commonly found in American novels of war. Combatants who risk catastrophic injury and death need a chemical release, and that release is often the legal drug of choice, alcohol. Most American novels of war present a motif of alcohol in some manner, and beer is the most frequently used aperitif, while various liquors are common, too (in novels of the First World War, wine is often featured — when in France). Getting drunk between combat episodes is understandable enough, as is drinking whenever booze is readily available, as the pressure of life in war is hardly imaginable. Many novels also have a tobacco motif, most often in the form of cigarette use; if one has ever been around the uniformed military, one is aware that this tobacco use absolutely common, and in a war zone, where death is pervasive, and one can die at any moment, who cares about tobacco-related disease? Further, the tobacco companies' "gift" of free tobacco to the uniformed during wartime is factually verifiable, and thus tobacco use is common to American novels of war. War means combat, and combat means traumatic injury and medical care. As such, American novels of war that present medical themes or motifs also offer two types of pharmaceuticals — narcotic pain relievers and antibiotics. Most often, the narcotic of choice is morphine sulfate. And the presence of prostitution leads to the distribution of antibiotics secondary to prophylactic or post-infection sexually transmitted disease. Finally, in the texts of the Vietnam War, marijuana use is rampant. Weed is so conjoined with the Vietnam War, in reality and in popular culture, that an American novel of the Vietnam War sans some form of marijuana motif is incomplete, untrue, or penned by a former officer. All in all, though, the presence of alcohol and drugs — legal and not, commercial and pharmaceutical — is a very common, nearly omni-text, motif in the American novel of war, and (not coincidentally) in novels of war authored by writers of other nationalities. Therefore, the drug and alcohol motif in the American novel of war is worthy of further study and scholarship.

Also worthy of further study is the motif of man as animal in the American novel of war. The man as animal motif occurs in two manners: one, the combatants or the narrator dehumanize the self or the allied combatants; two, the combatants or the narrator dehumanize the enemy combatants and/or the indigenous civilians. In the first case, the combatant is transformed from man into animal — man into werewolf, for example, man into savage. For religious or social or cultural reasons, American man must become a non-human animal in order to kill the enemy. This transformation from man into animal makes the warrior a better, more efficient, more effective, non-human fighting entity. This transformation of man into animal also allows for the combatant to remove his "self" from the process: "I became an animal." After the war or combat, the man returns to his former self, or at least to a humanized self. In the second case, the combatant or narrator dehumanizes the enemy and/or the indigenous populace, both of whom are then killed secondary to the violence of war. Identifying the enemy as a non-human animal — or merely as "an animal" or "animals" — dehumanizes the enemy and creates an *en masse* villain, one sans home or name or family or history. In a similar manner, identifying the invaded or indigenous people with an animal — such as the Japanese labeling Chinese civilians "pigs" during the rape of Nanking — also dehumanizes those people and makes it easier to see them perish, and also to kill them when such action is deemed necessary. So, there is a self-dehumanization in war — for combat purposes, and there is a dehumanization of the other, both uniformed and civilian — for the purpose of less uncomfortable killing. Some American novels of war use this man as animal motif to the point that it becomes elemental, thematic in the text; most, though, keep the use at a motif level. Nonetheless, the presentation of man as animal in the American novel of war is quite interesting, and inherent, whether the presentation is offered as motif or thematic element.

In war, of course, one's olfactory sense is triggered repeatedly, as there are lots of unique smells in combat — the odors of war, odors one does not smell in civilian life. Explosive devices going off, various powders and chemical reactions, fire of all sorts and sources, burning flesh, rotting flesh, and indigenous foods, flora, and fauna — all pervade the combatant's olfactory nerves. As such, writers of the American novel of war (with emphasis here on combatant writers, of course) rarely fail to note the smell(s) of war. War smells; war stinks; the tolls of war smell; the results of war smell. There is no other way of stating this: Chemistry and violence and explosions and decomposing flesh and burning flesh and foreign countries and cook-sets and foods and forests and jungles and deserts and cities do not smell like the office or the school hall or the house in which one was reared and raised. War smells, and those authors who are skilled enough to do so create a sensory experience for the reader through the accurate and almost tactile description of the odors of war. War conjoins humanity and the natural world with chemical reactions and the results thereof, and the smells produced in war, the odors of war, are very important sensory imagery in the American novel of war.

Dreams and nightmares — peri-war dreams that can include pre-war life or post-war life, and post-war dreams often offered as post-traumatic nightmares — are also readily present in the American novel of war. Sleep-centric dreams, rather than "dreams of glory," are often situated in war texts, and are generally used by characters as a means of escape from the combat present. As such, a character will go to sleep and dream of his pre-war life or existence or of the girl "back home" with whom he is in love. Occasionally, too, the combatant will dream of his post-war life, of civilian glory or of a hero's parade in which he is the central character, the decorated and celebrated hero. Homecoming is rarely so glorious, though. More often, homecoming is a traumatic event, as the locals cannot empathize with the returning warrior, and, almost serially, the post-war combatant cum civilian is haunted by the war and by his own behaviors during the war. Thus, the post-war combatant is often post-traumatic, but is not helped by the post-war world, and thus is the victim of post–trauma-induced nightmares in which he revisits the war and the catastrophes thereof. In the postmodern era, a post-psychoanalytic era, a psychoanalytic reading — using both Freudian and Jungian concepts— of a number of these nightmares and the characters' experiences that produce the nightmares would be a valuable and interesting literary study.

And what is war without suicide? And what is the American novel of war sans a suicide motif? In the American novel of war, characters often have suicidal ideation, and occasionally — and noticeably — there are characters who move past ideation and do commit suicide, either during war or very soon thereafter. Sometimes suicide is motivated by fear — of combat, of survival in combat, of failure in combat. Sometimes suicide is an act of self-destruction secondary to a perceived or real failure of some sort, a failure in battle that leads to the loss of a peer, for example. Sometimes the character's hatred of service or of the military itself or of the given war is motivation enough. There are many contributing factors in the suicides or suicidal ideations of characters in these works, and this motif (rarely a thematic element) is in fact hard to pin down to a common mitigating factor. Something interesting, too, is the narrative ambiguity found in some suicidal situations: is a character's suicide a suicide or a fragging? Usually, a suicide is labeled a suicide (but there are some debatable exceptions). Also common in the texts, relative to a character's suicide, is the necessary ongoing of the fighting unit. Another guy is dead, by his own hand, but alas, the war is bigger than one man, one suicide, and thus the war — and the novel —continues. So while the suicide motif is not omnipresent in the American novel of war, it is sufficiently present in enough novels, to be a noticeable element.

As mentioned in the preceding chapter, humor — humor dark, humor black, the blackest — is found in many American novels of war. Within the text, humor is often used as a way to alleviate the deadly actions and omnipresent threat of death and being grievously maimed, and perhaps the best and briefest words on black humor in the American novel of war are Peter Aichinger's in the previously mentioned *The American Soldier in Fiction, 1880–1963*. Aichinger's brief chapter, "Black Humor" (95–99), contains the astute point that black humor is used in the American novel of war as a "counterpoint to the vivid realism" (98) present in the modern and postmodern American novel of war. So, in this way, the humor of war is quite different from is the absurdity of war, and the peri-textual jokes about the dead —civilians, peers, and enemy combatants alike — are countermeasures that aid in the characters' coping with the ghastly situations of modern and postmodern war. Additionally, the black humor allows the reader a respite from the horrors realistically presented within the text. Well-written or appropriate jokes are funny, regardless of the horrifying wrapping in which they come, and further, humor (black as it may be) is still humorous, even or especially because it is offered through the optic of the American novel of war.

Finally, and tragically, rape is a component of war, a weapon of war, a byproduct of war; therefore, many novels feature rape scenes, mention of rape, attempts at rape, or jokes about raping local women. A woman cannot escape her sexualized self when the person, the sexualizer, is a man existing within a life and death paradigm, one who sees no future, and thus no consequences for his actions. This rapist-to-be also uses the dehumanization of the victim to aid in the fantasy or reality of sexual assault; as such he does not see the rape victim as a human being, a woman with feelings and emotions and fears and family and a non-war, pre- or post-war life. Existentially speaking, there is no tomorrow, but for death, and thus there is no consequence for the brutalizing of a "non-human" woman. Therefore, the act of rape is undertaken, sometimes by a character who, perhaps, would never do so in civilian life, and sometimes by a character easily identified as anti-social. Historically, sexual violence against women is one of the atrocities of war, and, unfortunately, it is an ongoing tragedy, even in the twentieth and twenty-first centuries. As such, rape remains present in the modern and postmodern American novel of war.

And thus, this study closes, not looking backward but looking forward. As there is much more to read, much more to write, much more to argue about the American novel of war, and as war is endless (and as American participation in war is, it seems, endless), so is the American novel of war — as a literary genre, as a creative movement, as an act of artistic expression, and as a dynamic vehicle for debate, criticism, discussion, and scholarship. Thank you, and good day.

Bibliography

Aichinger, Peter. *The American Soldier in Fiction, 1880–1963: A History of Attitudes Toward Warfare and the Military Establishment.* Ames: Iowa State University Press, 1975.

Aldridge, John W. *After the Lost Generation: A Critical Study of the Writers of Two Wars.* 1951. Freeport: Books for Libraries, 1971.

al-Zaidi, Muntadar. "Perspectives." *Newsweek,* 23 March 2009: 25.

"American War Deaths Through History: From Independence to Iraqi Freedom." Military Factory.com, 2011. Accessed 29 June 2011.

Anderson, Maxwell, and Laurence Stallings. *What Price Glory: A Play in Three Acts. Three American Plays.* New York: Harcourt, Brace, 1926.

"Artillery." *Weapons of the American Civil War.* Civil War Home (online), 2002. Accessed 10 November 2010.

Associated Press. "Roadside Bombs Kill 12 Afghan Civilians." USA Today.com, 23 September 2009. Accessed 23 September 2009.

Axelsson, Arne. *Restrained Response: American Novels of the Cold War and Korea, 1945–1962.* New York: Greenwood, 1990.

Bates, Milton J. *The Wars We Took to Vietnam: Cultural Conflict and Storytelling.* Berkeley: University of California Press, 1996.

"The Battle of the Wilderness: Summary & Facts." Civil War.org. Civil War Trust, 2010. Accessed 30 December 2010.

Beehner, Lionel. "An Operation by Any Other Name." USA Today.com, 17 March 2010. Accessed 17 March 2010.

Beidler, Peter G. "Bloody Mud, Rifle Butts, and Barbed Wire: Transforming the Bataan Death March in Silko's *Ceremony.*" *American Indian Culture and Research Journal* 28, no. 1 (2004): 23–33.

Beidler, Philip D. "Introduction." In *Company K,* by William March (1933), vii–xxvi. Tuscaloosa: University of Alabama Press, 2006.

Berndt, Caroline M. "Popular Culture as Political Protest: Writing the Reality of Sexual Slavery." *Journal of Popular Culture* 31, no. 2 (1997): 177–87.

Bibby, Michael. "Fragging the Chains of Command: GI Resistance Poetry and Mutilation." *Journal of American Culture* 16, no. 3 (1993): 29–38.

Bierce, Ambrose. "Chickamauga." In *The Complete Short Stories of Ambrose Bierce* (1970), edited, with commentary, by Ernest Jerome Hopkins, foreword by Cathy N. Davidson, 313–18. Lincoln: University of Nebraska Press, 1984.

_____. "Two Military Executions." In *The Complete Short Stories of Ambrose Bierce* (1970), edited, with commentary, by Ernest Jerome Hopkins, foreword by Cathy N. Davidson, 380–82. Lincoln: University of Nebraska Press, 1984.

_____. "What I Saw of Shiloh." In *Phantoms of a Blood-Stained Period: The Complete Civil War Writings of Ambrose Bierce,* edited and introduced by Russell Duncan and David J. Klooster, 93–110. Amherst: University of Massachusetts Press, 2002.

Bishop, Ryan, and John Phillips. "Sighted Weapons and Modernist Opacity: Aesthetics, Poetics, Prosthetics." *Boundary 2: An International Journal of Literature and Culture* 29, no. 2 (2002): 157–79.

Bolchoz, Cole. *A Medic in Iraq: A Novel of the Iraq War.* Cambridge: ebooksonthe.net/Write Words, Inc., 2007.

Bonadeo, Alfredo. "War and Degradation: Gleanings from the Literature of the Great War." *Comparative Literature Studies* 21, no. 4 (1984): 409–33.

Bonner, Thomas, Jr. "Experience and Imagination: Confluence in the War Fiction of Stephen Crane and Ambrose Bierce." *War, Literature, and the Arts,* Special Edition: Stephen Crane in War and Peace (1999): 48–56.

Bowman, Peter. *Beach Red: A Novel.* New York: Random House, 1945.

Boyd, Thomas. *Through the Wheat: A Novel of the World War I Marines.* 1923. Introduction by Edwin Howard Simmons. Lincoln: University of Nebraska Press, 2000.

Boyer, Marilyn. "The Treatment of the Wound in Stephen Crane's *The Red Badge of Courage.*" *Stephen Crane Studies* 12, no. 1 (2003): 4–17.

Bradbury, Malcolm. "The Denuded Place: War and Form in *Parade's End* and *U.S.A.*" In *The First World War in Fiction,* edited by Holger Klein, 193–235. London: Macmillan, 1976.

Bradley, James, with Ron Powers. *Flags of Our Fathers.* 2000. New York: Bantam, 2006.

Broyles, William, Jr. "Why Men Love War." *Esquire* (online), November 1984. Accessed 21 April 2008.

Buitenhuis, Peter. "Writers at War: Propaganda and Fiction in the Great War." *University of Toronto Quarterly: A Canadian Journal of the Humanities* 45 (1976): 277–94.

Burdick, Eugene. "Cold Day, Cold Fear." In *Retrieving Bones: Stories and Poems of the Korean War*, edited and introduced by W.D. Ehrhart and Philip K. Jason, 53–62. New Brunswick, NJ: Rutgers University Press, 1999.

Burke, James Lee. "We Build Churches, Inc." In *Retrieving Bones: Stories and Poems of the Korean War*, edited and introduced by W.D. Ehrhart and Philip K. Jason, 43–52. New Brunswick, NJ: Rutgers University Press, 1999.

Buzzell, Colby. *My War: Killing Time in Iraq.* 2005. New York: Berkley Caliber, 2006.

"Canada's Secret War: Vietnam." Canadian Broadcast Company *Digital Archives* (online), 2011. Accessed 4 July 2011.

Carpenter, Lucas. "'It Don't Mean Nothin': Vietnam War Fiction and Postmodernism." *College Literature* 30, no. 2 (2003): 30–50.

Chamberlain, Samuel. *My Confession: Recollections of a Rogue.* 1956. Unexpurgated and annotated edition. Edited and introduced by William H. Goetzmann. Austin: Texas State Historical Association, 1996.

Chang, Iris. *The Rape of Nanking: The Forgotten Holocaust of World War II.* 1997. Foreword by William C. Kirby. New York: Penguin, 1998.

"Chickamauga." *CWSAC Battle Summaries: The American Battlefield Protection Program.* Historic Preservation Services/National Park Service (online), 2009. Accessed 29 December 2010.

Chuman, Joseph. "Postmodernism and the Problem of the Modern Age." *Humanism Today* 8, no. 1 (1993): 7–18.

Clausen, Walter B. "Midway." In *Men at War: The Best War Stories of All Time* (1942), edited and introduced by Ernest Hemingway, 1070–72. New York: Bramhall, 1979.

Clausewitz, Carl von. *On War (1832).* 1976. Edited and translated by Michael Howard and Peter Paret. Princeton, NJ: Princeton University Press, 1984.

Cobley, Evelyn. "Violence and Sacrifice in Modern War Narratives." *SubStance: A Review of Theory and Literary Criticism* 23, no. 3 (1994): 75–99.

Cohen, Debra Rae. "Culture and the 'Cathedral': Tourism as Potlatch in *One of Ours.*" *Cather Studies* 6 (2006): 184–204.

Cohen, Milton A. "Fatal Symbiosis: Modernism and the First World War." In *The Literature of the Great War Reconsidered*, edited by Patrick J. Quinn and Steven Trout, 159–71. New York: Palgrave, 2001.

Cole, Sarah. *Modernism, Male Friendship, and the First World War.* New York: Cambridge University Press, 2003.

Colihan, Jane, and Robert J.T. Joy. "Military Medicine: How Our Wartime Experience Conquered a Wide Range of Problems from Hemorrhagic Shock to Yellow Fever." *American Heritage* 35, no. 6 (1984): 65–77.

Collette, Ann. "Vietnam Fictions, Memoirs, and Films." *San Francisco Review of Books* (May-June 1995): 20–24.

Cook, Matt. "Soldier." *Texas Monthly* (July 2008): 120–25; 156–65.

Cooperman, Stanley. "American War Novels: Yesterday, Today, and Tomorrow." *Yale Review: A National Quarterly* 61 (1972): 517–29.

_____. "Christ in Khaki: Religion and the Post–World War I Literary Protest." *Western Humanities Review* 18 (1964): 361–72.

_____. *World War I and the American Novel.* 1967. Baltimore: Johns Hopkins University Press, 1970.

Crane, Stephen. "A Mystery of Heroism." In *"The Little Regiment" and Other Civil War Stories* (1896), 1–8. Minneola, NY: Dover, 1997.

_____. *The Red Badge of Courage: An Episode of the American Civil War.* 1895. Edited and introduced, with notes, by Gary Scharnhorst. New York: Penguin, 2005.

Crawford, Bartholow V. "The Civil War and American Literature." *ESQ: A Journal of the American Renaissance* 44 (1966): 91–94.

Crawford, C.S. *The Four Deuces: A Korean War Story.* Novato, CA: Presidio, 1989.

Das, Santanu. "'Kiss Me, Hardy': Intimacy, Gender, and Gesture in World War I Trench Literature." *MODERNISM/modernity* 9, no. 1 (2002): 51–69.

Davis, Gary W. "*Catch-22* and the Language of Discontinuity." In *Critical Essays on Joseph Heller*, edited by James Nagel, 62–74. Boston: G.K. Hall, 1984.

Dawes, James. "The American War Novel." In *The Cambridge Companion to the Literature of World War II*, edited by Marina Mackay, 56–65. New York: Cambridge University Press, 2009.

_____. *The Language of War: Literature and Culture in the U.S. from the Civil War through World War II.* Cambridge, MA: Harvard University Press, 2002.

Der Derian, James. *Antidiplomacy: Spies, Terror, Speed, and War.* Cambridge, MA: Blackwell, 1992.

Dickson, Paul, ed. *War Slang: American Fighting Words and Phrases Since the Civil War.* 1994. 2nd ed. Washington, DC: Brassey's, 2004.

Doctorow, E.L. *The March: A Novel.* 2005. New York: Random House, 2006.

Dos Passos, John. *One Man's Initiation.* 1920. LaVergne: Kessinger, 2009.

Duffy, Michael. "Battles—The Third Battle of Ypres, 1917." First World War.com, 2009. Accessed 21 January 2011.

Duncan, Russell, and David J. Klooster. "Introduction: Fighting and Writing the Civil War." In *Phantoms of a Blood-Stained Period: The Complete Civil War Writings of Ambrose Bierce*, edited and introduced by Russell Duncan and David J. Klooster, 5–30. Amherst: University of Massachusetts Press, 2002.

Ehrhart, W.D., and Philip K. Jason. "Introduction." In *Retrieving Bones: Stories and Poems of the Korean War*, edited and introduced by W.D. Ehrhart and Philip K. Jason, xiii–xlii. New Brunswick, NJ: Rutgers University Press, 1999.

Empey, Arthur Guy. *Over the Top: By An American Soldier Who Went.* New York: G.P. Putnam's Sons, 1917.

Favret, Mary A. "War in the Air." *Modern Language Quarterly: A Journal of Literary History* 65, no. 4 (2004): 531–59.

Fox, Margalit. "Chaim Potok, Who Illuminated the World of Hasidic Judaism, Dies at 73." *New York Times* (online), 24 July 2002. Accessed 18 May 2011.

Frank, Pat. *Hold Back the Night.* New York: Lippincott, 1952.

Frankel, Ernest. *Band of Brothers.* 1958. New York: Signet, 1960.

Franklin, Edward. *It's Cold in Pongo-Ni.* New York: Vanguard, 1965.

Frederic, Harold. "A Day in the Wilderness." In *The Civil War Stories of Harold Frederic*, edited by Thomas F. O'Donnell, introduction by Edmund Wilson, 229–72. Syracuse, NY: Syracuse University Press, 1992.

Frederick, John T. "Fiction of the Second World War." *College English* 17, no. 4 (1956): 197–204.

Fussell, Paul. *The Great War and Modern Memory.* 1975. New York: Oxford University Press, 2000.

Garrison, Webb, with Cheryl Garrison. *The Encyclopedia of Civil War Usage: An Illustrated Compendium of the Everyday Language of Soldiers and Civilians.* Nashville: Cumberland House, 2002.

Gault, William Barry. "Some Remarks on Slaughter." *American Journal of Psychiatry* 128, no. 4 (1971): 450–54.

Getz, John. "Healing the Soldier in White: *Ceremony* as War Novel." *War, Literature, and the Arts: An International Journal of the Humanities* 9, no. 1 (1997): 123–40.

Goetzmann, William H. "Introduction." In *My Confession: Recollections of a Rogue*, by Samuel Chamberlain (1956), unexpurgated and annotated edition, edited and introduced by William H. Goetzmann, 1–25. Austin: Texas State Historical Association, 1996.

Granger, Jamie. "Love During Wartime: Adam and Eve and *Catch-22*." *Pleiades* 14, no. 2 (1994): 79–85.

Grant, Ulysses S. "Ulysses S. Grant to Jesse Root Grant." In *The Civil War: The First Year Told by Those Who Lived It*, edited by Brooks D. Simpson, Stephen W. Sears, and Aaron Sheehan-Dean, 590–91. New York: Library of America, 2011.

Gravett, Sharon L. "Novels and Other Fictional Accounts." In *The American Civil War: A Handbook of Literature and Research*, edited by Steven E. Woodworth, 603–12. Westport, CT: Greenwood, 1996.

Grimsley, Mark. "Modern War/Total War." In *The American Civil War: A Handbook of Literature and Research*, edited by Steven E. Woodworth, foreword by James M. McPherson, 379–89. Westport, CT: Greenwood, 1996.

Habegger, Alfred. "Fighting Words: The Talk of Men at War in The Red Badge of Courage." In *Fictions of Masculinity: Crossing Cultures, Crossing Sexualities*, edited by Peter F. Murphy, 185–203. New York: New York University Press, 1994.

Hagemann, Edward R. "Crane's 'Real' War in His Short Stories." *American Quarterly* 8, no. 4 (1956): 356–67.

Hantke, Steffen. "Disorienting Encounters: Magical Realism and American Literature on the Vietnam War." *Journal of the Fantastic in the Arts* 12, no. 3 (2001): 268–86.

_____. "The Uses of the Fantastic and the Deferment of Closure in American Literature on the Vietnam War." *Rocky Mountain Review of Language and Literature* 55, no. 1 (2001): 63–82.

Harmon, William, and Hugh Holman, eds. *A Handbook to Literature.* 10th ed. Upper Saddle River, NJ: Pearson Prentice Hall, 2006.

Harrison, Brady. "'That Immense and Bloodslaked Waste': Negation in *Blood Meridian*." *Southwestern American Literature* 25, no. 1 (1999): 35–42.

Hasford, Gustav. *The Short-Timers.* 1979. New York: Bantam, 1983.

Hass, Robert. "On Visiting the DMZ at Panmunjon: A Haibun; Study War No More: Peace, Violence and the Literary Imagination." *Pequod: A Journal of Contemporary Literature and Literary Criticism* 48–50 (2005): 9–31.

Hassan, Ihab. "Beyond Postmodernism: Toward an Aesthetic of Trust." *Angelaki* 8, no. 1 (2003): 3–11.

_____. "The Character of Post-War Fiction in America." *English Journal* 51, no. 1 (1962): 1–8.

_____. "Postface 1982: Toward a Concept of Postmodernism." In *Critical Essays on American Postmodernism*, edited by Stanley Trachtenberg, 81–92. New York: G.K. Hall, 1995.

Hayes, Kevin J. "How G.I. Joe Read Stephen Crane." *Stephen Crane Studies* 9, no. 1 (2000): 9–14.

Haynes, Terrence D. *Desert Norm: A Journal/Novel About the Gulf War.* Lincoln, NE: Writers Club Press, 2002.

Heller, Joseph. *Catch-22.* 1961. New York: Scribner, 1996.

Herr, Michael. *Dispatches.* 1977. Introduction by Robert Stone. New York: Everyman's Library, 2009.

Herzog, Tobey C. *Vietnam War Stories: Innocence Lost.* New York: Routledge, 1992.

Hetherington, Tim, and Sebastian Junger, dir. *Restrepo: One Platoon, One Valley, One Year.* Performed by 2nd Platoon, Battle Company. Virgil Films, 2010.

Heyman, Neil M. *Daily Life During World War I.* Westport, CT: Greenwood, 2002.

Higonnet, Margaret R. "Authenticity and Art in Trauma Narratives of World War I." *Modernism/Modernity* 9, no. 1 (2002): 91–107.

Hillenbrand, Margaret. "GIs and the City: Images of Urbanization in Some Postwar Taiwanese Fiction." *Asian Studies Review* 25, no. 4 (2001): 403–21.

Hoffman, Frederick J. *The Mortal No: Death & the Modern Imagination.* Princeton, NJ: Princeton University Press, 1964.

Hölbing, Walter. "The Second World War: American Writing." In *The Cambridge Companion to War Writing*, edited by Kate McLoughlin, 212–25. New York: Cambridge University Press, 2009.

Homberger, Eric. "United States." In *The Second World War in Fiction*, edited by Holger Klein with John Flower and Eric Homberger, 173–205. London: Macmillan, 1984.

Hooker, Richard (pseud.). *MASH.* 1968. New York: Perennial, 2001.

Hopkins, Ernest Jerome. "The World of War: Foreword." In *The Complete Short Stories of Ambrose Bierce* (1970), edited, with commentary, by Ernest Jerome Hopkins, foreword by Cathy N. Davidson, 261–63. Lincoln: University of Nebraska Press, 1984.

Hungerford, Harold R. "'That Was at Chancellorsville': The Factual Framework of *The Red Badge of Courage*." In *Critical Essays on Stephen Crane's* The Red Badge of Courage. Ed and Intro. Donald Pizer. Boston: G.K. Hall, 1990. 105–15.

Hunt, Nigel. "*All Quiet on the Western Front* and Understanding of Psychological Trauma." *Narrative Inquiry* 9, no. 1 (1999): 207–12.

James, Jennifer C. "African American War Literature." In *Encyclopedia of American War Literature*, edited by Philip K. Jason and Mark A. Graves. Westport, CT: Greenwood, 2001.

_____. *A Freedom Bought With Blood: African American War Literature from the Civil War to World War II*. Chapel Hill: University of North Carolina Press, 2007.

Jamjoon, Mohammed. "War Forces Iraqi Mom into Prostitution." CNN.com, 2 November 2009. Accessed 23 December 2009.

Janda, Lance. "Shutting the Gates of Mercy: The American Origins of Total War, 1860–1880." *Journal of Military History* 59, no. 1 (1995): 7–26.

Jason, Philip K. *Acts and Shadows: The Vietnam War in American Literary Culture*. New York: Rowman & Littlefield, 2000.

Jones, Thom. "Break on Through." In *The Pugilist at Rest: Stories*, 28–64. New York: Little, Brown, 1993.

_____. "The Pugilist at Rest." In *The Pugilist at Rest: Stories*, 3–27. New York: Little, Brown, 1993.

Junger, Sebastian. *War*. New York: Twelve, 2010.

Kaplan, Amy. "*The Red Badge of Courage* Redefined the War Novel." In *Readings on Stephen Crane*, edited by Bonnie Szumski, 117–27. San Diego: Greenhaven, 1998.

Kaufman, Will. "The American Civil War." In *The Cambridge Companion to War Writing*, edited by Kate McLoughlin, 148–59. New York: Cambridge University Press, 2009.

Kennard, Jean E. "Joseph Heller: At War with Absurdity." *Mosaic: A Journal for the Interdisciplinary Study of Literature* 4, no. 3 (1971): 75–87.

Key, Francis Scott. "*Star Spangled Banner Lyrics*." USA Flag Site.org, 2002. Accessed 2 June 2010.

Kinder, John M. "The Good War's 'Raw Chunks': Norman Mailer's *The Naked and the Dead* and James Gould Cozzen's *Guard of Honor*." *Midwest Quarterly: A Journal of Contemporary Thought* 46, no. 2 (2005): 187–202.

Klein, Holger. "Introduction." In *The First World War in Fiction: A Collection of Critical Essays*, edited and introduced by Holger Klein, 1–9. London: Macmillan, 1976.

Komunyakaa, Yusef. "The Edge." In *Pleasure Dome: New and Collected Poems*, 212. Middletown, CT: Wesleyan University Press, 2001.

_____. "Tu Do Street." In *Pleasure Dome: New and Collected Poems*, 209–10. Middletown, CT: Wesleyan University Press, 2001.

La Motte, Ellen Newbold. *The Backwash of War: The Human Wreckage of the Battlefield as Witnessed by an American Hospital Nurse*. 1916. LaVergne: Dodo Press, 2009.

Lawson, Andrew. "The Red Badge of Class: Stephen Crane and the Industrial Army." *Literature and History* 14, no. 2 (2005): 53–68.

Linderman, Gerald F. *Embattled Courage: The Experience of Combat in the American Civil War*. New York: Free Press, 1987.

Linhard, Tabea Alexa. "A Perpetual Trace of Violence: Gendered Narratives of Revolution and War." *Discourse: Journal for Theoretical Studies in Media and Culture* 25, no. 3 (2003): 30–47.

Liparulo, Steven P. "'Incense and Ashes': The Postmodern Work of Refutation in Three Vietnam War Novels." *War, Literature, and the Arts: An International Journal of the Humanities* 15, nos. 1–2 (2003): 71–94.

Luckett, Perry D. "The Black Soldier in Vietnam War Literature and Film." *War, Literature, and the Arts* 1, no. 2 (1989–1990): 1–27.

Lyon, Philippa. *Twentieth Century War Poetry*. New York: Palgrave Macmillan, 2004.

Mailer, Norman. *The Naked and the Dead*. 1948. New York: Henry Holt, 2000.

_____. "*The Naked* Are Fanatics *and the Dead* Don't Care." Interview by Louise Levitas. In *Conversations with Norman Mailer*, edited by J. Michael Lennon, 3–11. Jackson: University Press of Mississippi, 1988.

_____. "Norman Mailer: 'The Hubris of the American Vision.'" Interview by Eric James Schroeder. In *Vietnam, We've All Been There: Interviews with American Writers*, 91–105. Westport, CT: Praeger, 1992.

March, William. *Company K*. 1933. Introduction by Philip D. Beidler. Tuscaloosa: University of Alabama Press, 2006.

Marín, Pilar. "Alienation and Environment in the Fiction of Vietnam." *Revista Canaria de Estudios Ingleses* 15 (November 1987): 25–34.

Marlantes, Karl. *Matterhorn: A Novel of the Vietnam War*. New York: Atlantic Monthly Press, 2010.

Marsland, Elizabeth A. "The Combatant Experience Revisited: Two Comparatist Studies of First World War Literature." *Canadian Review of Comparative Literature/Revue Canadienne de Littérature Comparée* 24, no. 2 (1997): 352–58.

Matthews, John T. "American Writing of the Great War." In *The Cambridge Companion to the Literature of the First World War*, edited by Vincent Sherry, 217–42. New York: Cambridge University Press, 2005.

McCarthy, Cormac. *Blood Meridian, Or the Evening Redness in the West*. 1985. New York: Vintage, 1992.

McConnaughey, Janet. "U.S. Combats Bugs for Troops Abroad." *San Angelo Standard-Times*, 10 April 2009: A7.

McDonald, William. "Søren Kierkegaard: Kierkegaard's Rhetoric." *Stanford Encyclopedia of Philosophy* (online). Metaphysics Research Lab, Stanford University, 2009. Accessed 15 September 2010.

Miller, Paul W. "Anti-Heroic Theme and Structure in Midwestern World War I Novels from Cather to Hemingway." *Midamerica: The Yearbook of the Society for the Study of Midwestern Literature* 23 (1996): 99–108.

Misra, Kalidas. "The American War Novel from World War II to Vietnam." *Indian Journal of American Studies* 14, no. 2 (1984): 73–80.

Momaday, N. Scott. *House Made of Dawn*. 1969. New York: Perennial, 1999.

Moon, Katharine H.S. *Sex Among Allies: Military Prostitution in U.S.-Korea Relations*. New York: Columbia University Press, 1997.

Moreau, Ron, and Sami Yousafzai. "Pakistan Uprooted." *Newsweek*, 7 June 2010: 5.

Mulcaire, Terry. "Progressive Visions of War in *The Red Badge of Courage* and *The Principles of Scientific Management*." *American Quarterly* 43, no. 1 (1991): 46–72.

Murphy, John J. "Compromising Realism to Idealize a War: Wharton's *The Marne* and Cather's *One of Ours*." *American Literary Realism* 33, no. 2 (2001): 157–67.

Nabulsi, Karma. "Evolving Conceptions of Civilians and Belligerents: One Hundred Years After the Hague Peace Conferences." In *Civilians in War*, edited by Simon Chesterman, 9–24. Boulder, CO: Lynne Rienner, 2001.

"Navy Cross Citation for Karl A. Marlantes." Military Times.com, 2011. Accessed 19 May 2011.

Nelson, Robert. "Place and Vision: The Function of Landscape in *Ceremony*." *Journal of the Southwest* 30, no. 3 (1988): 281–316.

Newman, John. *Vietnam War Literature: An Annotated Bibliography of Imaginative Works about Americans Fighting in Vietnam*. Metuchen, NJ: Scarecrow, 1982.

O'Brien, Tim. *If I Die in a Combat Zone, Box Me Up and Ship Me Home*. 1975. New York: Broadway, 1999.

———. *The Things They Carried*. 1990. New York: Broadway, 1998.

———. "Two Interviews: Talks with Tim O'Brien and Robert Stone." Interview by Eric James Schroeder. *MFS: Modern Fiction Studies* 30, no. 1 (1984): 135–64.

———. "The Vietnam in Me." *New York Times Magazine* (online), 2 October 1994. Accessed 23 December 2009.

O'Donnell, Thomas F., and Hoyt C. Franchere. *Harold Frederic*. New York: Twayne, 1961.

Orwell, George. "Politics and the English Language." In *A Collection of Essays*, 162–77. New York: Doubleday Anchor, 1954.

Pachet, Pierre. "World War One and the Interpretation of Freud's Concept of the Event." *MLN* 88, no. 6 (1973): 1316–25.

Palm, Edward F. "James Webb's *Fields of Fire*: The Melting-Pot Platoon Revisited." *Critique: Studies in Contemporary Fiction* 24, no. 2 (1983): 105–18.

Parrish, Timothy. "Cormac McCarthy's *Blood Meridian*: The First and Last Book of America." In *From the Civil War to the Apocalypse: Postmodern History and American Fiction*, 80–116. Amherst: University of Massachusetts Press, 2008.

Peebles, Stacey. *Welcome to the Suck: Narrating the American Soldier's Experience in Iraq*. Ithaca, NY: Cornell University Press, 2011.

Pizer, Donald. "Introduction." In *Critical Essays on Stephen Crane's The Red Badge of Courage*, edited and introduced by Donald Pizer, 1–11. Boston: G.K. Hall, 1990.

Pollard, Tomas. "Gender Dynamics in *Catch-22*." *BELL: Belgian Languages on Language and Literature* (2003): 111–20.

Potok, Chaim. *I Am The Clay*. 1992. New York: Fawcett Crest, 1994.

———. "An Interview With Chaim Potok." By Elaine M. Kauver. *Contemporary Literature* 27, no. 3 (1986): 291–317.

———. "A *MELUS* Interview." By Laura Chavkin. *MELUS* 24, no. 2 (1999): 147–57.

Power, Mark. "Graves." In *Retrieving Bones: Stories and Poems of the Korean War*, edited and introduced by W.D. Ehrhart and Philip K. Jason, 115–26. New Brunswick, NJ: Rutgers University Press, 1999.

Pratt, Alan. "Nihilism: Existential Nihilism." In *Internet Encyclopedia of Philosophy* (online). University of Tennessee at Martin, 2010. Accessed 6 October 2010.

———. "Nihilism: Origins." In *Internet Encyclopedia of Philosophy* (online). University of Tennessee at Martin, 2010. Accessed 6 October 2010.

Quinn, Patrick. "The First World War: American Writing." In *The Cambridge Companion to War Writing*, edited by Kate McLoughlin, 175–84. New York: Cambridge University Press, 2009.

Rabe, David. *The Basic Training of Pavlo Hummel. The Vietnam Plays*. Vol. 1. New York: Grove, 1993.

Raghavan, Sudarsan. "War in Iraq Propelling a Massive Migration." Washington Post.com, 4 February 2007. Accessed 9 August 2011.

Robison, Mark A. "Recreation in World War I and the Practice of Play in *One of Ours*." *Cather Studies* 6 (2006): 160–83.

Roseman, Mark. "War and People: The Social Impact of Total War." In *The Oxford Illustrated History of Modern War*, edited by Charles Townshend, 245–63. New York: Oxford University Press, 1997.

Ross, Frank. "The Assailant-Victim in Three War-Protest Novels." *Paunch* 32 (1968): 46–57.

Ryder, Mary R. "'Dear, Tender-Hearted, Uncomprehending America': Dorothy Canfield Fisher's and Edith Wharton's Fictional Responses to the First World War." In *The Literature of the Great War Reconsidered: Beyond Modern Memory*, edited by Patrick J. Quinn and Steven Trout, 143–55. New York: Palgrave, 2001.

Sample, Maxine. "In Another Life: The Refugee Phenomenon in Two Novels of the Nigerian Civil War." *MFS: Modern Fiction Studies* 37, no. 3 (1991): 445–54.

Sanborn, Wallis. "The Accessible Postmodern American Novel." In *English 2307 Course Guide*, edited by Debra Nash, xiv–xxii. Lubbock: Texas Tech University Press, 2004.

Schaefer, Michael. "'Heroes Had No Shame in Their Lives': Manhood, Heroics, and Compassion in *The Red Badge of Courage* and 'A Mystery of Heroism.'" *War, Literature, and the Arts* 18, nos. 1–2 (2006): 104–13.

Schweitzer, Rich. "Troubled Water: The Wet Death Image as an Anglo-American Response to the Great War." *Weber Studies: An Interdisciplinary Humanities Journal* 6, no. 2 (1989): 5–24.

Scoggins, Michael C. "Joseph Heller's Combat Experiences in *Catch-22*." *War, Literature, and the Arts: An International Journal of the Humanities* 15, nos. 1–2 (2003): 213–27.

Seeger, Alan. "I Have a Rendezvous with Death." In *Poems by Alan Seeger*, 141. Charleston, SC: BiblioBazaar, 2007.

Seltzer, Leon F. "Milo's 'Culpable Innocence': Absurdity as Moral Insanity in *Catch-22*." In *Critical Essays on Joseph Heller*, edited by James Nagel, 74–92. Boston: G.K. Hall, 1984.

Sepich, John E. *Notes on Blood Meridian*. 1993. Revised and expanded edition. Foreword by Edwin T. Arnold. Austin: University of Texas Press, 2008.

Sharma, D.R. "War and the Individual Man in *The Red Badge of Courage*." *Literary Criterion* 9, no. 2 (1970): 56–64.

Shaw, Patrick W. *The Modern American Novel of Violence*. Troy, NY: Whitston, 2000.

Sheehan-Miles, Charles. *Prayer at Rumayla: A Novel of the Gulf War*. Cary: Cincinnatus, 2001.

Shelton, Frank W. "Robert Stone's *Dog Soldiers*: Vietnam Comes Home to America." *Critique: Studies in Contemporary Fiction* 24, no. 2 (1983): 74–81.

Shenon, Philip. "20 Years After Victory, Vietnamese Communists Ponder How to Celebrate." *New York Times* (online), 23 April 1995. Accessed 7 July 2011.

Siegal, Marcia Zoslaw. "The Prime of Chaim Potok." In *Conversations with Chaim Potok*, edited by Daniel Walden, 92–99. Jackson: University of Mississippi Press, 2001.

Silko, Leslie Marmon. *Ceremony*. 1977. New York: Penguin, 1986.

_____. "Preface." *Ceremony*. 1977. 30th anniversary edition, introduced by Larry McMurtry, xi–xix. New York: Penguin, 2006.

Simmons, Edwin Howard. "Introduction." In *Through the Wheat: A Novel of the World War I Marines*, by Thomas Boyd (1923), v–xv. Lincoln: University of Nebraska Press, 2000.

"Small Arms." *Weapons of the American Civil War*. Civil War Home (online), 2002. Accessed 10 November 2010.

Solomon, Eric. "From *Christ in Flanders* to *Catch-22*: An Approach to War Fiction." *Texas Studies in Literature and Language: A Journal of the Humanities* 11 (1969): 851–66.

Star-Spangled Banner Project. "Star-Spangled Banner and the War of 1812." *Encyclopedia Smithsonian* (online). Smithsonian Institution, 2004. Accessed 2 June 2010.

Stout, Janis P. "The Making of Willa Cather's *One of Ours*: The Role of Dorothy Canfield Fisher." *War, Literature, and the Arts* 11, no. 2 (1999): 48–59.

Swofford, Anthony. *Jarhead: A Marine's Chronicle of the Gulf War and Other Battles*. 2003. New York: Scribner, 2005.

Terry, Wallace, ed. *Bloods: An Oral History of the Vietnam War*. 1984. New York: Presidio, 2006.

"The Toll of War." NPR.org, 2011. Accessed 6 July 2011.

Trumbo, Dalton. *Johnny Got His Gun*. 1939. New York: Citadel, 2007.

Turner, Brian. "Hwy 1." In *Here, Bullet*, 6. Farmington, ME: Alice James, 2005.

United Nations Missions in Afghanistan (UNAMA). "Afghanistan: Civilian Casualties Up." *Time*, 23 August 2010: 14.

_____. "Afghanistan Civilian Casualties: Year by Year, Month by Month: Data Summary: Afghan Civilian Deaths." Guardian.co.uk, 2011. Accessed 7 July 2011.

Waldron, Randall H. "The Naked, the Dead, and the Machine: A New Look at Norman Mailer's First Novel." *PMLA: Publications of the Modern Language Association of America* 87, no. 2 (1972): 271–77.

Walsh, Jeffrey. *American War Literature, 1914 to Vietnam*. 1982. New York: St. Martin's, 1983.

_____. "American Writing of the Wars in Korea and Vietnam." In *The Cambridge Companion to War Writing*, edited by Kate McLoughlin, 226–38. New York: Cambridge University Press, 2009.

Washington, Ida H. *Dorothy Canfield Fisher: A Biography*. Shelburne: New England Press, 1982.

Wegner, John. "'Wars and Rumors of Wars' in Cormac McCarthy's Border Trilogy." *Southern Quarterly: A Journal of the Arts in the South* 38, no. 3 (2000): 59–71.

Weigl, Bruce. "Song of Napalm." In *Archeology of the Circle: New and Selected Poems*, 73–75. New York: Grove, 1999.

Wesley, Marilyn. "Truth and Fiction in Tim O'Brien's *If I Die in a Combat Zone* and *The Things They Carried*." *College Literature* 29, no. 2 (2002): 1–18.

Wharton, Edith. *The Marne*. 1918. Charleston: BiblioLife, 2009.

Whitman, Walt. "The Wound-Dresser (Originally titled The Dresser)." In *Drum-Taps*, 51–55. London: Chato and Windus, 1865.

Willis, J.H., Jr. "The Censored Language of War: Richard Aldington's *Death of a Hero* and Three Other War Novels of 1929." *Twentieth Century Literature: A Scholarly and Critical Journal* 45, no. 4 (1999): 467–87.

Wilson, Edmund. "Ambrose Bierce on the Owl Creek Bridge." In *Patriotic Gore: Studies in the Literature of the American Civil War*, edited by Edmund Wilson, 617–34. New York: Oxford University Press, 1962.

_____. "Introduction." *The Civil War Stories of Harold Frederic*, edited by Thomas F. O'Donnell, xi–xvi. Syracuse, NY: Syracuse University Press, 1992.

_____. "Introduction." *Patriotic Gore: Studies in the Literature of the American Civil War*, edited by Edmund Wilson, ix–xxxii. New York: Oxford University Press, 1962.

Wimmer, Adi. "Vietnam and the Death of Heroism? Critical Approaches to a Critical Era." *American Studies in Scandinavia* 30, no. 2 (1998): 30–42.

Winter, Michael. "Pentagon: Air Strikes Likely Killed 26 Afghan Civilians." USA Today.com, 19 June 2009. Accessed 20 June 2009.

"World War II Casualty Statistics." SecondWorldWarHistory.com, 2006–2010. Accessed 24 June 2010.

Index